Shaping the Emerging World

Shaping the Emerging World
India and the Multilateral Order

Edited by
Waheguru Pal Singh Sidhu
Pratap Bhanu Mehta
Bruce Jones

BROOKINGS INSTITUTION PRESS
Washington, D.C.

FOUNDATION® BOOKS

FOUNDATION®
BOOKS

Foundation Books is an imprint of Cambridge University Press India Pvt. Ltd.

Cambridge House, 4381/4 Ansari Road, Daryaganj, New Delhi 110 002

www.cambridgeindia.org

This edition was published by arrangement with the Brookings Institution on behalf of the Brookings Institution Press.

First South Asia edition 2014

Printed in India at Bhavish Graphics, Chennai

ISBN 978-93-82993-54-4 Hardback

Contents

Acknowledgments vii

PART I. INTRODUCTION

1 A Hesitant Rule Shaper? 3
Waheguru Pal Singh Sidhu, Pratap Bhanu Mehta, and Bruce Jones

PART II. PERSPECTIVES ON MULTILATERALISM

2 The Changing Dynamics of India's Multilateralism 25
C. Raja Mohan

3 India and Multilateralism: A Practitioner's Perspective 43
Shyam Saran

4 India as a Regional Power 57
Srinath Raghavan

PART III. DOMESTIC AND REGIONAL DRIVERS

5 The Economic Imperative for India's Multilateralism 75
Sanjaya Baru

6 What in the World Is India Able to Do? India's State Capacity for Multilateralism 95
Tanvi Madan

7 India's Regional Disputes 115
Kanti Bajpai

8 From an Ocean of Peace to a Sea of Friends 131
Iskander Luke Rehman

PART IV. MULTILATERAL POLICY IN PRACTICE

9 Dilemmas of Sovereignty and Order: India and the UN Security Council 157
David M. Malone and Rohan Mukherjee

10 India and UN Peacekeeping: The Weight of History and a Lack of Strategy 177
Richard Gowan and Sushant K. Singh

11 From Defensive to Pragmatic Multilateralism and Back: India's Approach to Multilateral Arms Control and Disarmament 197
Rajesh Rajagopalan

12 Security in Cyberspace: India's Multilateral Efforts 217
Sandeep Bhardwaj

13 India and International Financial Institutions and Arrangements 237
Devesh Kapur

14 Of Maps and Compasses: India in Multilateral Climate Negotiations 261
Navroz K. Dubash

15 India's Energy, Food, and Water Security: International Cooperation for Domestic Capacity 281
Arunabha Ghosh and David Steven

16 India and International Norms: R2P, Genocide Prevention, Human Rights, and Democracy 303
Nitin Pai

17 From Plurilateralism to Multilateralism? G-20, IBSA, BRICS, and BASIC 319
Christophe Jaffrelot and Waheguru Pal Singh Sidhu

Contributors 341

Index 343

Acknowledgments

The genesis of this edited volume was a workshop on Indian foreign policy organized by New York University's Centre on International Cooperation (CIC) in October 2010. Generously funded by the International Development Research Centre (IDRC), the workshop in New York provided an opportunity to chalk out the contours of the present book and establish a partnership between CIC and the Centre for Policy Research (CPR), New Delhi.

Subsequently, then IDRC President David Malone's scene-setting opus, *Does the Elephant Dance? Contemporary Indian Foreign Policy* (Oxford University Press, 2011), introduced many of the issues examined in detail here and provided a further impetus and inspiration for this volume.

We are very grateful for the generous funding provided to this joint CIC-CPR project by IDRC and CPR's core funders. Without their assistance the project would not have been possible. Our gratitude is expressed particularly to David Malone, Bruce Currie-Alder, and their colleagues at IDRC for unstinting intellectual, moral, and budgetary support throughout the project.

That support—and generous funding to CIC from the Norwegian Foreign Ministry—enabled us to assemble a stellar cast of authors—a mix of upcoming and established Indian and international scholars and experts—for a workshop at CPR in New Delhi in February 2012. The meeting helped to clarify the key research questions and elaborate on the scope of the volume and the chapters. Our sincere thanks to the authors for their insights, their diligence in drafting the chapters, and the numerous revisions to hone the chapters to perfection.

The publication of an edited volume can often become a long, tedious, and contentious process. So we are particularly grateful to Robert Faherty, Janet

Walker, and their colleagues at Brookings Institution Press for making the entire process smooth, efficient, and effortless. Thanks to their endeavors this volume is being published in record time.

We are also beholden to our colleagues at CIC and CPR for their dedication in keeping the project on schedule, within budget, and in good spirits. At CIC the hard work and commitment of Yvone Alonzo, Emily O'Brien, Lynn Denesopolis, Ben Tortolani, and Colette Jaycox were invaluable for the successful culmination of this ambitious project. At CPR the conscientious work of Srinath Raghavan, Sandeep Bharadwaj, and L. Ravi in keeping the project on track was crucial and much appreciated.

Finally, we thank our families for their love, support, and understanding. This book is dedicated to them and those who believe in India's ability to shape the emerging world order.

PART I

Introduction

WAHEGURU PAL SINGH SIDHU, PRATAP BHANU MEHTA,
and BRUCE JONES

1

A Hesitant Rule Shaper?

A Defining Period

India faces a defining period. As the world's biggest democracy with an economy among the world's ten largest, India's status as a reemerging global power is being not just recognized but increasingly institutionalized, with a seat on the G-20, increasing clout in the international financial institutions, entry into the club of nuclear-armed states, impending membership in the various technology and supply control regimes, and impressive peacekeeping credentials under the United Nations. As India reasserts itself economically on the global stage for the first time since the 1500s, it will inevitably wield greater international political and, possibly, military influence.[1]

At the same time, geopolitical shifts create simultaneous opportunities and challenges: the opening with the United States, the rise of China, the global financial crisis, the so-called Arab Spring, the mounting crisis between Iran and the West as well as key Gulf states, and the growing international tussles over energy, climate, food, cyber security, rivers and the oceans. India has experienced rapid growth through participation in the multilateral order, and its development strategy and energy requirements make it dependent on stable globalization. India has growing economic, trade, and energy stakes in literally every corner of the globe. Much of that trade and energy flows via the Indian Ocean, where India is an established maritime player but also faces enormous new demands and challenges. At this stage in its history, India has critical interests in just about every major multilateral regime and vital interests in several emerging regimes. The boundaries between Indian self-interest and the contours of the multilateral order have blurred. In short, India might have no choice but to influence the evolving multilateral order if it is to sustain its own interests.

Does India have the will to shape the changing multilateral order? If so, does it have the people, the tools, and the ideas to do so? How much do India's troubled neighborhood and complex domestic politics inhibit a forward-leaning stance on the multilateral order? Or do they demand it? How do India's elites—old and new—shape India's political options? How do the rising middle class and the growing urbanization influence India's multilateral outlook?

Many commentators on India's posture with regard to the multilateral order have argued that it has often been little more than a defensive crouch: that nonalignment was rooted in a geopolitical strategy, but Indian policy has neither fully reacted to changing geopolitics and geoeconomics nor genuinely sought to shape the resulting global order. To some extent, this is a caricature, although, like many caricatures, it contains an element of truth. What is certainly true is that India's posture on the multilateral order has not changed as quickly or as dramatically as the order itself.

Jawaharlal Nehru reportedly argued, as echoed by John F. Kennedy's famous charge to the American people, that states must ask not, what can the world do for us, but what can we do for the world?[2] This is the necessary question for a power that would seek to shape the order in which it finds itself. The history of the multilateral order is one of change from within driven by states willing to bear the costs. While India has been a key international actor since its independence in 1947, it practiced, according to one observer, "universalism of the weak."[3] This was evident during the early decades in its leadership of the Nonaligned Movement (NAM) and the G-77 countries and its championing of the cause of decolonization in Africa and Asia, which reflected a principled and ideological, but ineffectual, approach to multilateralism.

However, since the end of the cold war (which coincided with dramatic economic and political changes within India), New Delhi has exhibited "internationalism of the strong," which is apparent in its membership in the G-20, its quest for permanent membership in the United Nations Security Council (UNSC), its desire to provide leadership to international financial institutions, and its role in trade and climate negotiations, which has often been at odds with its membership in the G-77 and the NAM (although India's instinct to switch between the G-77/NAM and the G-20 limits its influence in both).[4] In addition, India's tacit endorsement of the "responsibility to protect" principle (though dampened by the Libyan experience) also indicates a shift from its traditional notion of unchallenged state sovereignty.[5] Post–cold war India has started to reflect a more pragmatic, realpolitik approach to multilateralism and multipolarity—which is evident in its multiple-alignment policy. While India continues to pay lip service to "nonalignment," its current articulation of the concept of "engaging with all with different degrees of proximity, but allying with none" and its insistence on maintaining "strategic autonomy" are unrecognizable from the original idea of a coalition of the third world as manifest in the NAM.[6]

Today, India increasingly has the financial strength to bear costs, as a rapidly growing middle class generates private and public resources. But what does it mean, politically, that India's per capita gross domestic product (GDP) is not just the lowest in the G-20 but more than 50 percent lower than that of the next lowest member, Indonesia, and a mere 3 percent of that of the United States? Or that only 32.4 million of its total population of 1.2 billion pay taxes and that the total tax revenue collected as a percentage of GDP is among the lowest in the G-20? Or that it has fewer doctors and nurses than even the World Health Organization benchmark of at least 23 medical personnel per 10,000 population? Or that India's Human Development Index (HDI) ranking of 136 (out of a total of 186 countries) is the lowest among all the G-20 countries. Or that it also comes in last among the G-20 in all of the other HDI indicators, except two—women's participation in national parliament and maternal mortality ratio.[7] Or that India ranks last among the G-20 in the number of police officers per capita and that only 77.1 percent of all police positions are filled nationally?[8] Or that India's 900-odd diplomats are around the same number as those of Singapore or New Zealand and about the same number as personnel employed by the U.S. embassy in New Delhi alone?[9] How will these constraints affect India's ability to influence the evolving multilateral order?

Despite these constraints, if India does focus on shaping the multilateral order, how will it attempt to do so? Will it be content with rule taking—adhering to the existing and emerging international norms and institutions? Will it focus on rule breaking—challenging the existing order primarily for effect and seeking greater accommodation for itself in existing global institutions? Will it be inclined to rule making—establishing new norms and institutions? Or will a more realistic strategy be one that focuses on rule shaping—contributing in partnership with others to emerging norms and building nascent regimes—for example, on climate, maritime security, and cyber security? Does India have the normative claims and the arguments with which to make them? Over the past few years, India has shown greater propensity as a rule taker and rule breaker than as a rule maker (an unlikely option in a multipolar world) or even a rule shaper.

Rule Taker: The Original Instinct

The rule-taker instinct is most apparent in India's unquestioning adherence to the dominant Western liberal economic and democratic model, albeit with Indian characteristics. India is unlikely to jettison parliamentary democracy or return to the state-dominated "license raj" economy, even if its practice of democracy remains imperfect and its efforts to dismantle the overbearing regulations that curtail economic growth are inept.

However, while practicing a vibrant multiethnic, multicultural democracy itself, India has not sought to promote democracy or to strengthen the rule of law as a strategic tool.[10] In fact, its support of democracy in its immediate neighborhood has been uneven.[11] For instance, India's 1971 intervention in Bangladesh set that country on the long and winding road to democracy, while its 1988 role in the Maldives helped to prolong the life of an authoritarian regime. More recently, New Delhi cozied up to the military junta in Myanmar, while voting against Sri Lanka's human rights record in the UN's Human Rights Council.[12]

National Security Adviser Shivshankar Menon's rumination on democracy promotion sums up the Indian dilemma:

> Do we not have a responsibility to spread democracy and fight for our values abroad? Yes and no. Yes, if we have the means to actually ensure that we are able to spread them. And yes if having democrats as our neighbours contributes to the peaceful periphery that we need. But please remember that a people cannot be forced to be free or to practice democracy. They have to come to these values themselves if they are to be lasting. Such a crusade for one's values is often mistaken by others as the pursuit of self-interest couched in high-tone words. We have seen how high-sounding phrases like the "right to protect" are selectively invoked and brutally applied in the pursuit of self-interest, giving humanitarian and international intervention a bad name.[13]

However, as India's economy becomes inexorably intertwined with countries out of its immediate areas of regional influence, its comfortable policy of masterly inactivity is likely to become detrimental to the promotion of its own national interests. Thus there is a need to recognize the strategic import of democracy promotion (beyond just increasing the contributions to the

UN's Democracy Fund) for strengthening the economy and furthering the national interests, particularly in areas undergoing profound political changes, such as the Middle East (a significant trade partner). For instance, while promoting democratic practices and the rule of law might be of limited relevance to the Indian economy in the short term, such practices are likely to benefit the country's economic interests in the long term as opposed to the interests of undemocratic powers, such as China.[14]

India's rule-taker (indeed rule-defender) instinct is also evident in its unstinting support of the peacekeeping and peacebuilding principles of the United Nations.[15] In fact, India has adhered to the existing Western liberal democratic norms, notably in Africa, even though these have been found to be wanting. At best India has sought to have a greater say in the peacekeeping mandates but has not challenged the established norms behind the UN's peacekeeping and even peacebuilding efforts.[16] In fact, in the United Nations India has been an absent-minded peacekeeper—deploying troops because it could and not because it needed to. Ironically, India's peacekeeping also benefited former colonial powers that did not contribute as many troops and whose interests Indian peacekeepers ended up defending through the various UN missions. This undermined not only India's own interests but also its principle of protecting the sovereign interests of the states where the peace operations were conducted.[17]

Clearly, then, India has not challenged the dominant Western liberal paradigm for peacekeeping and peacebuilding. In fact, it has staunchly defended this model, seeking the UN imprimatur for multilateral armed interventions. While some experts have called for India to reduce, if not entirely cut off, its contributions to UN peacekeeping, this is unlikely to happen for several reasons.[18] Instead, given India's economic rise and the growing risks of peace operations, which are now tasked with protecting civilians, among other duties, there is a need to align participation in UN peacekeeping operations with New Delhi's evolving strategic interests.[19] While India's increasing economic and political stakes in many of the countries that host UN peacekeeping operations further highlight the need for a strategic shift, New Delhi has sought only tactical adjustments so far.[20]

Rule Breaker: Seeking Greater Accommodation

There are some international organizations and institutions that India neither is a member of nor is interested in joining or associating itself with, even though it could do so. The North Atlantic Treaty Organization in the security sphere is one such institution and the Organization for Economic Cooperation and Development in the economic realm is another. There are other international institutions and arrangements where India either is an outsider or is seeking to have a greater role. India has displayed the rule-breaker trait toward the latter set of institutions. Perhaps the preeminent example of this is the quest for membership in the UNSC and reform of the international financial institutions, notably the International Monetary Fund (IMF) and the World Bank.[21] The rule-breaker approach is also evident with regard to various nuclear nonproliferation instruments, where India has sought to establish its exceptionalism by challenging the norm of the Treaty on the Non-Proliferation of Nuclear Weapons (NPT) and by seeking recognition as a nuclear weapon state. Recently, however, India has taken the rule-breaker route by seeking membership in the Nuclear Suppliers Group (NSG), the Wassenaar Arrangement, the Australia Group, and the Missile Technology Control Regime, which it had previously dismissed as "technology cartels."[22] In doing so, India reflects a curious dichotomy of being a rule breaker only to become a rule taker eventually.[23]

India has also proved to be a rule breaker or norm challenger even in international institutions where it has been a long-standing member. This is best exemplified by India's role in the collapse of the July 2008 World Trade Organization (WTO) negotiations on the Doha Development Round of trade liberalization. Speaking on behalf of the poor and subsistence farmers in the G-33 group of developing countries, India insisted on a "special safeguard mechanism" to protect them from the sudden surge of cheap food imports.[24] India's stance was prompted in part by the domestic opposition of thirty-five farmers groups. Besides, for the Congress-led coalition in power then, "Farm subsidies remain a crucial electoral clutch. Nearly 70 percent of the population lives in the countryside and the vast majority of Indians [about 700 million] derive their income directly or indirectly from farming, even though agriculture makes up less than a fifth of India's . . . economy."[25] As the noted Indian agronomist and director of the National Commission on Farmers, M. S. Swaminathan, cautioned, "If the government were to agree to something which will kill our agricultural sector, then their political futures will be finished."[26]

Some Indian scholars have argued that India's posturing at the WTO was the result of New Delhi's assessment that the United States would not be prepared to make a deal in an election year.[27] However, the U.S. trade representative, Susan Schwab, argued that India's impending election in April 2009 was, perhaps, more consequential in India's rule-breaker posture than the 2008 U.S. election. She noted, "It turned out that we were worried about the wrong election when we were negotiating Doha."[28] Yet other scholars have revealed that India's stance was inevitably the result of the lack of the Indian state's capacity for multilateralism.[29] While India's blocking of the negotiations can certainly be justified, it is not evident that this benefited either India or poor farmers. As the head of the WTO, Pascal Lamy, observed, the breakdown allowed a package of about $130 billion a year in tariff savings to "slip through their fingers."[30]

Despite the negative connotation of rule breaking, India is not seeking to destroy or even replace the existing international governance institutions with alternative or new institutions; it is merely knocking on the door to gain entry or have a bigger say or protect its interests. In fact, New Delhi has consistently argued for preserving, reforming, and strengthening these institutions and claims that its membership in these exclusive clubs will contribute toward those efforts. Were India to have a greater or permanent role in these institutions, it would most likely fall back into a rule-taker position rather than become either a rule breaker or a rule maker.

In practice, however, India has not been able either to attain membership in the UNSC or to reform the international financial institutions. The only exception is the unique exemption that it won from the NSG to circumvent the provisions of the NPT. This achievement was largely the result of the controversial 2005 Indo-U.S. nuclear agreement, which paved the way for the NSG exception. Although India has signed similar nuclear agreements with France, Russia, and other NSG members, there is no doubt that the Indo-U.S. agreement is more equal than these others.

India's efforts to reform the international financial institutions and seek a greater role for itself have made excruciatingly slow progress and even that only when it has joined forces with other emerging economies, notably Brazil, Russia, China, and South Africa (collectively the BRICS). However, even here India has been tentative to seize the opportunity, as in the race for leadership of the IMF. India and the BRICS are clearly eager to take the lead, as evident in their challenge of the "obsolete unwritten convention" of a European leading the IMF, and also have qualified and talented individuals to offer as candidates. However, they neither provided an alternative leadership model nor a consensus candidate who was acceptable to all BRICS at the very least. Their inability to do so again conceded leadership of the IMF to the Europeans.[31]

In retrospect, this is not surprising for at least three reasons. First, major differences among the BRICS make it difficult to create a united front. This is particularly true of the India-China relationship. Apart from the divergent political ideologies, the presence of the longest disputed border and the shadow of Tibet loom large and sustain mutual mistrust. This distrust is evident even in the 2012 BRICS Delhi Declaration, which calls for reform of the UNSC but falls well short of supporting the Indian case (along with that of Brazil and South Africa) for permanent membership in this exclusive club. Second, although the BRICS have started to challenge the dominant Western discourse on issues as diverse as leadership of the IMF and the World Bank and the crisis over Iran and Syria, they have been either unable or unwilling to formulate and lead an alternative approach. Thus even in the case of the World Bank leadership, their call for "an open and merit-based process" of selection does not reflect their democratic instinct, but rather the inability to agree on a consensus candidate. Finally, given that all BRICS have strategic partnerships with the United States and value their relationship with Washington more than with each other's capitals, they have no incentive to confront the leader of the Western bloc.

A similar story is unfolding over India's ambitions for a permanent seat on the UNSC. When India was overwhelmingly elected for a two-year tenure on the UNSC in 2010, it was clear that success would be measured against two criteria. First, could it contribute to restore the council's legitimacy by supporting resolutions that are effective and implementable? Although the UNSC has been prolific in passing resolutions, their implementation has been extremely uneven and detrimental to its credibility. This effectiveness will have to be proved across some of the most contentious issues: Iran, North Korea, the crisis in Sudan, and, closer to home, Afghanistan, Myanmar, Nepal, and Sri Lanka. Second, can India play with the big boys—the five permanent members of the UNSC? As these five, particularly China and the United States, have the ultimate say in any reform of the UNSC, including its enlargement and acceptance of new permanent membership, New Delhi has the unenviable task of assuring them that it can be a reliable partner.

At the end of the two-year term, India's performance has been mixed on both fronts. The UNSC has certainly not been united, let alone effective, in addressing some of these challenges. The only claim that India can make is the Presidential Statement on Syria, which was the only unanimous agreement achieved on this vexing issue (although Lebanon distanced itself later). As president of the UN's Counterterrorism Committee, India introduced the concept of "zero tolerance," and it remains to be seen whether this will be implemented successfully through the UN's actions. Similarly, India's initiative on anti-piracy is noteworthy. Apart from these, India's contribution to addressing urgent peace and security issues has been undistinguished.

Similarly, India has not done well to build on the initial support that it received from at least four of the five permanent members (P-5) for its candidacy, including Barack Obama's public endorsement during his visit to India in 2011. The primary reason for this is that the U.S. support was, as the joint statement noted, subject to making the UN (and the Security Council) more "efficient, effective, credible, and legitimate." While India's presence doubtless enhanced UNSC's legitimacy, it did not make the UN more efficient, effective, and credible. One indication of this is that while India was elected to the UNSC with an unprecedented 187 votes, it has not been able to get even a two-thirds majority of UN members to support its resolution calling for reform of the UNSC. The fact that it has done far better than Brazil, which lost Washington's support when it voted against a hard-won resolution on Iran in 2010, is no consolation. A related factor might well be that India remains hitched to the G-4 (Brazil, Germany, India, and Japan), despite the diminishing prospects of some of its members being admitted into the UNSC.

As National Security Adviser Menon noted, India's "tactical caution and strategic initiative, sometimes simultaneously," reflect not only a deep ambivalence but also the inability to take action that would be to India's advantage.[32] "Power," according to Menon, "is the ability to create and sustain outcomes." India has been unable to effect, let alone sustain, outcomes. As Menon candidly admitted in reference to the Kashmir issue, which also holds true for India's time on the UNSC, "We had underestimated the protean forms of power politics."[33] Sadly the same situation prevails even today.

Rule Maker Or Rule Shaper: Moving To A Realistic Approach

Some scholars have argued that India should aspire to the position of rule maker. This is an unreasonable standard. Historically no country has been a rule maker of global order primarily because no single country has had the overwhelming power and influence to do so. The only exception has been the United States, especially during the period between 1945 and 1949 when it was the sole superpower. During that time, the United States alone led the establishment of the UN and the related international financial institutions. Even later, when the Soviet Union was a competitor in strategic terms, the United States was the primary force behind the establishment of other rule-making institutions, such as the International Atomic Energy Agency. However, for most of the cold war even the United States alone could not play the role of rule maker; norms and institutions were made only if the interests of the two superpowers converged. Following the collapse of the Soviet Union and the end of the cold war, the brief "unipolar moment" disappeared in the wake of America's strategic overstretch. It was soon replaced by a rapidly emerging multipolar world in which "no longer the CEO [chief executive officer] of Free World Inc., the United States now holds a position akin to that of the largest minority shareholder in Global Order LLC."[34]

As leading Indian experts have argued, in this changing world,

> Alongside the U.S. and China, there will be several other centres and hubs of power that will be relevant, particularly in regional contexts . . . [which will] . . . require a very skillful management of complicated coalitions and opportunities—in environments that may be inherently unstable and volatile rather than structurally settled. This also provides India with rich opportunities, especially if it can leverage into the international domain some of its domestically acquired skills in coalition management and complex negotiation.[35]

Similarly, the 2012 U.S. National Intelligence Council also notes the shift from a U.S. dominated world to "networks and coalitions in a multipolar world." However, the report cautions that these rising powers, despite "strong fundamentals—GDP (gross domestic product), population size, etc.—will not be able to punch their weight unless they also learn to operate in networks and coalitions in a multipolar world."[36]

Thus in this non-unipolar world, no single power, including India, will be a rule maker by itself. A more credible ambition is for India to be a rule "shaper"—one of a small number of powers with the ability to play a major role in shaping the evolution of rules of the road.

Indeed, this "rule-shaping" notion is already in evidence, for example, in India's approach to climate, energy, and maritime security. In climate negotiations, as Navroz Dubash vividly illustrates, India has succeeded in shaping the international narrative about the principles for action, especially in its firm and sustained defense of the principle of "common but differentiated responsibilities."[37] India cannot simply dictate the rules of the climate change game; neither can the United States or China or any other actor. But India is both a significant enough economy and a skilled enough diplomatic actor that its policy and position cannot be ignored in climate negotiations. Particularly in the early years of the negotiations, India adopted a principled approach based on equity and differentiated responsibility around which it was able to mobilize a broad and supportive coalition. Seen from the European Union perspective, India could be counted as blocking action, along with China and the United States. But

India has been clear that it will act on climate issues, so long as such action does not violate its fundamental interests in tackling the deep poverty that characterizes a large swath of its population. As Dubash makes clear, the future challenge is to do a better job updating its principled stance in order to forge a renewed coalition more reflective of both shifts in the climate debate and in geopolitical context. This will allow India to contribute to shaping the emerging international regime.

The same is the case with maritime security. India has huge stakes in the evolving maritime arrangements, with regard to both terms of trade in the Indian Ocean and security concerns related to sea-borne terrorism.[38] What makes India distinct among major powers is the high percentage of Indian nationals who serve as merchant seamen in the vessels that are the subject of piracy concerns. India used one of its two presidencies of the UNSC in 2011–12 to seek a Presidential Statement calling for new approaches to delineating boundaries in high-risk areas. This kind of initiative represents a significant change in India's multilateralism and an important shift in global arrangements as a whole—one of the few times that one of the emerging powers, rather than a Western power, has led policy discussion on an issue of shared global concern. That it needed the support of the P-5 and other elected members of the Security Council—that it could shape, not simply make, the new rules of this particular part of the game—is simply a reality that India will confront, as will every other power. Rule shaping, along with other powers, is the maximum ambition that is achievable within the current distribution of power. Only on rare occasions will even the United States be able to act alone to shape new rules.

As National Security Adviser Menon admitted,

> In today's world we must also be ready to contribute within our capacity to the global public goods that are increasingly important to our well-being, such as freedom of the seas. Are we ready to shape outcomes on critical issues such as energy security and in areas such as West Asia? Not yet. We have internal hesitations due to what I would call the Partition syndrome and our fear of the communalisation of discourse. But more than that, our capacities, though growing, are still limited in certain fields critical to national security.[39]

In addition to its own capacities, another crucial element in India's rule-maker capabilities is its ability to manage "complicated coalitions." A review of India's participation in various existing and emerging coalitions, ranging from the G-4 to the India, Brazil, and South Africa (IBSA) group to the BRICS and the G-20, reveals a mixed record, at best.[40] This is partly on account of India's lack of capacity to manage these coalitions. It probably also reflects New Delhi's perception of the transient nature of these ad hoc groupings and, hence, its reluctance to invest more time and effort in their management.

In his thoughtful contribution to the compendium for the G-8 plus G-5 summit in L'Aquila, Italy, in 2009, titled *How the World Is Governed in the 21st Century*, Prime Minister Manmohan Singh gives pride of place to the UN-centered system of global governance, noting that "groupings [such as the G-8 plus G-5] do not have any special legitimacy within the UN System" and asserting that India "will continue to strive for the reform of the United Nations to make it more democratic." However, he also acknowledged that "efforts to reform the system have made little headway" and argued that the "unworkability of the existing structures [based around the UN system] has led to greater reliance on plurilateral groupings."[41]

Domestic Politics, Economics, and Multilateralism: A Symbiosis

There is broad agreement among scholars that India's approach to multilateralism and its role as a rule shaper will be determined by domestic economic and political drivers. As Sanjaya Baru argues, "India's biggest security challenge, in its journey to major power status, is largely internal, both economic and political."[42] Indeed, it could be argued that India's initial embrace of economic liberalization, globalization, and renewed engagement with multilateralism was directly related to the domestic political situation. As David Malone observes, in the 1990s at the domestic level there was the "growing pragmatism of political parties, which were compelled to engage in electoral alliances, more often ones of convenience than of ideological sympathy."[43] This "ideological unmooring of the domestic sphere was reflected also in the international arena," when India embarked on a pragmatic policy of multiple-alignment and built myriad strategic alliances in an uncertain world. Second, since 1991, foreign policy not only "assisted India in creating higher levels of economic growth" and allowed global opportunities to benefit "domestic constituents in the hope of ameliorating poverty," but also provided a "pathway to great-power status." Thus the Indo-U.S. nuclear deal was sold in Parliament not as a "strategic alignment" with the United States, but as an essential step to ensure energy security.[44]

This positive attitude toward liberalization, globalization, and multilateral engagement was made possible by three premises. First, it served the objectives of India's national power, grew out of sophisticated nationalism, and did not in any way negate it. Second, globalization depended heavily on the ability of elites to manage domestic politics. Finally, globalization also required a broad ideological consensus, a compact among global elites in favor of certain modes of regulation.[45]

In turn, globalization and economics are subtly transforming Indian politics. India's integration into the world economy, contrary to most fears, has lessened, not increased, the politics of anxiety. Politics is often shaped by subtle changes of mood, and India's self-image has changed considerably. It is beginning to have a sense of being able to change its own destiny for the first time in modern history. Some of this sense of self-importance is exaggerated. But there is a palpable sense in which India is less anxious and more hopeful as a nation. And nations in such a frame of mind are less likely to be hostages to a politics of resentment. At one level, India being a repeated target of terrorism is a grim reminder of how incompetent its state can sometimes be. But the fact that, despite all that, there was no significant internal backlash or politics of reprisal is a sign, not of apathy but of quiet self-confidence, which makes for more equanimity in politics. Again, this is an area where politicians, out of desperation, may try to score their own goals; but the undercurrent is toward creating a more sophisticated Indian nationalism, not one swayed by momentary frenzies.

Economics and liberalization have subtly transformed Indian democracy and the state. The Indian state is still often corrupt, venal, incompetent, and fragile. But under the surface a quiet transformation is taking place. First, Indian growth has been made possible by a high savings rate, which is now touching Chinese and East Asian levels. But 40 percent of the increase in the savings rate has come from enhanced government savings; the last decade was the first in which government went from being a net drain in narrow financial terms to a net contributor. The recent profligacy of spending and irrational subsidies and avoidance of the Fiscal Responsibility and Budget Management Act notwithstanding, the state is becoming more responsible in its fiscal approach. Indian reform has not followed a first-principles template, and it never will, but in unexpected ways the general direction of growth will prevail.

Similarly, identity politics will not disappear. But the default template is beginning to shift to performance. Economics has brought about this shift. The scale of government spending is altering the incentives for politicians. Until the late 1990s, even the best-performing government could not make much of a difference in the lives of the poor. A scheme worth about 1,000 crores (about $180 million) used to be considered a big scheme. So the default position of both voters and politicians was that the marginal impact of the state was low; it did not really make a difference who came and who went. Now schemes are of a greater order of magnitude; in some cases, more than 100 times bigger. This is leading some Indian politicians to conclude that if they perform well, the voters will reward them; they have enough resources to send credible signals to large sections of the population. There is an old argument in political science that, with the exception of India, serious democracy can only take root in a middle-income country. Political scientists often interpreted this to mean that a middle class is essential to sustain democracy. An alternative interpretation is that a politics of accountability kicks in only when the state is of a sufficient size.

And for voters as well, paradoxically, the stakes of politics are becoming higher, not lower. Although scholars bemoan political apathy in India, voters, particularly at the state level, are for the most part becoming more discriminating, and the vicious cycles of knee-jerk anti-incumbency are over. This will set up a healthier politics of accountability. The scale of government spending is making possible a shift away from the politics of identity to the politics of development. Although there is a long way to go, this change has been made possible by economic growth and globalization.

Moreover, although India's infrastructure remains woefully inadequate, the quality of roads, ports, and airports is improving. There is a real revolution in rural roads, although the energy scenario remains bleak. While corruption will not disappear, politicians have found innovative ways of extracting rents while at the same time ensuring that the quality of construction improves.

In addition, for the first time in India's history, if the universal identity scheme is successful, states will have the means to identify the poor; the main source of corruption in services to the poor has been that the state simply could not identify them. The universal identity scheme will improve the government's ability to deliver social services and subsidies. Consequently, the coming decade is likely to see higher growth, higher government spending (particularly if a general sales tax is put in place and India's ratio of tax to GDP increases), more elements of a welfare state, and therefore a greater interest in accountability. There will be ups and downs, but there is good reason to believe that India's current despair over accountability and its dismal prospects might become relics of the past by 2020.

The last phase of the deepening of India's democracy centered on greater representation for marginalized groups in politics. India will now need a different kind of deepening as a result of its success. India is among the most centralized societies in the world, and decentralization is important for various reasons. First, it is a much more effective mechanism of accountability than centralization. India's experience with decentralization has been mixed primarily because it has not decentralized properly; decentralization requires the devolution of powers and financing and the building of capacity. Despite the seventy-third constitutional amendment, India has not done any of these things properly. Second, decentralization is a better way of accommodating identity aspirations. Third, the biggest challenge India will face is coping with rapid urbanization. Global experience shows that unless there is clarity over what functions of government should be performed at which level, it is very hard for societies to manage rapid urbanization.

The elements of a virtuous cycle between politics and economics are now coming into place. They are often not the product of conscious design but a consequence of the cunning of unreason, intelligently exploited. India's growing inequalities may lock it into a growth trap. This can happen through several mechanisms. Growing class inequality can produce new forms of social conflict; the legitimacy of growth may begin to be questioned. These are genuine and serious worries, although they represent opportunities as well. Some degree of enhanced class conflict is not only desirable but also necessary to produce a politics of accountability. There cannot be a healthy capitalism without an intelligent left-wing critique, and despite the governance perfidies of the left-wing parties, this will emerge in due course.[46]

Against the backdrop of this dramatic domestic transformation, India is forging a new and sophisticated understanding of the currency of power in the modern world. For decades, India's approach to the world was hostage to fundamental misconceptions. It confused autonomy with autarky, sovereignty with power, and interdependence with a lack of independence. Its insecurities and inhibitions created a conceptual fog around how power operates in international society.

That fog has been decisively lifted. Today there is more recognition of the fact that the more India engages with the global economy, the more its power and security will grow. This is not just because of the obvious fact that an increasing share of world trade and investment will make India more important. It is also because the only sure path to peace is to create powerful constituencies in other countries that have a vested interest in supporting a nation's cause. Trade and investment create the lobbies that transform relations among states. Even more remarkably, a new way of thinking is emerging in some quarters in India that links foreign policy with pluralism and a new kind of multilateralism. Ask the question: What aspects of societies will, over the long haul, best prepare India to take advantage of globalization? Part of the answer is going to be pluralism and openness. Japan's economy is suffering because the country has in some senses remained a closed society incapable of accepting immigration as a solution to its demographic woes. Europe is struggling to acknowledge that it has become multicultural, and some of its nations' sense of identity is so fragile that a headscarf can put it at risk. Even China's capacity to negotiate pluralism remains an open question. For all its warts, a multicultural, multiethnic, and multireligious India has the capability to position itself as a mediator among different civilizations and ways of life. Although India can be vulnerable to intolerance and extremism, it is one of the few societies in the world capable of negotiating a deep pluralism. This inheritance is an asset in a globalizing world; it ought to be the cornerstone of India's foreign policy.

Both economic globalization and social pluralism need to be linked to what can be described as a multicentric multilateralism. This is not the multilateralism centered on a moribund United Nations. It is a multilateralism that enduringly binds nations in webs of interdependence through a series of overlapping institutions. India is now seeking to join almost any multilateral arrangement that will admit it as a member, from the Asia-Pacific Economic Cooperation organization to the G-8. These arrangements involve sovereignty trade-offs. But the underlying vision is that any sovereignty trade-offs are more than compensated for by the real power that accrues from participation in these institutions. The three elements of this emerging approach—economic openness, pluralism, and membership in multilateral institutions—reinforce each other. Genuine economic openness is not sustainable without an open society, and a willingness to participate in regional arrangements signals a commitment to openness and dialogue.

Conclusion

When the first wave of globalization began half a millennium ago, India accounted for around a quarter of global GDP. However, India's insular outlook, its lack of interest, and lack of capacity to play the role of rule maker or even rule shaper meant that the rising European powers stepped in to create a global order that reflected their norms, interests, and powers and resulted in the economic, political, and even ideational subjugation of India.[47] Today India's economic, political, and even social future is inexorably linked to the latest wave of globalization. This linkage, coupled with the changing world order, provides, perhaps, a once in a millennium opportunity to shape the norms and institutions that will govern the global order. Despite severe limitations, India increasingly has the ideas, people, and tools to shape the global order, "not wholly or in full measure, but very substantially" (to quote from Nehru's stirring first Independence Day speech on August 15, 1947).[48] Will India keep its "tryst with destiny" and emerge as one of the shapers of the emerging world order? This volume seeks to answer that question.

Notes

1. See Pranab Mukherjee, "India's Strategic Perspective," speech given at the Carnegie Endowment for International Peace, Washington, June 27, 2005, and Angus Maddison, *The World Economy: A Millennial Perspective* (Paris: OECD Development Centre, 2001).

2. "Nehru Worked for One World—Until He Felt Let Down," *Deccan Herald*, July 30, 2012. See also Manu Bhagavan, *The Peacemakers: India and the Quest for One World* (New Delhi: HarperCollins India, 2012), and Manu Bhagawan, "One World 2020: A Decade-Long Vision for India's Relations with the United Nations," in *Grand Strategy for India: 2020 and Beyond*, edited by Krishnappa Venkashamy and Princy George (New Delhi: Pentagon Press, 2012), pp. 253–60.

3. C. Raja Mohan, "Rising India: Partner in Shaping the Global Commons?" *Washington Quarterly*, July 2010: 134.

4. Ibid., p. 138. See also chapter 2 by C. Raja Mohan in this volume.

5. See chapter 16 by Nitin Pai in this volume.

6. See Centre for Policy Research and National Defense College, *Nonalignment 2.0: A Foreign and Strategic Policy for India in the Twenty First Century* (New Delhi, 2012) (www.cprindia.org/workingpapers/3844-nonalignment-20-foreign-and-strategic-policy-india-twenty-first-century), and Shyam Saran, "An India Allying with None," *Business Standard*, March 21, 2012 (www.business-standard.com/india/news/shyam-saran-an-india-allyingnone/468441/). See also chapter 3 by Shyam Saran in this volume.

7. See W. P. S Sidhu, "India and the Ascendency of the Global South," *Yojana* (May 2013).

8. See Milan Vaishnav, "India: State Capacity in Global Context" (Washington: Carnegie Endowment for International Peace, November 2, 2012) (carnegieendowment.org/2012/11/02/five-truths-about-india/ebjq); Milan Vaishnav, "Resizing the State," *Caravan*, October 1, 2012 (www.caravanmagazine.in/perspectives/resizing-state).

9. Shashi Tharoor, "Our Diplomatic Deficit," *Indian Express*, August 24, 2012 (www.indianexpress.com/news/our-diplomatic-deficit/992257).

10. "Avoid Unauthorised Intervention in Internal Affairs: India," *Hindu*, September 25, 2012.

11. See Nitin Pai, "The Paradox of Proximity: India's Approach to Fragility in the Neighbourhood," Policy Paper (New York University, Center on International Cooperation, April 2011).

12. See chapter 16 by Nitin Pai in this volume.

13. Shivshankar Menon, "India and the Global Scene," Sixteenth Prem Bhatia Memorial Lecture, New Delhi, August 11, 2011 (www.maritimeindia.org/article/india-and-global-scene).

14. W. P. S. Sidhu, "Learning to Preach What They Practise," *Mint*, April 30, 2012 (www.livemint.com/Opinion/9dChFE4uE0Zk38jkl8xesN/Learning-to-preach-what-they-practise.html). See also Daniel M. Kliman, "Advantage India: Why China Will Lose the Contest for Global Influence," *Global Asia* 7, no. 2 (Summer 2012): n.p.

15. See "India and the United Nations: Peacekeeping and Peacebuilding" (www.un.int/india/india_and_the_un_pkeeping.html), and Satish Nambiar, "UN Peacekeeping and India's National Strategy," National Strategy Lecture, Institute for Defense Studies and Analyses, New Delhi, March 4, 2011 (www.idsa.in/event/INSPInt/UNPeace keepingIndiasNationalStrategy).

16. See W. P. S. Sidhu, "India's Evolving Role in Development and Security in States at Risk," in *Engagement on Development and Security: New Actors, New Debates*, edited by Jake Sherman, Megan Gleason, W. P. S. Sidhu, and Bruce Jones (New York University, Center on International Cooperation, September 2011), pp. 27–28.

17. W. P. S. Sidhu, "An Absent-minded Peacekeeper, So Far," *Mint*, July 21, 2011 (http://103.1.112.210/Opinion/TOBPhkCEBZXNN3nyP5MoXK/An-absentminded-peacekeeper-so-far.html).

18. For discussions on India's UN peacekeeping role, see Nitin Pai and Sushant K. Singh, "Bring the Troops Back," *Indian Express*, July 10, 2008, and Anit Mukherjee, "Keep the Troops There," *Indian Express*, July 12, 2008.

19. See Varun Vira, "India and UN Peacekeeping: Declining Interest with Grave Implications," *Small Wars Journal*, July 13, 2012, and Kabilan Krishnasamy, "A Case for India's 'Leadership' in United Nations Peacekeeping," *International Studies* 47, no. 2-4 (April-July 2010): 225–46.

20. See chapter 10 by Richard Gowan and Sushant Kumar Singh in this volume.

21. See chapter 9 by David Malone and Rohan Mukherjee and chapter 5 by Sanjaya Baru in this volume.

22. See chapter 11 by Rajesh Rajagopalan in this volume.

23. W. P. S. Sidhu, "A New World Order: Make, Take, or Break," *Mint*, January 10, 2011 (http://103.1.112.210/Opinion/IbFW8gAjj7MVHHbZUfcCqK/A-new-world-order-make-take-or-break.html).

24. Heather Stewart, "Tariffs: WTO Talks Collapse after India and China Clash with America over Farm Products," *Guardian*, July 29, 2008, and Anthony Faiola and Rama Lakshmi, "Trade Talks Crumble in Feud over Farm Aid," *Washington Post*, July 30, 2008.

25. Bruce Einhorn and Mehul Srivastava, "WTO: Why India and China Said No to U.S.," *Businessweek*, July 30, 2008.

26. Ibid.

27. See chapter 5 by Sanjaya Baru in this volume.

28. Robert Wolfe, "Sprinting during a Marathon: Why the WTO Ministerial Failed in July 2008," Working Paper (Paris: Groupe d'Economie Mondiale, Sciences Po, April 2009), p. 27.

29. See chapter 6 by Tanvi Madan in this volume.

30. Stewart, "Tariffs."

31. See chapter 13 by Devesh Kapur in this volume.

32. Menon, "India and the Global Scene."

33. Ibid.

34. Bruce D. Jones, "Largest Minority Shareholder in Global Order LLC: The Changing Balance of Influence and U.S. Strategy," Foreign Policy Paper 25 (Brookings, March 2011), p. 2. See also Joseph Nye, *The Paradox of American Power: Why the World's Only Superpower Can't Go It Alone* (Oxford University Press, 2002).

35. See Centre for Policy Research and National Defense College, *Nonalignment 2.0*, p. 9.

36. National Intelligence Council, *Global Trends 2030: Alternative Worlds* (Washington, 2013) (www.dni.gov/nic/globaltrends).

37. See chapter 14 by Navroz Dubash in this volume.

38. See chapter 8 by Iskander Rehman in this volume.

39. Menon, "India and the Global Scene."

40. See chapter 17 by Christophe Jaffrelot and Waheguru Pal Singh Sidhu in this volume.

41. Manmohan Singh, "PM's Vision of How the World Is Governed in the 21st Century," press release (New Delhi, July 7, 2009).

42. Sanjaya Baru, "Strategic Consequences of India's Economic Performance," in *Globalization and Politics in India*, edited by Baldev Raj Nayar (Oxford University Press, 2007), p. 326. See also Amit Bhaduri and Deepak Nayyar, *The Intelligent Person's Guide to Liberalization* (New Delhi: Penguin Books, 1996), particularly the chapter entitled "Sensible Economics and Feasible Politics," pp. 159–81.

43. David M. Malone, *Does the Elephant Dance? Contemporary Indian Foreign Policy* (Oxford University Press, 2011), pp. 51–52.

44. Ibid.

45. Pratap B. Mehta, "Circle on the Globe," *Indian Express*, October 26, 2010 (www.indianexpress.com/story-print/702423/).

46. Pratap B. Mehta, "Nationalism Is So 2000," *Indian Express*, January 1, 2010 (www.indianexpress.com/story-print/562071/).

47. See Pankaj Mishra, *From the Ruins of Empire: The Intellectuals Who Remade Asia* (New York: Farrar, Straus, and Giroux, 2012).

48. See *Essential Writings of Jawaharlal Nehru* (Oxford University Press, 2003).

PART II

Perspectives on Multilateralism

C. RAJA MOHAN

2 The Changing Dynamics of India's Multilateralism

Introduction: Four Phases of Multilateralism

The evolution of India's multilateralism remains one of the underexplored domains of India's foreign policy. This is surprising given the pressing nature of the multilateral agenda in recent years—international trade negotiations, nuclear nonproliferation, global warming, humanitarian intervention, and the promotion of democracy—and India's complex responses to it. As New Delhi confronted these issues in the last few years, its multilateral positions encountered much criticism at home and abroad. Yet there has been no systematic effort to record, assess, historicize, and theorize about India's rich multilateral experience. Meanwhile, the popular, policy, and academic discourses on New Delhi's multilateralism are clouded by the political presumption of a default Indian position. Some critics of India's multilateralism argue that India is too wedded to the ideology of nonalignment, third world solidarity, Westphalian sense of national sovereignty, and the principle of nonintervention to make effective contributions. Other critics attack current Indian foreign policy for deviating too far from India's presumed gold standard of multilateralism. Neither view is backed by solid empirical evidence. Nor have systematic efforts been made to codify the multilateral tradition of India, its approach to various regional and international organizations, and the domestic contestation over these policies. Even a preliminary look at India's multilateral record reveals that it is by no means monochromatic. There is much variation in India's position on critical issues over time and across space.[1]

This chapter presents a broad overview of the evolution of India's multilateralism in four phases. It points to considerable difference between the presumptions about India's multilateralism and its practice in the real world. It suggests that India has begun to adapt to the new imperatives of multilateralism, while the pace and direction of change are questioned at home and abroad, and concludes with a reflection on how India's multilateralism could develop in the coming years.

Expansive Internationalism

The first phase, covering the final decades of India's independence movement and early years of independence, was a period of *expansive internationalism.* While India's emerging worldview had diverse elements in it, a strong streak of internationalism did indeed stand out. Rabindranath Tagore's critique of Western materialism and Indian nationalism formed the basis for the conception of a humanist internationalism. His ideas on Asian cultural unity and a shared spiritual civilization helped to construct Asian universalism as an alternative to the dominant Western one.[2] The discovery of Indian influence on Southeast Asia at the turn of the twentieth century had a big impact on India's own sense of historic linkages with the world and led to the notions of a "greater India."[3] The Indian communists and socialists joined various streams of left-wing internationalism. This period also witnessed a more centrist internationalism—a notion of a world federation or a "one world." Jawaharlal Nehru was at the forefront of making the Indian National Congress aware of the changing world in the interwar period and recognizing the importance of the external for India's own struggle for independence. The interwar period proved decisive for the emergence of an internationalist consciousness of the Indian national movement, which in turn laid the foundation for India's independent foreign policy under Nehru.[4]

The first diplomatic act of the new India was to convene the Asian Relations Conference in New Delhi in March 1947, a few months before formal independence. The proposal for such a conference can be traced back to 1930, when the Indian National Congress called for a meeting of all Asiatic people to promote greater solidarity and laid the foundation for an "Eastern Federation."[5] India's international role in the first decade after independence—as a champion of Asian solidarity and decolonization, opposition to racism and apartheid, rejection of militarism and call for general and complete disarmament, contributor to international peacekeeping, and proponent of peaceful coexistence between different political systems—is widely noted. A closer look, however, reveals much complexity in India's multilateral positions and occasional conflicts between positions held dear on various issues. These positions are at considerable variance with the contemporary understanding of a "Nehruvian foreign policy" and its default positions.

Consider, for example, India's current wariness of Western efforts to promote human rights; its strong commitment to universally applicable human rights is less appreciated or integrated into the understanding of India's internationalism. As Manu Bhagavan's work shows, in the drafting of the United Nations (UN) Universal Declaration of Human Rights, India did not emphasize nonintervention and the primacy of national sovereignty. India's negotiating position in the framing of the UN declaration between 1946 and 1948 moved in the opposite direction.[6] Nehru's mandate to the negotiators was to focus on the universalism of human rights rather than to undertake a narrow defense of the Westphalian understanding of sovereignty. The European colonial powers, which wanted to retake their old territorial possessions, sought to dilute the universalism of the UN declaration. If the European powers thought that colonialism and postwar international institutions could coexist comfortably, India was at the forefront of destroying that illusion.

Nehru's imposition of sanctions against South Africa, in protest of its apartheid policies, and the mobilization of international support against apartheid in the United Nations General Assembly (UNGA) underlined India's commitment to the universal application of human rights.[7] Nehru's decision to take the Jammu and Kashmir (J&K) question to the United Nations Security Council (UNSC) voluntarily underlined India's belief in the possibilities of collective security.[8] His decision to join the Commonwealth does not square with the widespread equation of India's foreign policy with "third worldism" or anticolonialism.[9] Nehru did not allow his notions of solidarity and anticolonialism to degenerate into crude third worldism. In the run-up to the first and only nonaligned summit in Belgrade (1961) that he attended, the Indian prime minister insisted that the peace question was more important than decolonization. Under Nehru's prodding, the first Nonaligned Movement (NAM) summit did something that is inconceivable today—attempt to promote a nuclear dialogue between the major powers and act as an honest broker between them.[10] Nehru's championing of global nuclear arms control and disarmament was not tempered, as it is today, by narrow considerations of national security. Recall that Nehru's India was the first country to sign the Partial Test Ban Treaty after the three negotiating powers—Great Britain, the Soviet Union, and the United States—presented it to the world in 1963. In signing the treaty, India was voluntarily forgoing the option to conduct atmospheric testing of nuclear weapons barely a year before China conducted its first nuclear test.

By the end of the Nehru era, however, India's expansive internationalism had weakened. While maintaining an impressive universalist approach to many issues, there was no escaping the imperative to reconcile principled internationalism with mundane questions of self-interest and realpolitik. India's inconsistent positions on the Suez and Hungarian crises in 1956 reflected India's ambiguities and the need to differentiate between friends and others in taking international positions. Nehru strongly criticized the attack on Suez by Britain, France, and Israel, while remaining ambivalent on the Soviet invasion of Hungary. Nehru and Egypt's Gamal Abdul Nasser were close partners in building Afro-Asian solidarity and the Nonaligned Movement, and the mid-1950s saw the Soviet Union support India in the UNSC on J&K at a time when London and Washington were tilting toward supporting Pakistan. Nehru's use of force to liberate Goa in 1961 was seemingly at odds with his relentless hectoring of the great powers on the peaceful resolution of disputes. While India was right in justifying it as an anticolonial war, there was no denying that it stood against the principle of peaceful resolution of disputes.[11] Nehru's expansive internationalism was also questioned at home when the political elites found little international support from the developing world in India's conflicts with China and Pakistan. Nehru himself had to turn to the United States for help in coping with the Chinese aggression in 1962, undermining the much-vaunted policy of strategic autonomy and nonalignment. Nehru, who began his stewardship of independent India's external engagement with the world with a major initiative on engaging Asia, ended his tenure by turning largely away from it. After the New Delhi and Bandung (1955) conferences on Asian relations, Nehru was deeply disillusioned and focused more on addressing global issues than on uniting Asia. The notions of integrating Asia and building an Eastern Federation soon disappeared from Nehru's international agenda. While universalism and internationalism marked the Nehruvian foreign policy in the 1950s and 1960s, Indian diplomacy had its downside as well. Its prickliness in multilateral fora and a tendency to get carried away with its own rhetoric steadily distanced India from its friends in the West.

Dysfunctional Multilateralism

The post-Nehru period in India's international engagement, extending from the mid-1960s to the late 1980s, constitutes the second phase and might be called the period of *dysfunctional multilateralism*. India survived the many difficult years that followed the death of its first prime minister. The 1960s, called

India's dangerous decade, saw two wars (with China and Pakistan), extended famine, profound economic instability, and deepening internal political divisions. India came out of the 1960s stronger, acquiring self-sufficiency in food production and overcoming political fragmentation with the revitalization of the Indian National Congress under the leadership of Indira Gandhi. If the wars of the 1960s seemed to diminish the image of India, its successful liberation of Bangladesh in 1971 and the demonstration of nuclear capability in 1974 seemed to restore some of India's political prestige. Its de facto alliance with the Soviet Union in response to the Sino-U.S. rapprochement seemed to generate a reasonably stable balance of power in India's immediate neighborhood. The new third world majority at the UNGA opened the door for India to play a larger role at the United Nations. The détente between the two superpowers provided an opportunity to move the UN beyond the political paralysis of the 1950s and 1960s and to construct a more cooperative world order.

Yet in retrospect the period was counterproductive for India on the international stage.[12] India's approach to multilateralism moved from the idealistic orientation of the Nehru years to a more ideological one in the 1970s and 1980s. In this phase, India's internationalism was increasingly less liberal and its posturing was more radical. In part this was due to the radicalization of the Nonaligned Movement in the 1970s and its increasingly anti-Western orientation. To be sure, India's positions were less extreme than others in the NAM, and India consistently sought to promote cooperation between the developed and developing countries rather than a confrontation between the North and the South. In the 1950s and early 1960s, Nehru had the strength to resist the radical forces seeking a strong anti-Western orientation for the movement. His successors did not. In the 1970s, India drifted along with the radical rhetoric in the NAM, the UNGA, and the G-77. This, in turn, steadily distanced India from the West and limited its freedom for maneuver on the global stage. In the 1950s, India's internationalism allowed it to win favors from both the East and the West. Its increasing tilt toward radicalism and the Soviet Union also cost India politically with many moderate states in the developing world and in the NAM.

On the economic front, India's leftward drift at home in the late 1960s coincided with the radicalization of the NAM and the virulence with which it championed the causes of the developing world or, as it came to be known, the Global South. The greater emphasis on economic autarchy at home sat nicely with the external emphasis on "collective self-reliance" of the third world. But here is the paradox. India's focus on constructing the New International Economic Order peaked at precisely the time when India began to delink itself from the flows of global commerce and capital. The more limited India's economic engagement became with the world, the more passionate was its call for reordering global financial and trading systems. While India's multilateral campaign bestirred the third world, it had little impact on the international trade and financial systems. Worse still, India's historic economic links with fellow third world nations in Asia and the Indian Ocean steadily dissipated amid the inward turn of India's economy. Given the emphasis on import substitution, there was little prospect for deepening the commercial links with neighboring regions. This, in turn, meant the inevitable disappearance of the agenda for regional economic integration. Indian officials met their third world counterparts in Geneva and New York, drafting ambitious resolutions, but did little to promote trade links with each other. The talk of "South-South cooperation" was largely on paper, for the pursuit of "socialism in one country" in isolation was not conducive to beneficial economic engagement.

On the political security front, India's policy shifted away from urging the superpowers to talk and cooperate with each other and toward cautioning against collusion between them. India pointed to the severe limitations of the détente and the paradox of peace between the superpowers in Europe translating into more intensive conflict between them for influence in the third world. India held that superpower rivalry outside Europe was at the heart of the emerging instabilities in the postcolonial developing world. Nehru's belief in the possibilities of building collective security yielded place to skepticism about the UNSC in New Delhi. Following the successful war to liberate Bangladesh from Pakistan in 1971, India was no longer interested in international involvement through the United Nations or third-party mediation from the United States (1962–63) or Russia (1966).[13] Equally important was the emerging gap between multilateralist rhetoric at the international level and the emphasis on bilateralism in India's own neighborhood. Also important was the tension between India's seeming commitment to third worldism and the widespread perception that India was playing hardball power politics with its third world neighbors. No one combined the two better than Indira Gandhi, who presided over sweeping internationalist rhetoric in the 1970s and was grudgingly admired by her friends and adversaries as a hard-nosed practitioner of realpolitik.[14]

If Nehru pressed the United States and the Soviet Union to negotiate nuclear arms control and accepted constraints on India's own strategic programs, his successors took a very different approach. New Delhi now criticized the framework of superpower arms control as being fundamentally unstable and too narrowly focused on temporary palliatives and for failing to undertake sweeping measures. China's nuclear test in 1964, a few months after Nehru's death, compelled India to pay greater attention to national security in the nuclear debate. India's hopes that the Treaty on the Non-Proliferation of Nuclear Weapons would address its security concerns were dashed, and New Delhi deeply resented the superpower agreement on promoting it. India increasingly cited reasons of sovereignty and security to avoid putting its own nuclear activity under any international or regional control.[15] As the world reacted with sanctions after India conducted its first nuclear test in May 1974, the divergence between New Delhi and the global nuclear order steadily widened.

Some of New Delhi's populist positions in the multilateral arena in the second phase often worked against India's national interest. Consider, for example, India's multilateral positions on space and information issues. In the 1970s, when the UN Committee on Peaceful Uses of Outer Space was debating the impact of new space and communication technologies, India argued against the use of direct broadcast satellites by one country to beam television programs into another. It opposed the transborder flow of data outside the control of the state. India argued that satellite broadcasts into a country without its explicit permission would violate its territorial sovereignty, which extended inexorably into outer space. That India opposed a technological application in which it was among the pioneers and that would turn out to be an important instrument with which to project India's soft power underlined the conflict between ideology and self-interest in India's dysfunctional multilateralism during the 1970s and 1980s. Even more tragically, New Delhi's espousal of the new international information order coincided with India's curtailing of internal freedom of expression during the Emergency (1975–77).

Toward the end of this phase, in the second half of the 1980s, the youthful prime minister Rajiv Gandhi sought to rejuvenate India's multilateralism. As he moved toward exercising India's nuclear weapon option, he proposed a framework for nuclear abolition that would involve obligations from states both with and without nuclear weapons. He actively participated in the six-nation, five-continent peace initiative demanding an end to nuclear testing and the weaponization of outer space. Rajiv Gandhi also launched an active campaign against racism that contributed significantly to ending the apartheid regime in South Africa. However, his efforts to revive the NAM as the cold war drew to a close made little headway.

Defensive Internationalism and Renewed Regionalism

The end of the cold war, the disappearance of the Soviet Union, and the collapse of the old domestic economic order by the end of the 1980s saw India hunker down in the multilateral arena. At the same time, India shed many of its earlier inhibitions about regionalism and actively sought to integrate itself with Asian regional institutions. This third phase, encompassing the period from the turn of the 1990s to the mid-2000s, might be called the era of *defensive multilateralism and renewed regionalism.*

On the security front, India found the post–cold war international situation deeply disconcerting. Having lost a reliable political ally—the Soviet Union—and some distance away from building a new partnership with the United States and the West, India had to navigate a tricky international terrain during the 1990s. Amid the Western triumphalism at the end of the cold war, there was much enthusiasm for empowering the United Nations to intervene in the internal affairs of developing countries. As the prospect of war between the great powers receded and the focus shifted to civil wars and intrastate conflict in the developing world, the new "agenda for peace" generated deep anxieties in New Delhi. At the core of the new agenda was the conviction that the international community has an obligation to prevent civil wars within the sovereign jurisdiction of states from escalating to unacceptable levels of violence. The failure of states to offer either minimal governance or security, it was argued, threatens international peace and security. Moreover, the territories of failed states become havens of international terrorism and criminal mafias and facilitate the spread of weapons of mass destruction. These concerns translated into doctrines of humanitarian intervention and the international "responsibility to protect."

The new humanitarian agenda raised Indian apprehensions about potential international meddling in Jammu and Kashmir, which were going through a troubled phase. New Delhi also had to face considerable diplomatic pressure from Pakistan for the internationalization of the issue. The Clinton administration questioned the accession of J&K to India and mounted pressure on New Delhi over the question of human rights violations by Indian security forces. The fear of external intervention at a time when India's internal security was facing turbulence led inevitably to New Delhi's rejection of the new international interest in downplaying territorial sovereignty and developing an expansive interventionist agenda. India's concerns about the international intervention in J&K were further reinforced by the post–cold war international emphasis on nuclear proliferation. The declaration by the UNSC in early 1992 that the proliferation of weapons of mass destruction posed a threat to international peace and security put India's own nuclear and missile programs under the international scanner.

The Clinton administration added to these concerns by declaring its policy goals of freezing, reversing, and ultimately eliminating the weapons of mass destruction programs in the subcontinent. Worse still from New Delhi's perspective, Washington began to see the nuclear and J&K issues as part of a single problem. The common refrain in Washington in the 1990s was, "Kashmir is the world's most dangerous place."[16] This, in turn, meant that the American and Western policies in the multilateral arena were running headlong into two of India's most important national security issues: the question of New Delhi's sovereignty over J&K and the future of India's nuclear missile programs. Seen in this context, India's anxieties about Western intervention—recall the past American tilt toward Pakistan on the Kashmir question—were not unreasonable and provided the basis for a strong rejection of the new notions of intervention and a defense of the traditional notion of sovereignty.

In the third phase, India also had to cope with the far more sweeping and immediate economic demands from the "Washington Consensus" on globalization. Unlike the J&K and nuclear questions, the external pressures on India's economic policy played out in a different framework. As India's economic crisis deepened at the turn of the 1990s, its political class had no choice but to embrace reform. This involved the liberalization and globalization of the Indian economy and shedding of many shibboleths from the past. While the political leadership understood the importance of reorientation, it was loath to be seen as acting under external pressure. Given the strategy of political stealth in pushing economic reforms forward, there was much posturing in New Delhi on standing up to the West and questioning the direction of negotiations—for example, at the World Trade Organization. India often seemed to act against its own long-term interests in international negotiations on trade, investments, and intellectual property.[17] Quite a bit of this had to do with the tension between the new international imperatives generated by the Indian economic reform and the reluctance of the political establishment to confront the costs of inertia.[18] This is not unique to India; all major countries confront difficult challenges in coping with trade liberalization. In India the concerns of the political class for the rural poor and the agriculture sector were driven by cold electoral calculus rather than ideology.

The third phase of India's multilateralism saw Indian leaders trying to cope with competing requirements. On the one hand, they had to befriend the West after the collapse of the Soviet Union and to reconnect with the international economic system led by the United States. On the other hand, they had to protect India's core national security interests, especially on J&K and nuclear issues, at a time of great flux in India's relations with the great powers and a period of intense domestic political vulnerability. On the economic front, the governments in New Delhi after the 1990s understood the imperatives of reform, but insisted on having the freedom to conduct liberalization and globalization on their own terms. As a result, India's approaches to multilateralism oscillated between adapting to the new requirements and holding on to past positions. This tension between the logic of the new and inertia of the old was reinforced by the deep domestic political divisions over the pace and direction of reform. If the centrist political formations were opportunistic—proposing reforms when in power and opposing them when out of it—the right and left flanks of the political spectrum were unrelenting in their resistance to change. On the diplomatic front, too, there were sharp divisions within the political class as well as the permanent bureaucracy on how best to adapt to the new international context and to define the nature of India's multilateralism in the new circumstances.[19] The situation began to change somewhat as rapid economic growth and steady improvement in the relations with the major powers cut India the necessary slack to move forward on the multilateral front without making too many compromises on its core national interests. This set the stage for the fourth phase of India's multilateralism, when New Delhi was far more comfortable in recasting its approach to international organizations, including the United Nations.

If India's global multilateralism had acquired a measure of ambivalence in the third phase, there was some enthusiasm in New Delhi for regionalism in the subcontinent and beyond in Asia. India was deeply suspicious of the initiative of Bangladesh at the turn of the 1980s to form a regional association for South Asia, concerned as it was with being encircled by the smaller states of the region. As it opened up the Indian economy and began to look for markets for its exports, New Delhi began to shed some of its inhibitions about the South Asian Association of Regional Cooperation (SAARC) and to emphasize the importance of promoting trade and economic cooperation within the subcontinent.[20] While progress was slow in the SAARC during the 1990s, India was more enthusiastic about partaking of East Asia's economic boom. For the policymakers in New Delhi, there was no escaping the fact that India had lost much ground in comparison to East Asia, which was enjoying the benefits of an economic miracle. India unveiled its policy of looking east and focused on becoming a full partner in the Association of Southeast Asian Nations (ASEAN) and its associated institutions such as the ASEAN Regional Forum. The economic transformation of ASEAN made it a model and benchmark for India's own economic reforms in the 1990s. All of this involved discarding some of the old superiority complex toward the region that Nehru once described as consisting of "Coca Cola Republics." Gone was the 1950s ambition of "leading" Asia. The focus was now on following the ASEAN, maintaining a low profile, and regaining India's weight in East Asia. The "Look East" policy became one of India's most successful foreign policy initiatives during the 1990s. "Regionalism," which was conspicuous by its absence in India's foreign policy lexicon from the late 1950s to the 1980s, now became an important component of the nation's economic and diplomatic engagement in the 1990s. It also marked a return to the Asianism that had animated India in the immediate aftermath of independence.[21]

Toward Responsible Multilateralism

At the turn of the 2000s, India entered the fourth phase of its multilateralism, which might be characterized as *responsible multilateralism*. Central to this new phase has been the erosion of traditional third worldism in India's approach to multilateral issues. A persistent claim of special responsibility to defend the interests of the developing nations had been the central element of India's sense of exceptionalism in the past. While some of that rhetoric endures, India has begun to discard much of that theology in practice. The NAM and G-77 are no longer the preferred instruments of India's multilateral diplomacy. While India does participate in them in a pro forma manner, they no longer are the focus of India's multilateral diplomacy. Smaller forums like the India, Brazil, South Africa group (IBSA), which includes three democracies from the South, and the BRICS, which also includes the emerging economic powers China and Russia, have become far more consequential for Indian foreign policy. On the international economic front, the G-20 has become a major arena of activity for India. Meanwhile, the third world itself has become a differentiated mass with sharply divergent interests in relation to trade, global warming, and arms control. In all of these areas, there has been growing divergence between India's national interests and the presumed default positions of the developing world.

As the pace of India's economic growth has picked up momentum, India's relations with most major powers have improved; cooperation in multilateral forums is at the very top of political engagement between India and the major powers. In previous decades, India's aspiration to play a larger role in the global multilateral arena was not matched by support from other power centers; today most major powers are urging India to undertake a larger role in regional and international organizations. For its part, the establishment in New Delhi has not been carried away either by the hype about India's rise or by the demands to take up greater global responsibilities. What India has done is to signal a strong commitment to a new and responsible multilateralism. The last decade has seen India adapt to the new imperatives of multilateralism. While the pace of progress does not satisfy India's external critics, domestic critics feel that India has already gone too far.

On the nuclear front, India has moved away from taking "all or nothing" positions to supporting partial arms control measures, even as it holds onto the rhetoric on global disarmament. The accommodation of India's own interests to the historic civil nuclear initiative with the United States, implemented during 2005–08, has allowed India to become part of the nuclear mainstream and contribute effectively to management of the global atomic order.[22] On climate change, India has moved away from the position that it did not contribute to the problem and therefore will not do anything about it. Through a series of actions that have elicited a strong domestic reaction, India has begun to take more constructive positions on addressing the challenge of global warming.[23] On trade issues too, India has moved toward significant liberalization vis-à-vis its neighbors and Asian partners, including the ASEAN, Japan, and South Korea. On the military front, India has ended its isolationism and embarked on an active military engagement with countries big and small. Looking beyond its focus on territorial defense, the Indian armed forces are eager to contribute to the maintenance of collective public goods in the security sector.[24] More broadly, India is willing to join other powers in defending the freedom of movement in maritime spaces and negotiate new rules in regulating the activity in outer space.[25] All of these strands underline India's incremental adjustment to its changing power potential and recognition of its new responsibilities.

As India grew to join the world's top-tier economies, in terms of aggregate size and not per capita figures, New Delhi began to sense that many of its traditional multilateral positions could no longer be sustained. When Rajiv Gandhi came to power at the end of 1984, India's total annual trade was barely $30 billion. In 2011 it touched $700 billion and is expected to reach $1 trillion within the next few years. India's two-way trade, counting only goods, now accounts for nearly 40 percent of its gross domestic product. A very different economy drives India, and New Delhi's international concerns are likely to be very different from those that dominated during the era of third worldism and nonalignment.

Future Trajectory

Although "strategic autonomy" remains the Holy Grail of India's international relations and is seen by its external interlocutors as the principal obstacle to a more vigorous role for India on the world stage, its extraordinary economic interdependence has begun to generate a whole new set of policy imperatives. In the past India's focus was on preventing the world from intruding too strongly; it is now under pressure to shape the multilateral system to protect its national interest. As economic self-reliance yields place to growing interdependence with the rest of the world, multilateralism is bound to acquire greater salience in India's engagement with the world. In the past, India had the luxury of resisting international rules and norms that did not fit with its worldview or national security needs. Today it needs to work with other powers in developing new rules and do its part in enforcing them. Consider, for example, that India needs to import more than 80 percent of its oil and a growing share of its coal. This extraordinary dependence on natural resources for sustaining India's economic growth and the well-being of its people demands greater collaboration with other powers and an active contribution to the development of plurilateral and multilateral mechanisms for resource security.

When India returned to the UNSC as a nonpermanent member in 2011, with nearly unanimous support in the General Assembly, it was widely assumed that the two-year period would herald the arrival of India as a great power playing its due part to maintain the global order. The West, including the United States, had endorsed India's candidature for a permanent seat on the UNSC, a major diplomatic objective of New Delhi since the end of the cold war. Yet there is deep disappointment in the West at India's reaction to the series of crises that have broken out in the Middle East since 2011. India's ambiguities about international intervention in Libya, reluctance to support regime change in Syria, and criticism of unilateral Western sanctions against Iran suggest that India is returning to its default nonaligned positions on sovereignty and nonintervention. Academic and policy scholarship has posited that India's emphasis on sovereignty and nonintervention is a big obstacle to New Delhi's future role on the world stage. It points to the "paradox of India's commitment to democracy internally and its dedication to principles of sovereignty and noninterference internationally. This situation creates confusion and potential conceptual obstacles for Indian development of distinctive contributions to the operation of legal rules and governance mechanisms."[26]

The framing of this paradox, however, does not stand close scrutiny. Whatever its rhetoric might be, India has not been squeamish about intervening in the internal affairs of its South Asian neighbors. Bangladesh, the Maldives, Nepal, Pakistan, and Sri Lanka have all experienced India's interventions to differing degrees. India has long considered this region as its own sphere of influence and affirmed its responsibility to maintain peace and stability there.

India, however, has tended to oppose unilateral interventions beyond its own periphery but has contributed to UN-mandated peacekeeping operations. What this practice tells us is that India's emphasis on "nonintervention" is not a high principle cast in stone. India is quite flexible on when and how it will apply this principle.

India's wariness about Western interventionism, however, has several sources. For one, as a former colony, India's strategic memory is indeed informed by the legacy of anti-imperialism. India has not forgotten how the imperial powers have used international organizations to legitimize their use of military force by framing it in high moral terms. Second, India is especially ambivalent about Western interventions in the Middle East, because of their perceived consequences for India's own large Muslim minority (close to 200 million). This has a long history and can be traced back to the concerns of the British Raj that its European rivals might foment the Muslims to revolt against Calcutta and the opposition of the Indian nationalist movement to the use of Indian forces for imperial objectives in the Middle East.

Third, New Delhi believes that India does not become a "responsible" multilateral actor by merely raising its hand in support whenever the Western powers decide to intervene. India is unwilling to be bulldozed by references to democracy, human rights, and other higher principles. After all, New Delhi has not forgotten the widespread international opposition to its "humanitarian intervention" in East Pakistan and the Western condemnation of Vietnamese intervention in Cambodia that ended the genocide by Pol Pot. Put simply, despite framing the logic of intervention in terms of moralpolitik, New Delhi believes that the use of force cannot be separated from the considerations of realpolitik in understanding the motivations and the consequences, intended and unintended. Fourth, the mixed results from the post–cold war interventionism call for a measure of humility in the Western debates about the use of force to promote presumed good in other societies. India's caution reflects the importance of making prudent judgments about the use of military force and when and where it might be successful. It is also about defining sensible norms for such interventions.

Fifth, India is aware that academic and policy fashions keep changing in the West. What seems absolutely the right thing to do one day might look foolish another. As Washington reflects on its occupation of Afghanistan and Iraq, many are questioning the wisdom of reflexive interventionism that has defined Western political instincts in the two decades since the end of the cold war. American president Barack Obama throughout his campaign for reelection in 2012 emphasized the importance of "nation building" at home and signaled that the era of interventionism should be brought to an end. "Nation building" at home is also at the very heart of Indian reluctance to be drawn into external military adventures. Pointing to the huge developmental challenges confronting India, National Security Adviser Shivshankar Menon argued, "India's primary responsibility is and will remain improving the lives of its own people for the foreseeable future. In other words, India would only be a responsible power if our choices bettered the lot of our people."[27] Menon went on to raise the question of India's democratic values and whether India should promote them abroad:

> Do we not have a responsibility to spread democracy and fight for our values abroad? Yes and no. Yes, if we have the means to actually ensure that we are able to spread them. And yes if having democrats as our neighbors contributes to the peaceful periphery that we need. But please remember that a people cannot be forced to be free or to practice democracy. They have to come to these values themselves if they are to be lasting. Such a crusade for one's values is often mistaken by others as the pursuit of self-interest couched in high-tone words.[28]

India's current attitudes with regard to the use of force and the promotion of its values are rooted in prudence and realism, qualities that the West might need as it redefines its international strategy in an era of austerity. To construct the problem of sovereignty and intervention in terms of a conflict between Western powers and rising powers in the multilateral arena would do an injustice to the complex considerations that must go into using military force to change the internal structures of other countries. As the debate evolves, it is possible to imagine the emergence of common ground between the Indian and Western positions on the use of force. The United States and its allies will have to move toward doing less, and India will have to consider doing more for the maintenance of international peace and security. Through the last many decades, India has had to intervene consistently in the internal affairs of countries in its immediate neighborhood given its high stakes in regional stability. As India's political interests are becoming more globally dispersed, thanks to the globalization of its economy since the early 1990s, New Delhi will find it increasingly difficult to take pure positions on nonintervention far from its homeland. The Western nations, in contrast, are facing growing domestic political resistance to stepping into conflicts around the world. A measure of burden sharing between the rising and established powers in maintaining regional and global stability is becoming unavoidable. Such a burden sharing, in turn, must be rooted in a new consensus, not necessarily universal, but with sufficient breadth and depth, with regard to when, where, and how to intervene in internal conflicts that threaten regional and global peace.

Notes

1. For a recent comprehensive discussion on the evolution of India's multilateralism, see Rohan Mukherjee and David M. Malone, "From High Ground to High Table: The Evolution of Indian Multilateralism," *Global Governance* 17 (2011): 311–29.

2. Stephen Hay, *Asian Ideas of East and the West: Tagore and His Critics in Japan, China, and India* (Harvard University Press, 1970).

3. Susan Baily, "Imagining 'Greater India': French and Indian Visions of Colonialism in the Indic Mode," *Modern Asian Studies* 38, no. 3 (July 2004): 703–44; see also Kalidas Nag, *India and the Pacific World* (Calcutta: Greater India Society, 1941).

4. Bimal Prasad, *The Origins of Indian Foreign Policy: The Indian National Congress and World Affairs, 1885–1947* (Calcutta: Bookland, 1962); see also T. A. Keenleyside, "Prelude to Power: The Meaning of Nonalignment before Indian Independence," *Pacific Affairs* 53, no. 3 (Autumn 1980): 461–83.

5. T. A. Keenleyside, "Nationalist Indian Attitudes towards Asia: A Troublesome Legacy for Post-Independence Foreign Policy," *Pacific Affairs* 55, no. 2 (Summer 1982): 210–30.

6. Manu Bhagavan, "A New Hope: India, the United Nations, and the Making of the Universal Declaration of Human Rights," *Modern Asian Studies* 44, no. 2 (2010): 311–47; see also Mark Mazower, *No Enchanted Palace: The End of Empire and the Ideological Origins of the United Nations* (Princeton University Press, 2009).

7. Mazower, *No Enchanted Palace*, pp. 149–89.

8. For a discussion, see Michael Brecher, "Kashmir: A Case Study in United Nations Mediation," *Pacific Affairs* 26, no. 3 (September 1953): 195–207; see also Aiyaz Hussain, "The United States and the Failure of UN Collective Security," *American Journal of International Law* 101, no. 3 (July 2007): 581–91.

9. For a discussion, see S. Gopal, "The Commonwealth: An Indian View," *Round Table* 60, no. 240 (1970): 613–17.

10. Homer A. Jack, "Nonalignment and a Test Ban Agreement," *Journal of Conflict Resolution* 7, no. 3 (1963): 542–52.

11. See Arthur G. Rubinoff, *India's Use of Force in Goa* (Bombay: Popular Prakashan, 1971).

12. For a critique of India's foreign policy during this period, see Shashi Tharoor, *Reasons of State: Political Development and India's Foreign Policy under Indira Gandhi, 1966–77* (New Delhi: Vikas, 1982).

13. See chapter 7 by Kanti Bajpai in this volume.

14. See, for example, Surjit Mansingh, *India's Search for Power: Indira Gandhi's Foreign Policy, 1966–82* (New Delhi: Sage, 1984).

15. Michael J. Sullivan III, "Reorientation of Indian Arms Control Policy, 1969–72," *Asian Survey* 13, no. 7 (July 1973): 691–706.

16. The phrase is attributed to a remark by Bill Clinton in 2000.

17. Amrita Narlikar, "Peculiar Chauvinism or Strategic Calculation? Explaining the Negotiating Strategy of a Rising India," *International Affairs* 82, no. 1 (2006): 59–76.

18. For a discussion, see Aaditya Mattoo and Robert M. Stern, eds., *India and the WTO* (Washington: World Bank, 2003); see also Suparna Karmakar, Rajiv Kumar, and Bibek Debroy, eds., *India's Liberalization Experience: Hostage to the WTO?* (New Delhi: Sage, 2007).

19. For a passionate defense of the traditional Indian view of multilateralism, see Muchkund Dubey, *Multilateralism Besieged* (Geneva: South Center, 2004).

20. See, for example, S. D. Muni, "India in SAARC: A Reluctant Policy Maker," in *National Perspectives on the New Regionalism in the South*, edited by Bjorn Hettne, Andras Inotai, and Osvaldo Sunkel (New York: St. Martin's, 2000), pp. 108–31.

21. See Christophe Jaffrelot, "India's Look East Policy: An Asianist Strategy in Perspective," *India Review* 2, no. 2 (2003): 35–68.

22. For a discussion of the origins of the deal and the strategic logic that moved it, see C. Raja Mohan, *Impossible Allies: Nuclear India, United States, and the Changing Global Order* (New Delhi: India Research Press, 2006).

23. See Lavanya Rajamani, "India and Climate Change: What India Wants, Needs, and Needs to Do," *India Review* 8, no. 3 (2009): 340–74; see also Joachim Betz, "India's Turn in Climate Policy: Assessing the Interplay of Domestic and International Policy Change," GIGA Working Paper 190 (Hamburg: German Institute of Global and Area Studies, March 2012).

24. See Institute for Defense Studies and Analyses, *Net Security Provider: India's Out of Area Contingency Operations* (New Delhi: Magnum Books, 2012).

25. See C. Raja Mohan, "Rising India: Partner in Shaping Global Commons?" *Washington Quarterly* 33, no. 3 (July 2010): 133–48.

26. David P. Fidler and Sumit Ganguly, "India and Eastphalia," *Indiana Journal of Global Legal Studies* 17, no. 1 (Winter 2010): 163.

27. Shivshankar Menon, "India and the Global Scene," Sixteenth Prem Bhatia Memorial Lecture, New Delhi, August 11, 2011 (www.maritimeindia.org/article/india-and-global-scene).

28. Ibid.

SHYAM SARAN

3 India and Multilateralism: A Practitioner's Perspective

Introduction

While multilateralism is a broad concept, encompassing relations among states beyond the bilateral context, for the purposes of this chapter I confine myself to India's approach to the United Nations (UN) and its institutions and processes. In order to highlight how India has conducted itself in this specific multilateral context, I draw on my experience as a professional diplomat, representing India in two different UN forums and at two different time periods. The first part draws on my experience as India's representative at the Conference on Disarmament in Geneva (earlier known as the forty-nation Committee on Disarmament) from 1980 to 1983. The second part comments on the more contemporary multilateral climate change negotiations, this time using my experience as India's chief negotiator on climate change from 2007 to 2010. In the concluding part of the chapter, I make general observations about the role of the UN as the premier multilateral institution and instrument of global governance in a rapidly changing world and India's place in it.

India has been an early and mostly enthusiastic supporter of the United Nations and the principle and practice of multilateralism. Despite the fact that India was not included as an original permanent member of the United Nations Security Council (UNSC), India's first prime minister, Jawaharlal Nehru, accorded an unqualified endorsement of the UN charter and the establishment of the United Nations in 1945, even before India had formally gained independence from British colonial rule. India has been one of the most active members of the UN right from its inception, often playing a role beyond what may have been warranted by its economic or military capabilities.

Its role has been wide ranging, covering several domains. During the early years, particularly in the 1950s, India played a critical and influential role in the negotiations on the Universal Declaration of Human Rights, the mobilization of international opinion against apartheid in South Africa, and the promotion of decolonization and peace throughout the world, becoming an early contributor of armed forces for UN peacekeeping operations. The same activism was visible on issues of general and complete disarmament, the promotion of a more equitable international economic order, and the negotiation of several complex international legal instruments such as the law of the sea. This tradition of activism continues today, although it is manifest in a posture different from that of the cold war era, responding to a vastly transformed international geopolitical terrain and a greatly transformed India itself.

What has been the main driver behind this activism in multilateral forums, in particular, the United Nations? In a world dominated by major powers deploying significant economic and military capabilities, India saw in the UN and the multilateral processes encompassed within it a useful support for its own search for relative strategic autonomy. There has been an enduring preference for multilateral, rule-based international regimes that would limit, though not fully constrain, the resort to unilateralism, which is the hallmark of great-power behavior. The United Nations also provided a useful platform on which India could mobilize the numerically growing constituency of newly emerging independent states in support of its own policy objectives, thus making up for its own limited economic and military clout. Finally, the UN and its agencies and the Bretton Woods institutions associated with it—the International Monetary Fund and the World Bank—became significant sources of financial and technological resources to support India's own economic and social development. Multilateral support, it was felt, entailed a lesser political price than bilateral assistance.

This chapter examines how these principles were put into practice and with what success in two multilateral processes—one involving international security and disarmament and the other involving climate change.

The Conference on Disarmament: 1980–83

In January 1980 I joined India's permanent mission to the United Nations as the country's alternate representative to the Committee on Disarmament, now known as the Conference on Disarmament (CD). Its mandate was to negotiate multilateral arms control and disarmament agreements. In 1980 it had forty members. The CD was an autonomous multilateral negotiating body, which set its own rules of procedure and working agenda. Nevertheless, it did report to the First Committee of the General Assembly, and its secretary was appointed by the UN secretary general. The CD was also serviced by the UN and met on the UN premises. The nonaligned and neutral countries together formed the Group of 21, which was an informal consultative forum of members who belonged neither to the United States–led North Atlantic Treaty Organization (NATO) alliance nor to the Soviet-led Warsaw Pact. In a typical week, the CD would meet twice in formal plenary meetings and once or twice in informal meetings, and the Group of 21 would meet informally at least once.

When I took up my assignment, four working groups had been set up to negotiate specific instruments. These groups covered four agenda items: (a) Chemical Weapons, (b) Radiological Weapons, (c) Negative Security Guarantees, and (d) the Comprehensive Program on Disarmament. Of these four groups, only the one on chemical weapons one led to a successful outcome (in the form of the Chemical Weapons Convention); the other three issues still remain on the CD agenda. The head of the Indian delegation would attend the plenary meetings and some of the informal meetings; as the alternate representative, I would participate in the working group sessions, each meeting at least once a week. I would also cover the Group of 21 meetings, although the permanent representative would attend whenever important policy matters would be discussed. In a typical week, my records show, I would attend nine to ten separate meetings and several as the sole Indian representative. Both Western and Socialist bloc delegations typically were large, deploying diplomats and domain experts for each of the working groups. Even the Chinese delegation sent sixteen or seventeen representatives to the CD. Most of the other developing countries, like India, had one- or two-member delegations and certainly no domain experts. Thus developing countries, despite their theoretical advantage in numbers, faced an asymmetrical situation in multilateral forums because they could not afford to field large delegations and, in most cases, did not have the specialized knowledge or background that negotiations on sometimes complex technical issues required.

It is true that by the end of my tenure at the CD, I had, through compulsion, acquired a working knowledge of some of the intricacies involved in the issues under negotiation, but I was always at a disadvantage when the negotiations had to deal with complex technical issues.

The period from 1980 to 1983 saw a sharpening of East-West tensions, particularly with the inauguration of the Reagan presidency in the United States. Despite a great deal of activity in the CD, there was little or no progress in the negotiations because of these tensions. The Group of 21 saw its role mainly as a vocal pressure group, constantly reminding both East and West of their responsibility to maintain international peace and security and to deliver on their commitment to achieve nuclear disarmament. One of the encouraging features was the sense of solidarity among the Group of 21, despite divergent interests on specific issues such as nuclear nonproliferation. It was mainly as a result of this solidarity and close cooperation among the nonaligned countries that the second UN Special Session on Disarmament in 1983 was able to prevent the erosion of the international consensus achieved in the declaration of the first special session convened in 1979. As a delegate representing a leading nonaligned country, I certainly felt confident and empowered to articulate positions that were critical of both the East and the West. It was exciting working together with some very gifted and eloquent diplomats from countries like Argentina, Brazil, and Mexico from Latin America, Pakistan and Sri Lanka from South Asia, and Algeria, Egypt, and Nigeria from Africa. The Mexican representative, Ambassador Alfonso García Robles, was already a legend, while Ambassador Oluyemi Adeniji from Nigeria commanded immense respect. Mohamed El Baradei from Egypt was a most persuasive colleague, whose qualities as a diplomat already marked him for greater things in the future. The Nonaligned Movement (NAM) did exercise a moral influence in the domain of international peace, security, and disarmament. It carved out a space for peace and moderation in a world riven by ideological and great-power conflict. The subsequent weakening of the NAM and its eventual enfeeblement marked the end of the global movement for peace and disarmament. Step by step, India, too, began to look at its own security interest through the narrower prism of nationalism, moderated less and less by an earlier spirit of internationalism.

What is worthwhile noting is the fact that the UN, during that time, saw itself as a custodian of the interests of the international community, as articulated in UN declarations and consensus documents. Its role was not that of an impartial referee or, worse, a mute and mechanical service provider, but that of an active facilitator in achieving the objectives set forth by the UN. Thus, in his own quiet way, the UN secretary to the CD, Ambassador Rikhi Jaipal, actively assisted in finding solutions, facilitating compromise, and even encouraging the Group of 21 to insist that the major powers, from East and West, fulfill their commitments to the UN. It was a different UN then. It had a different view of its role and its responsibility toward the international community.

In my days at the CD in Geneva, the Group of 21 nations looked on the UN system as a source of support and advice. Conscious of the fact that there was a lack of expertise and capacity among the delegates of developing countries, the UN offices servicing the CD provided much-needed expertise and guidance. This has changed. Today, more often than not, the UN Secretariat and its personnel are viewed as working for the major donor countries and advancing the latter's interests, rather than as custodians of the interests of the international community, in particular, its large constituency of developing countries.

In the last several years, the United Nations system has barely been able to meet its establishment expenses from its regular budget, which is financed by contributions from members. Virtually the entire operational and activity budgets of the UN and its specialized agencies are financed by ad hoc funds made available by its affluent members or the Organization for Economic Cooperation and Development (OECD) countries. It is no surprise, therefore, that in recent years the UN system has been perceived as the handmaiden of its more affluent members, dictating its agenda as well as the scope of its activities. The relatively democratic functioning of the UN, which was its hallmark in the early years, is a thing of the past.

Multilateral Climate Change Negotiations: 2007–09

I was appointed special envoy of the prime minister on climate change in January 2007 and in that capacity served as India's chief negotiator in the multilateral negotiations under the UN Framework Convention on Climate Change (UNFCCC) up until the Copenhagen climate summit in December 2009.

The UNFCCC is a remarkable international legal instrument adopted by consensus at the historic Rio summit in 1992. In mobilizing an international, collaborative effort to deal with the global challenge of climate change, the UNFCCC embedded the principle of equity in the phrase "common but differentiated responsibilities and respective capabilities." Recognizing their historical responsibility for the accumulation of greenhouse gases in the Earth's atmosphere since the dawn of the industrial age, the industrial countries agreed to take the lead in reducing their carbon emissions and to transfer both financial and technological resources to developing countries to enable them to undertake climate change action. The UNFCCC explicitly recognized that economic and social development and poverty eradication constituted an "overriding priority" for developing countries and that their greenhouse gas emissions would inevitably rise in the course of their development.

The UNFCCC was followed by the conclusion of the Kyoto Protocol, which incorporated legally binding emission reduction targets for the developed countries with a strict compliance procedure. The United States signed but did not ratify the protocol. In pursuance of the provisions of the UNFCCC, the protocol did not impose any emission reduction obligations on developing countries. The protocol set the emission reduction targets for a first commitment period ending in 2012, with subsequent targets to be negotiated later. In November 2007, the Thirteenth Conference of Parties to the UNFCCC was convened in Bali. It adopted, by consensus, a Bali roadmap, envisaging a two-year multilateral negotiating process on two interrelated tracks. An Ad Hoc Working Group on a Long-Term Action Plan was incorporated in the Bali Action Plan adopted at the conference. A parallel Ad Hoc Working Group on the Kyoto Protocol was formed to negotiate the emission reduction targets for developed countries in the second commitment period, commencing in 2013. These two tracks were mandated to come up with an "Agreed Outcome" at the Fifteenth Conference of the Parties (COP-15) scheduled to be held in December 2009 in Copenhagen. The objective of the "Agreed Outcome" was to "enhance the implementation of the principles and provisions of the UNFCCC," bearing in mind the increased urgency of dealing with the threat of global climate change.

When I took up my assignment as chief negotiator in January 2007, it soon became clear to me that I was engaged in something other than negotiations on climate change. It is important to keep in mind the broader international political and economic environment within which the multilateral negotiations on climate change had been taking place. First, there was the rapidly changing geopolitical landscape and changing relations among major powers, in particular, the growing profile of emerging powers like Brazil, China, India, and South Africa. Second, there was the global financial and economic crisis of 2008 and its continuing impact on economies around the world, but in particular the countries of the North. These factors transformed negotiations on climate change into full-fledged economic negotiations that focus instead on trade- and investment-related issues, economic competitiveness, intellectual property, and energy access. For developed, industrial countries, there is pervasive fear of losing economic ascendancy and affluent lifestyles; for emerging countries, there is fear of having their development prospects capped and retarded. In between are the large numbers of other developing countries, which believe that their very survival is being endangered. What was seen in 1992, at the time of the Rio convention, as the launch of a truly global and collaborative effort to deal with a cross-cutting challenge, on the basis of well-recognized principles of equity and equitable burden sharing, had now become a competitive process. The negotiating dynamic unleashed by this process could only yield a least-common-denominator outcome, not the "enhanced implementation" of the UNFCCC that had been originally envisaged.

What strategy did India adopt in these multilateral negotiations, and how far was it successful in safeguarding, if not promoting, India's interests?

In the initial phase of the negotiations, India argued strongly that the sanctity of the UNFCCC as an international legal instrument should be upheld. The "Agreed Outcome" from this round of negotiations would be not a new climate treaty, but rather the enhanced implementation of the existing agreement. It soon became clear, however, that the United States, the European Union (EU) countries, and other OECD countries were determined to eviscerate the UNFCCC by stripping it of its key principles, in particular, by obliterating the clear distinction between the obligations of the developed countries and those of developing countries. They introduced a new category of "major emitters" in which the emerging countries like China and India would figure and would be expected to accept emission mitigation obligations like the developed countries. The commitment to technology transfer was resisted on grounds that this would violate the intellectual property rights of technology holders in developed countries and lead to the loss of their industrial competitiveness. There was even less willingness to commit financial resources for developing countries to undertake climate change action. Private and public sources of funds were mixed together to dilute transfers of public funds from budgetary resources originally envisaged in the UNFCCC. There is no doubt that, despite its best efforts, India was unable to forestall the relentless attrition through which the UNFCCC was virtually hollowed out, beginning with COP-15 in Copenhagen and pushed further in subsequent meetings at Cancún, Durban, and Doha.

How and why did this happen? After all, India had built up an influential coalition in the BASIC group, comprising Brazil, South Africa, India, and China, which shared India's approach. The larger constituency of G-77 plus China constituted a looser coalition, but it, too, subscribed to the principle of upholding the UNFCCC. As pointed out earlier, India as well as other developing countries did not fully grasp the transformed character of the negotiations, which were now about economic interests rather than climate change. Insisting on the legal sanctity of the UNFCCC missed the point: this was about safeguarding economic interests in a world thrown into unprecedented turmoil, where appeals to legal rectitude had few takers.

The role played by the United States was a critical factor. It was clear from the outset that the United States would not accept a multilaterally negotiated emission target nor put itself under the discipline of an international compliance regime. In addition, neither on the issue of technology transfer nor on the extension of public funds to developing countries was it ready to adhere to the commitments made in the UNFCCC. At the most, it was ready to accept a voluntary "pledge and review" regime, with no compliance procedure. The United States set this very low bar quite early in the negotiations, and the choice before the other developed countries was either to reject the U.S. approach and forge a broad consensus with the developing countries, based on the Bali roadmap, or to race to the bottom and align with the United States. Once the EU decided that the United States had to be part of the "Agreed Outcome," it was no longer possible to forge a consensus with the rest in preserving the main elements of the UNFCCC, despite this being the preference of the key members of the EU. There was a point, early in 2009, when some understanding between BASIC and the EU seemed possible. The French were interested. However, this was not pursued vigorously enough. The prospect of alienating the United States made both the EU and BASIC nervous. As it turned out, the United States itself did not think twice about sacrificing EU positions on certain key issues once it got what it wanted in a late-night encounter with the BASIC leaders, enabling the adoption of the Copenhagen Accord.

The emergence of BASIC as an influential interlocutor at Copenhagen was not necessarily a positive from the Indian point of view. The United States–BASIC deal making may have alienated the larger constituency of developing countries, which have usually followed India's lead in most multilateral forums. This was very much in evidence at the subsequent meetings of COP-15 at Cancún, Durban, and Doha. Possible ways forward include promoting technological collaboration through a network of innovation centers, supporting the least developed countries, small island developing states, and Africa, encouraging extensive bilateral cooperation as well as cooperation under the auspices of the UN on climate change action and renewable energy, forging a commitment not to resort to trade protection, and making a firm commitment to the UN process.

What is becoming apparent is that India, as an emerging power, has interests that are decidedly more complex and differentiated than its earlier role as a champion of the South. This is related both to the changes in the global geopolitical landscape as well as to India's own impact on that landscape as an emerging power. For some time now, there has been a steady trend toward the diffusion of economic as well as political power. This diffusion of power has been accompanied by the rising salience of several cross-cutting and transnational challenges, such as energy security, food and water security, international terrorism, and global pandemics among others. Dealing with these global challenges in a world where power is becoming steadily more diffused and fragmented will require the active cooperation of all major emerging economies. Global regimes to address such challenges can no longer be imposed on the rest of the world by a handful of powerful countries. If the emerging countries are not always able to prevail in shaping the global regime in any particular domain, they are certainly able to prevent such a regime from being imposed without their assent. This was apparent at the Doha Development Round of multilateral trade negotiations and, to a lesser degree, at the climate change negotiations. This may create the impression that the emerging countries are being obstructive in such negotiations. Quite the contrary, they are becoming more effective in safeguarding their interests. And these interests do not always coincide with those of the larger constituency of developing countries either.

As India stands on the threshold of a single negotiating process under the Ad Hoc Working Group on the Durban Platform mandated to come up with a new climate change regime by 2015, it is imperative that New Delhi review its negotiating strategy so as to salvage some lost ground and safeguard its vital interests. To begin with, India needs to acknowledge that it is engaged in full-fledged economic negotiations rather than technical deliberations on climate change. India must ensure that it does not acquiesce in a climate regime that diminishes, not enhances, its prospects for economic development. If India has to take on emission reduction obligations post-2020, then it may be in its interest to link this with an insistence on a robust regime with a strong compliance procedure rather than accept the approach, exemplified by the U.S. position, which wishes to establish a "pledge and review" regime with no compliance mechanism. This is precisely because India will be the most severely affected by climate change.

It is also necessary to engage in sustained and vigorous diplomacy to build and maintain a critical mass of support among like-minded and developing countries for India's negotiating posture. Our lack of consistency in the recent past has confused and even alienated some of our partners. Our display of flexibility to gain support from some of the developed countries has led to even greater erosion of our position in the negotiations without any tangible gains.

While reassessing its strategy at the multilateral negotiations on climate change, India must nevertheless continue to pursue the vigorous implementation of its ambitious National Action Plan on Climate Change. The plan constitutes a visionary blueprint for sustainable development of our country and has its own compelling rationale. This would also lend greater credibility and confidence to our negotiating posture in the multilateral negotiations.

Three Scenarios and Four Lessons

The Indian Planning Commission has undertaken an innovative exercise in scenario building for the country as part of the approach to the Twelfth Five-Year Plan. The results are available in a document titled "Scenarios: Shaping India's Future."[1] The merit of the document lies in the fact that it clearly spells out the domestic and external challenges that define India's development space as well as the choices we confront in leveraging our strengths and overcoming our weaknesses in order to emerge as a successful nation in the decade and more ahead.

The document provides a rigorous and detailed rationale for embracing the "politics of empowerment" as against the prevailing and eventually self-defeating "politics of entitlement." It would be worthwhile to disseminate "Scenarios" widely in a language that is easy to grasp and to generate a wide-ranging public debate over its contents.

The document envisions three possible scenarios for India in the years ahead. These are "muddling through," "falling apart," and the "flotilla advances." Over the past several decades, India's default position has been "muddling through." It is the preferred choice for our governing elite, with significant policy departures occurring only episodically in response to crises. Hence the penchant for "reform through crisis," as we are witnessing today, or "reform through stealth," where change is slipped through, hoping no one will notice. Neither approach is likely to work for very long. This is because mobilizing political consensus behind change is indispensable in a democracy. And, surely, change ought to be embraced in the positive expectation of achieving better livelihoods rather than out of fear of "falling apart."

If "muddling through" is hard-wired into our political and bureaucratic elites, how do we change this? In a democracy, the politician responds to public opinion. He espouses policies that bring in votes and discards those that do not. Logically, therefore, we must create a critical mass of compelling demand in the electorate favoring reform and buying into what the document has put forward as a vision of the Indian flotilla advancing in relative harmony. The good news is that recent experience in several states tends to validate the proposition that the politics of empowerment can attract votes, transcending both anti-incumbency as well as lingering caste and parochial divides. Nitish Kumar in Bihar, Shivraj Singh Chouhan in Madhya Pradesh, and Sheila Dikshit in Delhi are examples. Regrettably, national political parties, and sometimes the national leadership of these parties, are out of touch with the changing aspirations of the people of India—the youth in particular—and will end up paying the price for their myopia at the hustings.

It is not enough to change the political calculus of political parties. The vast and entrenched instrument of governance, the Indian bureaucracy, must also be aligned with the reform agenda. This may be difficult, when much of the reform may involve its lighter and receding footprint and greater accountability. The current structure of incentives and disincentives that drives bureaucratic behavior does not encourage innovative thinking and effective decisionmaking. An act of commission that involves even a minor departure from the rules, or a less-than-successful result, may invite unwelcome penalties. Very rarely would an act of omission, even with a high opportunity cost of inaction, constitute a setback to one's career. The prevailing system engenders a risk-averse, decision-deflecting mind-set, which can frustrate any spirit of bold reform of a far-sighted political leadership. Without aligning career advancement with performance and capabilities, bureaucracy may become a drag on reform, when it could be transformed into a powerful engine.

The Planning Commission document brings home another important factor in successful nation building in a rapidly transforming domestic and external environment: a constant awareness that most of the challenges we confront today are cross-domain and cross-cutting in nature. The failure of our governance structures, indeed our societies, to comprehend this could lead to contradictory policies and failed strategies. We witness this in the energy sector, where different ministries, agencies, and public and private sector entities adopt policies that work mostly at cross-purposes and undermine our energy security. There is no energy ministry to take a comprehensive view and look at the energy challenge in an overall perspective. Nor is there an appreciation of how developments in other domains, such as climate change or changing trends in power consumption, affect energy security.

What is true of the energy sector is equally valid for other sectors such as agriculture, water, and urban development. The old silo approach and the ordering of governance activities around the outdated Allocation of Business Rules will frustrate any attempt to fashion integrated, multidisciplinary approaches to current challenges. Ministerial or departmental turf battles in both the public and private sectors consume the energy required to fight the much larger battles threatening the country.

"Muddling through" is no longer a steady-state phenomenon with minimal risk, as many of us seem to believe. As surely as night follows day, it will lead us into the scenario of "falling apart," which the Planning Commission document rightly warns against. In that perspective, the latest reform measures can only be a modest opening gambit. To sustain reform, a vigorous public debate is necessary, which will help to evolve a broad political consensus on where India should be headed and what means are necessary to get there. These scenarios could be a good starting point for such a debate.

This, in turn, will inform our evolving approach on critical issues that are presently on the global agenda. On each item on the global agenda, India will have to seek an item-specific balance, where our role as a global actor does not undermine our ability to deliver the basic development needs of millions of our citizens. The balance we seek must be relevant to their interests. We have done this before, but in a very different kind of world and confronting a different set of challenges. Multilateral, rule-based regimes remain our preference, but achieving the appropriate balance will test India's multilateral diplomacy for years to come.

What should India's strategy be to deal with this period of heightened uncertainty and rapid and unexpected change? One, I would once again repeat a mantra that I have put forward: "Engage with all major powers, but align with none." We need to become adept at forming and working through coalitions that are issue based and sometimes event specific. Dealing with uncertainty demands flexibility of response. It also demands contingency planning, the working out of alternative scenarios and Indian responses that are appropriate to each. For example, a prolonged disruption in oil supplies from the Persian Gulf is a contingency that could very well confront India, and we need to explore alternative sources of supply before that happens. Is it possible to redirect some of our sources of supply to Southeast Asia and the Russian Far East? Is Latin America an option? Could some of our demand for oil be converted to natural gas, which may be easier to access? As we look into these alternatives, new alignments will suggest themselves; perhaps a much greater emphasis on our relations with Russia; the possibility of turning IBSA (comprising India, Brazil, and South Africa) into an energy partnership or tapping into Iran's huge gas reserves if that country manages to escape the current turmoil in its Arab neighborhood.

Two, India remains a relatively stable political entity in an arc of instability stretching from the edge of Europe to the western edge of the Pacific. In an atmosphere of pervasive uncertainty, this attribute of stability is a strong asset that can be leveraged to India's advantage. It can serve to attract investment, and it can project India as a reliable and predictable partner. An international situation in flux creates the space for an emerging power like India to consolidate the geopolitical gains it has already made and expand its strategic space vis-à-vis other powers. This requires a degree of strategic boldness that is not always characteristic of the Indian temperament.

Three, for India, the geopolitical focus will be Asia and, in particular, the Asia-Pacific region. The emerging strategic order in the region is, in the words of one analyst, "profoundly maritime," and "geopolitically speaking the maritime balance would appear to be the key to further stability in Asia." With its significant and steadily growing naval capabilities and its geographic location, straddling the western and eastern reaches of the Indian Ocean, India is very well placed to be a decisive element in this maritime balance. A reordering of our security priorities in favor of our naval capabilities is essential if we are to consolidate and expand our role in the region. This will enable us to create the kind of countervailing presence that is necessary in order to ensure that Asia remains as multipolar as the world that is emerging.

Four, I repeat what I have advocated on many occasions in the past: we need to have a long-term and effective neighborhood policy. The Indian subcontinent is a single, interconnected, and cohesive geopolitical and geoeconomic unit, although it is divided politically. It constitutes India's strategic realm. The challenge for Indian diplomacy is to transcend the region's political divisions and enable a shared security and strategic perspective to emerge. Regional economic integration and promotion of cross-border physical and digital connectivity must become urgent priorities, because they may help to foster the shared security perspective to which I have referred. Without progress in this direction, India's larger role regionally and globally will encounter a constant constraint nearer home.

Conclusion

India today is an emerging power displaying all the attributes of a "transitional power" or a "premature power." The hallmark of such a power—in terms of overall gross domestic product, share of global trade and investment, and even absolute size of its middle class—is a large global footprint. However, in terms of domestic economic and social indexes, India is still very much a developing country, with modest average income per capita. A "premature power" still confronts major challenges of widespread poverty, illiteracy, malnutrition, and disease, although the country appears to be rich. Therefore, in playing a global role, emerging economies like India display an acute dichotomy. On the one hand, they are expected to take on greater responsibility in managing the so-called "global commons" and contributing global public goods. On the other hand, they continue to seek a global order that will deliver to them the resources and instruments they require to tackle significant domestic challenges. An Indian diplomatic practitioner confronts this tension all the time. I experienced this during the climate change negotiations. This was very different from the role I played more than thirty years ago at the CD, where no such ambiguity clouded my perceptions. Today, finding the right balance between the demands of a global role and the imperatives of domestic challenges is never easy.

Note

1. Planning Commission, "Scenarios: Shaping India's Future" (New Delhi: Government of India, June 2012).

SRINATH RAGHAVAN

4 India as a Regional Power

Introduction

Since independence and partition in 1947, India has largely been seen as a regional, more specifically subcontinental, power. India's core interests and its capacity to secure these have apparently been bounded by the geography and politics of South Asia. Over the past two decades, however, India's economic reforms and opening up have unleashed unprecedented entrepreneurial energy and sustained economic growth. The Indian state is steadily, if slowly, translating some of this economic tissue into military muscle. And as with most states, India's growing power has resulted in a corresponding widening of its own conception of its interests as well as its role on the global stage. Then again, the subcontinental considerations that limited India's strategic horizons in the past have hardly become irrelevant. India, therefore, is at an interesting juncture, where it needs to strike a balance between regional interests and its global aspirations—considerations that are not easy to reconcile. In consequence, the tension between these will remain a key feature of India's external engagements in the short- to medium-term future.

This chapter focuses on this key tension at the heart of Indian foreign policy. It begins with a brief examination of how India sought but failed to balance these in the past. It then looks at India's evolving approach to dealing with subcontinental problems and fault lines and suggests that New Delhi has attempted something novel in recent years. The chapter suggests that India's conception of its "region" has expanded over the past two decades and considers the principal issues on which India's new regional and global interests could be most problematic to resolve, arguing that, as India moves closer to achieving great-power status, these tensions will acquire greater urgency and edge.

Looking Back

India's foreign policy in the immediate aftermath of independence was undoubtedly shaped by subcontinental considerations. The disputes with Pakistan over Hyderabad, Junagadh, and Jammu and Kashmir (J&K), the treaties with Bhutan, Nepal, and Sikkim, and the problems over Tibet and the boundary with China all consumed India's attention and circumscribed its strategic vision to the subcontinent. Yet it is misleading to assume that India did not have larger aspirations during these years or that these aspirations were driven simply by a dreamy idealism about anticolonial solidarity, pan Asianism, or third worldism. In fact, from the outset, India regarded its engagement with multilateral institutions, particularly the United Nations (UN), as central to its foreign policy.

India's first prime minister, Jawaharlal Nehru, certainly thought that the UN could pave the way for a new form of internationalism in the postwar world. But he also recognized that it afforded a concrete opportunity for an emerging India to brand its image on the international stage and so pursue its interests with legitimacy. Nehru's approach toward the UN reflected his awareness of the multidimensional character of power. The use of military and economic power certainly enables a state to constrain the options of its adversaries and advance its own interests. But power is also exercised when a state devotes its efforts to creating or reinforcing political norms and practices that influence and shape the behavior of other states. This process of setting and cementing norms requires a keen sense of the sources of legitimacy in international politics and a willingness to work with and strengthen international institutions. This awareness lay at the core of postcolonial India's early stance toward the UN.

Thus India was an early and vocal opponent of the racial laws introduced by South Africa. Although the latter sought to take refuge under the cover of domestic jurisdiction, India forced the UN to express its displeasure with these policies.[1] Subsequently, New Delhi was active in the various international campaigns against apartheid in South Africa. India also played a prominent role in the UN's attempts to draft the Universal Declaration of Human Rights and the human rights covenants that were supposed to follow the declaration.[2]

From the outset, however, there was a tension between India's desire to promote global norms such as human rights and its wish to prevent the derogation of the principle of sovereignty. As a newly independent state, it is not surprising that India laid considerable emphasis on the latter. During the Nehruvian period, India sought to reconcile these tensions by advocating a thin version of human rights: principally nondiscrimination on the grounds of race, religion, or sex. This approach predated India's involvement with the UN on the issue of Jammu and Kashmir, but the latter reinforced the importance of protecting sovereignty and forestalling external intervention in issues of core strategic interest to India.

This did not mean that India entirely forsook its earlier attempts at engaging the UN to shape the agenda of international politics and to further India's own interests. During the 1950s and early 1960s, India continued to play an active role on issues such as race relations, decolonization, mediation, and assistance for UN efforts in Congo, Korea, and Vietnam. The payoff from these efforts was evident when the UN General Assembly approved of India's military action against Portuguese Goa in 1961—an action that was almost unanimously condemned by the North Atlantic Treaty Organization member-states.

Nevertheless, there was a greater wariness about permitting the great powers that sat on the UN's high table to override the sovereignty of postcolonial states. Equally important was the growing weariness with the inability of the UN to pull its weight owing to differences between the superpowers. Perhaps the key turning point was the Bangladesh crisis of 1971, when the UN refused to criticize—never mind initiating other forms of action—the Pakistan army's murderous crackdown on the Bengalis and the ensuing flow of refugees into India. The 1971 war underscored India's strategic superiority within the region but also left New Delhi with the abiding impression that the great powers were actuated by considerations of power, not norms. Be that as it may, in the years ahead, India remained an active contributor to peacekeeping missions under the UN umbrella. Although India was not particularly active on normative debates in the UN, its increasing profile in peacekeeping operations coincided with a period in which human rights were firmly on the global agenda.

India in South Asia

Throughout this period, India remained enmeshed in a series of problems with its subcontinental neighbors—problems that persist to date. These thorny relationships stem from a combination of historical and structural factors. To start with, there is the lasting and ramified impact of the partition of India in 1947. It is not an exaggeration to say that the subcontinent is yet to come to terms with the implications of partition. The economic, political, and psychological fallouts of partition interacted in ways that have greatly complicated the prospects for cooperation and peace in South Asia.

A second and related factor is the structural asymmetry of South Asia. India is by far the largest, the most populous, and the most powerful country in the region. It shares a boundary with every country in the neighborhood, but most of them do not share a border with another South Asian country. It is not surprising that most of India's neighbors regard it with wariness and resentment, if not suspicion and fear. These sentiments have been accentuated by the arrogance and condescension with which India occasionally treats its smaller neighbors.

A major casualty of this state of affairs has been the prospect for regional economic exchange and integration. South Asia was a largely integrated economic unit prior to 1947. But today it is among the least economically integrated parts of the world. The persistence of political and security problems has prevented a cool assessment of the benefits of trade and economic integration. Reconciling these sets of considerations is not all that simple. Economic affairs tend to have a win-win logic. It is easy to see how cooperative exchange could work to the material benefit of all parties. But in politics, moral considerations such as identity and honor can outweigh material interests. This is a problem that India faces with almost every one of its neighbors. Further, if political differences have a national security angle to them, it becomes all the more difficult for the logic of economic integration to assume primacy. Economic affairs are about absolute advantages accruing from interchange, but security affairs are about relative advantages gained by one side or another. Here too India's immense lead in size and power as well as outstanding political disputes have worked to reduce the attraction of closer economic ties in the subcontinent.

Against this backdrop, India saw regional institutions like the South Asian Association for Regional Cooperation (SAARC) as akin to the attempt by the Lilliputs to tie down Gulliver. New Delhi not only remained cool toward SAARC but insisted on a strict principle of reciprocity in its dealings with immediate neighbors. However, India's stance began to change over the last decade. The impressive growth of the Indian economy since the early 1990s underscored the possibility of using economic integration to ameliorate political and security problems with its neighbors. This was paralleled by a growing realization that India's ambitions to play a greater role in world politics—

commensurate with its growing economic heft and political importance—could not be realized by turning a blind eye to problems in South Asia. A troubled neighborhood will shackle India's ability as well as its credibility in operating on the global stage.

Speaking at a SAARC summit in 2011, Prime Minister Manmohan Singh observed, "Complete normalization of trade relations will create huge opportunities for mutually beneficial trade within South Asia." He added that India had a "special responsibility" in fostering regional economic integration owing to "the geography of our region and the size of our economy and market."[3] In another speech that year, he stated, "India will not be able to realize its own destiny without the partnership of its South Asian neighbours."[4] This turn in India's approach to its immediate periphery is significant. India sees closer economic ties as a way of indirectly addressing neuralgic relationships. By allowing its neighbors to partake of its economic growth, New Delhi apparently hopes to draw the sting from these relationships, secure a degree of stability, and pave the way for eventual resolution of knotty problems. This seems a more cautious approach than the standard liberal assumption equating free trade and economic integration with peace.

This shift in Indian foreign policy is also important because India is, for the first time, credibly poised to play the role of a regional dynamo. India's neighbors are gradually realizing the unprecedented opportunity that India presents for their growth prospects. India's free trade agreements with Bhutan and Sri Lanka and the trade and transit agreement with Nepal have showcased the potential benefits of regional economic integration. In this context, it is not surprising that Bangladesh wants to enhance trade and connectivity with India or that Pakistan has given most favored nation status to India. Bilateral initiatives have had a demonstration effect even in the more sensitive areas of potential cooperation. Until a few years ago, Nepal was chary of developing its hydroelectric power potential with Indian support. This development would not only have met Nepal's own energy requirements but also become a major export to India. The issue, however, was seen in Nepal as one of water sharing with India and hence as politically problematic. Such inhibitions were overcome only after Kathmandu saw the benefits accruing to Bhutan from embarking on such ventures and exporting power to India. Also significant is the fact that India—once the largest recipient of foreign aid—now has a growing profile as a donor. Afghanistan, Bangladesh, Bhutan, the Maldives, Nepal, and Sri Lanka have benefited from this turn in Indian foreign policy.

Another factor contributing to this shift in India's regional policy is the increasing presence of China on India's periphery. Since the late 1950s, India and China have had a fraught relationship. Central to this are the unsettled boundary dispute and the question of Tibet. Although progress has been made in the decades following the Sino-Indian War of 1962, the two sides are nowhere close to reaching agreement on the boundary. The question of Tibet is a related and thorny one. The presence of a vocal and active community of Tibetan émigrés in India is a cause for some concern to China. Although India does not recognize the Tibetan government-in-exile, it does not prevent the Dalai Lama and his followers from carrying out their activities so long as these are nonviolent. Until Beijing decides to come to terms with the aspirations of the Tibetans, this issue will remain a point of contention in China's ties with New Delhi.

Against this backdrop, the strengthening—in some cases, the cementing—of ties between India's neighbors and China is hardly surprising. Given their structural asymmetry vis-à-vis India, most of these countries have looked for countervailing influences. At different points in the last six decades, Bangladesh, Nepal, Pakistan, and Sri Lanka have sought and obtained varying degrees of assistance from external powers. The current Chinese footprint in South Asia is largely economic, although there are potential—in some cases, immediate—security implications as well. In the past, India has invested inordinate levels of diplomatic effort to stanch the flow of any external assistance that could impinge on its security. New Delhi now realizes that it is operating in a competitive marketplace: instead of shouting itself hoarse about the Chinese presence, it should focus on rejuvenating its ties with neighbors and increasing its influence in South Asia.

In short, India's approach to tackling political and security problems in the subcontinent now hinges on its ability to foster deeper economic integration not just with individual neighbors but with the subcontinent as a whole. In parallel, though, India's conception of its "region" has also expanded and introduced fresh challenges in its attempt to reconcile its regional and global interests.

The Extended Neighborhood

The expansion of India's regional interests has been primarily in two areas: Southeast and East Asia and the Middle East. This is not surprising. Prior to 1947, the Indian subcontinent was tightly linked in political, security, and economic terms to these parts. Over the past two decades, India's growing interest in these areas has been driven largely by the needs and considerations of its own economic growth. Starting with the "Look East" policy in the mid-

1990s, India has sought to foster its ties with Southeast and East Asia and so benefit from the economic dynamism of these countries. More recently, China's rapid rise has underlined the importance of engaging with this part of Asia. For one thing, China's own economic growth and development have been enabled by the coupling of the Chinese economy with the integrated supply and manufacturing networks of East and Southeast Asia. For another, China's economic rise impinges on the geopolitical balance in this part of Asia, with concomitant implications for India.

After prolonged negotiations, India has concluded a free trade agreement with the Association of Southeast Asian Nations (ASEAN). The agreement has already been operationalized with Malaysia, Singapore, and Thailand—countries that account for an overwhelmingly large share of India's trade with the ASEAN states. India has also signed comprehensive economic partnership agreements, which go beyond a standard free trade agreement, with Japan and South Korea. Bilateral trade between India and South Korea has increased almost tenfold over the last decade: from a mere $2.5 billion in 2001 to $20.57 billion in 2011. In the wake of the comprehensive economic partnership agreement, it could easily touch $40 billion by 2015. Trade between India and Japan has seen a similar expansion over the past decade and is poised to grow in the years ahead. Then again, India's trade with China is bigger than its trade with both of these countries put together.

Both of these countries have also emerged as important investors in India. South Korea made an early entry into the Indian markets in automobiles, electronics, and consumer goods, and its companies have carved a distinct place for themselves in India. India and Japan concluded agreements for an ambitious $77 billion Delhi-Mumbai industrial corridor project. Spanning six states, the corridor is projected to become a global manufacturing and trading hub—one that will foster closer economic and commercial relations between the two countries. Other areas of emerging cooperation include renewable energy and ecologically sustainable urban spaces.

India's growing relationship with these countries has also benefited from their concerns about China's growing economic and military clout in Asia. Take the case of Japan. China has been the favored destination of Japanese investment and exports. But deepening economic relations have not always worked in Japan's strategic interests. In dealing with China, Japan is seeking to diversify and strengthen its portfolio of economic and political relationships. From this standpoint, India seems an increasingly attractive partner. India, too, sees better ties with Japan as important both in its own terms and in increasing India's room for maneuver in Asia. The two countries announced a strategic and global partnership in December 2006. This was upgraded last year to include closer security cooperation and military exchanges. South Korea too is seeking to enhance its strategic ties with India. Seoul's decision to sign an agreement on civilian nuclear energy cooperation with India signaled its desire to inject a more strategic component into ties with India. In the future, there will be increasing scope for cooperation in the maritime domain—not just in conducting naval exercises but also in drawing on South Korean expertise in related areas such as shipbuilding and construction of ports.

Bilateral efforts apart, India is also engaged in multilateral efforts to craft a regional architecture for East Asia. Prime Minister Singh has explicitly stated that India stands for "an open, inclusive, and transparent architecture of regional cooperation in the Asia-Pacific region."[5] New Delhi regards the East Asia Summit as providing the institutional base for this architecture to take shape. India's interests lie in an Asian architecture that is neither dominated by China nor explicitly aimed at it. This gives New Delhi ample space and opportunity to work not just with Southeast and East Asian countries but also other extra-regional powers like Australia and the United States.

On several questions, India's own interests in East Asia are entirely compatible with larger multilateral interests and global norms. For instance, India has made it clear that while it does not take any stand on the merits of territorial disputes in the South China Sea, it abides by and upholds the principle of freedom of navigation. India has also insisted that its interest in exploring natural resources in the South China Sea does not conflict with competing territorial claims of the parties to the dispute. In fact, when Oil and Natural Gas Commission Videsh, the public sector company, signed production-sharing contracts with Vietnam for two production blocks in 2006, the Ministry of External Affairs was unaware of the potentially sensitive implications of the deal. Only in November 2007, after China lodged a formal protest, did the ministry realize that these two blocks were in disputed territory. New Delhi then took the view that the exploration should continue. After all, for many years China had a presence in disputed territory that India regarded as its own. Yet there are other ways in which India's interests might not align with the plans of regional architecture being drawn up by the United States and its allies.

For example, the Trans-Pacific Partnership (TPP) promoted by the United States as a new economic architecture for the Asia-Pacific region may not work to India's advantage. Signed in 2005 by Brunei, Chile, New Zealand, and Singapore, the TPP has drawn the interest of five other countries: Australia, Japan, Malaysia, Peru, and Vietnam. The TPP has an ambitious tripartite agenda. It aims to achieve a free trade agreement with provisions for protecting intellectual property, to create investor-friendly regulatory frameworks and policies, and to address emerging issues, including measures to ensure that state-owned companies "compete fairly" with private companies and do not put the latter at a disadvantage. While some of these provisions are evidently aimed at China, it is unlikely that India will find them palatable. Similarly, Washington's attempts to rejuvenate its existing alliances in the region and craft new ones could work to India's advantage. Yet the willingness of the United States to interpose itself in regional disputes could well embolden China's smaller neighbors to take stances that might not be conducive to regional stability. Adjusting India's regional interests in East Asia with its wider global ones may not be all that easy. Nor will it be simple to strike the right balance between deepening bilateral cooperation and building a stable regional architecture.

India and the Middle East

As in East Asia, India's interests in the Middle East turn on economic issues. The region accounts for more than 60 percent of India's crude imports and more than $90 billion of trade; it also comprises 6 million Indian expatriate workers who remit more than $35 billion every year. These factors make the Middle East central to India's core interests. In recent years, this region has also been in the throes of various crises and upheavals, ranging from the U.S. invasions of Afghanistan and Iraq to the various manifestations of the "Arab Spring." Recent crises in the Middle East brought sharply into focus the various tensions between India's regional and global interests. And the ones that loom on the horizon, particularly over Iran, could well pose major challenges for India.

Afghanistan is the most proximate country in India's extended western neighborhood. India's interests in Afghanistan stem from a variety of factors: its strategic location between Central and South Asia, the threats posed to India's security in the past from developments in Afghanistan, and the need to ensure that Afghanistan is not destabilized by its immediate neighbors, especially Pakistan. Since the overthrow of the Taliban regime in 2001, India has sought to carve out a distinctive space for itself in Afghanistan. The emphasis in Indian policy has been on cultivating strong political ties with Kabul and on reaching out to the people of Afghanistan. The principal—but not the sole—instrument deployed by India in pursuit of these objectives has been economic and developmental assistance. India has emerged as the largest nontraditional donor to Afghanistan and has already extended aid to the tune of $1.6 billion. Much of this aid has gone toward the reconstruction of infrastructure (especially roads and electricity), health, education, and community development projects. Successive opinion polls and surveys have shown that the Indian effort is viewed positively by an overwhelming majority of the Afghan people. President Hamid Karzai has remarked more than once that India provides "emotional strategic depth" to the Afghan people.

More recently, India has pledged an additional $500 million for developmental activities. The focus will be on increasing its contribution in the areas of health, education, transportation, agriculture, and small developmental projects. Further, India will also scale up its assistance in building the capacity of the Afghan state at various levels. Equally significant is the decision to embark on a "comprehensive economic partnership." These efforts, together with New Delhi's willingness to participate in the Turkmenistan-Afghanistan-Pakistan-India pipeline project, underline the new instruments of statecraft being deployed by India.

On the political front, India has focused on building links with the elected government of Afghanistan. After 2001, New Delhi has sought to shed its image as solely a patron of the non-Pashtun groups who had opposed the Taliban (the so-called Northern Alliance). It has not only built close ties with the government of President Karzai, but also urged the other non-Taliban groups to work with him. It is no coincidence that many of India's developmental projects have been undertaken in the Pashtun-dominated areas. Indeed, India has systematically sought to refurbish its standing among the Pashtuns as well as other ethnic groups in Afghanistan. Similarly, India has sought to steer clear of the Western coalition and focused on interacting directly with the ministries in Kabul and in the provinces.

India's relationship with Afghanistan has an explicitly strategic dimension as well. The two countries signed a strategic partnership agreement in 2011. The agreement reaffirms India's commitment to the reconstruction and development of Afghanistan. But it goes beyond the existing relationship and caters to closer economic and security ties. On the economic front, the agreement aims to facilitate the economic integration of Afghanistan with other South Asian countries. This is in keeping with New Delhi's recent efforts to foster better trade and connectivity in the subcontinent and so enable its neighbors to partake of its economic growth.

The agreement also caters to security cooperation. Afghanistan and India engage in a regular "strategic dialogue" led by their national security advisers. This provides a systematic framework for consultation and coordination of policies. More important, India has agreed "to assist, as mutually determined, in the training, equipping, and capacity-building programs for Afghan National Security Forces."[6] At this writing, India's assistance on the security front has been focused largely on training Afghan officers and the police. Looking ahead, the evolution of this dimension of the relationship will depend heavily on the nature and quality of the insurgency in Afghanistan after 2014 as well as the political dispensation in Kabul.

A key problem, of course, is Pakistan's concerns about India's security footprint in Afghanistan. In the past, Pakistan has urged the United States not to allow India to play any role in Afghan security matters and has even offered to train Afghan forces. Afghanistan and the United States have been sensitive to Pakistani concerns, not least because of the need for Pakistan's cooperation in dealing with the Taliban. However, this position has shifted toward looking at a larger role for India. This has largely been due to the increased friction between Pakistan and the United States over the last couple of years, especially since the killing of Osama Bin Laden. There is also a greater appreciation of the importance of getting on board key regional players like India. But much will turn on how the efforts to negotiate with the Taliban play out.

In any event, it seems reasonably certain that the Taliban will return to the governing structures of the country sooner rather than later. It has been clear for some time now that the U.S. exit strategy will entail a negotiated settlement between the Afghan government and the Taliban. The only questions are on what terms such a settlement will be struck and how long it can reasonably be expected to last. So far, both Kabul and Washington have held that the Taliban will have to adhere to "red lines" for any negotiated solution to evolve. These include forsaking violence, cutting ties with al Qaeda, and abiding by the Afghan constitution. Now these positions are at best seen as the end points of a settlement. It seems almost certain that they will be considerably diluted in the attempt to bring in the Taliban.

It would, however, be incorrect for India to conclude that either Pakistan or the Taliban has "won" in Afghanistan. Unlike the 1990s, the Taliban or its Pakistani patrons are unlikely to attempt a direct overthrow of the elected government. Rather, they will try to work within the government and undermine it. This insidious strategy will, in many ways, make it more difficult for friends of Kabul to respond to the evolving situation. Even so, India remains well placed to contribute to the stability of the elected government in Afghanistan. The strategic partnership agreement provides the requisite framework for such cooperation.

By contrast, other flashpoints in the Middle East are likely to present more of a challenge for maintaining a balance between regional and wider interests. This is already evident in Syria. From the Indian standpoint, the continuing crisis in Syria is problematic for a variety of reasons. Given India's dependence on West Asia for its energy needs and the huge presence of Indian expatriate workers in the region, there is concern that continued conflict in Syria will affect the entire region and that this protracted instability is highly undesirable. More worrying, the Syrian crisis is in danger of becoming the focal point for two axes of regional rivalries.

First, Iran has remained steadfast in its support for the Syrian government. Not only has Iran sent its own troops to bolster the embattled Assad regime, it also has pressured other allies in the region, such as Hamas, to come out in support of the Assad government. Responding to Iran's activism, Saudi Arabia and other Gulf Cooperation Council countries have stopped assisting the rebel groups. As Syria descends in a downward spiral of civil war, the sectarian overtones of the conflict could reverberate across other parts of the Middle East and even in the subcontinent. Unlike similar situations in the past—during the decade-long Iran-Iraq War, for instance—India has a much larger expatriate presence in the region, with ripple effects back home. Second, there is the danger of renewed fighting between Israel and the protégés of Syria and Iran, Hezbollah and Hamas. This could set the stage for a wider conflagration in the region, which would threaten Indian interests.

India's response to the crisis, particularly in the UN, has been to condemn the violence perpetrated by the regime as well as the rebels and to call for a Syrian-led peace process. In consequence, India has supported Security Council statements and resolutions calling for an end to violence or criticizing the regime's actions, but has refrained from supporting calls for President Assad to step down.

New Delhi clearly does not favor any form of external intervention aimed at regime change. India is concerned that, following Libya, Syria risks becoming a testing ground for new ideas and principles on international intervention. New Delhi believes that ideas like "responsibility to protect" have been deployed, especially in Libya, in ways that go beyond the consensus in the UN Security Council. Besides, there is concern about the selective application of international norms and the organized hypocrisy of the great powers. India's stance sets it apart both from the United States and other Western powers, on the one hand, and from China and Russia, on the other. Unlike the former, India does not believe that the norm of sovereignty can be easily trumped. But unlike the latter its identity as a democracy makes it difficult for India to diminish the importance of human rights. Such a stance is unlikely to endear New Delhi to either side of the divide. But it represents the kinds of situations India is likely to confront in the future.

Nowhere is this more likely than in Iran. Since the late 1970s, Indian foreign policy toward Iran has been pragmatic and attuned to the pursuit of its interests in Southwest Asia. Successive Indian governments have leveraged the differences between a Shiite Iran and a Pakistan that is increasingly a haven for Sunni extremists. New Delhi and Tehran also have cooperated in stiffening the resistance to the Taliban regime in Afghanistan. Iran remains a key source of energy imports for India. As with Afghanistan, its strategic location lends it considerable importance, in terms of both India's interests in the Persian Gulf and India's efforts to tap into the resources of Central Asia.

A key irritant in India's relationship with Iran has been the latter's nuclear program. New Delhi does not want another nuclear power in its neighborhood. India has voted against Iran in the International Atomic Energy Agency and has urged Tehran to comply with its obligations under the Treaty on the Non-Proliferation of Nuclear Weapons. The problem is not that a nuclear Iran would pose an existential danger to its Arab neighbors and Israel. The U.S. nuclear umbrella and the Israeli nuclear arsenal are more than adequate to ensure that Iran does not even contemplate using nuclear weapons. Nor will a nuclear Iran trigger a chain reaction of nuclear proliferation in West Asia. The Arab countries have, after all, lived with the Israeli bomb for decades. The problem is that the acquisition of nuclear weapons might embolden Iran in using its proxies to advance its influence in the region. The fear of nuclear escalation would constrict the options open to Iran's rivals. The resulting instability would undermine India's interests in the Middle East.

Further, a determined push by Tehran to acquire the bomb will catalyze the incipient rivalry between Iran and Saudi Arabia. This dynamic is currently playing out in third countries like Bahrain and Syria, where Iran and Saudi Arabia are supporting their respective clients. India has important interests in its relations with both Iran and Saudi Arabia. Saudi Arabia is now the largest supplier of oil to India. India, in turn, is the fourth largest importer of Saudi oil—after China, the United States, and Japan. The "Delhi Declaration," signed during the Saudi king's visit in 2006, called for a closer economic engagement and energy partnership. The latter will remain a critical component of the relationship in the years ahead. New Delhi is also looking to attract Saudi companies and investment in the infrastructure sector. Equally important is the presence of nearly 2 million Indians in Saudi Arabia. Indians constitute the largest community of expatriates in that country and play an important role in its domestic economy.

It is no coincidence that in recent years New Delhi has attempted to infuse a more strategic dimension into its relationship with Riyadh. Saudi Arabia has cooperated with India on counterterrorism and has helped to apprehend and extradite key terrorists wanted by India. The two countries have also begun discussing defense-related issues. From Riyadh's standpoint, the backdrop to this is the concern generated by Iran's determination to persist with its nuclear enrichment activities. The Saudis fear that a nuclear Iran will overturn the precarious regional strategic balance. Notwithstanding the differences in perception about Iran's goals and capabilities, this has provided an opening for India to build its relationship with Saudi Arabia.

At the same time, India has refused to go along with U.S. orchestrated sanctions on Iran. The cumulative impact of these sanctions could be to set back Iranian exports by as much as 35 percent, leaving China and India as the two largest buyers of Iranian crude. Iran currently accounts for more than 11 percent of India's oil imports, amounting to $12 billion a year. Faced with such sharp sanctions, Iran has agreed to a rupee payment mechanism for 45 percent of its oil exports to India. This, of course, works rather well for New Delhi, providing a major opening for Indian exports. Iran is already the largest importer of rice from India, accounting for half of the 2.2 million tons exported by India last year. New Delhi hopes to use this opportunity to push ahead with exports in other, higher-value sectors. India also aims to upgrade the Chahbahar port and its transportation links with Afghanistan and other Central Asian countries. India has used Chahbahar to send food aid to Afghanistan. Investing further in its development will considerably increase India's economic footprint in these parts.

More generally, as the Western coalition prepares to pull out of Afghanistan in 2014, Iran will assume a more important role there. From India's standpoint, it is not clear how the United States hopes to leave behind a reasonably stable setup in Afghanistan without Iran's cooperation. The deterioration of American ties with both Iran and Pakistan portends greater instability in Afghanistan in the run-up to 2014. A better working relationship with Iran will be important to preserve India's interests in Afghanistan.

Yet as the United States and its allies attempt to tighten the noose of sanctions on Iran, India's options will be constrained. For a start, the agreement on the payment mechanism does not spell the end to the problems in importing oil from Iran. There is the major issue of insurance for tankers shipping Iranian oil to India. European firms insure more than 90 percent of the world's tanker fleets. Their refusal, following the imposition of sanctions, to cover shipments from Iran poses serious problems for India. New Delhi has extended sovereign guarantee to Indian ships that fetch Iranian crude. But the extended cover falls far short of what is required. In the event of an accident or crisis, India could come a cropper.

In any event, as the standoff between Iran and the United States continues, there will be political pressure on India to follow suit with sanctions. So far, India has spoken out against these steps and has held that it is not bound to comply with unilateral sanctions. But the choices for India could become more pointed if a crisis looks imminent in the region, for India also has a stake in curbing the proliferation of nuclear weapons. Moreover, New Delhi has an important strategic relationship with Israel, which could be undercut in the event of a standoff between Tehran and Tel Aviv.

Iran, then, could be a potential flashpoint that casts into sharp relief the complexities of Indian interests as a regional power and its desire to play a more prominent role on the global stage. The Middle East remains central to India's economic growth and security. India has considerable interests at stake on all sides of the divide between the Shia and the Sunni countries, between Iran and Saudi Arabia, and between Iran and Israel. At the same time, these interests will have to be set against wider considerations of the norms of international politics: nonproliferation versus rights to the peaceful use of nuclear technology, unilateral versus multilateral sanctions, and sovereignty versus intervention. Balancing these interests will be akin to walking a tightrope. But like all tightrope walkers, India will have to move ahead simply to avoid falling.

Conclusion

India's role as a regional power has undergone significant changes over the past two decades. In its immediate neighborhood, India has sought to use its economic growth to mitigate security problems. By contrast, in its extended neighborhood in East and West Asia, India's increasing footprint has been driven primarily by economic considerations, but it finds itself involved, if minimally, in a series of problems ranging from the South China Sea to Syria. In dealing with these, India has been active in several multilateral forums such as the UN Security Council and the East Asia Summit. Like most other powers, India's stance on these issues is a compound of interests and normative considerations. More specific to India is the tension between its interests, which are primarily regional, and its aspirations, which are more global. The latter require India to engage in normative debates about the nature of the international system and to shape the normative consensus emerging on issues such as human rights. At the same time, India remains wary of new doctrines of intervention being used as a fig leaf for the pursuit of great-power interests—especially in ways that could undermine India's regional interests. So, while India is unlikely to dilute the importance of human rights in international politics, it is equally unlikely to support the notion that the sovereignty of states can be set aside without considerable deliberation and consensus. Similarly its stance on issues such as nonproliferation and freedom of navigation is likely to entail substantive support for this agenda without embracing the notion that the use of force will advance these in all cases. India's ability to straddle these positions and, more important, to convince other states of the merits of its stance will be a key determinant of its rise to great-power status.

Notes

1. For an interesting treatment, see Mark Mazower, *No Enchanted Palace: The End of Empire and the Ideological Origins of the United Nations* (Princeton University Press, 2009), pp. 149–89.
2. Manu Bhagavan, *The Peacemakers: India and the Quest for One World* (New Delhi: HarperCollins India, 2012), pp. 82–93.
3. Manmohan Singh, statement at the inaugural session of the Seventeenth SAARC Summit, Addu City, the Maldives, November 12, 2011 (www.saarc-sec.org/statements/Statement-by-Prime-Minister-of-India-Dr.-Manmohan-Singh-at-the-Inaugural-Session-of-the-XVIIth-SAARC-Summit/15/).
4. Manmohan Singh, speech at Dhaka University, September 2, 2011 (http://pmindia.gov.in/speech-details.php?nodeid=1057).
5. Manmohan Singh, speech at the Sixth East Asia Summit Plenary Session, Bali, November 19, 2011 (http://pib.nic.in/newsite/erelease.aspx?relid=77331).
6. Text of Agreement on Strategic Partnership between India and Afghanistan, October 4, 2011 (www.mea.gov.in/outoging-visit-detail.htm?5383/).

PART III

Domestic and Regional Drivers

SANJAYA BARU

5 The Economic Imperative for India's Multilateralism

Realism and a Rule-Based Regime

India has been a strong advocate of multilateralism even when it has preferred a bilateral approach to the political challenges it confronts in South Asia. India is not alone among major powers in adopting such a paradoxical stance. However, the Indian view of multilateral institutions and of multilateralism has evolved over time, with the approach adopted in the political and security field different from that adopted in the economic field. While India has always sought to achieve a "rule-based" multilateral order, it has sought with equal vehemence rules that recognize India's place as the world's largest democracy, the biggest developing-country democracy, and a pluralist, secular, and constitutional democracy. India's view of its place in the multilateral political and security order, whether seeking membership on the United Nations Security Council (UNSC) or participation in the Treaty on the Non-Proliferation of Nuclear Weapons, has been defined by this outlook.[1]

This chapter discusses India's approach to multilateralism in the realm of economic organizations and regimes. It examines, in particular, India's approach to multilateral economic institutions, namely, the International Monetary Fund (IMF), the World Bank, and the General Agreement on Trade and Tariffs (GATT)/World Trade Organization (WTO).

It is useful to remember that while a country may have national institutions that help to create a common approach to international issues and institutions, and this may be even more so under powerful national leaders (like

I am grateful to the editors of this volume and to Montek Singh Ahluwalia and Shivshankar Menon for comments on an earlier draft.

Jawaharlal Nehru and Indira Gandhi), there is always the possibility that the approach to national policy can differ in different segments of government, especially in a plural democracy like India. Analysts in other democracies, such as the United States, are all too familiar with finding that different wings of the administration—the State Department and the Pentagon or the White House and Congress—adopt different, even conflicting, approaches to international issues.

In the early years after independence, India's approach to international institutions like the United Nations and its various organs had the clear imprint of its first prime minister, Jawaharlal Nehru, and his key foreign and strategic policy advisers. This was equally the case with both domestic and external economic policy. However, the thinking within the foreign and strategic policy establishment was greatly influenced by those, including Nehru, who opted for an admittedly "idealist" posture, seeking a larger international role for India commensurate with its standing as a leading postcolonial democracy inspired by the idea of the solidarity of developing countries, especially the postcolonial nations of Africa and Asia.

However, the thinking on external economic policy was also shaped by another set of Nehru's disciples who were more "realists" than "idealists" in their appreciation of India's capabilities and needs. They understood the need for external assistance, even if India were to pursue a more inward-looking strategy of industrial development with less emphasis on foreign trade. India's approach to external economic assistance, in general, and to multilateral and bilateral economic assistance, in particular, was pithily stated in the first chapter of the First Five Year Plan (1950), written under the direct supervision of Nehru. Having noted that such assistance could only be a residual and that economic planning must be based on harnessing domestic resources, it summed up the dilemma in these words:

> That a plan of development today must, in the main, rely on domestic resources can hardly be over-emphasised. In the first place, the conditions governing international investment are no longer what they were when some of the highly industrialised countries of today like the United States, Australia, and Canada began their career of development. Secondly, external assistance is acceptable only if it carries with it no conditions, explicit or implicit, which might affect even remotely the country's ability to take an independent line in international affairs. There are also obvious risks in excessive reliance on foreign aid which depends on the domestic political situation in lending countries and

> which might be interrupted by any untoward international developments. And yet, external resources at strategic points and stages can be of so much assistance in a period of rapid development that it is desirable, consistently with other objectives, to create conditions favourable to their inflow.

The plan document went on to state that while priority would be given to investment through multilateral financial institutions, one must recognize that far more investible funds would be available from foreign governments and from private corporations. It then added the understandable caveat that all such foreign investment would have to be in accordance with "the country's development programme."[2]

However, even while India's economic planners moved increasingly to an "inward-oriented" import-substituting strategy of industrial development, they were not averse to seeking either foreign investment or multilateral economic assistance. Aid was preferred over trade, partly because of an inherent "export pessimism" among policymakers and partly on account of the historically inherited, but flawed, view that much of Indian export trade was "forced" on India by the East India Company and its inheritors, European multinationals.[3] Even though the Indian subcontinent was at the crossroads of pan-Asian trade for centuries before the arrival of European traders in the Indian Ocean, the Indian independence movement was greatly influenced by its more recent historical experience, wherein trade was viewed as "exploitative" and "enforced" rather than as beneficial to development and growth.[4]

Thus, after independence, even as India's share of world trade declined from 2.0 percent in 1950 to 0.5 percent by 1980, India's share of both bilateral and multilateral aid increased significantly, with India emerging as a major beneficiary of such assistance. In the 1960s and 1970s India's share of total official development assistance was 10 percent, with South Asia as a whole receiving as much as all of Africa. In the period 1960–2003, India received 5.6 percent of the official development assistance of Norway and the United States, ranking as the third largest recipient, next to Israel and Egypt.[5]

On foreign direct investment, India initially adopted a more open stance until the end of the 1950s, with Nehru actively soliciting it. What this open stance meant was that even as the share of exports in India's national income fell from more than 6.0 percent in the early 1950s to less than 4.0 percent by the end of the 1950s, the share of imports in national income rose from around 6.0 percent to nearly 8.0 percent in the same period. This resulted in a sharp fall in India's sterling reserves. The resulting balance of payments crisis, in 1958–59, altered perceptions about the role of external flows in aiding economic development. While the government's initial response to the foreign exchange shortage of the late 1950s was to open up the economy further to foreign investment, India became less open to foreign investment by the end of the 1960s.[6]

All of this explains, in part, the difference in India's approach to multilateral financial institutions—that is, the IMF and the World Bank—and to the global trading system, especially under GATT. The Indian independence movement's concern with deindustrialization and the national leadership's focus on protecting domestic industry against external competition shaped policy with respect to external trade. However, the planners' desire to bridge the resources gap meant that they remained open to the possibility of using external aid to finance development. India was not interested in seeking a more open trading system; hence it vacillated between indifference and active resistance to GATT and free trade.[7]

Differences in approach to India's relations with the world have also persisted between India's External Affairs Ministry and foreign policy strategists, on the one hand, and its economic ministries and economic policymakers, on the other. Ironically, in the 1950s the foreign policy strategists were more internationalist in their orientation, while economic policymakers were more nationalist, while by the 1980s the reverse seems to have been the case.[8] While critics of the multilateral financial institutions and of recent trends in multilateralism remain dissatisfied,[9] Prime Minister Singh best summed up India's approach to multilateral institutions and to multilateralism in his very first address to the United Nations General Assembly in September 2004.[10] Stating that democratic principles should govern international institutions as much as national ones, Singh underscored the importance of what he dubbed a "culture of genuine multilateralism," adding,

> The United Nations and its specialised agencies are the only instruments available for responding effectively to the challenges we face collectively. But what is missing is our sustained commitment to democratising the functioning of the United Nations. It is common knowledge that the UN is often unable to exert an effective influence on global economic and political issues of critical importance. This is due to what may be called as "democracy deficit," which prevents effective multilateralism, a multilateralism that is based on a democratically evolved global consensus.[11]

He embedded India's support for UN reform within this wider context of the UN's democratization. Thus, while advocating reform of multilateral institutions and seeking a greater say in their functioning, India has reaffirmed its commitment to working with them. While "idealism" still marks India's approach to multilateralism in general, "realism" characterizes its approach to multilateral economic institutions.

"Realistic Restructuring" of the Bretton Woods Institutions

British India was represented by both British and native Indian officials at the Bretton Woods conference, where the International Monetary Fund and the World Bank were created. However, a key member of the Indian delegation, A. D. Shroff, complained that India had not secured its due in the shareholding structure of the IMF and the Bank. He complained to John Maynard Keynes, head of the British delegation, who had fought hard to increase India's quota from $300 million to $400 million. Shroff's main complaint, which is being echoed even today, is that the United States was more accommodative of China, which was granted a higher quota share than India. It is worth quoting at length from the detailed account of the episode in Robert Skidelsky's authoritative biography of Keynes:[12]

> Raymond Mikesell, who served under White in the U.S. Treasury, had worked out a complicated formula for allocating 90 percent of the available money, leaving $800mn, "to be added to any place we wanted to." White had told him that the formula should yield a quota of $2.5bn for the USA, about half of that for Britain and its colonies, with the Soviet Union and China assured third and fourth places. To "cook" the results White wanted, Mikesell had to introduce data for national income. "These last had to be approximated and their uncertainty afforded opportunities for making minor adjustments to the suggested quotas when these did not conform to political realities." The quotas were made public for the first time at Bretton Woods, but the basis for their calculation remained secret. When the figures became known, there were explosions of affronted pride. Russia, which wanted quotas to reflect military as well as economic prowess, said it would not accept a quota smaller than Britain's. Britain said that if Russia got a larger quota, so should India. India wanted equality with China. France would accept a smaller quota than China, "for political reasons," but insisted on a larger quota than India.[13]

Skidelsky's biography of Keynes goes on to elaborate the outcome of the China-India tussle over quotas and seats:

> Keynes confined his efforts to getting the Indian quota raised from $300mn to $400mn. His success was not received with much satisfaction. "Indian *amour propre* in connection with China," wrote Lionel Robbins, "was still far from satisfied; and it was very vocal. Moreover, they are still ambitious for a permanent seat on the Executive. Keynes, who received them lying on his couch, railed them on their ingratitude and urged with much force that they now had an excellent case to present at home, which he proceeded to outline in the form of an imaginary speech which might be delivered by Mr. A. D. Shroff (an Indian delegate to the conference). All this was without much visible effect."[14]

Independent India took seriously its participation in both the United Nations system as well as multilateral financial institutions. It sent some of its best officials and diplomats to these institutions. While India did not always like and accept the policy advice they offered, Nehru did not shy away from tapping into the best talent available worldwide as far as economic planning and management were concerned. Thus he consulted many policy advisers, including experts from the multilateral financial institutions, Milton Friedman from the University of Chicago, and Poland's Michal Kalecki; a wide range of external policy advice was available, given, and taken.[15]

India's relations with the Bretton Woods sisters deteriorated only after the infamous devaluation of 1966.[16] The unprecedented drought of 1965–66 had forced India to import food grains, thereby exerting pressure on the balance of payments. India approached the United States, the IMF, and the World Bank for support. A combination of bilateral U.S. assistance and multilateral funding was offered, but India was forced to devalue the rupee and was advised to reverse its policy of import-substituting industrialization. The political backlash in India forced Prime Minister Indira Gandhi to abandon the program halfway. The 1966 devaluation constituted a turning point in how India viewed the Bretton Woods sisters. Opinion was sharply divided both politically and among economists. India became a critic of the world economic order, cemented a new relationship with the Nonaligned Movement, created the G-77 and other developing-country forums, and became an advocate of the New International Economic Order, a platform that was critical of the Bretton Woods institutions and the so-called "Washington Consensus"—conservative macroeconomic policies that were aimed at encouraging debtor nations to reduce fiscal and budget deficits, privatize public enterprises, liberalize external trade, and open up capital markets to external flows.[17]

Wary of such policies in the 1970s, India did not approach the IMF for balance of payments support until 1981, when Indira Gandhi chose to seek IMF support once again. Returning to office in 1981, Indira Gandhi was a changed political animal. Her nuanced position on the Soviet invasion of Afghanistan in 1979, which India did not endorse, and her meeting with the U.S. president Ronald Reagan in Cancún, Mexico, in October 1981 were indicative of this change in her view of the United States and, therefore, of what India perceived as "U.S.-led institutions." However, in response to a renewed political attack against her by the Left Front, which targeted her decision to seek IMF assistance, she opted to give up the last installment and to prepay the loan, making it a symbol of her independence of action.[18]

The 1981 episode is instructive. India's application for IMF lending met with initial resistance from the United States. India's case was presented starkly by her executive director on the IMF board, M. Narasimham, who told his U.S. counterpart that if the United States blocked IMF support India would have no option but to turn to the Soviet Union for financial assistance.[19] The United States chose to abstain on the vote of the board, enabling India to get access to IMF support while at the same time expressing its disapproval of Indian policies by not voting in favor of the loan application.

It was only in 1991, a decade later and under very different circumstances, that India returned to the IMF for balance of payments support and secured this on the condition that India would put in place policies approved by the IMF and its principal shareholders, especially the European Union and the United States. The "new turn" in India's economic policies and the reconfiguration of its foreign policy in the post–cold war era mark a turning point in India's approach to the Bretton Woods institutions.

The new Indian view was that, as a founding member of the IMF and the World Bank, it was entitled to financial support from these institutions and that the policies then advocated by the institutions were in India's own interests and reflected the thinking within the Indian government. As the Indian finance minister, Manmohan Singh, told Parliament, in his budget speech of February 1992,

> It has been alleged by some people that the reform programme has been dictated by the IMF and the World Bank. We are founder members of these two institutions and it is our right to borrow from them when we need assistance in support of our programmes. As lenders,

> they are required to satisfy themselves about our capacity to repay loans and this is where conditionality comes into the picture. All borrowing countries hold discussions with these institutions on the viability of the programmes for which assistance is sought. We have also held such discussions. The extent of conditionality depends on the amount and the type of assistance sought. However, I wish to state categorically that the conditions we have accepted reflect no more than the implementation of the reform programme as outlined in my letters of intent sent to the IMF and the World Bank, and are wholly consistent with our national interests. The bulk of the reform programme is based on the election manifesto of our Party. There is no question of the Government ever compromising our national interests, not to speak of our sovereignty.[20]

This assertion of sovereignty, combined with a realist approach to the institutions and to the policies being adopted, has since become the leitmotif of the Indian approach to the multilateral financial institutions. India has not approached the IMF since 1991, and, since the Asian financial crisis of 1997–98 as well as the experience with U.S. and Japanese sanctions in the aftermath of the nuclear tests in May 1998, it has opted to build adequate foreign exchange reserves to insulate itself from the need to do so. This is a tactic adopted by many other Asian economies, although India has continued to assert its right to tap the World Bank and other affiliates for development funding. Today India is the Bank's biggest borrower.[21] In 2010 the Bank's lending arms—the International Bank for Reconstruction and Development and the International Development Association—lent India a sum of $9.1 billion, compared with $6.4 billion to Mexico, $3.8 billion to South Africa, $3.7 billion to Brazil, and $3.0 billion to Turkey. Accordingly, the World Bank's India Country Strategy for 2009–12 "envisages a total proposed lending program of US$14 billion, for the next three years, of which US$9.6 billion is from the International Bank for Reconstruction and Development (IBRD) and US$4.4 billion (SDR 2.982 billion equivalent at the current exchange rate) [is] from the International Development Association (IDA)."[22] Half of the sums lent have been allocated to four sectors: agriculture, rural development, energy, and public transport.[23]

Summing up India's nuanced approach to multilateral assistance and external funding early in his tenure, Prime Minister Singh told a conference in New Delhi in 2005,

> As a developing economy we must draw on international resources to fuel our development. We should be more open to global capital flows and better prepared to take advantage of new markets for goods and services. India is wholly committed to multilateralism in trade. But we will seek the reform and democratization of multilateral institutions.[24]

One aspect of the new "realism" is that India has come to terms with the reality of China's larger quota, no longer complaining as Shroff did in 1944, but willing to live with a restructured IMF in which China has a much larger voting share than India. India therefore joined the BRICS—Brazil, Russia, India, China, and South Africa—consensus that has sought a reallocation of IMF quotas in favor of emerging economies. Having said this, the Indian proposal at the New Delhi BRICS summit for the creation of a BRICS Development Bank is aimed at encouraging China to divert some of its foreign exchange surplus into a BRICS-run bank in which India would have a larger say than it is likely to have in the IMF.[25]

In the interim, however, India has chosen to be pragmatic and accept the reality of Western dominance of the Bretton Woods institutions. When the IMF and the World Bank last selected new heads, some analysts adopted a revisionist view and urged India to play a more proactive role in selecting the heads of these institutions by putting up its own candidate for the posts of managing director of the IMF and president of the World Bank.[26] However, Prime Minister Singh took the "realist" view that since the IMF and the World Bank are "shareholder-driven" organizations, the majority shareholders will get the management of their choice as long as they remain majority shareholders. So there is no point in a marginal player like India sponsoring a candidate of its own until the shareholding structure itself is altered.[27] Thus, in seeking to restructure the quotas in favor of emerging economies, India accepted the existing shareholder structure and went along with the "majority" in supporting the nominee of the European Union, Christine Lagarde.

India will continue to maintain such a realist view, recognizing that no existing power voluntarily cedes power and any forced reallocation of quotas at this stage would benefit China more than India. India will, however, seek a "realistic restructuring" of the shareholding of these institutions that gives emerging economies a greater say in their functioning. Until that happens, India, like most other Asian countries, will seek to avoid tapping the IMF for balance of payments support, opting instead to maintain an adequately large foreign currency reserve.

Hedging Its Bets on the Multilateral Trade Regime

India was one of the twenty-three contracting parties to the GATT in October 1947. Yet, unlike with the Bretton Woods sisters, from which the Indian Ministry of Finance had always hoped to secure financial support, even in Nehru's time, India's interest in GATT was largely defensive. A combination of export pessimism and the strategy of import-substituting industrialization shaped India's trade and industrial policy, especially after the first balance of payments crisis in 1958. India saw its share of world trade diminish from 2.4 percent in 1948 to less than 1.0 percent a decade later and to a lowly 0.41 percent by 1981.[28] Economists have debated whether the decline in trade share contributed to the export pessimism or whether the import-substituting industrialization strategy contributed to the decline. Whatever the causal factors, the consequence was a general neglect of external trade and therefore a defensive approach to multilateralism in trade.[29] Prime Minister Singh's doctoral thesis at Oxford University was a critique of India's export pessimism and drew attention to the growth potential of foreign trade, but his view was ignored by policymakers at the time.[30] India's strategy in GATT was, therefore, defensive, aimed at minimizing exposure to a more open and intrusive multilateral trade regime.

In fact, one could argue, India was adept at deploying "diplomatic cover" and promoted developing-country unity to secure a less open multilateral trading regime that enabled it to protect its own markets and promote its domestic industrialization process. This, however, is not how Indian diplomats viewed the country's GATT strategy.[31] Rather, the dominant view in the 1950s and 1960s was that India had played a leadership role in securing protection for developing countries in the GATT system. Dubey notes with pride India's robust activism in securing benefits for developing countries, such as the Generalized System of Preferences and the Multifiber Agreement, rejecting criticism that India was a "free rider" in GATT and claiming credit for India's activism in rule making under GATT, which aimed to protect the interests of developing countries.[32]

As Mattoo and Subramanian observe, "India's stance in the GATT/WTO has always tended to be defensive, seeking freedom to use restrictive policies, which has been one of the two prongs of the so-called special and differential (S&D) treatment embraced by developing countries as a whole."[33] Indeed, one could argue that by the 1970s and into the early 1980s India had a minimal stake in the real policy outcome in various rounds of GATT negotiations given its small share of world trade. However, active participation and strenuous bargaining for fair outcomes may have yielded foreign policy benefits with developing countries. While this approach made eminent "diplomatic" sense, since it gave India a leadership role among developing countries, it did not help India to increase its share of world trade. Since India's economic strategy was based on import substitution and export pessimism, planners did not consider its defensive approach to GATT and lack of interest in carving out a larger share of the world market as counterproductive.

Given this diplomatic background and the economic policy approach that lasted well into the 1980s, it is not surprising that India initially participated in the Uruguay Round of GATT negotiations (from 1986 to 1994), which eventually resulted in the dissolution of GATT and the creation of the World Trade Organization, with a plan to scuttle the round. India had strong reservations about bringing services into the GATT system. It had grave doubts about the purpose and consequence of replacing GATT with a formal institution, the WTO.[34] In the late 1980s and well into 1991, India fought hard to resist both creating the WTO and widening the scope of the multilateral trading system. Dubey, India's foreign secretary at the time and a key negotiator with a personal interest in multilateral economic diplomacy, claims that India agreed to support creation of the WTO only after the inclusion of a dispute settlement mechanism and the assurance that GATT's "special and differential treatment" for developing countries would continue.

India, however, remained strongly opposed to bringing new issues, such as intellectual property rights, and trade-related social policy issues, such as labor standards, into the WTO's ambit. India's official approach to multilateral trade negotiations in the early months of the Uruguay Round was no different from its approach to previous rounds, even though by the 1980s the share of foreign trade had begun to rise in India's national income and the export pessimism of the earlier era was no longer as prevalent.[35] The ratio of non-oil imports to GDP rose from around 4 percent in the early 1970s to more than 8 percent by the early 1980s. The ratio of total foreign trade (exports plus imports) to GDP rose from around 7 percent in the early 1980s to more than 12 percent in the early 1980s and to more than 25 percent in the mid-1990s.[36]

The shift in India's approach to multilateral trade negotiations and the WTO came with the adoption of a new policy of economic liberalization and reform in 1991. But this shift in thinking was on the part of a new team that had taken charge of economic policymaking in 1991, including the then finance minister, Manmohan Singh, and his key economic policymaking team of Montek Singh Ahluwalia, Shankar Acharya, and Rakesh Mohan.[37] The *ancien régime* represented by the then finance secretary, S. P. Shukla, who had earlier handled the Uruguay Round negotiations as India's commerce secretary, Muchkund Dubey, and Deepak Nayyar, the chief economic adviser who had earlier worked as an economic adviser in the Commerce Ministry, continued to advocate India's more defensive approach. By the end of the 1990s the dispute settlement mechanism was also seen as strategically important because China had secured entry into the WTO and its trade and fiscal policies were viewed as nontransparent and therefore supportive of anti-competition practices. As Nottage notes, "Ambassador Bhatia of India recently stated that the 'WTO dispute settlement system is certainly one of the most valuable achievements of the Uruguay Round.'"[38]

The critics of the WTO in the Indian government finally fell in line, so to speak, defending their change of heart as a response to the WTO's adherence to an important principle of multilateralism, namely, the principle of "one country, one vote," with decision making defined by the principle of consensus.[39] There is no doubt that this "democratic" principle set the WTO apart from the IMF and the World Bank and gave "voice" and "vote" to developing countries. It is a different matter that, in practice, real power—that is, real negotiations—has been restricted to major trading economies that form part of the "green room" process of informal discussions that define the final outcomes.[40] In fact, the core of the green room participants are the "quad"—Canada, the European Union, Japan, and the United States—that dominated GATT and seek to retain influence within the WTO.

In the past decade, the quad has been checked by the emergence of Brazil, China, India, and South Africa as important developing-country negotiators. With the entry of Russia as a WTO member, it is now possible that the BRICS could seek to balance the quad in the WTO.

But the shift in India's approach to multilateralism in trade came much before these structural changes in the global economy and the consequent shift in geopolitics. The new turn in India's economic policy had three elements: first, the end of the "licence raj" involving decontrol of production quotas and location and size restrictions on firms; second, fiscal stabilization aimed at reducing government deficits including through privatization; and third and most important, opening up of the Indian economy to easier flows of external trade and foreign direct investment.[41] India voluntarily adopted the sharp reduction in tariffs through its budget proposals for 1991–92 and 1992–93. This enabled India to negotiate with greater conviction as the Uruguay Round came to a close and the WTO came into being.[42]

Through the 1990s, and especially after the Singapore ministerial meeting of the WTO in 1996 and the Seattle meeting in 1999, India became an active participant in the WTO process. There is a misplaced view in the Western media and among Western analysts that the high profile and critical stance of Indian trade ministers in WTO meetings, especially in the ongoing Doha Development Round, are signs of India's resistance to multilateralism in trade. This is a superficial view based on appearances and a lack of understanding of India's domestic politics. The three trade ministers of the past decade—Murasoli Maran (in Doha, 2001), Arun Jaitley (in Cancun, 2003), and Kamal Nath (in Geneva, 2008)—adopted postures aimed at a domestic political audience knowing full well that an impasse between the United States and one or another country (on occasion the European Union or West African cotton exporters or someone else) would stall any agreement.

It would be an overstatement to suggest that Kamal Nath wrecked the ministerial meeting, as many in the West believed at the time.[43] It is entirely possible that Nath believed that the United States was not prepared for a deal months before a presidential election. Perhaps Nath rode a high horse to win accolades at home, as indeed he did for espousing the cause of the developing world![44] However, it is possible that Nath won these plaudits at the cost of securing an admittedly suboptimal deal. Prime Minister Singh was willing to arrive at a compromise that could have helped to conclude the round. While he never said so publicly, Singh believed that, as an essentially net food-importing country, India would benefit from cheaper imported agriculture products. However, the Commerce Ministry resisted yielding ground on the plea that "any 'bad' decision would 'haunt' them for having caused harm to future generations."[45]

Prime Minister Manmohan Singh has repeatedly emphasized India's stake in the multilateral trading regime. He has often referred to India's "strategic stake" in the multilateral trading system, a stake that has grown with the rise in India's share in trade in services and the WTO's embrace of services trade in the Uruguay Round.[46] In an address to foreign service officers, virtually on the eve of the 2008 Geneva WTO ministerial meeting, he summed up his own view on the importance of trade and the need for a multilateral regime in these words:

> When I talk about international environment, I have in mind the fact that what happens to the world trading system impinges on our capacity to grow at a faster pace. International trade particularly in the globalised world we live in has emerged as an important engine of

> growth of nations. And therefore we have to create an environment with which India's trade can grow, India's economy will benefit enormously if our exports are given a level playing field if we don't face barriers to increase exports of our country and therefore what happens to the multilateral trading systems, what happens to barriers to trade, barriers to commerce, is a very important indicator of what will be the pace of development of our country.[47]

Even as India has remained committed to multilateralism in trade, the continued impasse in the Doha Development Round has encouraged India to pursue, on a parallel track, a range of bilateral and regional free trade and comprehensive economic partnership agreements (including trade and investment treaties). Apart from the South Asian Free Trade Agreement, India has signed free trade agreements (FTAs) with the Association of Southeast Asian Nations (ASEAN) (and separately with its member-countries such as Singapore and Thailand) and South Korea. It has preferential trade agreements with a large number of countries and is presently negotiating one with the European Union.[48]

The range of FTAs that India has signed and is negotiating points to a new strategy on New Delhi's part. It has opted to engage widely and to secure market access to growing Asian markets, while continuing to support the multilateral trading system, especially with an eye on the WTO's dispute settlement mechanism.[49] India is willing to be part of as many plurilateral and regional groupings as necessary, building temporary coalitions when required. In climate change negotiations, India chose to be part of BASIC—an alliance of Brazil, South Africa, India, and China. India has become active in BRICS, has reactivated the South Asian Association for Regional Cooperation and the Indian Ocean Rim Association for Regional Cooperation, and has been an active member of the East Asian Summit process, signing on at the recent ASEAN-India summit to negotiate a regional comprehensive economic partnership agreement that could be a precursor to the creation of an Asian Economic Community.

In pursuing these regional trade agreements, Prime Minister Singh repeatedly emphasized India's commitment to multilateralism, defending the regional trade agreements on the grounds of geopolitical imperatives as much as economic benefits. Thus, for example, defending the ASEAN-India FTA against criticism from his own party, because of pressure from producer groups that felt they would be hurt by lower tariffs, he wrote to Congress Party president Sonia Gandhi:

> Our approach to regional trade agreements in general, and FTAs in particular, has been evolved after careful consideration of our geopolitical as well as economic interests. Although India has a large domestic market, our experience with earlier relatively insular policies, as also the global experience in this regard, clearly bring out the growth potential of trade and economic cooperation with the global economy.[50]

However, precisely because the WTO runs a consensus-based multilateral trade regime, it is limited from the point of view of developed and developing economies. Hence both have sought to explore parallel networks of regional and plurilateral free trade arrangements that are, in principle, "WTO-compatible," but in practice have sought to circumvent the multilateral system in seeking either a more or a less liberal trading regime. Bhagwati has dubbed them "the termites in the trading system."[51] The so-called "noodle bowl" or "alphabet soup" of FTAs and regional trade agreements has weakened the multilateral system, and the WTO is now at a crossroads, seeking renewal through completion of the Doha Development Round. Although India has been signing FTAs and preferential trade agreements with many of its trade partners, it has a strategic stake in strengthening the WTO mainly because of the competitive pressure exerted by China's rise as a trading power. [52]

The China Syndrome

The most important geopolitical factor shaping India's attitude toward multilateralism in general and multilateral economic institutions in particular is the rise of China and the challenge this poses to management of the global environment. While China continues to resist supporting India's claim for permanent membership in the UNSC, China and India have also been able to work together, for example, on seeking to reconstitute multilateral economic institutions and regimes, affirming Prime Minister Singh's assertion that the bilateral relationship would be characterized by both "cooperation and competition." India's "revisionist" stance toward existing multilateral institutions is balanced by a desire to seek a rule-based multilateral order. As a founding member of the G-20, India appreciates all the more the need to adhere to rule-based multilateralism, since the G-20 is really India's first major step away from being a "rule taker" and toward becoming a "rule maker" in multilateral institutions. For this reason, India attaches much importance to the G-20 as a plurilateral institution.[53]

Living through this transition in world affairs, India seeks a restructuring of multilateral institutions, while adhering to all of the inherited disciplines and articles of association. This paradoxical stance reflects the combination of aspiration and grievance, idealism and realism that informs the Indian approach.

Notes

1. For an elaboration of this view, see Sanjaya Baru, "Managing Multipolarity and Globalisation in the New World," in *Imagining Tomorrow: Rethinking the Global Challenge,* edited by Kamlesh Sharma (New York: United Nations, 2000), pp. 218–25.

2. Planning Commission, *First Five Year Plan* (Delhi: Government of India, 1950), ch. 1, para. 44–45 (http://planningcommission.nic.in/plans/planrel/fiveyr/index9.html).

3. On India's export pessimism, see Manmohan Singh, *India's Export Trends and the Prospects for Self-Sustained Growth* (Oxford: Clarendon Press, 1964); Jagdish Bhagwati and Padma Desai, *India: Planning for Industrialisation* (Oxford University Press, 1970). On the view that exports were a product of "forced commercialization," there is a vast postcolonial literature. In India this view found its earliest academic exposition in Dadabhai Naoroji's classic *Poverty and Un-British Rule in India* (London: S. Sonnenschein, 1901).

4. For a classic left-wing statement of this view, see Bipan Chandra, *The Rise and Growth of Economic Nationalism in India: Economic Policies of Indian National Leadership* (New Delhi: People's Publishing House, 1966). For a liberal academic presentation of both sides of the debate, see contributions by Dharma Kumar in *The Cambridge Economic History of India,* vol. 2, edited by Tapan Raychaudhuri, Dharma Kumar, and Irfan Habib (Cambridge University Press, 1982).

5. Sanjeev Gupta, Catherine Pattillo, and Smita Wagh, "Are Donor Countries Giving More or Less Aid?" IMF Working Paper WP/06/1 (Washington: International Monetary Fund, January 2006) (www.imf.org/external/pubs/ft/wp/2006/wp0601.pdf).

6. Arvind Panagariya, *India: The Emerging Giant* (Oxford University Press, 2008).

7. I. G. Patel, *Glimpses of Indian Economic Policy: An Insider's View* (Oxford University Press, 2002).

8. Possible reasons for this are discussed in Sanjaya Baru, "Can Indian Think Tanks and Research Institutions Cope with the Rising Demand for Foreign and Security Policy Research?" ISAS Working Paper 67 (National University of Singapore, Institute of South Asian Nations, June 2009) (www.isas.nus.edu.sg/Attachments/PublisherAttachment/ISAS_working%20paper_66_21102009181035.pdf).

9. Muchkund Dubey, *Multilateralism Besieged* (Geneva: The South Centre, 2004). See also Rohan Mukherjee and David M. Malone, "From High Ground to High Table: The Evolution of Indian Multilateralism," *Global Governance* 17 (2011): 311–29.

10. Manmohan Singh joined government service in India in 1972 as an economic adviser in the Ministry of Commerce. He then went on to occupy every important economic policymaking office in the government of India, including chief economic adviser,

secretary for economic affairs, governor of the Reserve Bank of India, deputy chairman of the Planning Commission, and finance minister in 1991–96.

11. Manmohan Singh, address to the United Nations General Assembly, New York, September 23, 2004 (http://pmindia.nic.in/speech-details.php?nodeid=18).

12. Robert Skidelsky, *John Maynard Keynes: Fighting for Britain, 1937–1946* (London: Macmillan, 2000), pp. 351–52.

13. Ibid., p. 351.

14. Ibid., pp. 351–52.

15. George Rosen, *Western Economists and Eastern Societies: Agents of Change in South Asia, 1960–1970* (Johns Hopkins University Press, 1986). See also Jagdish Bhagwati, *India in Transition* (Oxford: Clarendon Press, 1993).

16. Praveen K. Chaudhry, Vijay L. Kelkar, and Vikash Yadav, "The Evolution of 'Homegrown Conditionality' in India: IMF Relations," *Journal of Development Studies* 40, no. 6 (August 2004): 59–81 (http://people.hws.edu/vyadav/publications/jods.pdf).

17. See John Williamson, ed., *The Political Economy of Policy Reform* (Washington: Institute for International Economics, 1994).

18. Patel, *Glimpses of Indian Economic Policy*, ch. 7.

19. Author's interview with M. Narasimham and his executive assistant, Y. V. Reddy, circa 2000.

20. Manmohan Singh, "Budget Speech," Ministry of Finance, February 29, 1992 (http://indiabudget.nic.in/bspeech/bs199293.pdf).

21. World Bank, *India Country Strategy 2009–12* (Washington, 2010) (www.worldbank.org/en/news/2010/04/06/india-country-strategy).

22. Ibid.

23. See Indian Ministry of Finance website for details of fund allocation (http://finmin.nic.in/the_ministry/dept_eco_affairs/MI/sector_wise_ongoingProj.pdf).

24. Manmohan Singh, speech at India Today Conclave, February 25, 2005 (http://pmindia.nic.in/speech-details.php?nodeid=73).

25. This observation is based on conversations with Indian Ministry of Finance officials who were part of the BRICS Delhi summit preparatory work.

26. Aditya Mattoo and Arvind Subramaniam, "India and Bretton Woods II," *Economic and Political Weekly* 43, no. 45 (November 8, 2008): 62–70.

27. As told to the author by Prime Minister Singh at the time of the selection of Dominique Strauss-Kahn as managing director of the IMF.

28. T. N. Srinivasan and Suresh Tendulkar, *Reintegrating India with the World Economy* (Washington: Peterson Institute for International Economics, 2003). See also Bhagwati, *India in Transition.*

29. Jagdish Bhagwati and Padma Desai, *India: Planning for Industrialisation* (Oxford University Press, 1970).

30. Manmohan Singh, *India's Export Trends* (Oxford University Press, 1964).

31. See, for example, Muchkund Dubey, *An Unequal Treaty: World Trading Order after GATT* (New Delhi: New Age International, 1996).

32. Muchkund Dubey, "India and the WTO," in *Strategic Arena Switching in International Trade Negotiations,* edited by Wolfgang Blaas and Joachim Becker (London: Ashgate Publishing, 2007).

33. Aditya Mattoo and Arvind Subramanian, *India and the Multilateral Trading System after Seattle: Toward a Proactive Role* (Washington: World Bank, 1999).

34. Dubey, "India and the WTO."

35. Panagariya, *India: The Emerging Giant.*

36. Ibid., chs. 2, 3, 4, and 10.

37. While Ahluwalia was an "Oxbridge"-trained economist, like many in the post-independence generation of economic policymakers in India, Rakesh Mohan and Shankar Acharya studied at U.S. universities. All three had worked for the IMF and the World Bank before returning home to work for the government. From their perch in the ministries of finance and industry, they led the process of economic reform and liberalization in the 1990s.

38. Hunter Nottage, "Developing Countries in the WTO Dispute Settlement System," Global Economic Governance Programme Working Paper 2009/47 (Oxford: University College, 2009) (www.globaleconomicgovernance.org/wp-content/uploads/nottage-working-paper-final1.pdf). Remarks of Ujjal Singh Bhatia, ambassador and permanent representative of India to the WTO: "Settling Disputes among Members," presentation at the WTO Public Forum 2008, Session Six, September 24, 2008 (www.wto.org/english/forums_e/public_forum08_e/programme_e.htm).

39. S. P. Shukla, "From GATT to WTO and Beyond," Working Paper 195 (Helsinki: UNU-WIDER, 2000) (www.wider.unu.edu/publications/working-papers/previous/en_GB/wp-195/_files/82530864827082831/default/wp195.pdf).

40. World Trade Organization, "Understanding the WTO" (wto.org/english/thewto_e/whatis_e/tif_e/org1_e.htm).

41. Panagariya, *India: The Emerging Giant.*

42. Bibek Debroy, "India's Economic Liberalisation and the WTO," in *India's Liberalisation Experience: Hostage to the WTO?* edited by Suparna Karmarkar, Rajiv Kumar, and Bibek Debroy (New Delhi: Indian Council for Research on International Economic Relations, 2007).

43. Alan Beattle, "India's Local Hero Evokes Mixed Emotions in World Trade Circuit," *Financial Times*, December 3, 2008.

44. Rama Lakshmi, "Hard Line at WTO Earns India Praise," *Washington Post*, August 1, 2008.

45. This view of the Commerce Ministry was conveyed to the media in response to a statement that I had made speaking at the India Global Forum of the International Institute for Strategic Studies in New Delhi on April 8, 2008. Believing at the time that I reflected the prime minister's thinking, I had suggested that India should soften its resistance to U.S. and European Union farm subsidies and help to break the logjam in the Doha Development Round. See www.iiss.org/conferences/iiss-citi-india-global-forum/igf-plenary-sessions-2008/first-plenary-session-economic-and-financial-outlook/first-plenary-session-dr-sanjaya-baru/. For a news report of the discussion, see www.financialexpress.com/news/baru-calls-for-softening-of-india-s-stance-on-us-eu-farm-subsidies/299053/0.

To quote the *Financial Express* report, "Speaking at the IISS-Citi India Global Forum here, Baru argued that since domestic consumption of food is rising without an increase in supply, the country should welcome cheap food imports. Underlining that he was speaking in his personal capacity and not as a government spokesman, Baru said, 'We may not be able to make the same argument against the U.S. subsidies. It would be in the interest of India to favour continuation of farm subsidies by the U.S. and the European countries so that import prices remain low.'"

46. Rohan Mukherjee and David M. Malone, "Global Responsibilities: India's Approach," *Jindal Journal of International Affairs* 1, no. 1 (October 2011): 182–203 (www.jsia.edu.in/JJIA/RMDMbstract.html).

47. Manmohan Singh, speech to foreign service officers, June 11, 2008 (http://pmindia.nic.in/speech-details.php?nodeid=666).

48. See www.india-briefing.com/news/indias-free-trade-agreements-4810.html/.

49. Mukherjee and Malone, "Global Responsibilities."

50. "No Disagreement on FTA: Congress," *Economic Times*, May 9, 2006 (http://articles.economictimes.indiatimes.com/2006-05-09/news/27437763_1_india-asean-fta-india-asean-free-trade-agreement-prime-minister).

51. Jagdish Bhagwati, "The Doha Round's Premature Obituary," *Project Syndicate*, April 28, 2011 (www.project-syndicate.org/commentary/the-doha-round-s-premature-obituary).

52. T. P. Bhat, Atulan Guha, and Mahua Paul, *India and China in WTO: Building Complementarities and Competitiveness in the External Trade Sector*, report of a study sponsored by the Planning Commission, Government of India (New Delhi: Institute for Studies in Industrial Development, April 2006) (http://planningcommission.nic.in/reports/sereport/ser/stdy_indch.pdf).

53. Agnès Bénassy-Quéré, Rajiv Kumar, and Jean Pisani-Ferry, eds., *The G20 Is Not Just a G7 with Extra Chairs* (New Delhi: Indian Council for Research in International Economic Relations, 2009).

TANVI MADAN

6 What in the World Is India Able to Do? India's State Capacity for Multilateralism

Introduction

As India aspires to move from a rule-taker to a rule-maker or at least a rule-shaper role in the multilateral order, the main question being asked is, "What will India do"? Perhaps an equally relevant question is, "What is India able to do?" This question is directly related to India's state capacity, which this chapter defines as a state's ability to develop and implement policy.

This chapter begins with a look at why capacity matters, as well as an assessment of the people and ideas available to the Indian state that could help it to shape the multilateral order. Discussions about the state's ability to operate and to exercise influence in the external realm often start—and sometimes end—with the numbers question. The factoid most often quoted is that India and Singapore have about the same number of foreign service officers.[1] Capacity, however, also involves other components that are often overlooked.

The chapter lays out four such elements that are affecting the ability of Indian policymakers to formulate and implement policy broadly related to the external arena: the changing nature of policy issues; domestic politics; the media and public opinion; and the corporate sector's increasing international interests and involvement. The chapter then provides examples of how these elements have affected the Indian government's ability to act on some multilateral questions, examining multilateral trade negotiations in particular. It also looks briefly at their impact on climate change negotiations, as well as a few other multilateral issues. Finally, it suggests some ways in which the capacity-related challenges to India's effective participation in the multilateral order can be mitigated.

People and Ideas

There continue to be calls at home and abroad for India to do more to shape and enforce global rules, norms, and institutions.[2] Yet there is a realization that India does not necessarily have the numbers and expertise to do so, especially in its Ministry of External Affairs (MEA)—the ministry that often takes the lead on these questions or at least plays a starring role. Various observers have noted that India's foreign service and the ministry's budget are "remarkably small," especially when compared with those of other countries.[3]

The MEA's capacity—personnel and budget—to conduct external relations was a concern of the Indian leadership from the early days of independence.[4] However, historically, compared to other developing countries, India had "relatively more advanced diplomatic resources"[5]—this capacity was indeed one reason why the country could play an international role perhaps disproportionate to its capabilities. The Indian state today has significant capacity to develop and formulate external policy in terms of individuals, idea generation, and institutions. However, now it is this capacity that is disproportionate to its capabilities and the role to which India aspires. With economic growth, the MEA's resource situation has improved considerably, but budget constraints and personnel shortages continue to be a problem—one that is likely to get more acute as India's international footprint grows.

For some of India's interlocutors, the Indian situation turns on its head Henry Kissinger's apocryphal question about engaging Europe, "Who do I call if I want to speak to Europe?"[6] The problem reflected in that question was that too many actors were involved with not enough clarity about who was in charge. In India's case, foreign officials express the opposite problem: not enough counterparts with whom to engage.[7] A European diplomat, for example, commented that, when engaging Indian counterparts, "We may have 10 people on our team, but the Indian side comprises just one or two persons."[8] A Southeast Asian diplomat noted a related problem: not enough high-level personnel to participate consistently and effectively in regional dialogues.[9]

Many foreign officials note the high quality of the Indian officials with whom they interact in bilateral and multilateral settings.[10] However, as the scale and kind of activities that India is seeking and expected to be involved in at the bilateral, regional, and multilateral levels expand, the availability of expertise has also become a concern. Most MEA officials, like many of their counterparts in other ministries, are generalists by recruitment and training.[11] There are questions about their ability to meet effectively the demands of dealing with counterparts on a range of complex issues that require specialized knowledge and skills. Rotations or deputations—one way of involving those from other ministries with specialized knowledge—are an option, but this option is only exercised to a limited extent. The National Security Council Secretariat and some ministries do bring on specialists through lateral entry (perhaps the most famous being Prime Minister Manmohan Singh in the 1970s, first as adviser to the Ministry of Foreign Trade, then as chief economic adviser and secretary in the Finance Ministry), but this is a road rarely taken, especially in the MEA.[12] Lacking the expertise and time, most ministries have limited research and long-term planning capabilities. The government does "outsource" some research and analyses to industry groups, think tanks, universities, and even consultancies. However, the think tanks and universities researching foreign policy are "underdeveloped" and "short of resources."[13] Moreover, with limited access to officials and lack of information about the policymaking process, many experts at these organizations feel hamstrung.[14]

Why do limited numbers and expertise—or capacity more broadly—matter? First, inadequate capacity can limit the range of issues—geographic and functional—on which already stretched officials can focus. Second, it can lead to a concentration on day-to-day imperatives, a tactical or parochial focus, and, as Malone notes, case-by-case policy formulation. This leaves little time for identifying priorities, assessing trade-offs, or engaging in strategic thinking or long-term planning. Third, the quality of the work undertaken by overburdened officials can suffer. Fourth, it can decrease the time or inclination to engage with and mobilize other stakeholders. Fifth, it can put officials in reactive mode, with little time or incentive to take the initiative. Sixth, it can affect other countries' perceptions of whether India is a country with which they can effectively engage in a sustained manner.[15] They might question not just India's willingness to engage—and the quality of that engagement—but also its ability to meet the commitments it makes.[16] Capacity limitations can also negatively affect India's ability to nurture bilateral relationships with key actors—relationships that can help or hinder the country's prospects and leverage in the multilateral realm. Seventh, inadequate capacity can impede progress in bilateral, regional, or multilateral relations if foreign officials hesitate to act for fear of overloading the Indian system.[17]

On the multilateral stage, the numbers and expertise problems are exacerbated by "the sheer number of institutions." Add to these the informal networks that are playing an increasing role in setting norms and standards.[18] In some multilateral settings, there is "significant asymmetry" between the capacity of India and that of other countries, which can circumscribe India's role.[19] Indian officials can find themselves at a disadvantage when faced with other delegations that have specialists from different fields, limiting their ability to contribute to policy formulation.[20] A recent Finance Ministry paper on trade negotiations acknowledging this problem noted that in order to be able to "set [its] own agenda and make others . . . react instead of [India] reacting as has been the case till now," the government would need to undertake in-depth advanced study of various issues, as well as involve trade policy experts in the negotiations to a greater degree.[21] Saran also outlines the potentially negative impact of the "major shortage of capacity, both in terms of human resources and available expertise," on India's ability to play an effective role in a forum like the G-20, for example, whose agenda seems to be getting broader and deeper.[22] On the flip side, when India has available expertise, it can play an effective and significant role in multilateral settings—as Kapur points out in his contribution to this volume, this has been the case in multilateral financial negotiations and institutions.[23]

"New" Factors Affecting Policymaking Capacity

Complicating the capacity situation are a few additional factors that have affected and will continue to affect the ability of the Indian state to formulate and implement external policy. Two points should be kept in mind about these factors: first, their role and impact are not new, but India's policymakers have to grapple with them to a greater extent than ever before; second, they are not exclusive to India.

The Blurring of Horizontal and Vertical Policymaking Lines

Today, there is a blurring of both horizontal and vertical policymaking lines. In terms of the former, there are few policy issues that do not span foreign and domestic jurisdictions. As Sunil Khilnani points out, global developments, institutions, and regimes affect domestic interests and options.[24] Similarly, domestic interests and capabilities affect foreign policy. In addition, while foreign policy might "rarely" be a factor in domestic political and electoral calculations,[25] domestic political calculations are definitely a factor in foreign policy calculations. Within India, the lines between the "central" and "state" lists are also increasingly fading, with many issues falling, in practice at least, in the "concurrent" list. As for the vertical lines, there are few—if any—issues that do not "cut across [functional] domains."[26]

The horizontal and vertical policymaking lines are especially blurred on issues of multilateral interest: nuclear policy, climate change, trade, maritime security, cyber security, and resource security (food, energy, water).[27] These issues cut across the domestic and international spaces and involve the interests and jurisdictions of multiple government agencies (including the military services). The capacity of the Indian state to engage effectively on any of these issues in the multilateral realm will be affected by each of these agencies' preferences as well as the lead agency's ability to factor them into policymaking. Often the lead agency is the MEA, where a former minister of state notes that even intra-agency coordination continues to be a challenge, further hindering interagency communication and coordination.[28]

On the one hand, if the lead agency ignores other relevant actors and their preferences and does not communicate or coordinate policy with them, this will negatively affect the quality of India's multilateral engagement as well as its ability to make sustainable commitments or deliver on them. In addition, external actors can take advantage of interagency differences and turf wars—especially if they play out publicly—to undercut India's negotiating position and leverage. On the other hand, coordination not only can help the government assess priorities and trade-offs better but also can strengthen Indian policymakers' hands vis-à-vis those of their interlocutors. Devesh Kapur's chapter in this volume, for example, outlines how India's participation in international regimes to control illicit finance has benefited from such coordination.[29]

Permanent or temporary venues for communication and coordination, such as the Groups or Empowered Groups of Ministers, the Committee of Secretaries, cabinet committees, and a range of issue-specific bodies (like the Energy Coordination Committee, the Trade and Economic Relations Committee, or the Council on Climate Change) exist in India and bring together some of the stakeholders.[30] However, communication and coordination are often ad hoc, informal, and concentrated at the senior levels.

There are numerous examples of the consequences of unresolved interagency differences. They delayed the establishment of a single agency to oversee and coordinate India's growing overseas development assistance programs.[31] Such differences in the energy policymaking space in India led to questions in the mid-2000s from energy and foreign policy officials in other countries about who in India was taking the lead in formulating and implementing India's international energy activities. Indian energy companies on their part complained about the negative impact that the lack of interagency coordination was having on their ability to secure assets and resources abroad.[32] In another instance, different perspectives of the MEA and the Ministry of Home Affairs have led to delays in issuing research visas for foreign scholars and students, affecting, according to a foreign secretary, India's ability to "build constituencies" abroad.[33] Differences have also reportedly stalled the addition and promotion of personnel in the MEA, affecting the crucial numbers and expertise questions mentioned above.[34]

Coalition Politics, Surging States, and Oppositions That Oppose

A debate exists on the extent of the influence of domestic politics on those handling India's external relations and especially on decisionmaking. As Rudra Chaudhuri notes, however, politics has played a role in limiting executive capacity and "more than a marginal role in shaping policy outcomes."[35]

What some have called "political fragmentation" has especially affected the capacity of the Indian state to make external policy.[36] This is playing out in three dimensions. First, fragmentation has meant that the Congress Party no longer dominates at the center, and no "national" party is likely to do so in the near future. The party in power has to deal with a vocal opposition—one that often sees its role as literally opposing the government's foreign and domestic policies, even those it might have supported when in power. Second, coalition governments and coalition politics more broadly have an impact on policymaking capacity. Feigenbaum has written about the time and effort that coalition management requires, restricting available capacity to develop policy. He also notes the substantive policy constraints that members of a ruling coalition can impose. Both aspects, he argues, increase the difficulty of "mov[ing] big ideas and big policies through the Indian system."[37]

The rise of regional parties, in particular, has concerned some observers who argue that their presence in coalitions at the center can lead to the privileging of parochial concerns and interests, consigning external and strategic considerations to the dust heap.[38] However, given the blurring of horizontal policymaking lines—something that is evident to regional parties who seek power and influence at both the state and central levels[39]—even regional parties can and do have preferences with regard to foreign policy and multilateral issues and organizations that need to be considered. Coalition politics means that these interests and preferences—as well as those of nonregional coalition members—matter and that these actors can affect state capacity.[40] Even if they do not have an active view, they can serve as a brake on policy.

A third dimension is the evolving center-state dynamic. While still a fairly centralized country, the changing role of states in India, their engagement with the global economy, their influence at the center, and state governments' authority and responsibility for implementing key policies mean that state preferences can also have an impact on capacity. Foreign officials have recognized the role of the states, visiting them and meeting state officials.[41] Indian chief ministers, in turn, have made clear that they have interests—largely economic—abroad, for example, with visits to China, Israel, and the United States. They have also been vocal on issues like foreign direct investment, a national counterterrorism center, and a goods and services tax—each of which has the potential to affect India's relations with other countries or its capacity to act in multilateral negotiations or organizations.

Domestic politics affected policymaking capacity on "foreign" questions even before the current coalition era. Chaudhuri has noted the impact of domestic politics on Indian decisionmakers during and after the 1962 Sino-Indian War.[42] Mukherji has examined the effect of domestic politics on decisions on trade and economic liberalization in the aftermath of Indira Gandhi's 1966 decision to devalue the rupee.[43] Domestic political dynamics also contributed significantly to Gandhi's decision to alter her stance on multilateral negotiations on Vietnam.[44] Observers have also noted the impact of domestic political factors on the Indian government's capacity to make policy toward Sri Lanka as well as West Asia.[45] More recently, the effect of domestic politics—coalition politics and the center-state dynamic—on the government's decisionmaking capacity was perhaps most prominently evident in constraining the ability of the central government to strike a deal with Bangladesh on the sharing of water from the river Teesta.[46]

However, fragmentation does not have to mean lack of capacity to take the initiative in the external realm—between 1989 and 1998, India had seven coalition governments, but this was also a period of some policy departures and innovations.

The Media and Public Opinion

Most observers acknowledge that the media environment in which Indian policymakers are operating has undergone a major transformation. Along with a vibrant print media, there are hundreds of television channels—some dedicated to news, others that include news programming.[47] In addition, there is the increasing use of social media platforms like Facebook and Twitter and technologies like mobile phones and the Internet. Overall, the distribution of news is mobile and real time or "instant," and government action is under constant scrutiny.[48] These technologies have also exacerbated the state's multiple-audience problem. Furthermore, along with the changed scale and nature of the media, there has also been a change, as Sanjaya Baru has noted, in the media's funding model—organizations are less dependent than before on the government (though not necessarily entirely independent from their private sector owners).[49]

This changed environment has had an impact on both the influence and effectiveness of government. The media play various roles. Basu has outlined three: observer, participant, and catalyst.[50] Raja Mohan has added another—venue—noting, "The media has become the principal theatre for intellectual and policy contestation on the direction of Indian foreign policy."[51] Opposition parties have used media and public pressure to attack the government's bilateral and multilateral polices on the grounds that it is giving up national sovereignty or strategic autonomy. Further, the media can not only reflect but also exacerbate political differences.[52] When he was defense minister, George Fernandes accused the media of "stoking partisan fires."[53] In addition, various government stakeholders or coalition members use the media to push their preferred policy or personal interests, which can deepen internal differences.[54]

Through these roles, the media have put the "brake" on some new initiatives and played "facilitator" on others.[55] They have affected the policy options available to government, including on multilateral relations and issues.[56] They can also shape other countries' views of government policy, which when inaccurately represented can cause problems for the government. The media have also helped to set the terms of the public debate, although government officials complain that the search for ratings and the dearth of journalists who specialize in foreign policy mean that these debates are often not very sophisticated. Finally, the media play a significant role in shaping public opinion.[57]

An oft-heard contention is that public opinion does not matter in foreign policy. This is not really borne out by Indian history. While perhaps less influential on foreign policy questions, there is little doubt that public opinion can have an impact—even if that effect is primarily through its impact on the domestic political debate on foreign policy questions.[58] Public opinion has affected state capacity by ruling out certain avenues: perhaps most prominently in 1959–62 on the China-India border question.[59] More recently, the media, reflecting and shaping public opinion, pushed the government to act on issues, such as the alleged killing of two Indian fishermen by Italian marines, that potentially have repercussions for multilateral efforts to combat piracy.[60] The impact of this factor on trade and climate change policies is discussed below.

The Corporate Sector

As the Indian economy and its corporate sector—both the private sector and state-owned companies—have grown and globalized, so have the sector's interests in foreign policy.[61] As their footprint has expanded—Indian companies' outward investment has grown significantly, both in scale and geographically[62]—Indian businesses' interest in multilateral policy has also grown. Affected by global economic standards and rules to a greater extent than in the past, the sector has strong preferences about the decisions made in this realm, including on market access and visa regimes.[63] Thus it has an interest in the Indian government playing a part in rule making or at least rule shaping. It also has an interest in specific issues. Indian companies like Reliance and ONGC, for example, have a deep interest in developments vis-à-vis Iran in the U.S. Congress, at the United Nations (UN) Security Council, and in the European Union. Moreover, with their success, domestic and international clout, and access to the media (and sometimes ownership of them), overall these companies can make their voices heard.[64]

Corporations are playing different roles in India's external relations. First, they are stakeholders with an interest in influencing foreign relations and policy. Second, they are constituents wanting the government to help them to secure resources, technology, capital, expertise, investments, and markets abroad as well as to protect their interests there. Third, they are assets, whose investments and partnerships in some countries have created opportunities for the pursuit of broader Indian interests there. Nirupama Rao, India's ambassador to the United States, for example, recently called Indian business "both a cheerleader and a star player" in that relationship.[65] They also can be liabilities if their activities abroad create complications for India's foreign policy. Fourth, they are providers of expertise, with a crucial role in the development of policy on issues like energy and cyber security. Finally, they have played a role in implementation, performing some functions that traditionally are undertaken by diplomats or perhaps think tanks: public diplomacy, convening, economic diplomacy, information collection, and analysis. Through public diplomacy and public relations activities, the corporate sector has also shaped debate and opinion both in India and abroad.[66]

While the Indian government has used corporations instrumentally in the past—for example, getting private sector leaders to make the case in the United States for aid to India in the 1950s[67]—the scale of this activity has increased tremendously. The government often works with the two major Indian chambers of commerce—the Confederation of Indian Industry (CII) and the Federation of Indian Chambers of Commerce and Industry (FICCI)—in what it calls "public-private partnerships." With offices in Australia, China, France, Germany, Italy, Japan, Singapore, South Africa, the United Kingdom, and the United States, these organizations help the government to publicize brand India, attract investment, undertake bilateral or multilateral dialogues, serve as "listening posts," and even write policy papers and provide advice.[68]

The corporate sector has enhanced Indian state capacity to develop and implement foreign policy, especially in its implementation role. However, it can also have a negative impact on that capacity at times. The perception of India—especially public perception—in other countries, for example, can be negatively affected by the activities of Indian companies. A senior MEA official acknowledged this challenge a few years ago, noting the government's efforts to urge public and private sector companies operating in Africa not just to pursue their corporate interests but also to contribute to local development.[69] Recently, the potential complications that corporate activity can create for the Indian state were evident over the question of the Indian company GMR's contract to build an airport in the Maldives.[70]

Impact on Multilateral Realm

Each of the elements mentioned above can have an effect on state capacity to make and implement policy related to the multilateral realm. The impact of these elements has, for instance, been evident in the multilateral trade and climate negotiations as well as in policy related to Iran and the South China Sea disputes.

Trade Negotiations

The elements mentioned above have affected Indian state capacity in multilateral trade negotiations. They have had an impact on the ability of the lead Indian ministry—commerce and industry—to develop and implement multilateral trade policy. This was evident during the Doha Development Round negotiations of the World Trade Organization (WTO), which began in late 2001. The negotiations collapsed in July 2008 over differences between the developed and developing countries on issues like market access and agricultural subsidies. Many abroad held Kamal Nath, the Indian commerce minister, responsible for the breakdown.[71] From the Indian negotiators' perspective, they had to factor in the views of different ministries, domestic political interests, as well as the preferences of the corporate sector. The experience left a sense that "complex multilateral agreements" just required too much domestic "consensus-building."[72] Indeed, many countries seem to have come to this conclusion, preferring instead to seek bilateral or regional preferential trading agreements.[73]

The Indian negotiating stance during the Doha Round had to take into account various domestic interest groups: given the range of stakeholders and activities they affect, the trade negotiations required input and buy-in from numerous ministries in addition to Nath's own, including the foreign, finance, agriculture, rural development, and communications and information technology ministries. It also required the state to factor in the interests of state governments, farmers, and the corporate sector (both the manufacturing and services sector). These various interests, along with domestic politics and public opinion, affected the state's capacity and flexibility to negotiate—and interest in negotiating—a deal. The fact that "no deal" was an acceptable option—or even a preferred option because of domestic politics and public opinion—affected everyone's capacity to get a deal done.[74]

The impact of domestic politics on India's stance was evident to India's interlocutors. At an early stage of the round, India's commerce and industry minister, Murasoli Maran, bluntly told his Egyptian counterpart, "Look, in the domestic politics of India, it is in my political interest that this thing fails."[75] A few years later, Nath told his interlocutors that a bad deal (anything that seemed like it was sacrificing the interests of farmers) would be detrimental to his party's political chances.[76] The Congress-led coalition government had come to power arguing that the previous Bharatiya Janata Party–led coalition had put in policies that benefited India's urban middle classes and the services sector, but ignored the interests of the rural population—many believed that argument was the basis of its victory.[77] The final set of negotiations in July 2008 took place just after the Congress Party faced a no-confidence vote and before elections in 2009. Thus it was hardly surprising that the government was factoring in politics. Nath observed that while his actions during the trade negotiations were not a major concern of voters, he benefited politically from the position he took during trade negotiations.[78] Indeed, at home he highlighted his stance, which many abroad held responsible for the collapse of the negotiations, and was feted for it.[79]

State-level politicians made sure their voices were heard at the center as well. Using the megaphone that the media provided, in advance of the Doha Round, the Madhya Pradesh deputy chief minister Subhash Yadav raised the possibility that the central government would succumb to pressure and lower agricultural subsidies, stating that this would be disastrous for small Indian farmers.[80] Also, in 2001 Punjab chief minister Parkash Singh Badal, a member of the ruling National Democratic Alliance coalition at the center, noted his state's fear of the WTO.[81] A few years later, with a different coalition in power at the center, he went further, asserting that the agreements the Indian government had made during another negotiation "will sound the death knell of [the] farm sector."[82] Just before the Indian delegation left for the July 2008 talks, the Kerala chief minister V. S. Achuthanandan released his letter to the prime minister asserting that a WTO agreement would harm Indian farmers and manufacturers, and it was better not to reach any agreement.[83]

Before 1991, Indian industry had actively campaigned against trade liberalization through the WTO. That approach changed somewhat with the reforms of 1991, but industry continued to have strong views on other issues being discussed during trade negotiations.[84] It was active in the lead-up to the Doha Round and not hesitant to express its preferences publicly.[85] In the early stages of the Doha Round, an industry group publicly urged the government not to negotiate on investments, expressing its concerns to the commerce minister (Arun Jaitley) about being "exposed to international competition" prematurely.[86] However, as Indian companies—especially, but not solely, in the services sector—grew and globalized, their interests changed. Overall, they continued to make their views heard on issues like intellectual property rights, access to markets, industrial tariffs, and labor standards, although, as different sectors evolved in different ways, some cleavages became evident in the last stages of the negotiations.[87]

Climate Negotiations

The way "new" factors mentioned above can have an impact on the Indian government's multilateral climate policymaking capacity was evident during the run-up to the Copenhagen summit in December 2009, when countries gathered for global climate negotiations. Earlier that year, differences among India's negotiating team had become apparent after the prime minister endorsed a multilateral statement aiming to limit global temperature increase to 2° Celsius.

These differences became even more evident in the fall of 2009. Remarks made by Jairam Ramesh, the Indian minister of environment and forests, in China and a letter he wrote to the prime minister that was leaked to the press outlined a proposal to alter India's traditional stance on climate negotiations and suggested a different position vis-à-vis the developed and G-77 countries than India had traditionally taken. The letter also laid out the option of accepting some emission cuts.[88] Abroad the note was seen as suggesting negotiating flexibility and elicited approval. At home, there was a feeling that Ramesh not only had changed Indian policy substantively without consulting other stakeholders but also had weakened the country's negotiating position.

The prime minister's climate change envoy reiterated publicly that India's main challenge at the summit would indeed be countering any "attempt by rich countries to . . . remove the distinction between developed and developing." Some suggested that this challenge had just become more acute because of Ramesh's proposal. Two of India's climate policy negotiators indicated that they would withdraw from the negotiating team if the Indian position reflected the approach outlined in the memo. Some members of the government reportedly were also unhappy with the minister's proposal. Opposition parties took to the airwaves to accuse the government of weakening India's negotiating position. State chief ministers expressed concern about the government's stance and its impact on economic development. Gujarat chief minister Narendra Modi criticized the insufficiency of the role given to state governments in the policy process on this question. Some environmentalists and the business community also criticized the proposal. The minister found himself having to provide an explanation in Parliament, denying that he had suggested legally binding emission reduction targets and qualifying some of his proposals. Other negotiators later noted that all this had indeed negatively affected India's negotiating position in Copenhagen.[89]

Other Areas

The four elements—the involvement of various government agencies, domestic politics, media and public opinion, and the corporate sector—have affected Indian state capacity to formulate and implement policy on other multilateral questions as well. For example, when Indian policymakers had to decide whether or not to vote against Iran at the International Atomic Energy Agency, they had to factor in domestic politics, public and media reaction, as well as Indian companies' investments in and exports to Iran. With ramifications for energy security concerns, the health of the Indian economy and India's relations with several countries, including the United States, the decision and India's policymaking space were also affected by the interests of multiple ministries. Some of these elements also played a role in the Indian debate and decision on whether or not to participate in the United States–led multilateral coalition's "armed intervention" in Iraq in 2003.[90]

Even if one looks beyond traditional multilateral activities and forums toward "new" multilateral issues, these various elements will affect India's state capacity. The issue of freedom of navigation and the South China Sea dispute, for example, involves not only India's relations with various countries and regional organizations but also multiple ministries— foreign, finance, petroleum and natural gas, defense—as well as the Indian military and state-owned companies. With various entities making public statements about the dispute, policymakers will likely have to factor in domestic politics and the media and public opinion when making decisions on this issue as well.

The Way Ahead

The building of robust state capacity to act externally does not always precede the acquisition of power or an increase in external activity. As Daniel Markey and C. Raja Mohan point out, in the United States much of the institutional and intellectual infrastructure of foreign and security policymaking was put in place after the need for it was felt as the U.S. footprint and its interests expanded.[91] Perhaps necessity will lead the Indian state to strengthen its capacity to make external policy broadly and multilateral policy particularly. However, India may not have the luxury of time. While external observers note with surprise how much the Indian state has achieved with limited capacity,[92] India cannot continue to rely on *jugaad* (improvising solutions in the context of limited resources) alone. Without effective state capacity, it will miss opportunities, especially in shaping the multilateral order, and have a difficult time tackling challenges that come its way.

Numbers matter and, despite the proliferation of stakeholders, the state will remain the key actor in developing and implementing India's external policy. The government needs to find a way to overcome resistance and hire additional skilled personnel to develop, conduct, and implement policy. These increased numbers will help to ease the burden on current officials. Some specialized recruitment and a revised training program should be considered, as should mid-career training and increased rotations through different ministries. The government can also supplement career officials with experts brought in through a lateral entry process. This is not a silver bullet, but it can be a crucial component of increasing state capacity as long as it is used to bring in qualified specialists on a meritocratic basis.

The government can also reach outside to organizations—think tanks, universities, corporations, and industry groups—that can provide expertise and enhance state capacity to develop, explain, and implement policy. The corporate sector can also provide tools and expertise to aid the government, and the government should continue to collaborate with this sector. However, it needs to find the right business-government partnership balance; overreliance on business can lead to corporate interests taking precedence over other interests, perhaps more strategically important ones. As Indian policy research institutions become more effective, the government should consider reaching out to them for certain activities instead.

These research institutions—think tanks and universities—need to be brought into the process on a more systematic basis. They need funding—from the state and from other sources—but in a manner that protects the integrity and independence of their work. In addition, giving researchers access to policymakers and allowing them to learn more about the policy process will give them a better understanding of policymakers' constraints and increase their ability to produce feasible policy advice. Experts at these institutions, for their part, have to engage not just with each other but with the media, private sector, and government. They have to make their analyses and recommendations feasible and communicate them in an accessible way. They need to fill in the capacity gaps, especially providing work that government officials do not have the time or expertise to undertake: for example, in-depth policy-relevant research as well as contingency, scenario, and long-term policy planning. Through programs designed to prepare students and junior scholars for a multidisciplinary, multilateral policy world, they also need to train a new generation of experts to work on and in external policymaking.

As far as the "new" factors mentioned above, their potentially negative impact can be limited with effective planning, consultation, and coordination. Managed well, each of these factors can indeed be leveraged, enhancing Indian state capacity. The media, for example, can be a useful tool to explain policy, anticipate and address criticism, pressure opposition parties, solicit views, and shape the policy debate. This requires the government to engage actively, consistently, and directly with the media and via social media platforms. The hesitation to speak publicly on certain multilateral issues—which can be sensitive and complex—and to insulate policymaking on them from public discussion is understandable, given that that they can benefit from less visibility. But the state cannot depend on these issues remaining low-key. If it does not engage with the media and in the public debate (or at least prepare to do so), others will fill the vacuum and instead shape the state's options and capacity to act. If the government shapes and harnesses public opinion, it can strengthen its own hand vis-à-vis other stakeholders—internal and external. This engagement, however, cannot just be reactive. It has to be an integral part of policymaking, from the formulation stage itself.

Consultation with various stakeholders should also be an integral part of the policy process from the onset—rather than an afterthought. Both internal and external consultations are important. It is better to deal with any differences through the policy-formulating process, rather than leave them to the end to sort out. On the one hand, if not dealt with, these differences can seriously impair the ability to implement policy. On the other hand, getting other stakeholders to buy in to policy can enhance state capacity. There are often hesitations about bringing additional stakeholders into the process—because of reduction of influence and questions about whether their inclusion will hurt more than help or be at all effective in limiting the role of some of the elements mentioned above. However, if the process of consultation is institutionalized and consistent, the state has a better chance of making and implementing policy effectively. Indian governments have shown an ability to build political constituencies and coalitions; they now have to work on building policy ones.

Policy coordination is also crucial. It allows priorities to be identified and trade-offs to be considered. Better-coordinated policy at home also translates well abroad. The state cannot effectively play a global "chess grandmasters' game, where each move will have to be mindful of several other pieces on the board and the game is played as part of a long strategic interaction,"[93] if it cannot keep track of the pieces. Interagency coordination needs to be institutionalized and not left to personal initiative and networks. Coordination mechanisms need to be established at different levels and not just at the senior ones.

Taking the steps outlined above to build state capacity will not be easy because of internal resistance and inertia, but it is an effort worth making, with long-term payoffs for India's multilateral interests and influence.

Notes

1. Shashi Tharoor, *Pax Indica: India and the World of the 21st Century* (New York: Penguin Books, 2012), p. 319.

2. C. Raja Mohan, "Rising India: Partner in Shaping the Global Commons," *Washington Quarterly* 33, no. 3 (July 2010): 139.

3. Daniel Markey, "Developing India's Foreign Policy 'Software,'" *Asia Policy* 8 (July 2009): 73–96; Tharoor, *Pax Indica*, pp. 319, 336–37. Also see David M. Malone, *Does the Elephant Dance? Contemporary Indian Foreign Policy* (Oxford University Press, 2011).

4. Tharoor, *Pax Indica*, p. 317.

5. Raja Mohan, "Rising India," p. 136; Arvind Gupta, "Tasks before Indian Foreign Policy," *IDSA Comment*, May 9, 2012 (http://idsa.in/idsacomments/TasksbeforeIndianForeignPolicy_ArvindGupta_090512).

6. Gideon Rachman, "Kissinger Never Wanted to Dial Europe," *Financial Times*, July 29, 2009 (http://on.ft.com/hVM9ew).

7. Senior U.S. official at a roundtable, Washington, October 2011.

8. Amit Baruah, "MEA to Double Its Strength in Five Years," *Hindustan Times*, June 3, 2007 (http://goo.gl/x3Zd5).

9. Conversation with the author, Washington, January 2013.

10. Tharoor, *Pax Indica*, p. 319, Malone, *Does the Elephant Dance?*, p. 8.

11. Tharoor, *Pax Indica*, pp. 321–22

12. Markey, "Developing India's Foreign Policy 'Software,'" p. 78. C. Raja Mohan, "The Making of Indian Foreign Policy: The Role of Scholarship and Public Opinion," ISAS Working Paper 73 (National University of Singapore, Institute of South Asian Studies, July 13, 2009), p. 11.

13. Markey, "Developing India's Foreign Policy 'Software,'" pp. 75, 79.

14. Tharoor, *Pax Indica*, pp. 337–39.

15. Malone, *Does the Elephant Dance?*, p. 7; Baruah, "MEA to Double Its Strength"; Indrani Bagchi, "In the Service of Indian Diplomacy," *Times of India*, April 14, 2011 (http://goo.gl/0Dees); Markey, "Developing India's Foreign Policy 'Software,'" pp. 90–92; "Interview with Jorge Heine, Chile's Ambassador to India," *FPRC Journal* 3 (2012): 6.

16. Centre for Policy Research and National Defense College, *Nonalignment 2.0: A Foreign and Strategic Policy for India in the Twenty First Century* (New Delhi, 2012), p. 33 (www.cprindia.org/workingpapers/3844-nonalignment-20-foreign-and-strategic-policy-india-twenty-first-century).

17. Conversation with U.S. military officer, Washington, November 2012.

18. Centre for Policy Research and National Defense College, *Non-Alignment 2.0*, pp. 34–35. For more on informal networks, see Anne-Marie Slaughter, *A New World Order* (Princeton University Press, 2005).

19. Shyam Saran, "The Evolving Role of Emerging Economies in Global Governance: An Indian Perspective" (London: King's College, King's India Institute, June 7, 2012), p. 45.

20. See chapter 3 by Shyam Saran in this volume.

21. "Failure of Doha Round to Impact India in Services Sector: Study," *Mint*, November 21, 2007 (http://goo.gl/w4YSC).

22. Saran, "The Evolving Role," p. 35.

23. See chapter 13 by Devesh Kapur in this volume. Malone also notes India's strength in "finance diplomacy." Malone, *Does the Elephant Dance?*, p. 267.

24. Sunil Khilnani, "When Local Meets Global," *Times of India*, March 10, 2012 (http://goo.gl/921Ul).

25. Ashok Malik and Rory Medcalf, "India's New World: Civil Society in the Making of Foreign Policy" (Sydney: Lowy Institute for International Policy, May 2011), p. 3.

26. Khilnani, "When Local Meets Global."

27. Chellaney provides a glimpse of the number of agencies involved in water policy. See Brahma Chellaney, *Water: Asia's New Battleground* (Georgetown University Press, 2011). For a similar survey on the energy policy front, see Tanvi Madan, *India*, Brookings

Energy Security Series (Brookings, Foreign Policy Studies Program, 2006) (http://brookin.gs/luHj).

28. Tharoor, *Pax Indica*, pp. 328–31.

29. See chapter 13 by Kapur in this volume.

30. Malik and Medcalf, "India's New World," p. 9.

31. Shubhajit Roy, "MEA Drops Aid Agency Plan as DoPT Objects," *Indian Express*, May 17, 2010 (http://goo.gl/Iz44Y); Ivy Mungcal, "India's Long-Delayed Development Agency Takes Form," *Development Newswire*, July 2, 2012 (http://goo.gl/6a6M9).

32. For details, see Madan, *India*.

33. Vikas Dhoot, "Menon to Home Secy: Image at Stake, Need to Simplify Visa Rules for Foreign Students," *Indian Express*, January 19, 2007 (http://goo.gl/3UAG4); Pratap Bhanu Mehta, "Our Insecurity Syndrome," *Indian Express*, February 13, 2007 (http://goo.gl/WVQB6).

34. Tharoor, *Pax Indica*, p. 321. Dipanjan Roy Chaudhury, "MEA Pushes for Creation of New Posts in Foreign Ministry," *Mail Today*, July 16, 2012 (http://goo.gl/9xj5m). Also see Iftikhar Gilani, "IAS-IFS Battle Hits India's March to Global Power Status," *DNA India*, August 3, 2012 (http://goo.gl/QSG3Q).

35. Rudra Chaudhuri, "The Limits of Executive Power: Domestic Politics and Alliance Behavior in Nehru's India," *India Review* 11, no. 2 (2012): 96.

36. Rohan Mukherjee and David M. Malone, "Indian Foreign Policy and Contemporary Security Challenges," *International Affairs* 87, no. 1 (2011): 90.

37. Bernard Gwertzman, "Interview with Evan A. Feigenbaum on India's National Elections and Improved U.S. Relations" (New York: Council on Foreign Relations, April 15, 2009) (http://goo.gl/Zn2Hp).

38. Poorvi Chitalkar and David M. Malone, "Democracy, Politics, and India's Foreign Policy," *Canadian Foreign Policy Journal* 17, no. 1 (March 2011): 82.

39. Mukherjee and Malone, "Indian Foreign Policy," p. 91.

40. Mohan, "The Making of Indian Foreign Policy," p. 10. Also Khilnani, "When Local Meets Global."

41. Bharat Bhushan, "Why the US Is Chasing India's Regions," BBC News, May 8, 2012 (http://bbc.in/IESFL5); "Israel Ambassador Calls upon Narendra Modi," *Hindustan Times*, January 30, 2013 (http://goo.gl/kHWBp).

42. Chaudhuri, "The Limits of Executive Power," pp. 104–07.

43. Rahul Mukherji, "India's Aborted Liberalization—1966," *Pacific Affairs* 73, no. 3 (Autumn 2000): 375–92, and "The Political Economy of Development in India," conference paper (Canberra: Australian National University, November 20, 2009).

44. Tanvi Madan, "With an Eye to the East: China and the U.S.-India Relationship, 1949–1979," Ph.D. dissertation, University of Texas at Austin, 2012, pp. 408–09.

45. Mukherjee and Malone, "Indian Foreign Policy," p. 91. Also see Chitalkar and Malone, "Democracy, Politics, and India's Foreign Policy," p. 81.

46. Arvind Gupta, "Tasks before Indian Foreign Policy," *IDSA Comment*, May 9, 2012 (http://goo.gl/97qZ0); "Teesta Pact with Bangladesh Put off after Mamata Sulk," *Times of India*, September 6, 2011 (http://goo.gl/9DfLL); Arindam Sarkar, "Mounting Pressure on CM to Sign B'desh Water Treaty," *Hindustan Times*, February 21, 2013 (http://goo.gl/WvCKl).

47. Malik and Medcalf, "India's New World," p. 12.

48. Tharoor, *Pax Indica*, pp. 299–301.

49. Sanjaya Baru, "The Growing Influence of Business and Media on Indian Foreign Policy," *ISAS Insights* 49 (February 5, 2009), p. 13.

50. Partha Pratim Basu, *The Press and Foreign Policy of India* (New Delhi: Lancers Books, 2003).

51. Mohan, "The Making of Indian Foreign Policy," p. 8.

52. Baru, "The Growing Influence," p. 11.

53. George Fernandes, "National Security and the Role of the Media," *Strategic Analysis* 22, no. 6 (1998): 819–28 (www.idsa-india.org/an-sep8-1.html).

54. Mohan, "The Making of Indian Foreign Policy," p. 8; Malik and Medcalf, "India's New World," p. 15. Mukherjee and Malone, "Indian Foreign Policy," p. 102.

55. Mohan, "The Making of Indian Foreign Policy," p. 8.

56. Baru, "The Growing Influence," p. 2.

57. Mohan, "The Making of Indian Foreign Policy," p. 1. Sadanand Dhume, remarks on a panel on "Recent Political Developments in India: The Other Leadership Transition" at Brookings, Washington, February 14, 2013; Malik and Medcalf, "India's New World," p. 12.

58. Baru, "The Growing Influence," p. 1; Mohan, "The Making of Indian Foreign Policy," p. 7. Tharoor notes the greater flexibility that decisionmakers have vis-à-vis the media and public opinion on foreign policy; Tharoor, *Pax Indica*, p. 314.

59. Srinath Raghavan, *War and Peace in Modern India: A Strategic History of the Nehru Years* (Ranikhet, India: Permanent Black, 2010), pp. 273–77, 285–92.

60. "Fishermen Killing Case: Italy Recalls Ambassador to India," *Indian Express*, May 18, 2012 (http://goo.gl/VDGqf).

61. Malik and Medcalf, "India's New World," p. 8.

62. Harun R. Khan, "Outward Indian FDI: Recent Trends and Emerging Issues," speech by the deputy governor of the Reserve Bank of India before the Bombay Chamber of Commerce and Industry, Mumbai, March 2, 2012 (http://rbi.org.in/scripts/BS_SpeechesView.aspx?Id=674). Also see Malik and Medcalf, "India's New World," p. 5; Baru, "The Growing Influence," p. 6.

63. Baru, "The Growing Influence," p. 7.

64. Markey, "Developing India's Foreign Policy 'Software,'" p. 90.

65. Nirupama Rao, remarks at a reception of the Confederation of Indian Industry, India Business Forum, Washington, February 22, 2013 (http://goo.gl/mhg64).

66. Mohan, "The Making of Indian Foreign Policy," p. 9.

67. Madan, "With an Eye to the East," p. 199.

68. Markey, "Developing India's Foreign Policy 'Software,'" p. 82. Mohan, "The Making of Indian Foreign Policy," p. 9; Baru, "The Growing Influence," pp. 7–9; Malik and Medcalf, "India's New World," pp. 6–8.

69. Nalin Surie, keynote address by secretary (West), Ministry of External Affairs, Government of India, International Conference on "Africa and Energy Security: Global Issues, Local Responses," Institute for Defense Studies and Analyses, New Delhi, June 23, 2008 (www.idsa.in/node/1579).

70. Indrani Bagchi, "GMR-Maldives Spat: India Loses Strategic Advantage in Indian Ocean," *Economic Times*, December 9, 2012 (http://goo.gl/w5foF); Elizabeth Roche, "Indian Firms' Global Footprint Adds New Dimension to Diplomacy," *Mint*, November 29, 2012 (http://goo.gl/dNXpA).

71. See also chapter 5 by Sanjaya Baru in this volume.

72. Centre for Policy Research and National Defense College, *Non-Alignment 2.0,* p. 26.

73. Paul Blustein, *Misadventures of the Most Favored Nations: Clashing Egos, Inflated Ambitions, and the Great Shambles of the World Trade System* (New York: Public Affairs, 2009), p. 293.

74. Ibid., p. 265.

75. Ibid., p. 112.

76. Ibid., p. 267.

77. Ibid., p. 186.

78. Alan Beattie, "Kamal Nath: Showmanship at the WTO That Plays Well with the Poor," *Financial Times*, January 30, 2009 (www.ft.com/intl/cms/s/0/64a23b8c-ecdd-11dd-a534-0000779fd2ac.html).

79. Malone, *Does the Elephant Dance?*, p. 263.

80. "WTO Terms, a Blow to Indian Farmers," *Hindu*, August 14, 2001 (www.hindu.com/2001/08/15/stories/14152124.htm).

81. "Primal Fears," *India Today*, June 4, 2001 (http://goo.gl/eVn8s).

82. "Explain WTO Pact to Farmers, Badal Tells PM," *Hindu*, December 23, 2005 (www.hindu.com/2005/12/23/stories/2005122304130500.htm).

83. "WTO Pact Will Hurt India: Achuthanandan," *Hindu*, July 19, 2008 (www.hindu.com/2008/07/19/stories/2008071956550100.htm).

84. Malone, *Does the Elephant Dance?*, p. 261.

85. Baru, "The Growing Influence," pp. 5–6.

86. "CII Tells Govt to Say No to WTO Investment Talks," *Hindu Business Line*, August 25, 2003 (www.thehindubusinessline.in/2003/08/26/stories/2003082602070400.htm); Baru, "The Growing Influence," p. 4.

87. "Failure of Doha Round to Impact India in Services Sector: Study," *Mint*, November 21, 2007 (http://goo.gl/v0hXv).

88. For details, see chapter 14 by Navroz Dubash in this volume.

89. Chitalkar and Malone, "Democracy, Politics, and India's Foreign Policy," p. 83; Mohan, "Rising India," p. 139; Malone, *Does the Elephant Dance?*, p. 265; Bruce Stokes, "Countdown to Copenhagen," *National Journal*, October 30, 2009; Jeremy Kahn, "India Cleans Up Its Act," *Newsweek*, November 16, 2009; Ranjit Devraj, "India Ponders Way Forward to Copenhagen," *Inter Press Service*, December 1, 2009; "What India Has to Offer in Copenhagen," *The Economist*, December 3, 2009; "Modi to PM: Involve States in Climate Change Policy Process," *Indian Express*, December 12, 2009; Raj Chengappa, "Warming Up to a New Deal," *India Today*, December 21, 2009; "N-Deal Architect Shyam Saran Quits," *Indian* Express, February 20, 2010; Isabel Hilton, "In India, a Clear Victor on the Climate Action Front," *Yale Environment 360*, February 20, 2010.

90. Rudra Chaudhuri, "India and the Utility of Force in International Politics," conference paper for the annual meeting of the International Studies Association, Montreal, March 16, 2011.

91. Markey, "Developing India's Foreign Policy 'Software,'" pp. 88–89; Mohan, "The Making of Indian Foreign Policy," p. 14.

92. Mohan, "The Making of Indian Foreign Policy," p. 11; Tharoor, *Pax Indica*, pp. 320–21.

93. Centre for Policy Research and National Defense College, *Non-Alignment 2.0*, p. 9.

KANTI BAJPAI

7 India's Regional Disputes

Multilateralism and Third Parties: Yes, No, Maybe

From the 1970s onward, India has been regarded as being a difficult partner in multilateral settings. The end of the cold war may, as various commentators suggest, have effected a much greater degree of "pragmatism" in India's external dealings, but Indians themselves, as well as foreign commentators, recognize that India's attitude to multilateral negotiations and forums is ambivalent.[1] This would not matter much internationally if it were not for the fact that India's power and influence have increased since the early 1990s and are expected to expand as its economy continues to grow at between 6 and 9 percent annually. On numerous global commons issues, India's participation and assent seem to matter. Climate change, trade negotiations, reforms of international economic institutions, proliferation of nuclear weapons, maritime piracy, and transnational terrorism all increasingly require New Delhi to cooperate with major global and regional players. Interest in India's attitude to multilateralism therefore has grown.

Curiously little has been written on the subject, not the least by Indians themselves. If India is ambivalent about multilateralism, where does its conflicted view come from? The answer in part is its historical experience with multilateral institutions. In part, though, it arises from other third-party interventions on issues that affect its interests. To comprehend the Indian disposition to multilateralism, it is necessary to deal with its experiences both with international institutions and with other third-party interventions because the larger *problematique* is how India regards the costs and benefits of working with outside powers or institutions to solve national, bilateral, and global issues. This chapter argues that India's weighing of its experience with multilateralism and third-party engagement in Southern Asia (South Asia plus China) has made it wary of outsiders being involved in its neighborhood, and this has colored its view of multilateralism more generally. Yet, notwithstanding the rather jaundiced view that Indians have of multilateralism and third-party mediation, the record is much more mixed. Indeed, India has done quite well as a result of multilateral and third-party engagement in Southern Asia.

Outside agencies and powers have figured in India's relations in at least three ways:

—In territorial disputes,

—In river water disputes, and

—In times of crisis and war.

This chapter deals with these in turn to assess the role of outsiders and to ask whether or not India has benefited from extra-regional intervention. The broad conclusion is that outsiders have been involved quite significantly in India's disputes since 1947 and that their involvement in Southern Asia has frequently served Indian interests. This is an important conclusion since it suggests that India can be more confident about defending its interests in multilateral settings and can reasonably hope for multilateral interventions in Southern Asia that would help it to resolve disputes to its advantage. However, such a conclusion does not imply that India should mechanically and without careful consideration turn to multilateralism in regional disputes. It will take shrewd and sound diplomacy to use multilateral agencies in aid of India's goals and objectives.

Territorial Disputes

India has a history, at least until 1968, of working with multilateral institutions and other third parties to resolve territorial disputes. The most important cases are the Jammu and Kashmir (J&K) dispute and the Rann of Kutch dispute with Pakistan.

The J&K problem has been written about in great detail and depth, mostly in respect of the failure of the two countries to resolve their differences and the negative consequences for them as a result. The fact that the problem has still not been resolved should not obscure the fact that the two sides nearly came to an agreement during the 1950s under the auspices of the United Nations (UN). It was New Delhi that took the conflict over J&K to the UN, in the belief that its case on Pakistani aggression was strong and would get the backing of the UN. However, for various reasons, mostly to do with U.S. and British backing of Pakistan from the point of view of cold war alliances and with India's rather inept legal arguments, New Delhi found that the UN took a much more even-handed attitude toward the quarrel.[2] Nevertheless, India accepted the necessity of carrying out a plebiscite in the state in accordance with its own commitments and UN resolutions. The two countries were unable eventually to agree on various UN proposals to settle the dispute. These included the attempt to get India and Pakistan to accept arbitration under U.S. admiral Chester Nimitz in August-September 1949 as well as the mediation efforts of General Bruce McNaughton from December 1949 to February 1950, the jurist Owen Dixon from April 1950 to September 1950, and U.S. diplomat Dr. Frank Graham from late 1950 to February 1953.[3] The last time that outsiders became seriously involved in the J&K problem was in 1962–63, when the United Kingdom and the United States insisted that India reopen negotiations with Pakistan on the future of the state. Swaran Singh, the Indian foreign minister, and Zulfiqar Ali Bhutto, the Pakistani foreign minister, conducted the negotiations in 1963 without reaching agreement.[4]

A more successful case of international involvement in India's territorial disputes is the International Court of Justice's binding arbitration on the Rann of Kutch quarrel with Pakistan. In April 1965 the initial skirmishes in what was to become a full-fledged war between India and Pakistan (in September 1965, but over Kashmir) were fought in the Rann. The British government, led by Prime Minister Harold Wilson, succeeded in effecting a cease-fire and persuading the two countries to refer the dispute to an international tribunal.[5] In 1968 the tribunal handed down its decision, which gave India 90 percent of the disputed territory and Pakistan only 10 percent. The settlement was criticized in India on the grounds that the matter should never have gone to the tribunal in the first place.[6] Nonetheless, the two sides honored the award.

A dispute related to the Rann is the Sir Creek dispute, the creek being part of the Rann. The issue here is where the line between the two states should be drawn. Pakistan claims that the entire creek, up to the shores on the Indian side, belongs to it. India insists on a demarcation based on the *thalweg* principle, which has various technical meanings but essentially suggests drawing the line halfway between the two shorelines.[7] The dispute, long regarded as a minor issue, is now captive to concerns over its implications for demarcation of the maritime boundary (where the creek empties out into the sea). India and Pakistan continue to negotiate over Sir Creek in the composite dialogue that has been in progress since the early 1990s when Narasimha Rao was prime minister. The United Nations Convention on the Law of the Sea has mandated that all maritime boundary disputes be settled by 2009, failing which the areas in question will be deemed to be international waters.[8] That date has long expired, and India and Pakistan evidently have staved off the internationalization of the waters by continuing to negotiate bilaterally. If the two sides had allowed the international tribunal on the Rann of Kutch, back in the 1960s, to consider the Sir Creek case, they might well have been spared the difficulties they now confront.

India's boundary dispute with China remains unresolved despite fifteen rounds of negotiations between the special representatives and several rounds of talks in the Joint Working Group. Only in the middle sector of the boundary have the two sides exchanged maps. These maps do not demarcate the middle sector; they simply indicate how the two sides see the boundary line.[9]

Most countries have studiously avoided taking sides on the India-China boundary, including all the major powers. The United States, even at the height of its differences with China (in the 1950s and early 1960s), did not unambiguously endorse the Indian stand on the dispute.[10] However, a group of nonaligned Asian states, called the Colombo Powers (led by Sri Lanka), forwarded a proposal for resolving the dispute. India, albeit reluctantly, accepted the proposal. China rejected it.[11] Since then, no power or institution has tried to involve itself in the conflict. There is no evidence that India ever considered taking the dispute to the UN, unlike the India-Pakistan quarrel over J&K. After India's experience with the J&K dispute, New Delhi would have been wary of going to the UN. In any case, the People's Republic of China was not a member of the UN at the time, as the United States and its allies had installed republican China (Taiwan) in the international body instead. Even after the People's Republic assumed its position in the UN, New Delhi did not consider going to the UN. For its part, China has steadfastly refused to accept any third-party mediation or arbitration in its territorial disputes.

In sum, multilateral and third-party involvement in India's territorial disputes has a mixed record from the Indian point of view. On the one side, the UN's interventions came close to success in terms of organizing a plebiscite on Kashmir, which, however the plebiscite turned out, would have settled the matter, at least for a good number of years. On the other side, in the end, the UN failed to reach agreement on the plebiscite, and Indian hopes that it would come out of the dispute in a stronger legal and diplomatic position were confounded. As for India's arbitration experience, while there was domestic criticism of the Rann of Kutch award, in retrospect it was a good outcome for India, which got most of the territory in question and was left with one less dispute with Pakistan to worry about.

Why did India opt for multilateral mediation and arbitration on territorial disputes in the early years after its independence? There are four probable reasons. First, India clearly regarded the UN as a valuable asset in international society. As a weak state, entering the comity of nations, the UN and international law were potential resources against great-power domination. Investing in the UN was a sensible strategy for a weak state. New Delhi was also undoubtedly motivated by a concern over reputation. It wanted to be regarded as an international good citizen, and this was an opportunity to further both its material and symbolic interests. Second, New Delhi thought it had a very strong diplomatic and legal case over Kashmir and expected to get the international community's backing. It may also have calculated that it had a strong case in the Kutch dispute. Third, while it seems that India as the stronger power should have been able to integrate all of J&K through military means, the judgment at the time was that India would be hard pressed to advance much farther than the current line of control. In the case of Kutch, too, India was probably not strong enough to gets its way militarily. The 1965 war, which started with skirmishes in Kutch, was in fact a close run, and India at several times in the war was on the back foot. Sir Creek has never been militarized, but given the nature of the dispute, it is hard to imagine that it could be resolved militarily, especially when both sides have nuclear weapons and going to war risks escalation. Finally, bilateral negotiations over Kashmir and Kutch were bogged down, and there seemed to be no way of breaking the deadlock with Pakistan without outside help.

River Disputes

The greatest success with multilateral and third-party involvement has been over river waters. Indeed, perhaps the greatest cooperative venture in South Asia is the Indus Waters Treaty, which India and Pakistan signed in 1960. Despite three wars since then (1965, 1971, 1999), the treaty has held up and has largely been honored, even though, particularly on the Pakistani side, there are calls for its renegotiation and revision.[12]

The Indus waters problem arose almost immediately after partition. The two countries held to quite different positions. India wanted to be free to use the rivers, which run through Indian territory before flowing into Pakistan, more or less as it wished. Pakistan was nervous over the fact that it had little control over the upper reaches of the river. According to the Inter-Dominion Accord of 1948, India, in return for payments from Pakistan, would continue to allow the Indus waters to flow into its neighbor. Negotiations on a longer-term solution came to a halt by 1952, with Pakistan arguing for referral of the dispute to the International Court of Justice and India refusing to consider anything but a bilateral solution. The impasse was broken by David Lilienthal, former chairman of the Tennessee Valley Authority, and Eugene Black, president of the World Bank, who worked with both sides to bring engineers into the negotiation and to put the weight of the World Bank and the great powers, principally the United Kingdom and the United States, behind the successful completion of negotiations. The treaty divided the river system into two parts—the three western rivers, which went to Pakistan, and the three eastern rivers, which went to India. In addition, because Pakistan was to cede its rights to the eastern rivers, a series of canals and storage works would connect the eastern rivers to Pakistan to supplement the flow in the western rivers. When India refused to pay for these connecting works, the World Bank persuaded a consortium of Western powers led by the United Kingdom and the United States to pay for them. The treaty set up a permanent commission, which meets regularly to discuss matters relating to the rivers, including any disputes that might arise. The treaty also provides for dispute settlement by mediation and arbitration.[13]

The Indus Waters Treaty has held up quite well since 1960. In 1978 the two sides came to a further agreement—on India's plans to build the Salal Dam. The agreement was reached bilaterally and did not involve third-party efforts.[14] Several river water disputes related to the Indus have occurred since 1978. Two of them have been or are on their way to being resolved through international arbitration. These disputes originate in Indian plans to build storage or hydroelectric works on the rivers before they enter Pakistan. They include the Wullar Barrage/Tulbul Navigation Project, the Baglihar Dam, and the Kishenganga Dam. Pakistan would like arbitration on all three. Wullar/Tulbul is still under bilateral discussion. Baglihar was eventually referred to a neutral expert who, in 2007, found substantially in favor of India but also suggested, in line with Pakistan's concerns, that the height of the proposed dam be reduced.[15] The neutral expert was appointed by the World Bank. Similarly, when the Permanent Indus Commission was unable to find a solution to the Kishenganga Project, the two countries went to arbitration. The UN secretary general appointed a former judge of the International Court of Justice, Stephen Schwebel, to head a seven-person panel that included two nominees—an engineer and a legal expert—from the United Kingdom. In September 2011, in an interim order, the panel asked India to stop construction of "any permanent dam works on or above the river bed that might inhibit the flow of the river."[16] However, "It did not place any restriction on

India going ahead with construction of other components of the dam, namely the water conductor system, coffer dams, the temporary bypass tunnel, and excavation below the river-bed level. As per international law, India will do so at its own risk in case the final order provides for changes in the project design."[17] In September 2012 the two countries concluded their various submissions to the panel.[18] In February 2013 the arbitration panel handed down a partial award in which it allowed India to divert some water from the Kishenganga. A final award is expected in December 2013.[19]

Why did India turn to multilateral and other third-party involvements in its river water disputes, crucially, the Indus River dispute?

First of all, in 1948 when the Indus dispute broke out, India was well disposed to multilateralism (as noted in respect of India's reference of J&K to the UN). The offer by the U.S. expert David Lilienthal and the quick backing of his ideas by the World Bank occurred at a time when India was entering international society and eager to strengthen rules and norms to temper the hegemony of the big powers in international relations.

Second, once again India thought that it had a strong case in the court of international opinion, in this instance on the use of the entire Indus River system in cooperation with Pakistan, particularly with financial aid from the big powers. In the end, the agreement that was reached was a weak one, with the six rivers being divided three apiece, rather than, as Lillienthal had originally hoped, a strong one in which the rivers would be jointly and optimally exploited as a single system. However, New Delhi could be forgiven for thinking that the Lillienthal-Black team backed by the United Kingdom and the United States would deliver an integrated solution to river water use.

Third, the India-Pakistan river water dispute may have been tied up, in India's mind, with other riverine issues in the region. In the other river water cases in South Asia, India was in a weaker bargaining position. If India had asserted its upper riparian rights too strongly in the Indus case, it risked being hoist on its own petard with Bhutan and Nepal, where it was the lower riparian. Therefore, an implicit link between the various river water issues may have affected Indian calculations on the Indus.

Fourth, there was likely no appetite for a military confrontation over the issue. With India already embroiled in a fight over Kashmir and having found itself with little diplomatic support internationally against Pakistan, New Delhi was probably in no mood to get into a fight over the rivers as well and to lose even more diplomatic face.

Finally, the largely bilateral negotiations on the Indus waters, from 1948 to 1952, had been infructuous, and multilateralism offered a way out of the deadlock, one that could be financially attractive given the World Bank's backing for a solution. Since the original agreement on the Indus, India has continued to opt for arbitration (except in the case of Salal and Wullar/Tulbul), using the Indus Waters Treaty, which provides for this option if other means of resolving differences have not worked. Wullar/Tulbul may be the exception that proves the rule. It has been negotiated between the two countries bilaterally for twenty years without result; New Delhi may have felt that Baglihar and Kishenganga were better dealt with by third parties.

Crisis, War, and Regional Instability

India has accepted the intervention of, or actively worked with, multilateral institutions and third parties during bilateral crises and war and in other regional instabilities (typically internal violence in the smaller countries). Over time, the UN has become less important, and powerful outside powers have become more active in trying to manage conflict. South Asia has a rather impressive history of great powers trying to manage crises between India and its neighbors and to terminate war as well as broker postwar agreements. On the whole, these efforts have been positive from India's point of view.

Thus, immediately after partition in 1947, when war broke out between India and Pakistan over J&K, the Anglo-American powers and the UN tried to get both countries to accept a cease-fire and thereafter a solution to the quarrel. UN efforts eventually resulted in a cessation of hostilities. Was this intervention in India's interest? If the cease-fire had not occurred, would India not have taken control of the entire state of J&K and thus have put an end to the problem at its inception? This is clearly a what-if of history, but from the evidence available, it would seem that an Indian victory much beyond the present line of control was not ensured militarily.[20] Also, it is not clear that an Indian victory would have been the end of Pakistani efforts to contest India's control of the state. Pakistan, not India, might in this circumstance have gone to the UN for satisfaction and may have done what it subsequently did in any case—push insurgents into the state, instigate war, and internationalize the dispute.[21]

In 1965 first Britain in the Rann of Kutch in April and later the United States, other great powers, and the UN in the wider war in September tried to stop the fighting and bring about a cease-fire. India was criticized for enlarging the war by crossing the international boundary in order to relieve pressure on its forces along the line of control, but Indian attacks persisted until its forces stood at the gates of Lahore, at which point New Delhi heeded the call for a cease-fire.[22] After the war, in January 1966, India responded to an invitation by the Soviet Union to attend a bilateral summit with Pakistan. Prime Minister Lal Bahadur Shastri met President Ayub Khan under the watchful eye of Premier Alexei Kosygin to hammer out the Tashkent Declaration between India and Pakistan.[23] Once again, we might ask, was it in India's interest to stop fighting when it stood at the gates of Pakistan's largest city and thereafter to agree to a cease-fire? Here too, the evidence suggests that India would have been hard pressed to proceed much farther militarily, as it was running low on supplies.[24] Also, the fighting in and around Lahore might have become much fiercer. Finally, India would most likely have had to deal with much sterner international diplomatic reaction to any attempt to take the city. The point is that the call for a cease-fire gave India a way of ending a war that was likely to become increasingly costly.

In 1971 the international community including the UN tried once more to manage the worsening relationship between the two countries over the deteriorating situation in East Pakistan. The United States was particularly keen to see an end to the war, at least in part to reassure China that it stood by its allies.[25] However, in this instance, India was relatively impervious to international calls to stop fighting, doing so only after Pakistani forces had surrendered in East Pakistan. International involvement may have played a role in terminating the conflict in the western sector though. There were quite direct pressures on India to stop its campaign in the west as soon as the eastern campaign was over. The United States sent an aircraft carrier, the USS *Enterprise*, ostensibly in aid of Pakistani troops and U.S. citizens in East Pakistan who might need to be evacuated, at least in part to send a warning to New Delhi.[26] The Soviet Union may also have pressured New Delhi. There is evidence of Soviet pressures on India to stop the fighting in the western sector as soon as East Pakistan had fallen.[27] The evidence is murky on what motivated Prime Minister Indira Gandhi to stop the war in the west. Several factors, including rough military parity on the western front, the resoluteness of Pakistani forces in defending West Pakistan, a desire not to alienate the international community including the United States beyond a point, and a desire to preserve the moral high ground against Pakistan, probably contributed to her decision. In addition, India's closest ally in the crisis, the Soviet Union, appears to have been quite firm on this issue. As New Delhi was dependent on the Soviets for the veto in the UN and for military supplies, Moscow's views could not be ignored.

In the 1980s and 1990s the great powers were involved once again in helping to manage an India-Pakistan conflict. In 1986–87, during the Brasstacks crisis, Washington tried to ensure that, in the wake of India's military exercise, the two countries would not find themselves in a shooting war. New Delhi did not refuse U.S. help during the crisis. General Krishnaswami Sundarji, the army chief, briefed U.S. military attachés in New Delhi on the nature and scale of the Brasstacks exercise as a way of reassuring the Americans that nothing sinister was afoot. Three years later, in 1990, when India responded to a Pakistani military exercise, *Zarb e Momin*, by mobilizing its forces, Robert Gates, deputy national security adviser, and Richard Haass, of the National Security Council, were sent to the region to urge de-escalation. They met senior officials in the Indian government as part of U.S. intervention in what Washington regarded as the prelude to another dangerous crisis, this time possibly involving nuclear weapons.[28] In 1999, when Pakistani troops were found on the Kargil Heights, on the Indian side of the line of control, the United Kingdom, the United States, and several other powers, including China, issued statements condemning Pakistan's military presence and urging caution on both sides. During the war, President Clinton communicated by phone with both the Indian prime minister, Atal Behari Vajpayee, and the Pakistani prime minister, Nawaz Sharif, to help end the war. Indian troops were slowly and at some cost engaged in recovering territory along the Kargil Heights. The U.S. intervention got Pakistan to withdraw its troops and restore Indian control of the heights.[29]

The United States and the international community were also involved in a series of crisis management interventions in the 2000s. In 2001–02 the United States played a pivotal role in defusing a crisis that played itself out over six months. After terrorists had attacked the Indian Parliament on December 13, 2001, India blamed Pakistan for the attacks and mobilized its forces all along the border and line of control. The United States dispatched a series of officials, including the secretary of state, secretary of defense, and assistant secretary of state, to try and head off what looked like Indian preparations for an attack on Pakistan.[30] In November 2008, with a different Indian government and a different U.S. administration in power, when terrorists attacked Mumbai and killed more than 200 people, the United States and its allies once again sent high-level emissaries to India and Pakistan to urge calm, particularly on the part of New Delhi.[31] U.S. officials included the national security adviser, chairman of the joint chiefs, deputy secretary of state, and assistant secretary of state.

In the 2000s India was far more acceptant of U.S. and other involvement not only in India-Pakistan crises but also in regional crises elsewhere—in a way that New Delhi would have vociferously opposed during the 1990s and certainly during the cold war. In Nepal, India worked closely with U.K. and U.S. officials and also the UN to bring about a transition to stability and democracy in the midst of the Maoist insurgency.[32] And in Sri Lanka in 2000 New Delhi accepted Norwegian mediation efforts, whereas India had intervened in 1986–87 to ensure that powers from outside the region did not become involved in the island's civil war.[33] The Nepalese intervention was relatively successful, although instabilities continue to mark Nepal, especially on the issue of integration and rehabilitation of Maoist forces and the nature of federalism in the new constitution. The Norwegian intervention, ultimately, was not a success. India, nonetheless, stayed largely out of Sri Lankan affairs, until the end of the civil war, when it more or less turned a blind eye to growing Pakistani and, which was important, Chinese involvement.[34]

This review of India's experience with third-party efforts on behalf of crisis management, war termination, and regional instabilities suggests that New Delhi has, over the years, become far more open to the involvement of non-regional powers, including the great powers, in Southern Asia. Broadly, also, third-party efforts have been positive from India's point of view: they have played a role in fostering communication between India and Pakistan at critical times, in putting pressure on Pakistan diplomatically and politically, and in suggesting to the Indian public that its government was not isolated from the international community. In helping to stave off hostilities and to terminate actual shooting wars, these interventions have saved Indian lives and, arguably, have promoted and protected Indian interests.

Why did India allow powerful outside powers to intervene in crises, war, and internal instabilities in its neighboring countries, and why did it work with them to manage conflict when its rhetoric typically voices opposition to "external involvement" in bilateral disputes and regional instabilities? Both during and after the cold war, India worked with the UN and the great powers to resolve regional crises, wars, and instabilities for a variety of reasons.

First, during bilateral crises and war with Pakistan, India did not want to alienate the international community and great powers beyond a point, and it therefore accepted their diplomatic interventions. In 1948, in the J&K case, as suggested earlier, India wanted to strengthen international institutions and law as a counterpoise to the great powers. Working with the UN to establish a ceasefire with Pakistan over J&K partly reflected this larger cosmopolitan interest. In the later cases, New Delhi had to consider whether it was politic to ignore the United States and Soviet Union, in particular. At various times and to varying degrees, both were supportive of India—the Americans economically and the Soviets as quasi-diplomatic and military allies through much of the cold war.

Given India's relative weakness internationally, it would have been dangerous to resist their interventions beyond a point. If either or both had switched their support to Pakistan, India would have found itself isolated and even further weakened economically, diplomatically, and perhaps militarily.

Second, in all of the crises and wars with Pakistan, it is clear enough that India could not win an outright military victory, and once nuclear weapons made their appearance on the stage, there was always the fear of nuclear escalation. In these circumstances, New Delhi had an incentive to work with the great powers to control the military situation during the crises and wars and eventually to terminate hostilities.

Third, in the case of internal political instabilities in Nepal and Sri Lanka, India worked with outsiders to try and bring about an internal peace settlement between warring parties because (a) its degree of diplomatic and strategic comfort with the intervening outsiders—mostly Western states and the UN—was much greater than during the cold war, (b) it was preoccupied at various points with its own internal economic and political problems, but most important (c) its efforts at resolving the conflict directly had stalled, partly because of the suspicions that India evoked among the warring parties (Nepalese government and the Maoists; Sri Lankan government and the Liberation Tigers of the Tamil Eelam, LTTE).

Conclusion

This analysis of India's past suggests that New Delhi has worked with multilateral institutions and third parties with varying degrees of enthusiasm. On territorial issues, arbitration is the only multilateral/third-party intervention that has had any success (Kutch). It is hard to imagine any leadership in India, now or in the foreseeable future, having the political courage to agree to international involvement on J&K. With respect to river disputes, of which there are plenty, India has had reasonable success with external involvement—with the World Bank initiative on the Indus River in 1960 and with arbitration on the Baglihar and Kishenganga projects (although the latter has not been altogether disposed of by the tribunal). Outside bodies and powers have helped India in times of crisis and war with Pakistan insofar as they have helped to damp down the escalation of fighting and brought about an end to hostilities. In 1948, 1965, and 1971 external calls for India to stop its military campaigns had some impact in persuading New Delhi to stop its troops from going farther, but Indian leaders also had other reasons for stopping the fighting when they did. Except for the fact that the UN did not come out unequivocally in

India's favor in the J&K dispute in the early years, India has not done all that badly by third-party involvements in regional affairs. This conclusion goes against the traditional wisdom on the subject.

Under what circumstances does India turn to multilateral institutions or other third parties in its regional disputes? This chapter has suggested that New Delhi seems to be influenced by four broad factors: (a) its desire to strengthen international institutions and rules against great-power domination and to project a reputation for international good citizenship; (b) its calculation that it has a good diplomatic or legal case and therefore will get the backing of multilateral institutions and the great powers and a decision in its favor; (c) its determination that its military power is limited or force cannot be used to resolve an issue and that its diplomatic or political influence is also limited; and (d) its perception that bilateral negotiations are stalemated.

What of the future? Suspicion of multilateralism or third-party involvement is strong in India—in the public, in the press, in Parliament, and in political and administrative institutions (the foreign service, the administrative service). This suspicion comes from a particular reading of post-independence history. In fact, as this chapter suggests, that history may not be as dark and dismal as Indians have been brought up to think. A reassessment of multilateralism and third-party involvement in regional affairs might change the largely negative attitude to outsiders playing a mediating role. Will India, as a rising power, be more willing to countenance outside involvement? As a bigger power, India might be more acceptant of third-party involvement, confident that its new status will temper any mediation efforts and that mediators will be more sensitive to Indian concerns. However, as a bigger power, India may well be even more negative toward mediation on the argument that the country has the ability to "stand up" to external "pressures." A fair bet is that it will be very difficult to get Indians to reread their history, that their sense of victimhood goes deep, and that with growing power they will continue to have a rather negative attitude to any kind of outside involvement in Southern Asia.[35]

River water issues, because they are highly technical in nature, may be the most susceptible to outside involvement. So far, arbitration decisions have not been politicized in India. India may continue to opt for arbitration on other river water issues, especially with Pakistan. Ad hoc crisis management may also continue to be an arena for third-party involvement, especially in the case of Pakistan. On the other hand, it is difficult to imagine the Kashmir dispute or the border quarrel with China being solved through arbitration or any multilateral or third-party process.

Notes

1. For various views on India and multilateralism, see Amrita Narlikar, "Peculiar Chauvinism or Strategic Calculation: Explaining the Negotiation Strategies of a Rising India," *International Affairs* 82, no. 1 (January 2006): 59–76; Amrita Narlikar, "India and the WTO," in *Foreign Policy Analysis in International Relations*, edited by Steve Smith, Tim Dunne, and Amelia Hadfield (Oxford University Press, 2008), pp. 269–84; C. Raja Mohan, "Rising India: Partner in Shaping the Global Commons," *Washington Quarterly* 33, no. 3 (July 2010): 133–48; and C. Raja Mohan, "India and the Asian Security Architecture," in *Asia's New Multilateralism: Cooperation, Competition, and the Search for Community*, edited by Michael J. Green and Bates Gill (Columbia University Press, 2009), pp. 128–53.

2. On India's original referral to the UN and the UN's initial responses, see Sisir Gupta, *Kashmir: A Study in India-Pakistan Relations* (New Delhi: Asia Publishing House under the auspices of the Indian Council of World Affairs, 1966), pp. 140–73.

3. On the various UN efforts, see the detailed account in Gupta, *Kashmir: A Study in India-Pakistan Relations,* pp. 194–98, 201–06, 211–23, and 235–54.

4. Robert G. Wirsing, *India, Pakistan, and the Kashmir Dispute: On Regional Conflict and Its Resolution* (New York: St. Martin's Press, 1994), pp. 193–94, on India-Pakistan talks in the wake of the India-China War of 1962.

5. See Ashutosh Misra, *India-Pakistan: Coming to Terms* (New York: Palgrave Macmillan, 2010), on the role of the British in bringing about a cease-fire, which included reference to arbitration. India had apparently agreed to arbitration as early as 1959 (pp. 93, 101–03).

6. See Sikandar Ahmed Shah, "River Boundary Delimitation and the Resolution of the Sir Creek Dispute between Pakistan and India," *Vermont Law Review* 34 (2012): 357–58, and Misra, *India-Pakistan*, pp. 103–06.

7. See Shah, "River Boundary Delimitation," p. 359, on India's stand.

8. Ibid., p. 361, on the 2009 deadline.

9. The maps were exchanged on November 14, 2001. See A. G. Noorani, "Maps and Borders," *Frontline* 25, no. 21 (October 11–24, 2008) (www.frontlineonnet.com/fl2521/stories/20081024252108000.htm).

10. The most recent statement by an American official is by U.S. ambassador Nancy Powell, which tilts toward India but not decisively so, leaving open the question of the final status of the border as needing to be decided by China and India. See Oinam Sunil, "India-China Border Row: US Sticks to McMahon Line," *Times of India*, December 15, 2012 (http://timesofindia.indiatimes.com/city/guwahati/India-China-border-row-US-sticks-to-McMahon-Line/articleshow/17620832.cms?).

11. See Steven A. Hoffmann, *India and the China Crisis* (Oxford University Press, 1990), pp. 226–28, on the proposals of the Colombo powers and the reactions of China and India to them.

12. India has been involved in other river water problems: for example, with Bhutan (relatively dispute free), Nepal (disputes largely over hydroelectric projects that India has or is supposed to build and fund), Bangladesh (the sharing of the Ganga), and China (the possibility that Beijing might divert the Brahmaputra within its territory toward its water-scarce northern provinces). I deal only with the Indus dispute here since it was the original quarrel and perhaps the most contentious.

13. See Misra, *India-Pakistan*, pp. 57–80, on the Indus Waters Treaty, and annex I, pp. 201–18, for the text of the treaty. Also see Jagat S. Mehta, *Negotiating for India: Resolving Problems through Diplomacy* (New Delhi: Manohar, 2006), pp. 197–204. Mehta was India's foreign secretary from 1976 to 1979.

14. Mehta, *Negotiating for India*, pp. 204–18. The Salal Dam Agreement was negotiated by Mehta. Mehta felt that arbitration could have interminably "internationalized" the dispute in the way that Kashmir had been internationalized (p. 206). He therefore changed India's stance and persuaded Pakistan to deal directly once more on Salal.

15. "Baglihar Cleared, India Has Its Way," *Times of India*, February 13, 2007 (http://articles.timesofindia.indiatimes.com/2007-02-13/india/27881332_1_india-and-pakistan-baglihar-dam-indus-waters-treaty).

16. Gargi Parsai, "Permanent Works on Kishenganga Dam Stayed," *Hindu*, September 25, 2011 (www.thehindu.com/news/national/permanent-works-on-kishenganga-dam-stayed/article2485108.ece).

17. Ibid.

18. Gargi Parsai, "India, Pakistan Await Kishenganga Award," *Hindu*, September 5, 2012 (www.thehindu.com/todays-paper/tp-national/article3860380.ece).

19. Mubarak Zeb Khan, "India Can Divert Only Minimum Water from Kishenganga: Tribunal," *Dawn.com*, February 19, 2013 (http://dawn.com/2013/02/19/india-can-divert-only-minimum-water-from-kishanganga-tribunal/).

20. Gupta, *Kashmir*, p. 139.

21. Gupta, *Kashmir*, p. 139, hints at the fact. He notes that a military decision in Kashmir would not have been easy and would not necessarily have settled the issue, since "Pakistani territory could be freely used by the [tribal] invaders [from the Pakistani side of Kashmir] for bringing reinforcements and essential supplies."

22. Sumit Ganguly, *The Origins of War in South Asia: Indo-Pakistani Conflict since 1947* (Boulder, Colo.: Westview, 1986), pp. 83–85, 88–91, on the war and UN and international efforts to stop the fighting.

23. Ibid., pp. 91–92.

24. On the military constraints facing India during the 1965 war that may have caused the attack on Lahore to stop, see the judgment of the official Indian military historian Anil Athale, "Did India Plant 1965 War Plans?" *Rediff.com*, June 2, 2005 (www.rediff.com/news/2005/jun/02spec11.htm). Athale notes that Pakistani equipment (mostly U.S.) was superior, that there was near military parity between the two sides, that the Indian commander lost his nerve at the rapidity of the advance, and that China had mobilized some of its troops along the border with India.

25. Henry Kissinger, *Years of Renewal* (London: Weidenfeld and Nicolson, 1999), p. 82.

26. Robert Jackson, *South Asian Crisis: India-Pakistan-Bangladesh* (London: Chatto and Windus for the International Institute for Strategic Studies, 1975), p. 137.

27. Ibid., p. 140.

28. Michael Krepon, *Crises in South Asia: Trends and Potential Consequences* (Washington: Stimson Center, September 2011), p. 20 (www.stimson.org/images/uploads/research-pdfs/Crises_Complete.pdf), refers to the visit of Gates and Haass and their role.

29. Bruce Riedel, "American Diplomacy and the 1999 Kargil Summit at Blair House," occasional paper (University of Pennsylvania, Center for the Advanced Study of India, 2002), pp. 6–16 (http://casi.ssc.upenn.edu/publications/occasional).

30. Polly Nayak and Michael Krepon, *U.S. Crisis Management in South Asia's Twin Peak Crisis* (Washington: Stimson Center, September 1, 2006), pp. 22–33, 35–38, on the U.S. role (www.stimson.org/books-reports/us-crisis-management-in-south-asias-twin-peaks-crisis/).

31. On the U.S. role during the 2008 crisis, see Polly Nayak and Michael Krepon, *The Unfinished Crisis: U.S. Crisis Management after the 2008 Mumbai Attacks* (Washington: Stimson Center, February 2012) (www.stimson.org/images/uploads/research-pdfs/Mumbai-Final_1.pdf).

32. On the UN's role in Nepal's transition to democracy, see Surya P. Subedi, "Post Conflict Constitutional Settlement in Nepal and the Role of the United Nations," paper presented at the international seminar on "Constitutionalism and Diversity in Nepal," Tribhuvan University, Centre for Nepal and Asian Studies, in collaboration with MIDEA Project and ESP-Nepal, Kathmanu, August 22–24, 2007 (www.uni-bielefeld.de/midea/pdf/Surya.pdf).

33. On India's and Norway's consultations on the peace process in Sri Lanka, see M. R. Narayan Swamy, *Sri Lanka and the Peacemakers: A Story of Norway and India*, Issue Brief 178 (New Delhi: Institute of Peace and Conflict Studies, December 2011).

34. International Crisis Group, "India and Sri Lanka after the LTTE," Asia Report 206 (Brussels, June 23, 2011) (www.crisisgroup.org/~/media/Files/asia/south-asia/sri-lanka/206%20India%20and%20Sri%20Lanka%20after%20the%20LTTE.pdf).

35. On India's enduring, postcolonial sense of victimhood, see Manjari Chatterjee Miller, "Re-collecting Empire: 'Victimhood' and the 1962 Sino-Indian War," *Asian Security* 5, no. 3 (2009): 216–41.

ISKANDER LUKE REHMAN

8 From an Ocean of Peace to a Sea of Friends

Introduction

The analysis of geopolitical trends in the Indian Ocean has always constituted a uniquely challenging undertaking. For decades, strategic pundits have cyclically recognized the region's growing importance, yet struggled to define both its boundaries and its precise geopolitical significance. Part of the difficulty lies, no doubt, in the very conceptualization of the region. Should the Indian Ocean be construed as a unified geopolitical space or simply as a series of overlapping, but distinct, strategic spheres? Is it an economic thoroughfare characterized first and foremost by trade and cooperation or a breeding pool for future great-power rivalry, where growing fears of resource vulnerability may come to exacerbate preexisting security dilemmas?

In such a light, India has demonstrated a remarkable consistency in its conceptualization of the Indian Ocean, viewing the region holistically—and as a potential launching pad for its rise to great-power status—rather than solely through a narrow geographic lens. Although New Delhi has long recognized the importance of the Indian Ocean, it has begun to display the underpinnings of a true maritime geostrategy only relatively recently. This chapter aims to explain the reasons behind such an evolution by examining one of its most central components—India's evolving attitude toward plurilateralism and multilateralism in the Indian Ocean.

The chapter proceeds in four parts, which are structured both thematically and chronologically. First, it examines the early years, when postcolonial India's approach toward its maritime environs was proprietary, exclusionary, and deeply rooted in the rhetoric of nonalignment. It argues that New Delhi's strong animus toward foreign presence in the Indian Ocean was not only normative in its groundings but also highly instrumental in its motivations and deeply intertwined with the young nation's particular set of strategic circumstances at the time.

The second section charts India's gradual move away from a reflexive sense of maritime embattlement and toward a more self-confident and inclusive stance in the Indian Ocean. A variety of factors explain such a shift in attitude, which occurred in an era when there was a singularly benign maritime environment. These favorable geopolitical conditions opened up a new era of opportunity—or *maritime peace dividend*—during which India could focus its growing naval capabilities first and foremost on projecting soft power throughout the Indo-Pacific maritime sphere. The Indian navy's embrace of its role in soft power projection became apparent via its involvement in a seemingly exponential array of plurilateral maritime efforts. On the multilateral front, India displayed a growing proclivity to shape both its maritime environment and the law of the sea.

The following section examines the various obstacles that could undermine New Delhi's attempts to use coordinated collective actions as a means of emerging as the prime integrative power in the Indian Ocean. These challenges range from the institutional to the political and take place under the strategic backdrop of the growing presence of powerful extra-regional actors. Building on such observations, the fourth and final section suggests that India's era of maritime opportunity in the Indian Ocean is rapidly drawing to a close. Various evolutions in India's tactical and strategic environment will compel New Delhi to adopt a more utilitarian attitude in the practice of its maritime diplomacy. This will express itself through a stronger emphasis on bilateralism, most notably with the United States, and through a reprioritization of the harder components of India's growing maritime power.

Moral Strength and Material Weakness

On December 16, 1971, the United Nations General Assembly (UNGA) adopted a resolution declaring the Indian Ocean "for all time a zone of peace." This came a year after the Lusaka Non-Aligned Conference, which had called for "states to consider and respect the Indian Ocean as a zone of peace from which great-power rivalries and competitions as well as bases conceived in the context of such rivalries and competitions . . . are excluded."[1] India, along with other nations, such as Sri Lanka, had spearheaded the initiative. Fearful of a destabilizing power vacuum following Britain's retreat east of Suez, India's attitude toward the Indian Ocean was both proprietary and exclusionary. It was also profoundly reflective of a strong sense of maritime embattlement, arguably inherited from the young nation's colonial past and considerably reinforced by various incidents, such as the dispatch of an Indonesian naval flotilla into the Bay of Bengal during the India-Pakistan War of 1965[2] or the well-known deployment of the USS *Enterprise* carrier task force in the Bay of Bengal in December 1971.[3]

Throughout much of the period, however, India's prime strategic concerns were situated on land rather than on sea. Indeed, after a series of brutal frontier conflicts in which navies played at best a secondary role, India's main priorities were to strengthen its land borders and build up its army and air force, which were the primary actors in the event of a conflict with China or Pakistan.

Some analysts have viewed New Delhi's seemingly excessive fixation on its continental borders as more than a simple response to strategic circumstances and as a complex form of strategic path dependency. One such thinker argued that India's continentalism should be interpreted as a legacy of the policies of the Raj,[4] whose administrators had historically privileged the Indian army over the air force, whose role was largely confined to air policing, and the Indian navy, which was almost systematically neglected. This vision is shared by numerous observers since, who tend to ascribe India's various maritime shortcomings to a wider malaise inherent to the nation's strategic culture.[5] Regardless of the debate over the supposedly continentalist character of Indian strategic culture, the empirical data clearly show that for the first decades following independence the navy remained severely underfunded. Nevertheless, even as it struggled to make its case vis-à-vis an occasionally sea-blind political leadership, it remained a carrier-centric force, with a service culture imbued with a strong understanding of the guiding tenets of sea power and geared toward blue-water operations and sea control.[6]

Faced with the dual reality of its relative material weakness and the increasing presence of powerful extra-regional navies in its maritime backyard, India resorted to a tactic typically employed by smaller powers fearful of foreign entanglement and desirous of focusing on internal development—strident moral opposition.[7] New Delhi's past embrace of the notion of the Indian Ocean as a "zone of peace" can therefore be viewed in much the same light as the former Yugoslav leader Josip Tito's call to designate the Mediterranean as a "Sea of Peace."[8] Both nations, desirous of maintaining a degree of strategic flexibility in a rapidly rigidifying bipolar world, attempted to use principles as a means of preserving a modicum of autonomy while inhibiting potential great-power aggression.

For India, the quest for greater agency was couched in the grammar of nonalignment and third world solidarity. Eminent scholars of the region have pointed to the complex, multifaceted nature of India's policy of nonalignment, which cannot solely be understood through an ideational lens. One observer, for instance, astutely notes that India's "policies had (both) normative and instrumental underpinnings," before adding that "at a systemic level, the policy made sense as it enabled a materially weak state to play a role that was considerably more significant than its capabilities would warrant."[9] Prime Minister Nehru himself noted that he "had not originated non-alignment" but that the policy was "inherent in the circumstances of India."[10] The fluid nature of the cold war environment meant that this same set of strategic circumstances evolved over the years, most notably when the Nixon administration's rapprochement with China in the 1970s induced India to draw closer to the Soviet Union. Both countries' navies substantively enhanced their cooperation, with the Indians importing and hybridizing an increasing amount of Soviet naval hardware and the Soviets assisting in construction of the Indian Eastern Naval Headquarters in Visakhapatnam. Despite this increased proximity, both navies never engaged in formal joint exercises, although they reportedly occasionally coordinated their antisubmarine warfare capabilities to monitor American submarine patrols.[11]

As U.S.-Soviet naval competition gradually spilled over into the Indian Ocean, U.S. analysts drew attention to the renewed importance of a region they had long considered to be something of a geopolitical backwater. In an eerie foreshadowing of today's geopolitical struggles, both superpowers sparred for influence over small, but strategically situated, island nations such as the Seychelles. With scant regard for the 1971 UNGA resolution, both Moscow and Washington gained access to naval facilities sprinkled at various points of the Indian Ocean.[12] After the Iranian Revolution and the energy crisis of 1979, the Carter administration decisively refocused America's attention on the Persian Gulf and the western Indian Ocean. U.S. national security adviser Zbigniew Brzezinski famously observed that "an arc of crisis" stretched "along the shores of the Indian Ocean with fragile social and political structures in a region of vital importance to us threatened with fragmentation," before warning that "the resulting political chaos could well be filled by elements hostile to our values and sympathetic to our adversaries."[13] This vision of an Indian Ocean marked by political fragility and riddled with potential maritime security gaps remains highly relevant to this day. The Soviet Union, for its part, also decided to expand its naval operations in the Indian Ocean, not only to ensure the safety of its sea lanes of communication but also to prevent the Indian Ocean from becoming its soft maritime underbelly. Indeed, many Soviet strategists at the time were concerned that the United States and its allies could attempt to "outflank" the Soviet Union by unleashing submarines capable of targeting the Soviet mainland from the balmy depths of the Indian Ocean.[14]

For much of the Indian strategic community, the dire warnings of the United States on the Indian Ocean's looming "arc of crisis" served to mask other, more insidious motivations. Indeed, a parsing of much of the strategic literature emanating from New Delhi at the time reveals the extent to which India's appreciation of its maritime environs was still permeated by a strong sense of embattlement and a lingering apprehension over the coercive effects of American sea power. This residual mistrust expressed itself through a strong indictment of the strengthening of U.S. naval presence in the region as well as through frequently relayed concerns over the enlargement of U.S. submarine pens in places such as Diego Garcia. During a joint Carnegie Endowment for International Peace and the New Delhi–based Institute for Defense Studies and Analyses event in 1985, an unnamed Indian participant gave voice to such feelings: "I have felt for many years that there is an overdetermination if exaggerated emphasis on the so-called vital economic interests of the West in the Indian Ocean . . . and based on this wrong assumption of the so-called vital interests, a large force structure has been projected into the Indian Ocean."[15] Such statements reflect India's overriding anxiety at the time over the nation's supposed vulnerability to maritime suasion, a concern that, paradoxically, often seemed to take precedence over more conventional fears of a naval defeat in combat on the high seas.

Despite the largely reactive nature of India's vision of maritime developments in its region, the instrumental and symbolic value of the Indian navy began to be more appreciated by India's political leadership in the mid-1980s, under the tenure of Rajiv Gandhi. During that period (1984–89), the Indian navy was a vital component of the Indian peacekeeping force's operations in Sri Lanka (ferrying troops, providing off-shore fire support, and combating suicide vessels of the Liberation Tigers of the Tamil Eelam, LTTE) and intervened successfully in support of the president of the small island nation of the Maldives, who was the victim of an attempted coup d'état. India's navy was bolstered by the induction of several high-end platforms, ranging from a nuclear attack submarine on lease from Russia to a new aircraft carrier acquired from the United Kingdom. This rapid accretion of Indian naval capability—and visibility—stoked fears in Canberra and some Southeast Asian capitals, whose denizens tended to view India, somewhat incorrectly, as little more than a South Asian surrogate of the Soviet Union. In April 1989 *Time* magazine's front cover featured a hybridized Indian frigate, INS *Godavari*, bristling with missiles and accompanied by the bold caption "Super India." For the first time, India's potential as a future maritime superpower was being noted, both at home and abroad. However, this recognition was not necessarily accompanied by the blossoming of a sophisticated form of Indian maritime geostrategy. As retired naval officer and strategic analyst Uday Bhaskar notes in an excellent study of the history of India's naval diplomacy, "While the rapid development of the Indian navy boosted India's image on the global scene, such development was not leavened in tandem with astute strategic communications and related naval diplomacy."[16] The Dutch American strategist Nicholas J. Spykman famously observed, "A land power thinks in terms of continuous surfaces surrounding a central point of control, while a sea power thinks in terms of points and connecting lines dominating an immense territory."[17] Until the end of the cold war, India's focus remained resolutely that of a land power, whose strategic outlook radiated outward from the central node of New Delhi rather than into the yawning maritime expanses of the Indian Ocean.

Understanding India's Turn toward Maritime Engagement

With the end of the cold war, India's foreign policy underwent a radical shift. The collapse of its erstwhile partner, the Soviet Union, and the crippling economic impact of recurring balance of payments issues moved New Delhi's decisionmakers toward greater pragmatism in their dealings on the world stage. This shift was ideological and substantive—ideological, as it represented, to a degree, a departure from India's former attachment to third worldism and Nehruvian ideals of nonalignment, and substantive, as it manifested itself through a desire to engage, both economically and strategically, with multiple partners.[18] On the economic front, India's reformist finance minister, Manmohan Singh, who gradually prized open India's statist and regulation-ridden economy to foreign investment and business competition, spearheaded reforms. As a result, the share of mercantile trade in India's gross domestic product (GDP) grew by leaps and bounds. Indeed, as of 2011, maritime trade constituted close to 41 percent of India's overall GDP.[19] Nearly 90 percent of India's trade in volume, and more than 77 percent of its trade in value, is maritime in nature.[20] This stands in stark contrast to the prereform era, when overall international trade accounted for little more than 16 percent of the country's GDP.[21] India's rapid economic growth has been fueled by steadily rising sea-borne energy imports. India now imports close to 73 percent of its oil, the bulk of which flows into India via the western Indian Ocean, from the Middle East and Africa.[22] As an element of comparison, China, which faces what former president Hu Jintao famously described as a "Malacca Dilemma," imports only 55 percent of its crude oil.[23] The underlying difference lies in each country's perception of its maritime environment. While Beijing, confined within its so-called "first island chain,"[24] fears that its seaborne trade and crucial energy flows could be imperiled by the initiation of hostile economic warfare by the United States and its allies, New Delhi does not appear, at first glance, to confront a similar array of potentially hostile actors—even though, arguably, it faces a "Hormuz Dilemma" of its own. The Indian navy has endeavored, in both iterations of its Maritime Doctrine, released in 2004 and in 2009, as well as in its Maritime Strategy, released in 2007, to alert the civilian leadership and the public writ large of the importance of the navy's role as the ultimate guarantor of India's economic growth, by virtue of its role in upholding freedom of navigation and ensuring the safety of the region's sea lanes of communication.[25]

Most significant, India has been increasingly proactive in its desire to shape the multilateral discourse pertaining to the law of the sea. Having ratified the United Nations Convention on the Laws of the Sea in June 1995, thirteen years after initially signing the treaty in 1982, India is now deeply involved in a bevy of UN bodies relating to maritime issues—whether it is the International Maritime Organization, the International Tribunal for the Law of the Sea (ITLOS), or the International Seabed Authority.[26] In addition to this, notes Indian naval analyst Vijay Sakhuja, Indian jurists have developed something of a niche expertise in maritime matters. For example, one of the judges of ITLOS is a well-known Indian legal expert—P. Chandrasekhara Rao.[27] Most recently, India has sought to capitalize on its presence within the United Nations Security Council (UNSC) in order to exhort the international community to craft a more comprehensive antipiracy strategy in the Indian Ocean. In November 2012 the UNSC adopted an India-initiated statement encouraging member-states to coordinate their efforts and to criminalize acts of piracy under their domestic legislations.[28] The statement was novel in the sense that it called for a more holistic appreciation of nonstate threats to the global maritime commons, whether they be in the Gulf of Guinea, which has experienced a recrudescence of acts of piracy over the past few months, or off the coast of Somalia. The statement also sought to lay the groundwork for the development of more stringent, and commonly accepted, rules of deployment for private security contractors. This issue has gained relevance in India after two Italian marines shot Indian fishermen in the Arabian Sea after purportedly mistaking them for pirates.[29]

While there is an animated discussion surrounding the issue of whether or not contemporary India has a readily identifiable grand strategy, there is a widespread consensus that sustained economic growth remains the nation's overriding strategic priority. As a result, notes a recent and much-discussed report, "India's primary strategic interest is to maintain an open economic order."[30] The clear prioritization of economic growth should therefore logically correlate with a decisive rebalancing in favor of its navy, which appears best placed among the three services to protect the nation's growing seaborne equities. For the time being, however, it remains unclear whether this is the case. Although the latest Ministry of Defense *Annual Report* observes, "There is a growing acceptance of the fact that the maritime domain is the prime facilitator of the development,"[31] this recognition has not yet been translated in budgetary terms. Indeed, from 2010 to 2011 India's "Cinderella Service" only captured 15 percent of the defense budget. In 2012 the navy's allocation was hiked to 18 percent.[32] Although this is an encouraging development, it remains to be seen whether it marks the advent of a new, more sea power–friendly era in Indian strategic planning or whether the additional funds will serve primarily to pay off previously acquired platforms. The underwhelming nature of these figures can be attributed, no doubt, to the absence of both a clearly discernible threat to Indian shipping and trade and an existential threat to the Indian navy.

India's overwhelming superiority over Pakistan enabled it to concentrate its eastern and western fleets in the Arabian Sea and engage in coercive maneuvering outside Karachi during the 1999 Kargil crisis without fear of severe repercussions. China's role in the Indian Ocean and its so-called "string of pearls" strategy is frequently discussed, often in sensationalistic terms, in the Indian press. Much is made of China's attempts to establish pockets of influence in the region, with several Indian commentators casting in a sinister light China's infrastructural undertakings in places such as Gwadar, a port along Pakistan's Makran coast, or Hambantota, on the southern tip of Sri Lanka. Most informed observers, however, believe that China, for the time being at least, is pursuing a strategy of "places rather than bases" in the Indian Ocean and that there is no compelling evidence yet to suggest that the Chinese navy has engaged in basing activities of an overtly military nature.[33] The Indian Maritime Strategy and the Maritime Doctrine, for their part, only mention China in passing, with fleeting—albeit foreboding—references to "some nations' attempts to gain a strategic toehold in the Indian Ocean Rim" or to "attempts by China to strategically encircle India."[34] The expansion of the Chinese navy and its presence in the Indian Ocean is taken seriously by both the navy and the civilian leadership, but is viewed, for the time being at least, as a long-term—rather than an immediate—challenge to India's maritime security. In short, India's oceanic surroundings are deemed secure from conventional threats for two reasons—one prospective naval adversary is considered too weak, while the other appears too remote. Both of these assumptions are dangerously flawed.

New Delhi's sanguine approach to maritime security has had a profound impact on how the nation has regarded the use of naval power. In a relatively threat-free environment, India's navy has focused on soft power projection and on benign and constabulary roles. This has been reflected both in words, via the 2004 version of the Indian Maritime Doctrine, which defined the navy as an "effective instrument of India's foreign policy by generating goodwill through maritime diplomacy,"[35] and in actions, as over the past decade the Indian navy has frequently displayed with a certain panache its desire and capacity to be viewed as a provider of public goods as well as a reliable partner. Indian ships have thus taken part in a wide range of humanitarian and disaster relief operations over the years, whether in the wake of the devastating 2004 tsunami or the 2008 cyclone Nargis. India has also engaged in noncombatant evacuation operations, such as in 2006, when four Indian ships successfully evacuated more than 2,000 Indian, Nepalese, and Sri Lankan citizens from war-torn Lebanon. More recently, Indian ships were dispatched to repatriate Indian citizens from Libya. The Indian navy is also engaged in multiple, increasingly institutionalized, naval exercises with a plethora of both regional and extra-regional navies, ranging from France to Singapore. During the first decade following the cold war, the Indian navy conducted close to fifty joint naval exercises with more than twenty countries. Since then, India's naval interactions have grown exponentially.[36] In order to better coordinate this plurilateralist surge, the Indian navy decided in 2004 to establish the Directorate of Foreign Cooperation, devoted to managing the service's diplomatic role and placed under the supervision a two-star admiral.

Large-scale collective naval maneuvers—such as the MILAN exercises (meaning "confluence" in Hindi), which include several navies from Southeast Asia and take place biennially off the Andaman and Nicobar islands, or the IBSAMAR exercises, which involve the navies from India, Brazil, and South Africa—form the most visible, high-profile examples of India's turn to maritime plurilateralism. New Delhi also engages in annual bilateral naval exercises with countries as varied as Japan (JIMEX), Singapore (SIMBEX),

France (VARUNA), and the United States (MALABAR). In 2008 the Indian navy took the lead in organizing and conducting the inaugural Indian Ocean Naval Symposium (IONS), which is loosely modeled on the Western Pacific Naval Symposium. The IONS hosts thirty-five members and provides a forum for discussion for all littoral navies of the Indian Ocean, through a series of seminars and workshops on issues of common concern such as piracy or the effects of climate change.

New Delhi also seeks to expand its custodial role in the Indian Ocean and to demonstrate its ability to provide security. It has thus helped to ensure the safety of key sea lanes of communication and the freedom of navigation, by deploying a small naval task force in the Gulf of Aden and off the coast of Somalia, escorting U.S. ships through the Malacca Straits after 9/11, or deploying vessels near Colombo during the 2008 South Asian Association of Regional Cooperation summit in order to provide protection against a possible LTTE attack. Significantly, India has chosen to accomplish such actions on a unilateral basis under the UNSC resolution and the Combined Multinational Taskforce (CTF) 151. This suggests that while New Delhi is increasingly apt to engage in naval cooperation, it remains leery of joining groupings with rotating command structures, which could curtail its operational autonomy.[37]

Finally, India is an active member of several regional forums and institutions, such as the Indian Ocean Rim Association for Regional Cooperation, which focuses on trade issues and was launched in 1997, or the Bay of Bengal Initiative for Multisectoral Technical and Economic Cooperation.

The Limits to India's Integrative Power

A subtle blend of economic and ideological factors has therefore underpinned India's maritime diplomacy in the Indian Ocean since the end of the cold war. Are these efforts being harnessed to serve a greater purpose? What are New Delhi's primary goals in the region, and what are the potential obstacles to the fulfillment of India's ambitions?

The question of whether India has a clearly defined Indian Ocean strategy is difficult to answer, given the absence of an official national security strategy or a publicly released triservice white paper. Nevertheless, judging by various statements or writings issued by both India's leadership and the country's vibrant strategic community, New Delhi seems to have a relatively coherent and structured vision of its present and future role in the Indian Ocean region. The study of such pronouncements suggests that India is animated by two desires:

—Enhance its global prestige by being viewed as a responsible stakeholder and custodian of the global commons and

—Favorably shape its maritime security environment by emerging as an integrative power within a largely disaggregated region.

The value of maritime diplomacy as a means of bolstering perceptions of India as a *compassionate* and *responsible* power has become something of a leitmotif among India's strategists. Thus, when Sakhuja commented on the Indian navy's performance in the wake of the 2004 tsunami, he also added, "The international community acknowledged India's capability and registered its presence in the tsunami-affected region as a compassionate power capable of helping its neighbors even when its own shores are troubled."[38] Underlying New Delhi's embrace of the political use of sea power is the age-old observation that states that orient their power seaward can more easily calibrate and shape perceptions, and therefore appear less threatening to their neighbors, than those that remain wedded to a more continentalist mindset.[39] In a region composed of a wide array of political regimes, many of which are characterized by severe democratic dysfunction or creeping authoritarianism, the Indian navy goes so far as to suggest that Indian ships compose not only "small mobile pieces of national sovereignty"[40] but also floating incarnations of the virtues of Indian democracy. The 2009 Maritime Doctrine thus posits that "the mere presence of an Indian warship, with its multi-ethnic and multi-religious crew in a foreign harbor, will contribute to India's image as a vibrant democracy abroad." The Indian navy's 2007 Maritime Strategy also emphasizes the need for the navy to be able to "project power" abroad. This aspiration is equally evident in the 2009 Maritime Doctrine, which outlines primary and secondary areas of maritime interest. The primary zone stretches as far as the Persian Gulf, whose narrow channels were once patrolled by the British Indian fleet, and the secondary zone extends all the way to the Red and South China seas.[41] This pan-oceanic vision is shared, to some extent, by elements of the civilian leadership. Former prime minister Atal Behari Vajpayee, for example, stated that India's "security environment ranged(s) from the Persian Gulf to the Straits of Malacca across the Indian Ocean . . . and Southeast Asia,"[42] and his expansive definition was reprised a year later by his successor, Manmohan Singh, who declared that India's "strategic footprint covers the region bounded by the Horn of Africa, West Asia . . . Southeast Asia, and beyond, to the far reaches of the Indian Ocean."[43]

In addition, maritime diplomacy is viewed as a means of favorably shaping India's wider security environment and its emergence as a leading integrative power within a region beset by numerous challenges, ranging from severe governance deficits to the risks associated with natural disasters and climate change.[44] India's ambition to form a more coherent and readily identifiable region with itself at the core is frequently manifested by both its political and military leadership. The 2011–12 Ministry of Defense *Annual Report* notes, "India's location . . . at the top of the Indian Ocean gives it a vantage point in relation . . . to the IOR [Indian Ocean Rim]."[45] A former chief of naval staff, Nirmal Verma, observed in his outgoing speech, "Given our [India's] geographical position, our natural paradigm is to architect the stability of our region via our maritime routes."[46] This ambition to foster greater stability within India's maritime backyard is being pursued via a two-pronged strategy. The first method is to discharge an increasing number of custodial duties within the Indian Ocean. The second is to implement a so-called "neo-Nixonian" strategy, which focuses on building regional capacity and helping smaller, weaker states to "help themselves."[47] The Indian navy's expertise in the area of hydrography has proven particularly valuable to smaller littoral states, which frequently call on Indian survey ships and hydrographers. New Delhi has also worked toward generating regional maritime capability by training personnel from several smaller navies in the region and by assisting countries such as the Maldives to set up maritime surveillance networks.[48]

Nevertheless, despite India's efforts to emerge as a leading, integrative power within the Indian Ocean, numerous obstacles risk jeopardizing the realization of its maritime vision, many of which are embedded within the very nature of its neighborhood. Indeed, theorists of regional security structures have identified preliminary conditions that must be met in order to ensure lasting, self-sustaining, regional stability. External actors with interests in the region must refrain from interference; interstate frictions must remain at a relatively low level or be dealt with in an effective manner by regional institutions, and regional states must display a measure of success in resolving their own internal tensions.[49] Unfortunately, none of these conditions has been met in the Indian Ocean. Extra-regional actors remain pivotal players, most notably the United States, which continues to boast the most powerful naval presence in the wider Indo-Pacific region. Although New Delhi and Washington have displayed a greater degree of strategic convergence over the past decade, as long as the United States remains the prime naval power in the region, India will be viewed as the foremost resident power—but not as the indispensable power—by smaller states within the region. Furthermore, China's growing economic influence among smaller archipelagic and littoral states considerably dilutes any Indian bid for uncontested control over its maritime environs. An additional obstacle to any integrative agenda lies in the fact that the Indian Ocean's waters continue to be roiled by a long succession of maritime territorial disputes and sporadic tensions over the nature and extent of countries' exclusive economic zones.

India is interlocked in several such disputes, and this abiding reality severely impedes its emergence as an integrative power within the Indian Ocean. For instance, New Delhi continues to differ with Colombo over the management of fishing in the Palk Strait and has joined Myanmar in a dispute against Bangladesh at the ITLOS over the demarcation of mutual maritime boundaries. Tensions between Bangladesh and Myanmar over the dispute remain rife and have recently led to small-scale naval jostling in the Bay of Bengal.[50] Most important, the Indo-Pakistani maritime territorial dispute, which centers on the delayed resolution of the land boundary in Sir Creek (a 40-kilometer-long spit of marshland in the Rann of Kutch) off India's Gujurat and Pakistan's Sindh provinces and the delineation of its maritime extension, has yet to be resolved. As for all territorial issues, India prefers to keep negotiations strictly bilateral and brooks no external interference. When it comes to questions pertaining to its own sovereignty, New Delhi is clearly not multilateralist at heart. Since 2007 leaders on both sides have frequently voiced their optimism over an eventual mutually advantageous accommodation. Yet both New Delhi and Islamabad continue to differ over the precise methodology for solving the dispute, and the latest round of talks was deemed unsuccessful.[51] More recently, and somewhat ominously, Pakistan announced its decision to increase substantially the number of its marines, who are tasked primarily with patrolling the Sir Creek area.[52] Both nations frequently arrest each other's fishermen for violating maritime boundaries, with Pakistan's Maritime Security Agency most recently detaining more than 100 Indian fishermen. These maritime tensions indicate a wider trend of Indo-Pakistani interactions, which have frequently led to standoffs and brinkmanship.[53] More generally, Pakistan remains profoundly hostile to the idea of India emerging as a natural leader within the Indian Ocean Rim. Pakistan's navy invariably portrays India's increased naval presence and activity as signs of New Delhi's latent hegemonistic tendencies[54] and continues to articulate its own, distinct, strategic vision for the Arabian Sea.

Finally, numerous internal tensions still ripple through the region, which hosts some of the world's most dysfunctional failed states. Somalia constitutes a prime example of how a glaring lack of governance ashore can lead to "yawning maritime security gaps" at sea.[55] The continued relevance of Brzezinski's notion of an Indian Ocean "arc of instability" suggests that the area may still be more of a "largely disaggregated oceanic and littoral zone and a collection of subregions than a coherent, unified region."[56] The World Bank, for its part, has singled out South Asia as being the "least integrated part of the world."[57]

In sum, three factors—the strong (and in the case of China, growing) influence of extra-regional actors; the persistence of interstate tensions, most notably the failure to resolve long-standing maritime disputes; and the continued lack of functional governance in some states—ensure that India's ambitions to emerge as the region's integrative power are likely to remain unfulfilled.

The End of an Era?

In addition to this depressing set of realities, India's maritime security environment is undergoing a profound transformation. India's more inclusive brand of maritime diplomacy will be superseded by a greater emphasis on utilitarian bilateralism. In particular, India will disproportionately strengthen its naval partnerships with the United States and U.S. allies such as Australia and Japan. This tilt toward naval bilateralism or select plurilateralism will grow to displace India's other more inclusive efforts and induce leaders in New Delhi to privilege the harder facets of the nation's growing maritime power.

Two major evolutions drive such a shift: first, the ongoing China-Pakistan maritime entente and the extension of India's two-front threat from land to sea and, second, naval nuclearization in the Indian Ocean.

The Extension of India's Two-Front Threat from Land to Sea

Pakistan's increasingly offensive strategy of sea denial, when combined with its deepening maritime partnership with China, will enable Islamabad, for the first time in decades, to genuinely contest India's freedom of maneuver in the Arabian Sea.[58] Moreover, China's progress in the field of anti-access and area denial (A2/AD) could result in the erection of an A2/AD dome that arches over the entirety of India's maritime backyard, from the Bay of Bengal to the Gulf of Karachi. Finally, China's future forays into the Indian Ocean could present New Delhi with a two-front threat extending from land to sea.

For Pakistan's naval planners, closer cooperation with China is desirable on many levels. At a time when relations between Islamabad and Washington are increasingly strained and Pakistan's economy is teetering on the brink of collapse, China's technological support and provision of warships at friendly prices are invaluable. Second, it is in Pakistan's interests to encourage Chinese naval power to move westward in order to counter New Delhi's growing influence. In private, Pakistani officials have relentlessly urged Beijing to enhance its naval presence in the Arabian Sea, suggesting that China's skyrocketing energy imports require that it stage some form of credible forward presence close to the world's busiest shipping lanes.[59] Another argument advanced is that by establishing a permanent naval presence along India's western seaboard, China would be able to neutralize India's attempts to exert greater influence west of the Malacca Straits.[60]

Chinese strategists, for their part, are increasingly concerned over India's growing maritime influence in Southeast Asia, and more specifically in the South China Sea, which they view as a veiled Indian attempt to "generate a southward gravitational pull on China's maritime strategy"[61] and to prevent China from enhancing its own presence in the Indian Ocean. Thus shoring up Pakistan as a proxy naval deterrent within India's own maritime backyard serves to divert New Delhi's attention from East Asia by keeping it focused on its immediate western maritime front. China's concerns are compounded by the fact that the Indian navy is currently revamping its naval presence along its eastern seaboard in response to what it perceives as a growing Chinese maritime threat. China's calculus may be that by increasing India's threat perception along its western front, it can compel the navy to stage a less sizable presence in the Bay of Bengal and Andaman Sea.[62] Finally, Beijing is also concerned that, in the event of a conflict, India or the United States may attempt to establish some form of a distant blockade of its energy supplies, a large portion of which originates from the Persian Gulf. While the effectiveness of such a blockade in times of conflict is debatable, there is no doubt that its possibility weighs heavily on Chinese strategic planning.

Naval Nuclearization in the Indian Ocean

In July 2009 India launched its first indigenously produced nuclear submarine, the S-2 (also known as an advanced technology vessel and ultimately named *Arihant*). It remains uncertain when the submarine will be truly operational. Recent statements from the chief of naval staff, however, indicate that the *Arihant* will be deployed on deterrent patrols as soon as it is commissioned, in early 2013. Pakistan, for its part, issued a press release in May 2012 publicizing the recent inauguration of the country's Naval Strategic Forces Command. In the course of the inauguration, it announced that the new headquarters would "perform a pivotal role in the development and employment of the Naval Strategic Force," which was defined as "the custodian of the nation's second-strike capability."[63] For the time being, however, there is a considerable degree of uncertainty over the form that this sea-borne capability would take. Most analyses concur that Pakistan does not have the technological or financial means to construct its own nuclear submarine. In all likelihood, Pakistan will opt to place nuclear missiles on surface vessels or, if it succeeds in the further miniaturization of warheads, aboard its growing fleet of conventional submarines.[64]

This development is highly troubling in many regards. Most notably, by blurring the lines between conventional and nuclear platforms, it risks leading to inadvertent or accidental escalation. The induction of tactical nuclear weapons in Pakistan's fleet would, in parallel, extend the more dysfunctional elements of current Indo-Pakistani nuclear interactions from land to sea. By threatening to use nuclear-tipped torpedoes or cruise missiles against advancing Indian carrier battle groups, Pakistan could inject uncertainty and, by so doing, drastically dilute the effects of India's overbearing advantage in the conventional naval domain.[65]

These twin developments, both of which are closely intertwined, signal the advent of a new, more threat-laden, maritime era. For the past two decades, India's navy has been able to maximize the strategic benefits derived from a relatively threat-free environment by engaging in an increasing array of multilateral exercises, forgoing any move toward the formation of alliances with countries such as the United States, and focusing on projecting soft power. Studies of the nature of military effectiveness indicate that diverse threat environments, where the challenges to national interests are numerous, low level, and not immediately perceptible, can complicate strategic assessments and result in uncoordinated policies. Moreover, the quality of threat (that is, its clarity) has more meaningful consequences for military effectiveness than the quantity or level of threat.[66] For the time being, India's maritime concerns are numerous, but diffuse, and none of them is existential. This is changing, and as a result the Indian navy could find itself confronted with what Edward Luttwak famously termed the "visibility/viability" paradox, whereby navies used to influencing opponents' perceptions by being "visible" struggle to refocus on their war-fighting role and be "viable."[67]

Applying Luttwak's paradox to contemporary India, one can assume that, in the future, the Indian navy, absent a major hike in funding, will find itself compelled to focus less on the "visible" components of maritime power, such as maritime multilateralism and soft power projection, and more on the "viable" aspects of developing an effective war-fighting capability in the face of rapidly coalescing threats to India's maritime lifelines.[68] The transformation of India's maritime environment will naturally also affect the conduct of New Delhi's maritime diplomacy, by privileging more utilitarian bilateral exercises over the more cosmetic effects of maritime inclusiveness. In particular, the

Indian navy's growing partnership with its U.S. counterpart will come to constitute the nation's defining maritime partnership. Astute observers have noted that whereas the MALABAR exercises started with only basic maneuvers and communication drills, they have since expanded in scope and scale.[69] Indian navalists have argued that the MALABAR exercises have "showcased the Indian navy's capability to be interoperable with the most advanced navy" in the world, by operating smoothly alongside U.S. nuclear submarines or by engaging in highly complex aerial refueling operations.[70] The growth of such an impressive level of synergy at an operational-functional level is perceived as a clear indicator of the Indian navy's own accretion in capability and hence is increasingly viewed as a core component of India's internal balancing and military capacity building. Former chief of naval staff Nirmal Verma openly acknowledged that through its "foreign cooperation initiatives" the Indian navy would gain "operational skills and doctrinal expertise."[71] The United States' unparalleled prowess in domains of growing importance to the Indian navy means that the Indo-U.S. naval partnership will naturally form the structural core of New Delhi's move toward a more utilitarian practice of maritime diplomacy. While this could never give birth to a formalized alliance, given New Delhi's profound attachment to its continued diplomatic maneuverability, one can well envision the emergence of a "tacit security compact"[72] or "an informal balancing arrangement of some type."[73] This evolution should not be viewed as a major departure from India's traditions. After all, during the cold war, New Delhi, perceiving its own vulnerability, did not hesitate to draw closer to the Soviet Union. Rather, the Indo-U.S. naval partnership should be construed as the natural result of two profoundly realist powers suddenly confronted with a markedly wide panoply of convergent aims in the maritime domain.[74]

The Triumph of Strategic Flexibility

From a somewhat neglected *zone of peace*, the Indian Ocean has become, in the words of Robert D. Kaplan, the noisy, crowded *center stage* for emerging great-power rivalries.[75] India, which used to engage in only an extremely limited form of naval cooperation, now takes part in an array of increasingly wide-ranging and complex exercises with a variety of countries. New Delhi, whose attitude was once governed by a reflexive sense of maritime embattlement, now embraces a more inclusive form of maritime diplomacy and plays an increasingly salient role in shaping the norms and rules that undergird the law of the sea. This oceanic overture has resulted in the navy growing, almost organically, into a vital component of India's multilayered diplomacy. India's Cinderella Service has suavely demonstrated its growing utility through the launch of highly visible soft power initiatives such as the IONS. This evolution toward maritime plurilateralism and the Indian navy's concurrent involvement in numerous humanitarian and custodian operations have been rightly heralded, both at home and abroad. Nevertheless, a closer examination of the substance of India's behavior at sea suggests that New Delhi's turn toward maritime multilateralism is far from absolute. The substance of India's naval interactions is to be found in its bilateral—rather than its collective—efforts. India's strategic elites remain as wedded as ever to their nation's freedom from foreign entanglement or interference. Long-standing tensions, governance deficits, and territorial disputes threaten to disrupt the rising nation's ambitions to emerge as the leading integrative power within a fractured maritime space. A future marked by growing competition, disruptive military developments, and rapidly calcifying security dilemmas will leave little time for the more vigorous and open engagement of these past two decades. More than nonalignment or the quest for autonomy, the governing principle of India's foreign policy since independence has been its extreme flexibility in the face of rapidly evolving, yet continuously challenging, strategic circumstances. Buffeted by increasingly choppy waters, India will be led—albeit reluctantly—to disproportionately privilege its bilateral naval partnership with the United States.

Notes

1. See B. Vivekandan, "The Indian Ocean as a Zone of Peace: Problems and Prospects," *Asian Survey* 21, no. 12 (December 1981): 1237–49.

2. At the time, President Sukarno described "India's attack on Pakistan as an attack on Indonesia." Two Russian-designed submarines and missile boats were sent to Pakistan, but arrived only after hostilities had come to an end. India's defense minister Y. B. Chavan clearly prioritized the defense of Andaman and Nicobar islands against a possible attack from Indonesia over the conduct of naval operations against Pakistan. Admiral B. S. Soman recounts this in the Indian navy's official history: "The defense of the Andaman and Nicobar islands from a possible attack from Indonesia . . . in the Government's order of priorities, was more crucial than naval operations against Pakistan." See Satyindra Singh, *Blueprint to Bluewater: The Indian Navy, 1951–65* (New Delhi: Ministry of Defense, 1992) (http://indiannavy.nic.in/about-indian-navy/blueprint-bluewater), p. 457.

3. During the Indo-Pakistani War of 1971, President Nixon dispatched a carrier task force, composed of the USS *Enterprise* and its escort vessels, into the Bay of Bengal. The task force had no orders to attack India, but was used as an instrument of naval suasion in order to prevent New Delhi from triggering the military collapse of West Pakistan. For much of India's strategic community during the cold war, the incident was perceived as

a potent symbol, both of the United States' supposed untrustworthiness and of India's susceptibility to foreign intimidation.

4. Raju Thomas, "The Armed Services and the Indian Defense Budget," *Asian Survey* 20, no. 3 (March 1980): 280–97.

5. George K. Tanham, "Indian Strategic Thought: An Interpretive Essay" (Santa Monica, Calif.: RAND Corporation, 1992).

6. A "blue-water" navy is a maritime force capable of operating across the deep waters of open oceans, in contrast to so-called "brown-water" or "green-water" navies, which are primarily oriented toward coastal defense and littoral operations. "Sea control" is a much-discussed concept in naval theory, which is essentially the attempt to control a maritime area for a limited amount of time. "Sea denial," in contrast, seeks to deny control of a maritime region to an adversary. For an in-depth discussion of these terms and their multiple applications in naval theory and history, see Geoffrey Till, *Seapower: A Guide for the Twenty-First Century,* 2d ed. (New York: Routledge, 2009), pp. 145–57.

7. David Vital, for instance, argues that, for small or weak states, it can be safer to "rely exclusively on political, psychological, legal, and moral factors" in order to "inhibit great-power aggression." See David Vital, *The Inequality of States, and the Survival of Small States* (Oxford University Press, 1971), p. 184. See also Robert L. Rothstein, *Alliances and Small Powers* (Columbia University Press, 1968), p. 33.

8. See Milan N. Vego, "Yugoslavia and the Soviet Policy of Force in the Mediterranean since 1961," Professional Paper 318 (Alexandria, Va.: Center for Naval Analyses, August 1981).

9. Sumit Ganguly, "Introduction," in *India's Foreign Policy: Retrospect and Prospect,* edited by Sumit Ganguly (Oxford University Press, 2010), p. 1.

10. Quoted in David Brewster, "Indian Strategic Thinking about East Asia," *Journal of Strategic Studies* 34, no. 6 (December 2011): 827.

11. Alexander O. Ghebhardt, "Soviet and U.S Interests in the Indian Ocean," *Asian Survey* 15, no. 8 (August 1975): 672–83.

12. For more on how India perceived U.S.-Soviet competition in the Indian Ocean, see Selig S. Harrison and K. Subrahmanyam, eds., *India, the United States, and Superpower Rivalry in the Indian Ocean* (Oxford University Press, 1989).

13. Interview with Zbigniew Brzezinski, *Time,* January 15, 1979.

14. See Harrison and Subrahmanyam, *India, the United States, and Superpower Rivalry.*

15. Quoted in "India, the United States, and the Indian Ocean: Report of the Indo-American Task Force on the Indian Ocean" (Washington: Carnegie Endowment for International Peace; New Delhi: Institute for Defense Studies and Analyses, 1985), p. 33.

16. C. Uday Bhaskar, "The Navy as an Instrument of Foreign Policy: The Indian Experience," in *The Rise of the Indian Navy: Internal Vulnerabilities, External Challenges,* edited by Harsh V. Pant (London: Ashgate, 2012), pp. 41–55.

17. Nicholas Spykman, "Geography and Foreign Policy I," *American Political Science Review* 32, no. 1 (February 1938): 28–50.

18. For a concise synthesis of this ideational shift in India's worldview, see C. Raja Mohan, *Crossing the Rubicon, The Shaping of India's New Foreign Policy* (Delhi: Palgrave Macmillan, 2003).

19. Nirupama Rao, speech on the maritime dimensions of India's foreign policy, National Maritime Foundation, India Habitat Center, New Delhi, July 28, 2011

(http://meaindia.nic.in/myprint.php?id=190017885&d=29&sz=c&m=&y=&pg=&flg=&searchdata1=).

20. Ibid.

21. See World Trade Organization, "India Trade Profile" (http://stat.wto.org/CountryProfile/WSDBCountryPFView.aspx?Language=E&Country=IN).

22. See Ernst and Young, "India's Energy Security: Key Issues Impacting the Oil and Gas Sector 3," report prepared for the Federation of Indian Chambers of Commerce and Industry, 2011 (www.ey.com/IN/en/Industries/Oil—-Gas/Indias-energy-security). This percentage is expected to reach a staggering 90 percent by 2030. Overall energy dependency (that is, including coal and natural gas) is expected to reach 80 percent. See Michael Kugelman, "Integrating Energy Concerns into India's National Security Strategy," *IAGS Journal of Energy Security* (December 2011) (www.ensec.org/index.php).

23. Marc Lanteigne, "China's Maritime Security and the Malacca Dilemma," *Asian Security* 4, no. 2 (April 2008): 143–61.

24. Chinese strategic writings frequently refer to the so-called "first" and "second" island chains, which act as geographic and strategic barriers to China's naval ambitions. The first island chain stretches from the Kurile Islands, through the main islands of Japan, the Ryukus, the Philippines, and then over to Borneo. The second island chain encompasses a far wider expanse reaching deep into the Pacific and skirting the Marianas and Micronesia.

25. For a detailed analysis of India's Naval Doctrine, see Iskander Rehman, "India's Aspirational Naval Doctrine," in *The Rise of the Indian Navy*, edited by Pant, pp. 55–81.

26. See Vijay Sakhuja, "Security in the Maritime Commons: India's Perspective," in *Crux of Asia: China, India, and the Emerging Global Order*, edited by Ashley J. Tellis and Sean Mirski (Washington: Carnegie Endowment for International Peace, 2013), pp. 155–65.

27. Ibid.

28. See Kristen Boon, "Security Council Debates Maritime Piracy," *Opinio Juris*, November 21, 2012 (http://opiniojuris.org/2012/11/21/security-council-debates-maritime-piracy/), and "November 2012 Monthly Forecast, Thematic Issues: Open Debate on Piracy," *Security Council Report*, November 1, 2012 (www.securitycouncilreport.org/monthly-forecast/2012-11/open_debate_on_piracy.php).

29. James Lamont and James Fontanella-Khan, "India Detains Italian Marines over Fishermen Deaths," *Financial Times*, February 19, 2012.

30. Centre for Policy Research and National Defense College, *Nonalignment 2.0: A Foreign and Strategic Policy for India in the Twenty First Century* (New Delhi, 2012), para. 99 (www.cprindia.org/workingpapers/3844-nonalignment-20-foreign-and-strategic-policy-india-twenty-first-century).

31. Ministry of Defense, *Annual Report of the Indian Ministry of Defense 2011–2012* (New Delhi, 2012), p. 34 (http://mod.nic.in/reports/welcome.html).

32. Jennifer McArdle, "India Eyes Its Cinderella Service," *The Diplomat*, April 22, 2012 (http://thediplomat.com/2012/04/22/india-boosts-its-cinderella-service/).

33. Daniel J. Kostecka, "Places Rather Than Bases: The Chinese Navy's Emerging Support Network in the Indian Ocean," *Naval War College Review* 64, no.1 (Winter 2011): 59–78.

34. Integrated Headquarters, Indian Navy, "Freedom to Use the Seas: India's Maritime Military Strategy" (New Delhi: Ministry of Defense, 2007), p. 41.

35. Integrated Headquarters, Indian Navy, "Indian Maritime Doctrine" (New Delhi: Ministry of Defense, 2004), p. 83.

36. See Walter C. Ladwig III, "Delhi's Pacific Ambition: Naval Power, Look East, and India's Emerging Influence in the Asia-Pacific," *Asian Security* 5, no. 2 (May 2009): 87–113.

37. At the time of writing, Pakistan has taken over the rotating command for CTF 151.

38. Vijay Sakhuja, *Asian Maritime Power in the 21st Century* (Singapore: Institute for Southeast Asian Studies, 2011), p. 197.

39. For an excellent study of the discussion of the virtues of sea power within classical philosophy and political theory, see Daniel Deudney, *Bounding Power: Republican Security Theory from the Polis to the Global Village* (Princeton University Press, 2007), pp. 114–36.

40. L. W. Martin, *The Sea in Modern Strategy* (London: Chatto and Windus for the Institute for Strategic Studies, 1967), p. 138.

41. Integrated Headquarters, Indian Navy, "Indian Maritime Doctrine" (New Delhi: Ministry of Defense, 2009), pp. 65–66.

42. Cited by S. Kapila in "India Defines Her Strategic Frontiers," SAAG Paper 832 (Selangor: South Asia Analysis Group, 2003) (www.saag.org/papers9/paper832.html).

43. Manmohan Singh, address at the Combined Commanders' Conference, October 24, 2004.

44. Rising temperatures have increased the likelihood of significant variances in the monsoon season, which could lead to severe droughts. In addition to this, meteorologists have noted an increase in the intensity and frequency of extreme weather occurrences in the Indian Ocean such as typhoons. Last but not least, rising water levels could have a devastating impact on millions of inhabitants throughout South Asia, ranging from the Maldives, whose archipelagoes are facing extinction, to Bangladesh, many of whose numerous inhabitants already live below sea level. See Lee Cordner, "Progressing Maritime Security Cooperation in the Indian Ocean," *Naval War College Review* 64, no. 4 (Autumn 2011): 66–88.

45. Ministry of Defense, *Annual Report*, p. 5.

46. Indian Navy, "Farewell Press Conference by Outgoing CNS" (New Delhi: Ministry of Defense, August 7, 2012) (http://indiannavy.nic.in/print/1433).

47. Walter C. Ladwig III, "A Neo-Nixon Doctrine for the Indian Ocean: Helping States Help Themselves," *Strategic Analysis* 36, no. 3 (May 2012): 384–99.

48. India has helped several smaller island nations, such as the Maldives or Mauritius, to set up coastal radar chains for monitoring all aspects of their maritime traffic.

49. Caroline Thomas, "Third World Security," in *International Politics: Enduring Concepts and Contemporary Issues*, edited by Robert Art and Robert Jervis (London: Longman, 2002), pp. 263–73.

50. For a listing of extant maritime territorial disputes and divergences of interpretation over the law of the sea in the Indian Ocean, see James Kraska, "Indian Ocean Security and the Law of the Sea," *Georgetown Journal for International Law* 43, no. 2 (June 2012): 433–95.

51. "India, Pakistan Discuss Sir Creek, Make No Headway," *Times of India*, June 19, 2012 (http://articles.timesofindia.indiatimes.com/2012-06-19/india/32316208_1_sir-creek-headway-amicable-solution).

52. "Interview of Admiral Asif Sandila, Chief of Naval Staff, Pakistan Navy," *Defense News*, February 20, 2012 (www.defensenews.com/article/20120220/DEFREG03/302200008/Interview-Adm-Asif-Sandila-Chief-Naval-Staff-Pakistan-Navy.)

53. "India and Pakistan Clash over Naval Ships," *Rediff News*, July 18, 2011; Sandeep Unnithan, "Stronger Tides: Pakistan Warship Violated Safety Norms, Damages Indian Frigate," *India Today*, June 25, 2011.

54. "Indian Navy Has 'Hegemonic Mindset': Pakistan Naval Chief," *Press Trust of India*, February 24, 2010.

55. Cordner, "Progressing Maritime Security Cooperation," p. 70.

56. Ibid.

57. World Bank, *Promoting Economic Cooperation in South Asia* (Washington, February 2010) (http://web.worldbank.org/WBSITE/EXTERNAL/COUNTRIES/SOUTHASIA EXT/0,,contentMDK:22470638~menuPK:2246552~pagePK:2865106~piPK:2865128~theSitePK:223547,00.html).

58. Iskander Rehman, "AirSea Battle's Indo-Pacific Future" (New Delhi: Observer Research Foundation, March 13, 2012) (www.orfonline.org/cms/sites/orfonline/modules/analysis/AnalysisDetail.html?cmaid=34446&mmacmaid=34447).

59. Fahran Bokhari, "Push and Pull: Pakistan's Navy Confronts an East/West Divide," *Jane's Navy International*, May 19, 2011.

60. Ibid.

61. Toshi Yoshihara, "Chinese Views of India in the Indian Ocean: A Geopolitical Perspective," *Strategic Analysis* 36, no. 3 (May 2012): 489–500.

62. Interview with former Chinese official, Beijing, September 2010.

63. "Naval Chief Inaugurates Naval Strategic Forces Headquarters," *Inter Services Public Relations*, May 19, 2012 (www.ispr.gov.pk/front/main.asp?o=t-press_release&date=2012/5/19).

64. For more on naval nuclear dynamics in the Indian Ocean, see Iskander Rehman, "Drowning Stability: The Perils of Naval Nuclearization and Brinkmanship in the Indian Ocean," *Naval War College Review* 65, no. 4 (Autumn 2012): 64–88; Andrew C. Winner, "The Future of India's Undersea Nuclear Deterrent," in *Strategy in the Second Nuclear Age: Power, Ambition, and the Ultimate Weapon*, edited by James R. Holmes and Toshi Yoshihara (Georgetown University Press, 2012), pp. 277–310.

65. Rehman, "Drowning Stability," p. 78.

66. Emily O. Goldman has described how, over the interwar period, a highly diverse threat environment complicated Britain's strategic assessment and undermined its political-military coordination. From this and other studies, she concludes, "In a diverse threat environment, one cannot easily focus on a single adversary and develop weapons optimized for a single purpose." Emily O. Goldman, "Thinking about Strategy Absent the Enemy," *Security Studies* 4, no. 4 (Autumn 1994): 40–85.

67. Edward Luttwak, *The Political Uses of Seapower* (Johns Hopkins University Press, 1974), p. 39.

68. This challenge has also been identified by an Indian security analyst who writes the following: "The danger, however, lies not so much in inability to win direct naval con-

tests. Rather, it lies in non-state threats blunting its [the Indian navy's] fighting edge, sapping morale, weakening resolve, and exposing naval personnel to moral dilemmas and dubious political economies. . . . Allocating naval resources for constabulary duties does come at the cost of preparing them for conventional naval warfare." See Nitin Pai, "Non-State Threats to India's Maritime Security: Sailing Deeper into an Era of Violent Peace," in *The Rise of the Indian Navy*, edited by Pant, p. 173.

69. Teresita C. Schaffer, *India and the United States in the 21st Century: Reinventing Partnership* (Washington: Center for Strategic and International Studies, 2009), p. 76.

70. Sakhuja, *Asian Maritime Power in the 21st Century*, p. 200.

71. Indian Navy, "Farewell Press Conference by Outgoing CNS."

72. Rehman, "AirSea Battle's Indo-Pacific Future."

73. James R. Holmes, "The US-India Naval Cooperation: Moving beyond Rhetoric," in *The Rise of the Indian Navy*, edited by Pant, pp. 139–57.

74. The United States has relentlessly encouraged India to take on a greater role within the Indian Ocean. This has become even more apparent under the Obama administration, which has vigorously pursued a rebalancing toward Asia. For a survey of growing Indo-U.S. strategic congruence in the Indo-Pacific, see David Scott, "The 'Indo-Pacific': New Regional Formulations and New Maritime Frameworks for U.S.-India Strategic Convergence," *Asia-Pacific Review* 19, no. 2 (November 2012): 85–109.

75. Robert D. Kaplan, "Center Stage for the 21st Century: Power Plays in the Indian Ocean," *Foreign Affairs* 88 (March-April 2009): 16.

PART IV

Multilateral Policy in Practice

DAVID M. MALONE *and* ROHAN MUKHERJEE

9 *Dilemmas of Sovereignty and Order: India and the UN Security Council*

Introduction

This chapter examines India's participation within and attitudes toward the United Nations Security Council (UNSC). In so doing, it confronts two empirical puzzles. First, contrary to what one might expect of a rising power, India's willingness to countenance violations of state sovereignty (through, say, multilaterally authorized intervention) as an international norm has diminished, rather than increased, as its power has grown—we call this India's *sovereignty paradox*. Second, contrary to what one might expect of a rising power that has benefited from the existing international order, India's commitment to maintaining this order has diminished as its position has improved—we call this India's *order paradox*. These two paradoxes offer intriguing insights relevant to the central concerns of this volume: the drivers of India's multilateral policies; India's orientation toward the existing rule-based international order; the balance between Delhi's conduct of regional and bilateral relations, on the one hand, and its multilateral engagement, on the other; and India's current—not necessarily fully coherent or cohesive—conceptions of a future world order.

The key argument we advance to explain the two paradoxes is that since the end of the cold war, India's multilateral engagements have increased in number and intensity on the global scale, but its security challenges have remained overwhelmingly internal and regional, in effect constraining India's ability to maneuver at the multilateral level. Moreover, although India's power and influence in world affairs have increased, the international order has not accorded India the status (most notably as a permanent member of the UNSC) to match the growing stature that some of its leading citizens desire. Therefore, due to concerns of national security and international representation, India has been more supportive of sovereignty and nonintervention in the internal affairs of states and less committed to an international order that, in the official Indian view, does not accommodate Indian interests or aspirations.

This chapter begins with a historical overview of India's relationship with the UNSC, discusses and analyzes two major vectors in official Indian views—on sovereignty and order—and reconnects with the core questions of this volume.

Historical Overview

India was among the fifty-one original members of the United Nations when the organization was formed in 1945, two years before the country's independence (mirroring an arrangement whereby India held membership in the League of Nations, albeit a membership controlled by the colonial power). Delhi's first major brush with the UNSC occurred in 1948 over what came to be known as the "India-Pakistan question," which arose as a result of the partition that attended the independence of both countries.

Early Lessons and Conflicts

The dispute centered on the status of the Princely State of Jammu and Kashmir (J&K), which both India and Pakistan claimed as integral to their territory and nationhood. Following an invasion by tribal forces backed by the Pakistani military, the ruler of Kashmir acceded to India, legally empowering India's military to fight the invaders. India's prime minister, Jawaharlal Nehru, referred the matter to the UNSC, hoping for a favorable outcome. He was soon disappointed, particularly by the Western great powers, which treated the matter as a dispute between two states rather than as the invasion of one territory by another. Indian leaders concluded from this painful experience, "The Security Council was a strictly political body and . . . decisions were taken by its members on the basis of their perspective of their national interest and not on the merits of any particular case."[1]

In 1950 India joined the UNSC in its first of seven terms to date through election as a nonpermanent member. During the following two years, the council focused mainly on the outbreak of the Korean War and the continuation of the India-Pakistan tussle over Kashmir. With regard to the former, India emphasized through its votes and statements the need for the UN to bring about a peaceful—that is, a nonmilitary—resolution to the conflict. In the event, the UNSC voted for armed intervention under a unified command led by the United States. Instead of troops, Delhi contributed a field ambulance unit to the UN effort. Following the war, India was instrumental in the repatriation of prisoners of war and refugees.

In subsequent years, India earned the reputation of being a "champion of peaceful settlement"[2] at the UN, variously contributing troops, senior officials, military observers, and humanitarian assistance to a diverse set of UN operations to resolve conflicts, including the Israel-Egypt conflict, the Congo, Cyprus, Indonesia, Lebanon, and Yemen.[3] However, India's own circumstances remained anything but peaceful during these years. In 1961 India used military force to wrest Goa from Portugal, a legally dubious yet politically feasible act given the prevailing climate of anticolonialism. India earned the particular disapprobation of the United States, which was allied with Portugal's military dictatorship. The U.S. representative to the UNSC, Adlai Stevenson, declared, "India's armed attack on Goa mocks the good faith of its frequent declarations of lofty principles."[4] Nevertheless, the Soviet Union vetoed a draft resolution sponsored by the Western powers calling on India to withdraw its troops.[5]

In October 1962 a border war broke out between China and India. Overlapping as it did with the Cuban missile crisis, the Sino-Indian conflict went entirely unnoticed in the UNSC's official record. Nonetheless, the United States came to a beleaguered India's aid militarily, and the Soviet Union intervened diplomatically to de-escalate the conflict. A few years later, in 1965, India found itself responding to Pakistani attacks across the border at Kashmir and in the Rann of Kutch. This conflict featured prominently on the UNSC's agenda, and the organization's demand for a cease-fire,[6] combined with Soviet mediation, helped to end the conflict.

India's Challenges to the System

India's second term on the UNSC occurred in 1967–68, when the council was faced with heightened tensions in the Middle East, notably a military conflict between Israel and its neighbors Egypt, Jordan, and Syria. In keeping with its staunchly pro-Arab policy and its third world identity, India criticized Israeli aggression and stressed the need to protect the sovereignty and rights of the Arab countries and peoples in the conflict.[7] India's tenure on the UNSC also coincided with the opening for signature of the Treaty on the Non-Proliferation of Nuclear Weapons (NPT) in 1968. India strongly opposed the NPT on grounds of fairness and the sovereign equality of states and consequently abstained from voting on a resolution calling for the five permanent members of the UNSC (the P-5) to protect states without nuclear weapons from nuclear attacks or threats.[8]

In 1971 India found itself in a tight corner at the UN due to its intervention in the East Pakistan conflict, which led to the creation of the independent state of Bangladesh. Most states considered the humanitarian issues that India invoked to justify its actions to be less compelling than Pakistan's territorial integrity, which was shattered. To its humanitarian concerns, India added the need for self-defense in the face of large flows of refugees across its borders.[9] Delhi narrowly avoided diplomatic isolation through Prime Minister Indira Gandhi's energetic diplomacy and the support of the Soviet Union, which vetoed three UNSC resolutions calling for a cease-fire in the immediate aftermath of India's entry into the conflict. Fortunately for India, its third term on the UNSC was already secure before the East Pakistan intervention, and India joined the council again in 1972–73, years during which the UNSC was preoccupied mainly with conflict in the Middle East and decolonization in Africa. India adopted a tough stance against Israel, notably in connection with its reprisals for the terrorist attack on Israeli athletes at the Munich Olympics.[10]

In 1974 India diverted foreign nuclear technology meant for civilian purposes to the first public nuclear test by a non-P-5 state. International reaction against India's defiance of the NPT regime was led by the United States.[11] The UNSC did not officially take note, leaving it to the International Atomic Energy Agency and individual states to respond, which they did at Washington's prompting by tightening their proliferation controls and forming what came to be called the Nuclear Suppliers Group. In 1975 India annexed the neighboring Autonomous Kingdom of Sikkim amid political unrest in that territory (which some argued India had fueled).[12] Although the People's Republic of China protested vociferously, the UNSC did not act on the matter.

A More Stable Engagement

India returned to the UNSC in 1977–78, where it co-sponsored a resolution following up on the withdrawal of Israeli forces from Lebanese territory,[13] a resolution condemning South Africa's involvement in Angola's civil war,[14] and three resolutions strongly condemning the minority white regime in Southern Rhodesia (Zimbabwe) for denying independence and self-rule to its citizens and using force against neighboring countries such as Mozambique and Zambia for severing ties with the regime.[15] India also joined in the unanimous condemnation of apartheid in South Africa, and in the imposition of an arms embargo on the South African government.[16]

Following a period of five years that witnessed the U.S.-Iran hostage crisis, the Soviet invasion of Afghanistan, the beginning of the Iran-Iraq War, armed conflict between Israel and Lebanon, the Falklands War, and the continuation of apartheid in South Africa, India was elected to its fifth term on the UNSC, 1984–85. Familiar themes predominated, with India focused on condemning the policies of South Africa toward nonwhites, the policies of Israel toward Palestinians in occupied territories, as well as the policies of both states toward their neighbors. Soon thereafter, in 1987, Prime Minister Rajiv Gandhi initiated a three-year period of India's engagement with Sri Lanka's civil war. The Indian peacekeeping force, sent to Sri Lanka further to an agreement between the two governments, proved an unmitigated failure and embarrassment for India, leading to its withdrawal by early 1990, leaving in its wake deep Indian reluctance to intervene militarily elsewhere in its neighborhood (even with the best of intentions).

Struggling to Keep Up

India was once again a nonpermanent member of the UNSC in 1991–92, at a time of seismic geostrategic change spurred by the end of the cold war. While some of the wreckage of the cold war (for example, conflicts in Central America and Indochina) proved amenable to resolution with UN assistance, new intrastate conflicts came to dominate the UNSC's agenda. During India's tenure, the UNSC dealt with conflicts involving a range of countries including Angola, Cambodia, Cyprus, Iran, Iraq, Israel, Kuwait, Lebanon, Liberia, Libya, Mozambique, Somalia, South Africa, and the former Yugoslavia (and its successor states). An overworked UNSC, unprepared for the complexity of civil wars, experienced an era of euphoria over the unshackling of its own bonds imposed by the cold war, but generated uneven results during this period of hyperactivity. Meanwhile, at the behest of the first UNSC summit in early 1992, UN secretary general Boutros Boutros-Ghali sought, notably in his report *An Agenda for Peace*,[17] to redefine and expand the UN's role in the security sphere to include a host of nontraditional situations, including coups, humanitarian crises, internally and externally displaced populations, and (indirectly) terrorism.[18]

India—internally riven by the necessity for coalition politics and an economic crisis and externally somewhat disoriented by the loss of its superpower ally—struggled to keep up with events. Delhi's reaction to the Gulf War, in particular, appeared haphazard, first condemning the U.S. invasion, then supporting it and allowing U.S. airplanes to refuel on Indian territory, and finally withdrawing this facility under domestic political pressure.[19] At the UNSC, India abstained on two crucial votes calling for an end to the Gulf War and Saddam Hussein's dictatorship, respectively.[20] In the words of Ramesh Thakur,

> India's confused response—which included a unilateral peace initiative to Baghdad—based on a faded image of itself as leader of the non-aligned nations, succeeded in alienating both Baghdad and Washington without winning any friends. Being bracketed with Cuba and Yemen in a UN Security Council vote at war's end calling for Iraq's surrender was less than edifying.[21]

Subsequently, India also abstained on four other resolutions dealing with an arms embargo on Libya (for the Lockerbie bombing), providing humanitarian assistance in Bosnia and Herzegovina, expanding the UN peacekeeping force in Bosnia and Herzegovina, and ending the membership of the former Yugoslavia in the UN.[22] There seemed to be no apparent pattern to India's stances at the UNSC during this period, except an inability to come to terms with American hegemony in global affairs (temporary though it turned out to be) and on the UNSC.

Nonetheless, as the UNSC rapidly expanded the scope of its activities, India voiced a consistent note of caution on the hazards of intervening in the internal affairs of sovereign states. (Although irritated by India's reserved position on military intervention at the time, Western powers might have given it more consideration, not least in light of the dubious outcome of their interventionist strategies in Somalia and the Balkans soon thereafter.)[23]

Through the 1990s, as the UNSC continued to authorize the use of force in domestic conflicts across the globe, India turned into something of a conscientious objector within the UN with regard to military and humanitarian interventions. This stance was especially familiar to international negotiators involved with nuclear proliferation and testing. India had long remained an obstinate holdout when it came to the NPT and remained so when the treaty was extended indefinitely in 1995. In addition, India frustrated its great-power interlocutors and also some other states the following year by opposing the Comprehensive Test Ban Treaty (CTBT) in the UN General Assembly. That same year, India lost the election for a nonpermanent position on the UNSC to Japan by a wide margin: Although India attributed Japan's success to "Yen Diplomacy,"[24] especially in relation to African states, India's unyielding positions on the NPT and in the CTBT negotiations clearly played a role in determining the outcome.[25]

Crossing the Rubicon

New Delhi had good reasons to oppose the CTBT. In May 1998 India burst onto the global stage (quite literally) with a series of nuclear tests—its first since 1974—that heralded its post–cold war status as a rising power. International reaction was sharply negative but surprisingly short-lived. In fact, as argued by C. Raja Mohan in his book *Crossing the Rubicon*, the nuclear tests made the world—and its remaining superpower—sit up and take notice of India as a major regional, if not world, power.[26] India thereafter developed an enhanced sure-footedness and confidence about its relations with the great powers and its involvement in international organizations. This new confidence was also supported by the rapid economic growth that post-1991 economic liberalization reforms had generated.

Increasingly, India began voicing a demand for greater representation in international organizations based on its national capabilities and contributions to the multilateral system over the decades. At the UNSC, this meant an expansion of the permanent membership to include India. After losing the election to Japan in 1996, India eschewed nonpermanent membership for a decade and a half, preferring to campaign for a permanent seat instead. During this period, and in particular in the run-up to the 2005 UN summit, India, with Brazil, Germany, and Japan, each a candidate for a permanent seat on the council, lobbied strongly for council reform.

Compared to its last tenure, India returned to the UNSC a far more self-assured interlocutor in 2011, which rapidly turned into an exceptionally challenging and active year for the UNSC. In addition to managing long-running conflicts, the council was faced with new crises in Côte d'Ivoire, Libya, and Syria. On Côte d'Ivoire, in March 2011, India exhibited a nuanced stance, joining a unanimous vote in support of multilateral military intervention while arguing for clear guidelines to prevent UN peacekeepers from becoming "agents of regime change" or getting embroiled in a civil war.[27] Libya and Syria, however, posed challenges for council cohesion, creating deep divisions within the P-5 as well as between the Brazil-Russia-India-China (BRIC) grouping and the Western powers. India—along with Brazil, China, Germany, and Russia—abstained on a resolution authorizing multilateral military intervention in Libya.[28] Later in the year, India abstained on a draft resolution—vetoed by China and Russia—condemning the Syrian regime for its brutal crackdown on antigovernment protesters.[29] In both cases, India offered clear and well-argued reasons for its decisions, but failed to provide any reasonable alternatives to the proposals put forward by the resolutions' sponsors. At best, India's argument came down to the need for a "calibrated and gradual approach"[30] that respected the sovereignty of the states in question, but it did little to elucidate the details of such an approach. In 2012, heeding events on the ground and perhaps due in part to representations from its Gulf oil suppliers (most prominently Saudi Arabia),[31] India adopted a multipronged approach to the Syrian drama, calling in the UN Human Rights Council for an end to the use of heavy weapons by that country's government against civilian populations, voting in line with essentially anti-Assad Arab League preferences, and expressing ever-stronger concern in the Security Council over the loss of life on the ground, but always proving leery of outside military intervention, direct or indirect, in the conflict.[32]

With India perhaps the strongest candidate among the four countries seeking a permanent seat through council reform, New Delhi was reminded that, ultimately, the composition of the council is controlled by the P-5, any of whose members can veto a proposal. Indeed, more than a subliminal message along these lines was reflected in strong comments made by the U.S. permanent representative Susan Rice over Washington's disappointment with India's stance on Libya and early position on Syria in light of the aspirations of several emerging powers to a permanent seat.[33] In effect, India was reminded that the deck remains heavily stacked in favor of the P-5 in the UN Charter's system of checks and balances, which to many today appears woefully outdated in some of its specifics but cannot be amended without unanimous consent of the P-5. Meanwhile, India and other emerging powers are perpetually "auditioning" for the P-5 during elected tenures on the council, a most frustrating reality (as Rice's remarks made clear).

Patterns and Paradoxes

India's interactions relative to the UNSC need to be viewed against the backdrop of the country's increasing power and influence in world affairs. What does India's power trajectory tell us about its engagement with the multilateral system for conflict management, and what clues would this insight give us to India's vision, willingness, and options for shaping the international order in the future?

India's Sovereignty Paradox

Acts or threats of aggression, which are the UNSC's primary focus, inherently involve violations or potential violations of sovereignty. A country on the UNSC contributes not only to collective responses to violations of sovereignty by other states in the international system but also to decisions regarding whether the UNSC itself must violate sovereignty in the service of peace and security.

In the modern state system, great powers have been more willing both to countenance third-party violations of sovereignty—although, of course, not against themselves—when important interests of their own are involved and to commit such violations themselves or through the UNSC.[34] The underlying premise is that the powerful face lower costs from violations of sovereignty in the international system. Conversely, weaker countries place great value in sovereignty because it is perhaps the only instrument they have with which to keep more powerful countries at bay.[35]

India, however, displays a peculiar paradox in its relationship with sovereignty. Not only did it become a stronger supporter of sovereignty as its power increased, but as a weak power India earlier defied theoretical expectation and supported a conception of sovereignty that in practical terms privileged intervention for the sake of protecting human rights. Recent historical scholarship argues that India's founding generation of leaders had an altogether different and somewhat utopian notion of sovereignty in the international system.[36] Mahatma Gandhi, Jawaharlal Nehru, and other leaders of the Indian nationalist movement espoused an ideology that can best be described as seeking "a post-sovereign-nation-state-dominated reality, a world of states governed by the meta-sovereign institution of the UN."[37] This vision, which they labeled One World, sought to use the UN as a vehicle for creating a world federation that would have the power and resources to prevent international conflict.

As its power and influence grew in international affairs, however, India sharply reduced its support for sovereignty violations. India consistently counseled restraint to the UNSC during the 1990s and opposed the violation of sovereignty except as a last resort, notably during debates over East Timor, Kosovo, northern Iraq, Sierra Leone, and Somalia. India was an even more vociferous critic of unilateral intervention, especially in the case of the North Atlantic Treaty Organization in Kosovo.[38] Overall, the Indian position was that the state ought to be the sole arbiter of domestic conflict; intervention, if at all necessary, must only be undertaken multilaterally, with the consent of the target state and only after all other avenues of conflict resolution have been exhausted. A similar stance pertained during India's tenure on the council in 2011–12.

India's Order Paradox

By maintaining international peace and security, the UNSC has helped to preserve the post–Second World War liberal institutional order established and underwritten by the United States and its allies. Over time, the UNSC has become a key pillar of that order, however inconsistent its decisions have sometimes been, conferring legitimacy (or not) on states and their policies.[39]

Potentially influential states that have traditionally been outside the great-power club that maintains this order—inadvertently or by design—have faced three choices: accept the order, challenge the order, or negotiate a rise within the order; that is, be a rule taker, a rule breaker, or a rule shaper aiming eventually to become a rule maker.

India does not seek dramatically to alter the international order but instead to realize its great-power ambitions largely within it (that is, to be a rule shaper); hence it has sought frequent election to the UNSC as a nonpermanent member. It follows that, as India's position improves within the order, New Delhi should increase its commitment to maintaining the global multilateral system so that India can continue benefiting from it and eventually become a rule maker within it. In the words of one scholar, "If the material costs and benefits of a given status quo are what matters, why would a state be dissatisfied with the very status quo that had abetted its rise?"[40]

However, apart from its long-cherished and generally admired leading role in UN peacekeeping, India has not exhibited such an evolution. Although India has gone from being a rule breaker—on Bangladesh, Goa, and nuclear testing, for example—to being a rule shaper, the definition of its interests and scope of its solutions to security problems have narrowed over time. New Delhi's willingness to shoulder the security burdens of the international multilateral system was noticeably higher when its position in the international system was weaker, that is, in the period between independence and the end of the cold war. Early on, India was an enthusiastic supporter of the United Nations, incorporating key elements of the UN Charter into the Indian constitution. Despite the initial setback over Kashmir, India remained committed to the UN. Throughout this period, India championed the interests of developing countries in various UN bodies and advocated in favor of the UNSC as the preeminent forum for resolving international conflicts. The latter was especially important to India's policy of nonalignment.

Since the end of the cold war, however, while the UNSC significantly expanded its mandate and operations, India's enthusiasm for multilateral solutions to international security problems has not kept pace. This discrepancy is evident not just from New Delhi's record on humanitarian intervention but also in its exclusively nonmultilateral approach to crises affecting its relations with neighboring countries, such as the 1999 Kargil War, the 2001 attack on the Indian Parliament, the 2008 terrorist attacks in Mumbai, the closing scenes of the Sri Lankan civil war, the conflict between the Maoists and the government in Nepal, and the 2011 coup in the Maldives, to name a few examples. On some of these it welcomed outside, mainly

Figure 9-1. *Size of Missions in the UN Security Council, 2011*

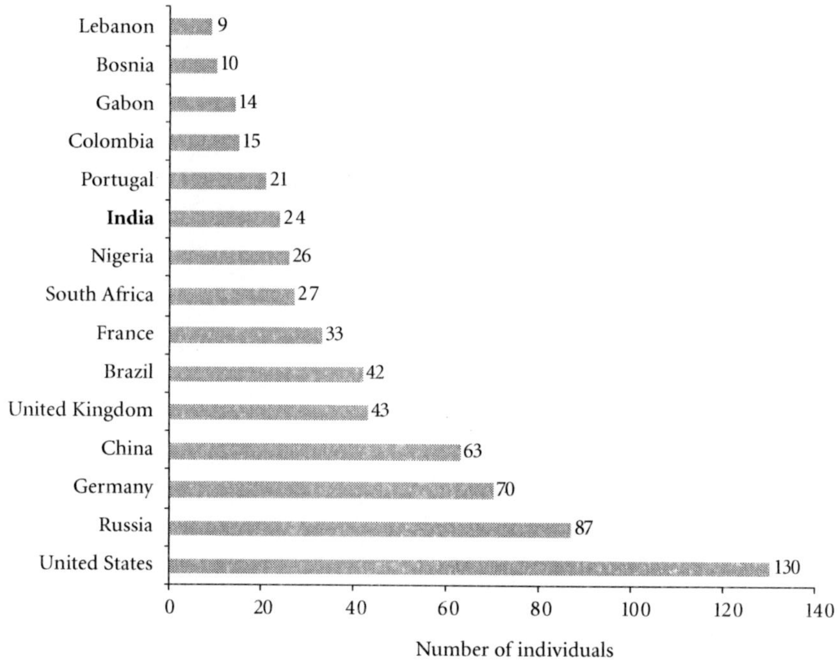

Source: Global Policy Forum (www.globalpolicy.org/images/pdfs/size_of_Missions2012_1.pdf).

U.S., mediation but mostly sought to avoid multilateral engagement. Even in the realm of peacekeeping, India's "altruistic and solidaristic objectives have been superceded by India's wider global ambition for recognition and influence on the world stage."[41]

With regard to upholding the foundational values of the UN and maintaining its legitimacy, Western observers have often lamented India's unwillingness to take on greater responsibilities or participate more meaningfully at the level of the UNSC. As shown in figure 9-1, in 2011 India's mission to the UN had twenty-four members, which was smaller than the missions of every other great or rising power on the council that year.

The data are symbolic of the curious lack of congruence between India's ambition to achieve great-power status within the existing order of norms and institutions and the resources it devotes to this in one of its prime forums. Although the world increasingly looks to India for leadership on the provision of global public goods, India's contributions to the UN, with some exceptions such as the UN Democracy Fund, are not perceived internationally as being those of an aspiring leader in the global order.

This view is also increasingly held by India's traditional constituency, the developing world, which has lately seen India pull away from its nonaligned solidarity and embrace a more independent path in the UNSC and some other forums. India has gone from articulating an expansive third world view of issues such as anti-colonialism and self-determination to defining its interests in terms beneficial to India alone. Therefore, India's current position in the UNSC is caught somewhere between countries courting the developing world—China and Russia—and those speaking for the developed world: Britain, France, and the United States.

Explaining India's Evolution

The end of the cold war was a watershed moment in modern Indian history, and the post-1989 world was one of great uncertainty for Indian foreign policy. Perhaps to the surprise of New Delhi (and many other capitals), the UNSC became a highly prized organization in which to wield influence, due to the actual and symbolic power it afforded its members.[42] How did these events affect India's approach to questions of sovereignty and order?

Sovereignty

Following the cold war, the heightened insecurity in Kashmir—a territory many Indians viewed as existentially vital in their nation's long-standing conflict with Pakistan—brought home the regional nature of India's security challenges and the need to protect India's territorial sovereignty. Soon India faced a more interventionist UNSC and a secretary general (Kofi Annan) who, egged on by Pakistan, attempted to internationalize the Kashmir conflict. The Indian military's ham-fisted approach to counterinsurgency and law-and-order in the Kashmir valley invited the censure of human rights groups both within and outside India. In addition, multiple insurgencies in the northeastern region of India that had remained dormant, as well as the peasant-based Maoist insurgency in several Indian states, threatened to undermine the government's authority. India's national security challenges also emanated from its periphery, sometimes relating to those within its own territory. For example, many rebel groups in northeastern India found safe havens in neighboring Bangladesh, Bhutan, and Myanmar.

As a result of these factors, India became far less willing to countenance violations of sovereignty as an international norm, lest the spotlight be turned on the several insurgencies within India. The Indian intelligentsia continues to echo this view: during the Syrian crisis, a prominent journalist, criticizing India's vote in favor of a draft UNSC resolution condemning the Syrian regime for using heavy weapons—vetoed by China and Russia—wrote, "Will India again vote with the West [in the future]? Before it does so, it would do well to remember that its own nation-building project is still incomplete. So whatever conventions it allows or helps the West establish on the right to protect or intervene may well come back to haunt it in the years that lie ahead."[43]

It may be no coincidence that, starting in 1992, as the Kashmir insurgency gained momentum, India began making statements at the UN that emphasized the inherent imbalance in an international norm that protected the human rights of terrorists and secessionists while censuring governments that attempted to fight them. Indeed, India gradually seized on terrorism as a frame within which to discuss human rights precisely because its greatest concern was that the norms of humanitarian intervention and the "responsibility to protect" could be applied to India's counterinsurgency and counterterrorism efforts.[44] Since 1989 India has also been wary of the UNSC's growing willingness to authorize the use of force and has sought to strengthen the role of the UN General Assembly and bring issues of economic development back into the UN's focus.[45]

International Order

While the Indian state remained weak at home, it was increasingly called on by the international community to take on roles of greater responsibility in managing the global order (a reasonable response to India's demands for greater representation in global governance institutions). While Indian security preoccupations remained regionally and internally focused, Indian diplomacy widened its scope tremendously to include issues and nations that New Delhi had not traditionally engaged with much. Although this new drive arguably worked well in international climate change negotiations and the General Agreement on Trade and Tariffs/World Trade Organization, it produced a mismatch in the UN where India did not perceive its own security needs being served by the ends that the UNSC often sought to achieve. India's commitment to maintaining a global conflict resolution architecture that emphasized greater humanitarian intervention—and gave a more prominent role to the International Criminal Court and the doctrine of responsibility to protect—began to diminish. Instead, India chose to secure its national interest via regional or bilateral arrangements, the former including the "Look

East" policy of 1992 and more recent overtures toward the Shanghai Cooperation Organization.

The Kargil conflict of 1999 is the clearest example of India's preference for resolving its own conflicts: faced with a Pakistani invasion, India chose first to respond militarily in a controlled manner and then to cooperate with the United States in back-channel negotiations with Pakistan to end the conflict. Nowhere was any mention made of referring the matter to the UNSC as Prime Minister Jawaharlal Nehru had done under similar circumstances in 1948. India's reaction to the Mumbai attacks of November 2008 was similar in many respects—essentially relying on the intermediation of a few foreign powers. These and other instances highlight the fact that, for the government of India, the usefulness of focusing on support of the liberal international order sponsored by the West seems unconvincing relative to other means of addressing its security needs.

India's Status Inconsistency

While India has been unable to view its security interests through a global prism, the P-5 have been unable or unwilling to oblige India in its quest for a permanent seat. Since the 1950s, when the issue of UNSC expansion first came up in the General Assembly, India has been a forerunning candidate in any scenario discussed by experts and statesmen alike.[46] India joined the chorus for expansion in the 1970s and renewed its activism in the early 1990s, when Prime Minister Narasimha Rao argued for expansion in order for the UNSC "to maintain political and moral effectiveness."[47] As a consequence of the efforts of India and other states, the UN General Assembly adopted a resolution in 1992 on questions of representation and expansion in the UNSC;[48] the Open-Ended Working Group was formed in 1993 to make recommendations on the issue. The working group remains open-ended, as the UN's 193 member-states continue in their attempts to reach a consensus.

India, like most other realistically eligible countries, had traditionally framed its arguments for a permanent seat in terms of the UN Charter's criteria for the election of nonpermanent members to the UNSC—that is, contribution to maintaining international peace and security and equitable geographic distribution. As a rising power, India has also emphasized *representation.* This claim is not geographic; rather, it is grounded in India's sizable population, growing economic clout, large military, and significant contributions to UN peacekeeping,[49] going so far as to present its claim as "natural" and "legitimate."[50] Indeed, India's overall dissatisfaction with its place in the international order has been couched in strongly normative terms. In 2006 Prime Minister Manmohan Singh stated, "Our goal should be to ensure a prosperous, secure, and dignified future for our people and to participate actively in contributing to the evolution of a *just* world order."[51] This statement is symbolic of a fundamental misalignment involving India and the UNSC (or at least its most powerful members)—the former seeks justice, equity, and representation; the latter focuses more narrowly on peace and security. The five permanent members, while claiming to be open to UNSC reform for the reasons laid out by India, strongly prefer the status quo, which emphasizes order over justice. The two positions are thus continually in conflict.

India's moral claims to permanent membership have often led it astray in what is essentially a political contest. For example, while India counted on its traditional role of developing-nation leader and crusader to win the support of the African nations, it did not take into account the significance of China's growing African connections. Beijing successfully pressured the African nations into proposing several permanent seats with veto power for Africa, thus complicating the joint campaign of India, Brazil, Germany, and Japan (known as the G-4),[52] among which China was deeply opposed to Japan's candidature and at best ambivalent about India's. China, however, is not the only obstacle to India's quest for a permanent seat. The question of the veto remains a powerful obstacle, with none of the P-5 willing to surrender the privilege or grant it lightly to additional countries. The veto is also not popular with the membership at-large, which does not seek to increase the number of veto-wielding countries. India recently signaled that it would be willing to accept permanent membership for an initial period without the veto, but such a proposal could still be stymied not only by the P-5 but also by political maneuverings within the various voting blocks of nations in the General Assembly, where any successful proposal for UNSC expansion would have to obtain two-thirds of the vote. Some of the other strong contenders for permanent seats face significant obstacles within their own regions: Brazil is quietly opposed by several Spanish-speaking Latin American countries, India by Pakistan, Japan by China, and South Africa by Egypt and Nigeria. In addition, some influential countries—Argentina, Canada, Italy, Mexico, Pakistan, and Turkey—prefer to expand the category of nonpermanent members only.[53]

From New Delhi's perspective, India's inability to obtain a permanent seat on the UNSC represents the overall inability of the global order to accommodate India's rise. Consequently, India's investment in a multilateral system that does not address its concerns or recognize its newfound status has diminished, even in the realm of peacekeeping.[54] This has been evident across various negotiating forums, including trade, climate change, and nuclear proliferation, where India has opted either for bilateral partnerships or for deals struck with small groups of influential countries such as the BASIC (Brazil, South Africa, India, and China) group in climate change negotiations.

Conclusion

Due to the expanding remit of the post–cold war UNSC and the persistent weakness of the Indian state in the face of serious internal and regional security threats as well as fragmenting domestic politics, an increasingly powerful India has become a stronger defender of sovereignty now than it was in the past. And due to India's aspiration for greater representation in international institutions and the UNSC's inability to accommodate this demand, an increasingly powerful India with rule-making ambitions has grown somewhat detached from the multilateral security system over time. What do these patterns suggest with regard to the central questions of this volume?

First, India envisages a more just and equitable multilateral order that takes into account the aspirations of a rising, democratic, and peaceful nation such as itself. In the UNSC, this means a permanent seat with veto power, which would allow India to temper the organization's impulse toward intervention and refocus attention on questions of economic development. It has not yet seriously faced the greater likelihood of second-class permanent-member status deprived of a veto, which it might prefer to eschew altogether.

Second, in a classic chicken-and-egg sense, India's willingness to shape the multilateral security order depends on the ability of the order's gatekeepers—the P-5—to accommodate India's interests and ambitions; this is nigh impossible unless India signals a willingness to shape the order in ways that are not detrimental to the P-5's interests (which are less congruent with each other's interests than they were during the immediate post–cold war period). India still lacks the tools and the strategy to convince each of the P-5 (notably China and the United States) that it will act "responsibly" from their perspective. With regard to strategy, New Delhi has yet to embrace a fully political calculus in negotiating its rise within the global order. With regard to ideas, although India can effectively argue within the UNSC against prevailing norms with which it disagrees, it is less capable of articulating credible alternatives.

Third, India's multilateral policy in the realm of international security will be driven largely by internal and regional security concerns rather than global, systemic considerations. When tensions arise between the demands of multilateralism and the exigencies of regionalism or bilateralism, India will tend to prioritize the latter, as it has done systematically in recent decades. In particular, given India's abiding interest in excluding great-power and third-party involvement in the Kashmir region, India's domestic and regional concerns will tend to eschew multilateral solutions rather than demand them.

Fourth, although India may have been a rule breaker at times in the past, it is essentially a rule shaper—that is, a state that will attempt to create exceptions for itself (nuclear testing) or modify rules that do not accord with its interests (the International Criminal Court). In this sense, India will remain largely compliant with the bulk of international law and international regimes, although it will occasionally seek to use its influence to shape the formation of new rules and the practice of existing rules. India does seek to comply with those treaties it ratifies and does not see why it should be bound by treaty regimes to which it has never agreed.

Finally, contemporary normative contestation exposes the growing gap between multipolarity (very much supported by India) and genuine multilateralism in the international system. A shifting balance of power is likely to create space for the emergence and growth of norms that are globally and regionally more appropriate to the circumstances of Asian powers such as China and India. In the future, a more powerful and strategically adept India might well press its normative claims in the UNSC with greater success.

The answers to this volume's core questions depend on the time horizon selected. India's conceptions of global order are likely to evolve as India's security environment changes and its economic and geostrategic weight increases. If immediate security threats can be addressed, India might begin to articulate a vision of global order that approximates the liberal ideal of democracy, human rights, and economic freedom. Until then, India will be content to fall back on a baseline conception that prioritizes national interest (narrowly defined), sovereignty, and autonomy.

Notes

1. Chinmaya R. Gharekhan, "India and the United Nations," in *Indian Foreign Policy: Challenges and Opportunities,* edited by Atish Sinha and Madhup Mohta (New Delhi: Foreign Service Institute, 2007), p. 200.

2. Charles P. Schleicher and J. S. Bains, *The Administration of Indian Foreign Policy through the United Nations* (New York: Oceana, 1969), p. 108.

3. Alan Bullion, "India and UN Peacekeeping Operations," *International Peacekeeping* 4, no. 1 (1997): 98–114.

4. Quincy Wright, "The Goa Incident," *American Journal of International Law* 56, no. 3 (July 1962): 618.

5. UN Security Council Document S/5033, December 18, 1961.

6. UN Security Council Resolution 211, September 20, 1965, adopted by ten votes to none, with one abstention (Jordan).

7. See UN Security Council Document A/6702: "Report of the Security Council, 16 July 1966–15 July 1967," Official Records of the General Assembly, 22nd Session, Supplement no. 2 (New York: United Nations, 1967), pp. 3–53.

8. UN Security Council Resolution 255, June 19, 1968, adopted by ten votes to none, with five abstentions (Algeria, Brazil, France, India, and Pakistan).

9. Nicholas J. Wheeler, "India as Rescuer? Order versus Justice in the Bangladesh War of 1971," in *Saving Strangers: Humanitarian Intervention in International Society* (Oxford University Press, 2000), pp. 55–77.

10. See UN Security Council Document A/9002: "Report of the Security Council, 16 June 1972–15 June 1973," Official Records of the General Assembly, 22nd Session, Supplement no. 2 (New York: United Nations, 1973), pp. 2–40.

11. George Perkovich, *India's Nuclear Bomb: The Impact on Global Proliferation* (University of California Press, 1999), pp. 183–87.

12. See Sunanda K. Datta-Ray, *Smash and Grab: Annexation of Sikkim* (New Delhi: Vikas Publishers, 1984).

13. UN Security Council Resolution 427, May 3, 1978.

14. UN Security Council Resolution 428, May 6, 1978.

15. UN Security Council Resolution 411, June 30, 1977; Resolution 423, March 14, 1978; and Resolution 424, March 17, 1978.

16. UN Security Council Resolution 418, November 4, 1977.

17. Boutros Boutros-Ghali, *An Agenda for Peace* (New York: United Nations, 1992).

18. David Malone, "The Security Council in the Post–Cold War Era: A Study in the Creative Interpretation of the UN Charter," *New York University Journal of International Law and Politics* (Winter 2003): 489.

19. See J. Mohan Malik, "India's Response to the Gulf Crisis: Implications for Indian Foreign Policy," *Asian Survey* 31, no. 9 (September 1991): 847–61.

20. UN Security Council Resolution 686, March 2, 1991, and UN Security Council Resolution 688, April 5, 1991.

21. Ramesh Thakur, "India in the World: Neither Rich, Powerful, nor Principled," *Foreign Affairs* 76, no. 4 (July-August 1997): 15.

22. Respectively, UN Security Council Resolution 748, March 31, 1992; Resolution 770, August 13, 1992; Resolution 776, September 14, 1992; and Resolution 777, September 19, 1992.

23. For some of the central debates and Indian positions on these issues, see Chinmaya Gharekhan, *The Horseshoe Table: An Inside View of the UN Security Council* (New Delhi: Longman, 2006).

24. Bullion, "India and UN Peacekeeping Operations," p. 108.

25. Rohan Mukherjee and David Malone, "For Status or Stature?" *Pragati*, February 4, 2011.

26. C. Raja Mohan, *Crossing the Rubicon: The Shaping of India's New Foreign Policy* (New Delhi: Viking, 2003).

27. Permanent Mission of India to the United Nations, "Explanation of Vote on Côte d'Ivoire Resolution by Ambassador Hardeep Singh Puri, Permanent Representative, at the Security Council on March 30, 2011" (www.un.int/india/2011/ind1843.pdf).

28. UN Security Council Resolution 1973, March 17, 2011.

29. UN Security Council Document S/2011/612. Subsequently, India voted for two draft resolutions that were again vetoed by China and Russia: S/2012/77, February 4, 2012, calling for the Syrian government to cease all violence; and S/2012/538, July 19, 2012, threatening sanctions for failure of the parties to the conflict to adopt former UN secretary general Kofi Annan's six-point peace plan.

30. Permanent Mission of India to the United Nations, "Explanation of Vote on the Resolution Adopted Concerning Libya by Ambassador Hardeep Singh Puri, Permanent Representative, at the Security Council on February 26, 2011" (www.un.int/india/2011/ind1831.pdf).

31. Atul Aneja, "On the Wrong Side of History," *Hindu*, March 23, 2012.

32. Indrani Bagchi, "India Takes Middle Path on Syrian Uprising," *Times of India*, August 31, 2012.

33. See Michele Kelemen, "U.S. Underwhelmed with Emerging Powers at UN," National Public Radio, September 17, 2011 (www.npr.org/2011/09/17/140533339/u-s-underwhelmed-with-emerging-powers-at-u-n).

34. On sovereignty violations generally, see Stephen D. Krasner, *Sovereignty: Organized Hypocrisy* (Princeton University Press, 1999). There are exceptions. In 1991 U.S. intervention to stem the humanitarian crisis in Somalia did not derive from compelling U.S. interests in that country.

35. See Robert H. Jackson, *Quasi-States: Sovereignty, International Relations, and the Third World* (Cambridge University Press, 1993).

36. Manu Bhagavan, "A New Hope: India, the United Nations, and the Making of the Universal Declaration of Human Rights," *Modern Asian Studies* 44, no. 2 (March 2010): 311–47.

37. Bhagavan, "A New Hope," p. 313.

38. Kudrat Virk, "India and the Responsibility to Protect," draft paper prepared for the International Studies Association Annual Convention, Montreal, March 16–19, 2011.

39. Inis L. Claude Jr., "Collective Legitimization as a Political Function of the United Nations," *International Organization* 20, no. 3 (Summer 1966): 367–79.

40. William C. Wohlforth, "Unipolarity, Status Competition, and Great Power War," *World Politics* 61, no. 1 (January 2009): 28–57.

41. Bullion, "India and UN Peacekeeping Operations," p. 99.

42. David Malone, "Eyes on the Prize: The Quest for Nonpermanent Seats on the UN Security Council," *Global Governance* 6, no. 1 (January-March 2000): 3–23; Ian Hurd, "Legitimacy, Power, and the Symbolic Life of the UN Security Council," *Global Governance* 8, no. 1 (January-March 2002): 35–51.

43. Prem Shankar Jha, "India Must Think before It Acts on Syria," *Hindu*, August 7, 2012.

44. Virk, "India and the Responsibility to Protect," pp. 12–13.

45. Andrew F. Cooper and Thomas Fues, "Do the Asian Drivers Pull Their Diplomatic Weight? China, India, and the United Nations," *World Development* 36, no. 2 (2008): 297.

46. See, for example, Norman J. Padelford, "Politics and Change in the Security Council," *International Organization* 14, no. 3 (Summer 1960): 390.

47. Bardo Fassbender, "All Illusions Shattered? Looking Back on a Decade of Failed Attempts to Reform the UN Security Council," *Max Planck Yearbook of United Nations Law* 7 (2003): 186; Tad Daley, "Can the U.N. Stretch to Fit Its Future?" *Bulletin of the Atomic Scientists* (April 1992): 41.

48. UN Security Council Resolution 47/62, December 11, 1992.

49. Yehuda Z. Blum, "Proposals for UN Security Council Reform," *American Journal of International Law* 99, no. 3 (July 2005): 638.

50. J. Mohan Malik, "Security Council Reform: China Signals Its Veto," *World Policy Journal* 22, no. 1 (Spring 2005): 19–29.

51. Manmohan Singh, "India: The Next Global Superpower?" speech given in New Delhi, November 17, 2006, cited in Xenia Dormandy, "Is India, or Will it Be, a Responsible International Stakeholder?" *Washington Quarterly* 30, no. 3 (2007): 118–19. Emphasis added.

52. Cooper and Fues, "Do the Asian Drivers," p. 300.

53. Fassbender, "All Illusions Shattered?," p. 200.

54. Richard Gowan, "Indian Power and the United Nations," *World Politics Review* 15 (November 2010).

RICHARD GOWAN *and* SUSHANT K. SINGH

10

India and UN Peacekeeping: The Weight of History and a Lack of Strategy

Introduction

India's involvement in United Nations (UN) peacekeeping operations is one of its most visible contributions to the multilateral system. More than 100,000 Indian military and police personnel have served in forty of the UN's sixty-five peacekeeping missions, dating back to their inception in the 1950s. As of April 2013, India had 6,851 troops and 1,038 police officers under UN command, representing just less than 10 percent of all uniformed personnel in blue-helmet operations. These overall figures arguably underrepresent the importance of India in peacekeeping, as it offers the UN a range of specialized military assets—such as combat helicopters and field hospitals—that peacekeeping missions urgently need. Yet despite these contributions, there is a curious ambivalence around India's participation in UN peace operations.

For many Western commentators observing India's rise, its leading role in blue-helmet missions is an obvious opportunity to brand itself as a responsible power.[1] China has effectively publicized its involvement in UN operations as a sign of its growing capabilities and commitment to multilateralism, although in numerical terms it still lags behind Ghana and Uruguay as a troop contributor. Brazil has also invested heavily in UN operations, providing the military backbone for the high-profile mission in Haiti and more recently sending units to trouble spots such as Lebanon. But while India still has more personnel serving with the UN than Brazil and China combined, it has not received a comparable quantity of political capital out of its role. It has received good publicity for some of its individual deployments, such as the dispatch of an all-female police unit (the first of its type in a UN mission) to

Liberia in 2007. But it has had to fend off recurrent reports of corruption among Indian units, especially in the eastern Democratic Republic of Congo (DRC). Meanwhile, advocates of UN operations complain that Indian policymakers have not made major conceptual contributions to discussions about peacekeeping strategies. India used its temporary membership in the Security Council in 2011–12 to convene a debate on peacekeeping, but as we note below, this generated no new insights or ideas.

There has been a growth in studies of non-Western powers and peace operations in recent years, but researchers have often been frustrated by India's relatively cautious approach. "Although India is developing a well-articulated discourse on peacekeeping issues and is critical of the Security Council's working methods," Thierry Tardy argues, "it has not acquired political influence commensurate with its massive field presence, nor has it given any indication that it intends to do so."[2] Some commentators have concluded that this passive posture presages a gradual disengagement from UN operations.[3] There is an ongoing debate within India about whether continued engagement in peacekeeping is in line with its national security priorities and status as an aspiring first-class power. But, as this chapter argues, this debate has only had a marginal effect on actual policymaking to date. India has linked its continuing participation in UN missions to receiving more command positions. But significant constituencies in India remain broadly satisfied with the status quo. A recent study by the Stockholm International Peace Research Institute concludes that the Indian military still perceives "a strong intrinsic value in deploying troops to showcase India's growing force-projection capabilities."[4]

India has also adopted an equivocal approach to the principles and norms that guide peace operations. In diplomatic debates about peacekeeping at UN headquarters, Indian officials are stout defenders of long-standing mantras such as the primacy of state sovereignty and need to limit the use of force by UN troops. Yet in the field, Indian contingents have participated in robust operations, some of which have blurred the boundary between peacekeeping and peace enforcement. As Varun Vira has observed, Indian soldiers "fall into the very narrow bracket of troop contributing countries willing and able to act kinetically" and have been praised for "operating with unprecedented force" in the eastern DRC.[5] Tardy concludes that "pragmatism often prevails over ideology" for Indian officers operating in tough places.[6]

This mixture of pragmatism and principle complicates efforts to define India a "rule maker" or "rule taker" in the field of peace operations. In some contexts, such as diplomatic debates at the UN, Indian officials adopt the role of "rule defenders," standing up for concepts including state sovereignty that resonate strongly with its traditional allies in the Nonaligned Movement (NAM). India also specializes in critiquing how rules concerning peacekeeping are made and applied, especially in the Security Council, as a way of highlighting imbalances in the distribution of power at the UN. This chapter identifies a narrow focus on the control of peace operations as an essential characteristic of Indian diplomacy at the UN, but this focus centers on tactical processes rather than strategies. Yet in other contexts, such as the eastern DRC, Indian officials are "rule benders," calibrating their actions to handle threats.

This chapter argues that this mixture of defending and bending the rules of peacekeeping reflects both the history of Indian involvement in UN operations and its current position as an emergent global power. The history of Indian peacekeeping (both during the cold war and in the ensuing decades) is ambiguous and a source of both pride and discomfort. If few nations are so closely associated with blue-helmet operations, few have experienced the limitations of those operations as viscerally. India has the unhappy distinction of losing more personnel on UN missions than any other nation. Its commitment to peacekeeping has been complicated by its disputes with other countries—including not only Western powers but also African nations—over the behavior of its personnel abroad.

Yet its commitment is also filtered through questions about India's identity as a major power and its network of established diplomatic relationships, especially with other members of the NAM. The appearance of the NAM as a significant factor in this chapter may come as a surprise. Most studies of Indian foreign policy emphasize India's gradual distancing from the NAM, even if some officials such as Prime Minister Manmohan Singh retain affection for the movement. In this volume David Malone and Rohan Mukherjee argue, "India has gone from articulating an expansive 'third world' view of issues such as anti-colonialism and self-determination to defining its interests in terms beneficial to India alone."[7] Other recent studies confirm this view. Developing countries have increasingly been drawn toward China as an ally and potential leader in the UN system. This has complicated India's efforts to win a permanent seat on the Security Council, which China has aimed to disrupt. "Despite the claims that India has much goodwill among the NAM countries," Saurabh Mishra warns, "it cannot get consistent support from them."[8] Yet when it comes to the politics of peace operations, there are still reasons for the NAM to stick together. Around 80 percent of all personnel under UN command come from NAM countries. They retain common interests in how these personnel are commanded and financed, even though there are growing disparities between the quality of forces that India can deploy and those sent by poorer NAM states. Peacekeeping also gives India a chance to take a leadership role in UN politics, and it has continued to project itself as the champion of UN troop contributors as a bloc.

This is one reason why some Indian commentators believe that India should cut its ties with peacekeeping: it cannot be taken seriously as a standalone great power at the UN while it continues to act as a ringleader for developing countries, usually in opposition to established Western powers. Equally, those commentators who would like to see India play a bigger role in shaping the strategic future of peace operations would also like it to detach itself from the constraints of the NAM. Kabilan Krishnasamy argues, "Instead of constantly criticizing the UN for not formulating appropriate peacekeeping mandates in line with changing ground realities, India as a peacekeeper should think of engaging with the UN at higher levels, directly or indirectly."[9] As this chapter concludes, India has not been ready to make this break to date, and it is not clear if it will do so soon. Affected by the legacy of past operations and diplomatic ties, India's approach to peacekeeping is characterized by inertia.

The Weight of History

Advocates of a strong Indian presence in UN operations often cite India's first prime minister, Jawaharlal Nehru. In the words of Anit Mukherjee, "India's participation in peacekeeping operations began under an ideal that was propagated by Nehru and earned it global goodwill with the conduct of the Indian army in Korea, Gaza, and in numerous missions in Africa."[10] Dipankar Banerjee argues that Nehru perceived peacekeeping as one element of a broader effort to demonstrate that India is a "great country" with international responsibilities.[11] However, a focus on the initial Nehruvian logic for peacekeeping may distract from the actual history of India's participation in UN missions. This has been complicated by political disputes over the control of missions and threats to its troops.

C. Raja Mohan has recently argued that Indian peacekeeping can be traced to the "legacy of the Raj" and the role Indian troops played in pacifying other parts of the British Empire.[12] Nonetheless, Mohan also endorses the view that Nehru played a crucial role in adapting this legacy after independence, not least through his response to the Korean War. India supported the UN's strong response to North Korea's invasion of the south in 1950. Nehru was convinced that this was a well-planned aggression that threatened to unravel the fabric of the UN if it was not stopped. He declined to send combat troops to fight under UN command but provided a medical unit (60 Parachute Field Ambulance), which served from November 1950 to May 1954. The highlight of its deployment was Operation Tomahawk in March 1951, when Indian personnel provided medical support for an airborne operation launched by U.S. army parachute forces. Toward the end of the war, India played an important role in breaking a diplomatic deadlock over the fate of Korean prisoners of war held by both sides. At the end of the conflict, it took the chair of a repatriation commission and deployed a large "custodian force" for almost two years to manage repatriations.

India dispatched troops to the UN emergency force deployed after the Suez crisis in 1956.[13] The UN mission to the former Belgian Congo in the 1960s proved to be a much greater test of Indian forces, one that raised questions over the use of force by peacekeepers that still resonate today. India deployed up to 4,700 troops as part of a UN mission—the United Nations Operation in the Congo, or ONUC—in addition to several light bombers. Nehru saw this deployment as an opportunity to demonstrate India's commitment to decolonization, which not only had domestic resonance but also was a project at the heart of the UN's mission in its first decades. India advocated a robust interpretation of its mandate to use "force, if necessary, under the last resort" in the secessionist province of Katanga. Indian aircraft helped to enforce a no-fly zone, bombed an airfield held by Katangan forces (which included significant numbers of Western mercenaries), and provided close air support to ground forces. Nonetheless, the Congo operation created rifts in the UN as France and Britain tried to rein in ONUC, fearing that its actions might destabilize their remaining African colonies. India objected to efforts by the permanent Security Council members to set limits on the operation, foreshadowing more recent debates over the control of peace operations. The Indian ambassador to the UN mocked the Security Council's equivocations over ONUC's use of force, asking why it had not sent "engineers, scientists, parsons, and preachers" rather than 20,000 troops to create stability in the Congo.[14]

These early cold war experiments in peace operations thus had both positive and negative legacies for India. They offered opportunities for the recently independent country to assert itself on the world stage and, in the Congolese case, to demonstrate its commitment to decolonization. One Indian officer in particular, General Inderjit Rikhye, became synonymous with the UN's cold war era peacekeeping efforts. Having served in the Middle East, Rikhye acted as a military adviser at UN headquarters and found opportunities for the organization to engage in conflicts despite the political limitations of the cold war. (During the Cuban missile crisis he tabled plans for UN aircraft to monitor the Soviet withdrawal of nuclear weapons, which the Kennedy administration came close to accepting.)[15] Yet the disputes over ONUC left difficult lingering questions about India's status vis-à-vis the old colonial powers at the UN.

But if India's experience in UN operations had an ambiguous legacy, its experiments with non-UN-led operations also left scars. During the cold war, India came under external and internal pressure to take unilateral military action to stabilize its neighborhood. In 1971 it defeated Pakistan and brought about the birth of Bangladesh as an independent country. In 1988 India sent a small military force, at the request of the Maldivian president, to thwart a coup attempt by his military officers and mercenaries. But India's attempt to act unilaterally in Sri Lanka in the late 1980s ended in disaster. Nearly 70,000 Indian troops were in Sri Lanka as the Indian peacekeeping force between 1987 and 1990. The mission failed and led to the assassination of former prime minister Rajiv Gandhi by Tamil terrorists. After Sri Lanka, India has been extremely wary of acting unilaterally even within its own neighborhood, and Indian analysts often argue that India's attachment to UN operations is related to an engrained fear of repeating the debacle.[16]

Nonetheless, India's experience of UN operations after the cold war was also problematic.[17] An Indian general, Satish Nambiar, acted as the first commander of the ill-fated UN protection force (UNPROFOR) in the former Yugoslavia from 1992 to 1993. However, India decided not to contribute a substantial contingent to UNPROFOR because of concerns that, in the words of one Indian official, "European powers had a pernicious finger in the Yugoslav pie."[18] Nambiar resigned after being accused of being too cautious and pro-Serb—in the poisonous atmosphere surrounding a failing mission, he was even accused of equating the breakup of Yugoslavia with the partition of India and Bosnia with Pakistan. This did not stop India from deploying peacekeepers to Rwanda and Somalia in the mid-1990s, but further questions about its commitment were raised when twelve Indian personnel died in Somalia. India also suffered a surprise diplomatic defeat in a race with Japan for a nonpermanent seat on the Security Council in 1996. This raised doubts about the diplomatic benefits accruing from India's heavy investment in UN operations, and India did not make another bid for a council seat until 2010.

After Rwanda and Srebrenica, UN peacekeeping appeared to be finished. But it regained momentum from 1999 onward as the Security Council mandated ambitious new missions in Kosovo, Timor-Leste, and a series of African countries. One of the first of the UN's new African operations came in Sierra Leone, and this was the stage for a particularly calamitous episode in Indian peacekeeping. An Indian general, V. K. Jetley, initially commanded UNAMSIL—the UN mission there.[19] UNAMSIL almost collapsed in early 2000 in the face of a rebel offensive and had to be bailed out by a British intervention. Jetley was accused of having deployed his forces too thinly in advance of the crisis, although a joint British-Indian operation to rescue a contingent of more than 200 Indian troops who had been besieged by rebel forces for more than two months was a success. But Jetley's travails were not over. Nigeria and other governments in the region demanded the general's removal after the leak of a report in which he accused African military commanders in the mission of colluding with rebel forces to mine diamonds illegally. Jetley accused Nigerian units and other UNAMSIL contingents of disobeying orders. New Delhi saved face by recalling Jetley on a "routine" basis and withdrew its troops from UNAMSIL altogether.

The Burden of Responsibility

India did not, however, withdraw from UN operations altogether, and its forces began to play an increasingly significant and robust role in major operations, including in the DRC. As the UN force attempted to restore order in the east of the country, Indian forces, including attack helicopters, provided a significant part of its military capabilities. From 2000 to 2007, the number of troops under UN command grew rapidly, and the demand for specialized assets such as helicopters and field hospitals grew concomitantly. India played a major role in meeting these needs. As of early 2011, for example, India provided more attack and utility helicopters to UN missions than any other country (although the UN relies heavily on commercial transport helicopters). The Indian army also maintains a 4,000-strong Standby Brigade Group for UN missions with a comprehensive all-round capability. An infantry battalion is deployable in thirty days, and the rest of the brigade can follow within eight weeks.

By many estimates, therefore, India is now the "backbone" of UN peacekeeping.[20] But this is not an entirely easy status to enjoy. Because India is such an important part of the UN peacekeeping system, its decisions over the deployment of its forces are subject to particular scrutiny. The government of Manmohan Singh learned this to its cost when it decided to withdraw some helicopters from UN missions in the DRC and South Sudan in 2011 to address an overall shortage of military aircraft in India. While this was driven largely by practical considerations—the Comptroller and Auditor General (CAG) had concluded that the Indian air force lacked around a quarter of the helicopters it needed—some Western commentators interpreted it as a sign of waning interest in the UN.[21] Under pressure to demonstrate its continuing commitment to peacekeeping, India decided to keep some of the helicopters in UN service.

India's willingness to deploy troops to challenging theaters such as the eastern DRC and South Sudan also involves a significant degree of risk.[22] Indian troops have not always appeared fully prepared for these risks, despite the range of assets New Delhi has offered the UN. In August 2010 "a militia outfit armed with spears, machetes, and other weapons" managed to launch a surprise attack on an Indian base in the DRC, killing three troops and wounding seven.[23] This raised questions about the preparedness of peacekeepers in the DRC. The concerns were compounded when it emerged that hundreds of women had been raped near a UN base that was manned by eighty Indian personnel. A series of internal UN reports found that the unit lacked vehicles and communications equipment and had not conducted night patrols that might have helped to prevent the rapes and that "the troops had not undergone specific training regarding the protection of civilians and interaction with communities in the context of the Democratic Republic of the Congo."[24] Once the scale of the atrocities became clear, the peacekeepers stepped up patrols, although local leaders still complained that they only had intermittent contact. This episode raised troubling questions about whether the Indian army was preparing all of its peacekeepers sufficiently for operations in difficult and unfamiliar terrain. Equally, as Krishnasamy points out, there has been a "steady stream of complaints from troops on the ground" about the constraints the UN puts on Indian forces.[25]

There have also been persistent stories of misbehavior by Indian peacekeepers. Charges of sexual misconduct by Indian soldiers and officers deployed in the DRC have been investigated by an Indian army court of inquiry.[26] It is sometimes alleged that, compared to the discipline and governance that keep Indian soldiers in line at home, UN assignments have bred a permissive culture in which activities such as smuggling are tolerated.[27] The Indian government has insisted that many of the charges are trivial, and these issues have only gained sporadic attention in the national media. Nonetheless, these episodes underline a theme in the history of Indian contributions to peace operations: whatever ideals the country's commitment to the UN serves, its deployments have often been costly and controversial.

Looking for Strategic Logic

Past and present costs and controversies may help to explain why India has not been as bold in presenting ideas about the strategic future of peacekeeping as some commentators might like. The experience of repeated political rifts and public criticism of Indian personnel—notably including senior generals—is a disincentive for innovative strategic thinking. To some extent India is trapped between two versions of its history as a peacekeeper. Its positive contributions to UN operations in Korea and the Congo (both in the 1960s and more recently) provide strong precedents for engagement. Yet its negative experiences in cases including the former Yugoslavia and Sierra Leone have left Indian officials skeptical of how the UN runs its missions. This skepticism has shaped recent Indian diplomacy over peace operations at the UN, which has focused on how missions are *controlled*. The issue of control links to the overall theme of this volume: whether India has acted as rule shaper, rule breaker, or rule taker in multilateral affairs. The next section of this chapter addresses this question by probing Indian diplomacy concerning peacekeeping in the UN system. But readers may wonder whether this approach is too narrow. While the UN provides a mechanism to mandate and manage peace operations, countries do not necessarily get involved in blue-helmet operations simply to keep diplomats in New York busy. To understand Brazil's engagement in peacekeeping in Haiti, for example, it is necessary to look not only at Brazil's behavior at the UN (where, like India, it has been an articulate and persistent critic of the way Western powers oversee missions from the Security Council) but also its far broader strategy for building up influence in its wider neighborhood. Similarly, South Africa has been an important player in UN peacekeeping in Africa, but this is part of a broader strategy for building up its regional leverage, which also involves working through the African Union and bilaterally.

So if we really want to understand India's political stake in UN peace operations, it is necessary to ask if this stake is part of a grander strategy. But if any such strategy exists, it is distinctly hard to identify. Unlike Brazil and South Africa, India has not concentrated its primary peacekeeping efforts in its own neighborhood. Indeed, it is deeply ambivalent about the UN's role in South Asia. It permitted but also set clear limits on a UN civilian mission to facilitate the end of monarchical rule in Nepal and maneuvered to ensure that the UN did not intervene effectively in the final stages of Sri Lanka's civil war. It has also taken a skeptical approach to the UN presence in Afghanistan and ensured that the organization has played no substantive role in the Kashmir dispute since the 1970s (New Delhi effectively ignores the UN peacekeeping operation in Kashmir altogether). India's peacekeeping deployments typically make little or no contribution to its national security or even its main security relationships.

The one possible exception to this is the maintenance of a battalion in the UN interim force in Lebanon (UNIFIL), India's largest contribution to a UN mission outside Africa. By keeping troops in Lebanon, New Delhi sends a reassuring signal to Israel, with which it has a far broader security relationship. There is often speculation that the Indian UNIFIL contingent is a source of information for Israeli intelligence. And since 2006, when a large number of European troops deployed to UNIFIL after the war in southern Lebanon, this has also been a theater in which Indian personnel can gain experience of working alongside North Atlantic Treaty Organization forces. But these benefits are specific to UNIFIL and do not apply to other operations.

Why, therefore, does India keep up its wider contributions to UN forces? One answer, found in official Indian policy statements, is that doing so keeps alive some of the Nehruvian ideals associated with cold war peacekeeping. We have already seen that this is based on a rather rosy telling of India's history in peacekeeping. But it is increasingly difficult to justify missions on the basis of these old ideals. When India sent troops to ONUC in the 1960s, for example, the logic of defending decolonization was clear. But its more recent participation in UN missions in the eastern DRC (MONUC and MONUSCO) cannot be based on the same justification. The DRC is undeniably still suffering the long-term effects of colonial rule, but its instability is also tied to regional interference and the weakness of the government in Kinshasa. President Joseph Kabila, who has relied heavily on UN support, has looked to China for economic patronage and criticized Indian peacekeepers for not taking a sufficiently aggressive approach to his opponents. At one point Kabila declared that he wanted no more Indian troops on his soil, and American diplomats reported that the "government officials paid crowds to hurl stones at the Indian peacekeepers."[28] The United States forced Kabila to back down. But under such circumstances, it is difficult to argue that India's continued participation in the UN force in the DRC is really in the service of an ideal.

An alternative explanation for India's behavior is that it is a mechanism to advance economic interests. Indian officials sometimes explicitly make this case in private. But it is not entirely convincing. Indian entrepreneurs have invested heavily in Africa, where the bulk of Indian peacekeepers are deployed. But it is hard to identify cases where UN troops have been specifically sent to safeguard Indian interests. In cases including Sierra Leone and the DRC, frictions around Indian deployments have arguably reduced local goodwill rather than increased it. India has a wide range of defense relationships with African states that go beyond peacekeeping and offer it greater leverage. As W. P. S. Sidhu notes, there is no clearly articulated Indian national strategy for economic peacebuilding in fragile states.[29] In 2012 Manmohan Singh visited Africa to offer new aid and investment. In doing so, he offered a small donation ($2 million) to support the African Union peace operation in Somalia, but did not make any similar gestures tied to blue-helmet operations. Overall, the economic rationale for Indian peacekeeping is weak.

By contrast, the Indian military sees "intrinsic value" in continued engagement in UN missions. But the argument that Indian deployments "showcase India's growing force-projection capabilities" is only partially satisfying. As we have seen, some Indian units in the DRC appear to have been underprepared and poorly equipped. This does not suggest that they were deliberately deployed to showcase Indian capabilities. At best, it can be argued that *some* Indian units—such as the attack helicopters in the DRC and female police officers in Liberia—provide useful advertisements for India's growing strength. Meanwhile, the Indian military has no need to send troops on foreign missions to expose them to life in an active operation, which is one reason that China has been interested in UN missions. Indian units can get all the experience they need closer to home on the border with Pakistan.

Some critics charge that India is interested mainly in peacekeeping as a source of financial gain.[30] In the past, income from UN peacekeeping duties was a source of hard currency when India was starved of foreign exchange. With foreign exchange reserves at nearly $300 billion, this is no longer valid. In fact, India's CAG contends that the national treasury now makes net losses for its deployment of men and equipment in UN operations. A recent study by the Center on International Cooperation highlighted particular uncertainties involving the reimbursement rate for helicopters deployed with the UN, which is worked out through a complex and unpredictable calculation of flight hours.[31] The growing "reimbursement gap" for helicopters has been a source of growing frustration to India and other states. We note in the next section that India has recently been active in efforts to improve the rates of reimbursement for peacekeeping units more generally, but this is of declining importance to the army.

This does not mean that peacekeeping is not of interest to members of the Indian armed forces. Indian soldiers are selected for UN assignments through a competitive process, and the slots are much sought after (Indian units on

UN missions have up to three times as many officers attached to them as they would at home, indicating how popular these assignments are). Besides the professional challenge of operating in unusual environments, additional financial remuneration also makes these assignments attractive for the soldiers. UN assignments also provide relief to soldiers after periods deployed in some of the harshest terrains, such as the Siachen Glacier, or after undertaking counterinsurgency operations in Jammu and Kashmir. Yet there are also signs of growing frustration among Indian officers about the limitations imposed by UN rules and regulations. As Indian forces grow more capable, they are likely to become increasingly skeptical of the benefits of UN service.

For now, it seems safe to say that the Indian military has a continuing interest in UN operations but that this is as much a product of habit or inertia as the result of conscious strategic choices. This may be an example of the "normative power of the status quo": the fact that individuals and bureaucracies assume that existing activities and routines are axiomatically positive. But while the benefits of peacekeeping for the Indian military are debatable, the country's status as a peacekeeper is still of diplomatic value for its representatives in New York. Having looked hard for a strategic logic beyond diplomatic routines for India's role in UN operations—and come up with at best somewhat convincing alternatives—we now return to the realm of multilateral diplomacy.

Diplomatic Dynamics

How do Indian diplomats view the making and breaking of rules concerning peacekeeping at the UN? The "rules" of peace operations are not set by a single arbiter, but in multiple forums. The basic directions for individual missions come from the Security Council. But missions are also shaped by budgetary discussions in the Fifth Committee of the General Assembly, while the systems and norms of peacekeeping are debated by a Special Committee on Peacekeeping Operations (colloquially known as the "Committee of the 34" or "C34") that is open to all states. Most of the C34's deliberations are prolonged yet pointless, but troop-contributing countries have more direct means of controlling events on the ground by placing caveats on the use of their forces or threatening to withdraw them altogether. As Gowan and his coauthors have argued, these options give major troop contributors such as India an "effective veto" over how operations function (Nigeria's insistence that General Jetley stand down as commander as UNAMSIL in 2000 is an example of this de facto veto).[32]

Meanwhile, the UN secretary general and his special representatives and UN force commanders maintain day-to-day direction over operations. India has recognized the leverage of these positions for some time, having sent a series of senior officers to the post of military adviser to the secretary general (at the time of writing in early 2013, a Senegalese officer holds this post, but he has an Indian deputy).

There is constant competition between the different actors and forums for control over peacekeeping. This competition involves not only writing the generic rules shaping operations but also making hard choices about actual forces on the ground, although the two can become blurred. India has often been at the center of tensions between the Security Council and the NAM in the General Assembly over how missions are managed. Thierry Tardy notes that there have been particularly intense debates between Western countries and the NAM—played out in the C34—over the level of force that peacekeepers can and should use. The NAM "expressed huge resistance" to proposals to make operations more robust: "Beyond the suspicion of a neocolonialist agenda behind increasingly intrusive peace operations, the argumentation put forward by the NAM group reflected genuine concerns about unrealistic developments in peacekeeping."[33] Close observers spotted a few hints of Indian flexibility on this issue, but ultimately Indian officials remained firmly on the side of its established NAM partners. Tardy highlights some of the practical and normative concerns affecting the NAM's positions, but they clearly are affected by concerns over the balance of power in the UN. While the Security Council has become increasingly willing to mandate robust peace operations since the cold war—a trend driven largely by the United States and its European counterparts, above all France and the United Kingdom—troop contributors such as India have feared that they are losing control over their units under UN command.

India continues to side with the NAM partly out of a desire to halt this loss of control. This raises difficult questions about India's attitudes to the rules around peacekeeping. In trying to block dramatic change, it is arguably defending one set of rules about peace operations against Western efforts to assert a new set of rules on issues such as the use of force. Tardy observes that India and the other BRIC countries (Brazil, Russia, and China) share this disposition and "advocate a 'light footprint' approach rather than a heavier approach that risks generating dependence; insist on local ownership and the responsibilities of the host state; and warn against transplanting models from one region to another."[34] As we have already observed, there are significant differences between these principles and realities in the field, and India has been the prime enabler of the UN's "heavy" approach in cases such as the DRC. Nonetheless, this sort of rhetoric provides a framework for India and other members of the NAM to resist Western efforts to rewrite the rules of peacekeeping through the Security Council.

But there is an irony here, as one of the most frequently stated reasons for India's continued contributions to UN operations is to strengthen its own claim to a permanent seat on the Security Council. Satish Nambiar, a trenchant defender of Indian participation in UN operations despite his experiences in the Balkans, argues that, through peacekeeping, "We must develop a stake in strengthening the Security Council setup, and such missions help do just that."[35] Paradoxically, India's role in peace operations still ties it to the non-Western states that make up the NAM, yet it is simultaneously meant to be a ticket to an elite status in the Security Council. How can India resolve this dilemma?

Western officials have long hoped that they could wean India away from the NAM, even if Security Council reform remains a distant hope. The United States has maintained a strategic dialogue with India on peacekeeping for almost a decade. The Obama administration and European Union members have made a point of courting India in an effort to develop better cooperation over peacekeeping. In some statements, Indian officials appear to have softened their line on peacekeeping principles—such as the use of force—in response to these overtures, but the shifts are very subtle indeed. India remains in the NAM camp.

In 2008–09, for example, India played an important role in demanding better consultations between troop contributors and the Security Council over the mandates for operations. This debate was overshadowed by a major crisis in the Congo in 2008, when militia forces outmaneuvered UN troops—displacing 200,000 Congolese civilians—and Indian units were widely accused of underperforming. India rotated in new contingents, but pushed back against criticism by accusing Western countries of failing to send their own troops to the DRC, arguing that it had been insufficiently consulted on the use of its troops in Congo and warning in private that it might even withdraw from UN operations altogether.

This diplomatic drive had some impact. The Security Council agreed to improve consultations with troop contributors on issues such as the renewal of mandates affecting their forces. This was generally agreed to be a success in procedural terms, although diplomats complain that the discussions are rarely substantive. The UN Secretariat also offered India a greater share of command posts in operations. The number of Indian officials in UN senior posts—such as that of force commander in the DRC—has increased in recent years only by a limited amount. As of early 2013, no Indian national was serving as the special representative of the secretary general in charge of a peace operation.

A bigger test for India came in 2011 and 2012, when it held a temporary seat on the Security Council for the first time since 1992. At the start of its term, there were expectations that its tenure would be dominated by peacekeeping issues, including crises in Côte d'Ivoire and Sudan. In reality, its time on the council was overshadowed by events in Libya and Syria, as Malone and Mukherjee describe in this volume. Peacekeeping issues did, however, still take up a good deal of the council's agenda. In March 2011 the council voted unanimously to mandate UN forces in Côte d'Ivoire to use force to defend civilians against attacks by heavy weapons as postelectoral violence worsened. India supported this, but its ambassador at the UN, Hardeep Singh Puri, warned, "Peacekeepers could not be agents of regime change."[36] He also returned to the procedural issues that India had highlighted about consulting with troop contributors, complaining about "the growing tendency to hurry adoption of resolutions." This indicated that, although now a member of the Security Council, India had not forgotten its NAM friends.

This perception was reinforced in August 2011, when India used the first of two turns as president of the Security Council to convene a thematic debate on peacekeeping. Here was a brief—if largely symbolic—opportunity to act as a rule shaper about peacekeeping by proposing new initiatives or principles. But the concept note prepared by the Indian mission for this debate returned to troop contributors' worries:

> The direct knowledge that troop- and police-contributing countries obtain of ground realities and their considerable experience in peacekeeping need to be factored into the decision-making process of the Security Council. It is also evident that the Council requires greater access to information in its vastly increased scope of functioning. Troop- and police-contributing countries, many of whom have not just troops but diplomatic presence, technical and economic cooperation activities, and sometimes a civil society or commercial presence in the field, are uniquely suited to provide credible and relevant information.[37]

The note then dug even deeper into diplomatic procedures:

> There has been progress in improving the consultations process but there is scope for forward movement in order to fully exploit the potential of this relationship. Consultative meetings should be structured and

predictable, in terms of timing and agenda. This will enable troop- and police-contributing countries to optimize their substantive contributions.

The concept note did raise other issues, including the shortage of resources affecting UN operations. Yet much of its analysis of the "rapid changes" under way in peacekeeping was a restatement of existing analysis of the state of UN operations. Analysts in New Delhi complained about this "not-so-impressive" debate, comparing its position unfavorably with the contributions of smaller Security Council members: "For a nation that has demonstrated impressive credentials with regard to peacekeeping, India's stand lacked teeth when compared to Guatemala's statement."[38] It would be a mistake to judge the debate too harshly: Security Council discussions of thematic issues in August are rarely intellectual treats, and New York was bracing for a hurricane just as the ambassadors met, which was presumably a distraction. More generally, India needed to be careful to satisfy the majority of members of the UN, as it had spent much of 2011 campaigning for a General Assembly resolution endorsing its vision of Security Council reform. This campaign had lost traction by August 2011, but India had no need to alienate the NAM.

Nonetheless, the Indian approach to peacekeeping reinforced two themes: its overriding focus on the *control* of peacekeeping forces and its tendency to identify more closely with troop contributors from the developing world rather than the big powers alongside it in the Security Council. In 2011 India also clashed with Western countries at the UN over the reimbursement rate for peacekeepers. India and other troop contributors argued that the reimbursement rate (which had been stuck at $1,028 per soldier per month since 2002) be increased 57 percent. The United States and European Union, responsible for paying most of the money involved, resisted fiercely. After a poisonous argument, the General Assembly agreed to raise the rate by just 7 percent for one year and appoint a Special Advisory Group (SAG) to discuss the issue further in 2012. India became a prime player in the SAG discussions, which generated a consensus report on better ways to fund peace operations in 2012. India negotiated on behalf of troop-contributing countries with counterparts from the United Kingdom and the United States, and the SAG arguably provided a better platform for India to show leadership on peacekeeping than the Security Council. Still, India had broadly failed to use its time on the council to shape the strategies affecting peace operations.

Conclusion

This chapter has made three basic arguments concerning India's approach to peace operations. First, Indian policy has been conditioned by a very mixed history of engagement in UN missions, which has taught policymakers to be very wary of how missions are run by the UN. Second, while India continues to maintain its contributions to the UN (despite occasional threats to pull out if it does not gain sufficient respect), it does so more out of habit than to fulfill any strategic goal. Third, these historical concerns and a lack of grand vision have led Indian diplomacy over peacekeeping to focus more on how missions are controlled than on what they can achieve in broader strategic terms. Indeed, the politics of the UN system pushes India to adopt highly conservative postures on many issues concerning peace operations to maintain a common front with other troop contributors from the NAM.

This is in spite of the fact that Western powers, including the United States, have consciously bid to develop an alternative relationship with India over peacekeeping. India has engaged in numerous dialogues with its Western counterparts but has not yet been willing to sacrifice its existing relationships with non-Western states. In part because of India's caution, political debates about the rules of peacekeeping at the UN often seem to emanate from another era, in which the cold war and NAM are still to the fore. In the meantime, Indian forces are willing to behave pragmatically in the field to handle actual challenges. But the longer the division between diplomacy in New York and realities on the ground persists, the greater it will become—and this may eventually prove a politically unsustainable dynamic.

What direction should India take with regard to peacekeeping? The authors of this chapter have distinctively different answers. Gowan believes that India should take the risk of breaking with the NAM for an enhanced dialogue with other big powers about future operations—boosting its status as a rule shaper.[39] Singh believes that the strategic vacuum around Indian peacekeeping requires a more radical response and that New Delhi should withdraw the bulk of its blue helmets, leaving only small contingents in strategically significant missions.[40] Although these are very different conclusions, they stem from a shared concern: India's contributions to the UN must be calibrated to meet future challenges rather than continue to be dictated by an often proud but sometimes uneasy history of peacekeeping.

Notes

1. Richard Gowan, "Peacekeeping: India's Chance to Lead," *Pragati* 37 (April 1, 2010); Thierry Tardy, "Emerging Powers and Peacekeeping: An Unlikely Normative Clash," GCSP Policy Paper 2012/3 (Geneva: Geneva Centre for Security Policy, 2012); Frank van Rooyen, "Blue Helmets for Africa: India's Peacekeeping in Africa," SAIIA Occasional Paper 60 (Johannesburg: South African Institute of International Affairs, May 2010).

2. Thierry Tardy, "Peace Operations: The Fragile Consensus," in *SIPRI Yearbook 2011* (Oxford University Press, 2011), pp. 106–07.

3. Nitin Pai and Sushant K. Singh, "Bring the Troops Back," *Indian Express*, July 10, 2008.

4. Sharon Wiharta, Neil Melvin, and Xenia Avezov, *The New Geopolitics of Peace Operations* (Stockholm: Stockholm International Peace Research Institute, 2012), p. 14.

5. Varun Vira, "India and UN Peacekeeping: Declining Interest with Grave Implications," *Small Wars Journal* (online), July 13, 2013.

6. Tardy, "Peace Operations," p. 106.

7. See chapter 9 by David M. Malone and Rohan Mukherjee in this volume.

8. Saurabh Mishra, "India amidst Increased Activity in the Security Council: A Few Observations," *Strategic Analysis* 36, no. 2 (2012): 202.

9. Kabilan Krishnasamy, "A Case for India's 'Leadership' in United Nations Peacekeeping," *International Studies* 47, no. 2-4 (2010): 242.

10. Anit Mukherjee, "Keep the Troops There," *Indian Express*, July 12, 2008.

11. Dipankar Banerjee, "India," in *Providing Peacekeepers*, edited by Alex J. Bellamy and Paul D. Williams (Oxford University Press, 2013), p. 227.

12. C. Raja Mohan, *India and International Peace Operations*, SIPRI Insight on Peace and Security 2013/3 (Stockholm: Stockholm International Peace Research Institute, 2013).

13. For further details on India's early commitment to peacekeeping, see Banerjee, "India," pp. 229–30.

14. Cited by Vira, "India and UN Peacekeeping."

15. David G. Coleman, *The Fourteenth Day* (New York: Norton, 2012), p. 53.

16. See P. R. Chari, "The IPKF Experience in Sri Lanka," ACDIS Occasional Paper (University of Illinois at Champaign-Urbana, Program in Arms Control, Disarmament, and International Security, 1994).

17. This paragraph draws on Alan James Bullion, "India," in *The Politics of Peacekeeping in the Post–Cold War Era*, edited by David S. Sorenson and Pia Christina Wood (Abingdon: Cass, 2005), p. 196ff.

18. Krishnasamy, "A Case for India's 'Leadership,'" p. 231.

19. This paragraph draws on Adekeye Adebajo and David Keen, "Sierra Leone," in *United Nations Interventionism, 1991–2004,* edited by Mats Berdal (Cambridge University Press, 2007), p. 246ff.

20. Wiharta, Melvin, and Avezov, *The New Geopolitics of Peace Operations*, p. 13.

21. Colum Lynch, "India Threatens to Pull Plug on Peacekeeping," *Foreign Policy* (online), June 14, 2011.

22. "Five Indian Soldiers Die as Rebels Ambush Convoy in South Sudan," *Hindu*, April 10, 2013.

23. "3 Indian Peacekeepers Killed in Congo," *Times of India*, August 19, 2010.

24. UN Joint Human Rights Office, "Final Report of the Fact-Finding Missions of the United Nations Joint Human Rights Office into the Mass Rapes and Other Human Rights Violations Committed by a Coalition of Armed Groups along the Kibua-Mpofu Axis in Walikale Territory, North Kivu, from 30 July to 2 August 2010" (Geneva: MONUSCO/OHCHR, July 2011), p. 10.

25. Krishnasamy, "A Case for India's 'Leadership,'" p. 226.

26. Bally Mutumayi, Ashish Kumar Sen, and Saikat Datta, "The Peacekeeper's Child," *Outlook*, August 8, 2011 (www.outlookindia.com/article.aspx?277848).

27. Omair Ahmad, "Rotting Olives," *Outlook*, June 2, 2008 (www.outlookindia.com/article.aspx?237577).

28. Cited by Lynch, "India Threatens to Pull Plug."

29. W. P. S. Sidhu, '"India's Evolving Role in Development and Security in States at Risk," in *Engagement on Development and Security: New Actors, New Debates,* edited by Jake Sherman, Megan Gleason, W. P. S. Sidhu, and Bruce D. Jones (New York: Center on International Cooperation, 2011), p. 23.

30. For a more detailed deconstruction of the financial benefits of Indian peacekeeping, see Banerjee, "India," pp. 240–42.

31. Jake Sherman, Alischa Kugel, and Andrew Sinclair, "Overcoming Helicopter Force Generation Challenges for UN Peacekeeping Operations," *International Peacekeeping* 18, no.1 (2012): 84–88.

32. Bruce D. Jones, Richard Gowan, and Jake Sherman, *Building on Brahimi: Peacekeeping in an Era of Strategic Uncertainty* (New York: Center on International Cooperation, April 2009), p. 18.

33. Tardy, "Peace Operations," p. 94.

34. Ibid., p. 100.

35. Quoted in Bullion, "India," pp. 202–03.

36. See UN Document SC/10215 (March 30, 2011).

37. See UN Document S/2011/496 (August 8, 2011).

38. Keerthi Sampath Kumar and Saurabh Mishra, "India's Presidency in the UN Security Council: An Evaluation" (New Delhi: Institute for Defense Studies and Analysis, September 19, 2011) (www.idsa.in/idsacomments/IndiasPresidencyintheUNSecurityCouncil_kskumar_190911).

39. Gowan, "Peacekeeping."

40. Pai and Singh, "Bring the Troops Back."

RAJESH RAJAGOPALAN

11

From Defensive to Pragmatic Multilateralism and Back: India's Approach to Multilateral Arms Control and Disarmament

Introduction

In the early days of India's independence, Prime Minister Jawaharlal Nehru, the architect of India's foreign policy, hoped that India would guide the world toward a more cooperative order in which multilateral discussion and debate would help to resolve international disputes. In a recent book, the historian Manu Bhagavan goes so far as to suggest that Nehru placed his faith in an eventual global government, "One World," and pushed his diplomats at the United Nations (UN) to pursue this ideal.[1] Nehru's multilateralist streak did not always benefit India: his decision to take the Kashmir dispute to the UN effectively internationalized the dispute in a manner that Nehru did not expect.

This tension between the multilateralist instinct and international political realities is a feature found in much of Nehru's global foreign policy, nowhere more so than in India's nuclear arms control and disarmament policy. The contradictory pulls between liberal notions of the benefits of multilateralism and the loss of control that any multilateral venture necessarily threatens lead to somewhat paradoxical and inconsistent policies. Hence India's traditional approach to multilateralism in arms control and disarmament has been defensive. It has primarily sought to protect India from ambitious multilateral arms control efforts that could potentially reduce India's military capacities or options. This has reflected India's natural incapacity to shape multilateral arms control and disarmament efforts to protect or promote Indian interests. Multilateral arms control efforts were often perceived as not just a nuisance but also as serious threat to Indian interests, requiring India's participation.

Has this traditional approach changed? Although India's attitudes in the aftermath of the 1998 nuclear tests moved toward a more "pragmatic multilateralism," the change was temporary and determined largely by two factors: initially, the need to mollify global partners, particularly the United States, and, second, a response to the opportunity of exploiting the Indo-U.S. nuclear deal. Over the last few years, since the major elements of the Indo-U.S. nuclear deal were concluded, India's arms control has backtracked toward the more traditional defensiveness. In this chapter, India's approach is characterized as "defensive multilateralism," suggesting a posture that is wary, almost suspicious, of specific multilateral efforts on arms control, while supporting multilateralism in the abstract. As a relatively weak state in the global system, India derives some benefits from multilateralism, including a voice in the deliberations of rules that affect its self-interest. But colonial history and more recent experience have also made India suspicious of the outcomes of such multilateral rule making.

This chapter is divided into four sections. The first briefly characterizes Indian behavior with regard to rule making in the multilateral arms control area. The next three deal with the evolution, drivers, and implications of India's multilateralism in this area; of these, the second briefly outlines the evolution of India's approach to multilateral arms control measures, tracing some of the changes in Indian attitudes since 1998. The third addresses six major drivers of India's multilateral approach to disarmament and arms control. The fourth outlines the implications for multilateral arms control efforts, specifically in three active policy areas where these implications are likely to be most visible: the Treaty on the Non-Proliferation of Nuclear Weapons (NPT), the Fissile Material Cut-Off Treaty (FMCT), and the resolution of the deadlock in the Conference on Disarmament (CD). India's intervention in these multilateral efforts is unlikely to be consequential because multilateral arms control efforts face significant other challenges.

India as a Rule Blocker?

It would be difficult to fit India into the broad threefold categorization used in this volume: rule maker, rule taker, and rule breaker. On the one hand, with the exception of proposals for nuclear disarmament, which can be seen as a form of "rule making," India has rarely attempted to lead the global community in setting new norms or rules with regard to nuclear arms control and disarmament. On the other hand, India has only rarely been accused of violating existing rules, making it difficult to characterize India as a "rule breaker."

There have been accusations that India imported heavy water to make up for shortfalls in its heavy water production, for example.[2] More recently, India's atomic agency was accused of having poor information security by revealing too much design information through its tendering process.[3] Most observers would agree with the overall judgment of David Albright and Susan Basu about India's nonproliferation record: India was not a "determined proliferator," which makes it difficult to characterize India as a "rule breaker."[4]

Finally, it is difficult to characterize India fully as a "rule taker" either. Although Indian officials repeatedly claimed, especially in the context of the debate over the Indo-U.S. nuclear deal, that India was a "responsible" nuclear power, this referred more to India's record in not transferring its nuclear technology to other states. The distinction being drawn was with Pakistan, which allowed the Abdul Qadeer Khan nuclear black market to flourish for decades.[5] But even while stridently campaigning for comprehensive nuclear disarmament, India has repeatedly refused to be drawn into global multilateral nuclear arms control regimes. India took part in the negotiations over the NPT in the 1960s, but in the end chose not to join it and has since been a strong critic of the treaty and its associated norms. Similarly, despite campaigning for more than four decades for a nuclear test ban treaty and joining the negotiations over the Comprehensive Test Ban Treaty (CTBT), India stood alone against it. In both cases, India had solid national security reasons for doing so: India worried about China's nuclear capability throughout the 1960s, but sought nuclear guarantees from global powers rather than build its own arsenal.[6] But while Indian decisionmakers were loath to build nuclear weapons, they were also reluctant to give up the option of building nuclear weapons should the situation warrant it, forcing them into the position of not joining the NPT while also refusing to proliferate nuclear weapons. In the case of the CTBT, Indian leaders similarly waffled until the treaty was upon them and then refused to sign because giving up the right to test would have put India in a position of permanent strategic disadvantage vis-à-vis China, which had conducted more than four dozen nuclear tests. India's reluctance to join these major multilateral arms control measures makes it difficult to characterize it as a rule taker either.

The best way to characterize India is as a "rule blocker" because India has repeatedly sought to prevent the making of new rules that might limit its security choices. Whether with regard to nuclear nonproliferation or the CTBT or the Landmine Ban Treaty, India has actively objected to and refused to join several multilateral arms control measures.

The Evolution of India's Multilateralism

India's experience with multilateral arms control and disarmament has been very mixed. Two types of multilateral engagements can be discerned with regard to India's approach—defensive and pragmatic multilateralism. India's multilateral engagements with nuclear disarmament represent an entirely different type (utopian multilateralism). However, since this has been a limited exercise of floating proposals rather than participating in actual negotiations, it is examined only briefly here.

Nuclear Disarmament: Utopian Multilateralism?

India has consistently pursued a nuclear disarmament agenda since its independence. Indian leaders, including Mahatma Gandhi and Jawaharlal Nehru, had expressed opposition to the use of nuclear technology for military purposes even before independence. After independence, nuclear disarmament became a signature element in Prime Minister Nehru's larger vision for a more peaceful global order. Nehru's call in 1954 for a nuclear test ban was proposed as a step in the direction of nuclear disarmament. Throughout the 1950s, Nehru consistently called for a negotiated end to the nuclear arms race.

Nevertheless, India's emphasis on multilateral nuclear disarmament was fairly nuanced: although India actively campaigned for nuclear disarmament, it was particular about the process through which multilateral nuclear disarmament would work. India was unwilling to accept multilateral efforts that potentially threatened its own nuclear program, which was still in its infancy. For example, India opposed the Baruch Plan, which the United States proposed as a means of both eliminating nuclear weapons and controlling nuclear material and technology, because it would have required India to submit its considerable thorium reserves to international control and potentially limit its nuclear development plans.[7]

In addition, India's multilateral diplomacy tended to be less than evenhanded, leaning toward Moscow and irritating Washington. The Soviet Union supported India's call for terminating nuclear tests; when the Soviet Union resumed nuclear testing in 1961, India took a sanguine view of Soviet behavior.[8] This imbalance probably gave Indian multilateral disarmament diplomacy less credibility than it might otherwise have had, although this was a minor issue compared to the unwillingness of both the United States and the Soviet Union to treat disarmament proposals as anything other than propaganda.[9]

Since the 1950s India has proposed negotiated but time-bound nuclear disarmament. De-legitimization of nuclear weapons and a nuclear test ban were seen as early steps in this process, which India put forward several times in the 1970s and 1980s. This would eventually become established in a formal and detailed proposal as the Rajiv Gandhi Action Plan for Nuclear Disarmament. The Rajiv Gandhi plan was a detailed multiple-decade, multiple-step plan that would begin with gradual confidence-building measures and eventually lead to nuclear disarmament, on the way to general disarmament and a more just world order. However, it suffered the vicissitudes of domestic political changes in India: after Rajiv Gandhi, the plan disappeared from Indian proposals, although it has recently been resuscitated by the Congress-led United Progressive Alliance government.[10]

What is most notable about India's nuclear disarmament proposals is their lack of any mooring in international political reality, but this is something that they share with similar proposals from other capitals. In addition, the multilateralism of these early proposals is suspect because there was nothing particularly "multilateral" about them. Indeed, many of these proposals were not even made in a multilateral setting, being made in press statements or in the Indian Parliament. Moreover, with the exception of Nehru's nuclear test ban proposal, most Indian interventions were more aspirational than programmatic. The Rajiv Gandhi proposal did set out in great detail a timetable for multilateral negotiations that were to lead to nuclear disarmament, but it was deployed with little concern about the international political context, which explains its lukewarm reception. Moreover, India does not appear to have pushed the Rajiv Gandhi plan much in multilateral forums, as the committee set up to reactivate the plan pointed out in its recent report. A subsequent effort, the Indian 2006 working paper on nuclear disarmament, was somewhat less elaborate, but equally ambitious, starting with acceptance of the idea of nuclear disarmament and ending with the total elimination of nuclear weapons.[11]

Over the last decade, India has consistently supported the idea of a nuclear weapons convention. Although India has placed great emphasis on this idea, it is unclear how India would proceed if an actual convention were to materialize because, as in the case of the NPT and the CTBT, very little assessment appears to have been done on the consequences of such a convention. Nuclear disarmament (and a nuclear weapons convention) is more an article of faith than a policy. How it would meet the test of multilateral negotiation remains to be seen.

Defensive Multilateralism

Defensive multilateralism characterized India's approach to multilateral arms control efforts from the late 1960s until the Pokhran 2 nuclear tests in 1998.

Multilateral arms control efforts began seriously with expansion of the Ten-Nation Committee on Disarmament into the Eighteen-Nation Committee on Disarmament (ENCD) with the inclusion of developing states. India played a major role in the deliberations of the ENCD, especially with regard to a nuclear test ban as well as nuclear proliferation. But India's efforts were not particularly fruitful, with New Delhi finding itself suddenly on the defensive because of how the NPT was finally framed. The consequence was a dramatic reduction in India's involvement in continuing multilateral arms control issues at the ENCD and a growing wariness about such multilateralism.[12]

As the NPT began to gather more adherents and the regime tightened, India's options declined. India's situation became even more constrained as the CTBT was concluded, further limiting India's strategic choices. However, India's Pokhran 2 nuclear tests and India's increasingly energetic economy changed the situation, offering India more choices as global powers sought to engage with it.

The Shift to Pragmatic Multilateralism

"Pragmatic multilateralism," another type of multilateral engagement with arms control and disarmament, characterized India's approach in the decade after the 1998 nuclear tests. Immediately after the tests, India announced a moratorium on nuclear tests and proposed multilateral measures to reduce the nuclear danger, including de-alerting and nontargeting of nuclear weapons, prohibiting the first use of nuclear weapons and their use against non-nuclear powers, and reducing the salience of nuclear weapons in military strategies. Most of these multilateral proposals were not particularly new, having appeared in various Indian and other proposals over the years, including the negative security assurance proposals. India's proposals clearly were an attempt to mollify international opinion after the nuclear tests.

More dramatic indications of India's pragmatic multilateralism were the efforts by the Bharatiya Janata Party government to find a modus vivendi with the CTBT.[13] The government made a serious bid to prepare India for accession to the CTBT, which, considering the level of domestic public opposition to the CTBT, indicated the seriousness of India's desire to seek a new compact with the NPT regime. Although that move ultimately petered out because of both domestic opposition and a reduction in international pressure after the Bush administration took over in Washington, the fact that India was willing to consider such a dramatic move on a treaty that resonated so negatively with the Indian elite and public opinion was an early indication of the pragmatic shift in Indian multilateral diplomacy.[14]

And the CTBT was only one among many examples. India also altered its earlier objection to ballistic missile defense, appearing to support the Bush administration when it discarded the Anti-Ballistic Missile Treaty.[15] India also came close to signing on to new counterproliferation efforts such as the Proliferation Security Initiative and joined the Container Security Initiative, both multilateral efforts designed to interdict contraband nuclear and other material. India also joined in efforts to counter the potential threat of nuclear terrorism, although this was mandated under UN Security Council Resolution 1540.

The Indo-U.S. nuclear deal also led India to seek closer working relationships with several multilateral technology-denial regimes with which India previously had antagonistic relations: the Nuclear Suppliers Group (NSG), the Australia Group, the Wassenaar Arrangement, and the Missile Technology Control Regime. India has yet to join these regimes, but this is as much because of continuing disagreement within these groups about whether to admit India than because of a lack of effort on India's part. India's interest in joining these regimes was highlighted by the foreign secretary, Ranjan Mathai, in 2012, when he stated unequivocally, "India's membership of the four regimes will be mutually beneficial on grounds of common nonproliferation objectives," a dramatic change in Indian views from even a decade back.[16] All of these reflected a new pragmatism in India's approach to arms control multilateralism that began after the 1998 nuclear tests.

Back to Defensive Multilateralism?

Since the conclusion of the Indo-U.S. nuclear deal, however, there appears to have been a slight slide away from pragmatic multilateralism. This is not very pronounced, partly because only one major multilateral arms control measure (the Arms Trade Treaty, or ATT) was negotiated over the last several years, which makes it difficult to provide indications of this change. On the ATT, India appeared both to seek a consensual position, which would be difficult to achieve, and to oppose any measure that might infringe on what India considered national sovereignty. Although India was not alone in opposing the treaty—many other great and small powers had various objections—what is more relevant here is that India continued to worry about multilateral arms control affecting national sovereignty.[17] Indian officials argued that the treaty as negotiated did not provide sufficient "balance of obligations between exporting and importing states," presumably because there was a possibility that even legally contracted arms transfers could be halted by the supplier countries.[18] India took this stand on an issue that it considers important because small arms trade helps terrorists, which indicates the conflicting pulls on India's choices in multilateral arms control.

The willingness to seek alternative and pragmatic ways around troublesome issues, much evident in the decade after the nuclear tests, is less evident today. Whether on resolving the deadlock in the CD or pushing India's membership in various multilateral technology control regimes such as the NSG, the language of India's diplomacy has returned to that of rights. A caveat is needed: a lot of what is characterized as "pragmatic" multilateralism did not necessarily lead to actual policy changes but was confined to the consideration of alternatives. Although this shift is slight, it might presage a return to defensive multilateralism.

Drivers of Indian Arms Control Multilateralism

Six drivers influence India's position on multilateral arms control and disarmament, and their importance has waxed and waned over the years: historical experience (previous experience with the NPT regime has made India cautious), material capabilities (India's weakness prevents it from being able to manage the multilateral agenda), national security concerns (India perceives significant security threats both in the nuclear and conventional realms that require it to maintain rather than surrender military options), domestic politics (nationalist opposition makes it difficult for the central government to compromise and a fractured polity supplements these difficulties), international opportunities (significant opportunities like the nuclear deal or the need to pacify global opinion after the nuclear test made India more accommodative), and, lastly, economic concerns (the need for domestic power generation, for example, was an important driver and justification for the Indo-U.S. nuclear deal).

Historical Experience

One of the key drivers of India's position on multilateral arms control is India's history both with multilateralism in general and with multilateral arms control in particular. Indian decisionmakers tend to be wary of multilateral approaches and to believe that the multilateral arena is treacherous and must be negotiated with extreme care, especially when critical national security issues are involved. Behind this wariness is a strongly held belief that Indian interests have been repeatedly undermined in multilateral settings. By the 1960s, even though India's rhetoric continued to emphasize multilateralism, India's behavior had cooled considerably toward multilateralism. This distrust was even more pronounced when it came to nuclear arms control measures, especially in the wake of India's experience with the NPT negotiations in the mid-1960s. The story of Indian participation in the NPT is a complex one, but in the Indian telling, which is shared across the political and administrative spectrum, India sought a balanced treaty that would have been equitable to both nuclear powers and non-nuclear ones with regard to promoting non-proliferation and nuclear disarmament. In reality, however, India hoped that the NPT would eventually constrain China's nuclear arsenal and protect India.[19] India was sorely disappointed with the final outcome. As Andrew Kennedy notes, "In the wake of this discouraging defeat, India's leaders seemed to have invested much less hope in nuclear diplomacy. As a result . . . New Delhi's approach became essentially defensive."[20]

The CTBT negotiations in the mid-1990s represented a similar experience for India. India had supported a test ban for more than four decades. But after China began building its arsenal and repeatedly conducted nuclear tests, India could no longer accept a test ban because doing so would permanently consign India to nuclear inferiority. Nevertheless, India's position on the CTBT did not change, probably because India did not expect that the treaty would come to fruition as quickly as it did. As the negotiations proceeded, India found that the process itself was part of the problem, especially the "entry into force" clause, which would have put pressure on India to sign the treaty or be blamed for its failure.[21] In addition, the indefinite extension of the NPT in 1995 further illustrated to Indian decisionmakers that the multilateral arms control process was tilted against Indian interests. Thus, for the first time, India cited national security concerns and refused to sign the treaty.[22]

India's foreign policy decisionmakers continue to support the idea of multilateral negotiations in arms control and disarmament. For example, although the deadlock in the Conference on Disarmament has persisted for more than fifteen years, India strongly supports the institution. In August 2012, India's permanent representative, Sujata Mehta, reaffirmed India's position on the Conference on Disarmament as "a forum with valuable expertise and unrivalled credibility," which "continues to have the mandate, the membership, the credibility, and the rules of procedure to discharge this responsibility. We hope that our debate today will reaffirm the critical role of the CD as the single multilateral disarmament negotiating forum and build a positive momentum for resumption of substantive work."[23] Nevertheless, India's experience made it more careful in dealing with such multilateral efforts. Indeed, even India's position on maintaining the consensus rule in the CD can be seen as a pragmatic move to ensure that India has some control over its deliberations. In short, although India was initially enthusiastic about multilateralism in arms control and disarmament and continues to support such multilateralism, it is today much more cautious and defensive about multilateralism in arms control.

Material Capabilities

India is undoubtedly a "rising" power, with an economy that has grown faster over the last two decades than that of most of the other major powers. But India continues to be a relatively weak global player. This relative weakness means that India's capacity to shape multilateral engagements in arms control is limited, which influences how India thinks of its role in these settings. As Deepa Ollapally notes, "The problem that has continually bedeviled India is that its material capabilities have been inadequate to meet its aspirations."[24]

This mismatch was not always so serious (and it is probably different in other multilateral settings such as climate change negotiations). In the 1950s and 1960s India was an active player in multilateral efforts, especially after the Eighteen-Nation Committee on Disarmament was set up in late 1961. India's rhetoric, the moral power of India's freedom struggle, and, most important, its potential power enabled India to punch above its weight in the international arena, including in multilateral arms control negotiations. But much of this ended with India's defeat in the border conflict with China in late 1962. With India's defeat in the war, India's potential power was suddenly less apparent, and with it both India's influence as well as its interest in multilateral negotiations declined.[25] This was, of course, relative to the 1950s: India continued to maintain a significant level of activism in multilateral disarmament negotiations through the 1960s. This was partly circumstantial: the Ten-Nation Committee on Disarmament, which was an east-west group, expanded in 1961 to include several developing countries, including India. The ENCD, as it was now called, was mandated with the task of multilateral arms control, and it took up the task of negotiating a test ban treaty and a nonproliferation treaty.

But India's activism in multilateral arms control negotiations was not necessarily matched by much success. Material power continued to determine the shape of the two key treaties negotiated by the ENCD. The Test Ban Treaty was whittled down to the Partial Test Ban Treaty; although India had wanted a comprehensive test ban treaty, New Delhi settled for a treaty that it hoped would still constrain China. India's failure in the NPT negotiations, of course, was much more serious. These cases demonstrate that rhetoric and moral power did not compensate for India's material weakness.

India played a significant role in the NPT negotiations in the 1960s, partly because it was worried about the consequence of China's nuclearization and hoped that the NPT would help to contain the threat.[26] India also contributed to the discussions around other major multilateral arms control efforts, such as the CTBT (which was eventually reduced to the Partial Test Ban Treaty) and the Seabed Treaty. Nevertheless, there was a significant drop in Indian activism in multilateral arms control negotiations by the late 1960s.[27]

The consequence of India's material weakness has continued. In 1995 the NPT was extended indefinitely. India had campaigned and argued vigorously for a quarter century about the inherent inequities in the NPT and had assumed that it had a sympathetic ear in the rest of the nonaligned developing world. But most of the nonaligned world nevertheless supported the indefinite extension. As the Indian analyst Giri Deshingkar noted, "That an overwhelming [majority] of non-aligned states had agreed to the NPT extension came as a shock to Indian nuclear opinion makers."[28] The power of India's argument mattered a lot less in the calculation of other states than the benefits that they could derive from the United States, which fought hard to get the indefinite extension. Not only did this have an immediate impact on India's negotiating position on the CTBT, but it made clear to Indian decisionmakers that they needed to be defensive in approaching multilateral negotiations: they simply did not have enough power to shape them.

If India becomes a leading power and its capacity to shape such engagements changes, it is possible that Indian attitudes will become more positive and less defensive. But unless and until India's relative power changes, Indian attitudes toward multilateral arms control negotiations are unlikely to change.

National Security Concerns

For most states, the idea of national security concerns playing a role in arms control negotiations would be unremarkable. Not so for India. India had always pitched its positions on arms control and disarmament in terms not of self-interest but of either the larger common interest or moral principles such as equity. Thus nuclear disarmament is a moral rather than a security issue, and the objections to the NPT were couched in terms of its inequity in the balance of rights and obligations.[29] From the 1950s until the denouement of the CTBT negotiations in 1996, India did not refer to national security as a concern in its arms control and disarmament policies.

This does not mean that India did not *consider* it a concern. Since the early 1960s, when China's nuclear program first became a factor in India's security calculus, India's positions on nuclear arms control have been deeply influenced by New Delhi's worries about China's nuclear capacity. In the 1960s India hoped that multilateral nuclear arms controls would limit China's nuclear progress. This influenced both India's acceptance of the Partial Test Ban Treaty in lieu of a more comprehensive test ban as well as India's position on the NPT negotiations and its eventual refusal to join the treaty.[30]

This coyness about national security concerns ended with the CTBT negotiations. Coming on the heels of the indefinite extension of the NPT, which cast India into a position of permanent nuclear outcast, India was less concerned about appearances and determined to ensure the survival of its "nuclear option." Since 1996 India has been more open in acknowledging the role of national security concerns in its policy postures. For example, the Indian government has stated that it has not signed the Ottawa Convention banning antipersonnel mines "as it does not adequately address its security concerns."[31]

As with most other states, India's primary concern is to prevent multilateral arms control from reducing India's military options. While India has always participated in multilateral efforts in the hope of shaping the outcome to suit its national security needs, as an unaligned middle power, it has also shown little reluctance to go it alone if the outcomes of such multilateral efforts are not to its liking. This is unlikely to change in the near future.

Domestic Politics

As a parliamentary democracy, the Indian government has always had to pay attention to public opinion on multilateral negotiations on arms control, especially when such opinion is reflected within the Parliament. As in any democracy, foreign policy issues are only occasionally salient in the public debate, but once a strong consensus emerges, the Indian government has found it difficult to overcome.

This is most evident in the debates over the NPT and CTBT. India's rhetoric about the inequities of the NPT has resonated with the public. In one of the few systematic public opinion polls conducted on nuclear issues, only about 13 percent of the respondents supported the idea of signing the NPT unilaterally, although that number rose to almost 40 percent if Pakistan also signed the treaty.[32] In turn, this has meant that no political party can take the risk of proposing that India accede to the treaty without suffering some political backlash. Such strong public opinion constrains the options available to Indian decisionmakers. For example, in the aftermath of the Indo-U.S. nuclear deal and the NSG waiver for nuclear commerce with India, India has sought to develop a more cooperative relationship with the global nonproliferation regime. While some Indian scholars have begun to consider such a relationship, the public antipathy to the NPT is likely to prevent India from making any radical departures from its existing policy.[33] Indian governments faced similar problems when they sought to reconsider India's opposition to the CTBT after the 1998 nuclear tests. So great was the domestic opposition that the Bharatiya Janata Party government in 1999 abandoned the effort.[34]

Such "veto" opinion is likely to become an even more prominent driver of India's arms control multilateralism because of the increasing fragmentation of the Indian party system, which leads to precarious political coalitions.[35] This is likely to make future Indian governments (over at least the next decade) cautious in shifting from the trodden path on national security and foreign policy issues.

International Opportunities

Any state would seek to benefit from international opportunities, and India is no exception. The Indo-U.S. nuclear deal provides a good illustration. Although the debate within India did not fully reflect it, the deal represented an opportunity for India to realign its relationship with the global nuclear order. In doing so, however, it also required some changes in India's position on multilateral arms control measures, including the NPT and the CTBT.

How likely are such opportunities in the future? If India continues to become a more influential player in the global balance and if the global system should shift toward a more bipolar direction between China and the United States, India could become an important prize. Although this scenario is by no means certain, such a system could present India with more opportunities and thus make India a more active player in multilateral arms control settings. This also depends, of course, on whether domestic politics will permit India to exploit such opportunities if they arise.

Economic Issues

Economic issues are the final driver of Indian arms control multilateralism. Economic factors have played a role at least in technology-related issues because India sees technology as an important factor in Indian development. India has sought to ensure as free a regime of technology transfers as possible in all areas of high technology, including nuclear and space capabilities.

Outside observers have generally seen India's civilian technology drive as simply a cover for its pursuit of military nuclear and space capabilities. Because there is no great distinction between civilian and military technologies in these areas, India has been able to build technological and industrial capacities that could easily be converted to military purposes. It is also possible that Indian leaders going back to Nehru saw the civilian efforts as *also* providing a cover for the development of such capabilities. But there is little doubt that India's enormous push in civilian nuclear and space technologies was driven by the needs of economic development. Thus from the beginning, India has consistently argued against any measure of technology controls, and this is likely to continue.

Despite Indian arguments, however, the global nuclear regime became progressively tighter by the 1990s. While India's traditional opposition to the NPT regime did not affect its nuclear commerce, this changed when the NSG modified its rules to require comprehensive nuclear safeguards as a requirement for nuclear commerce. This meant that India could no longer engage in nuclear commerce because it was unwilling to open itself up to anything more than safeguards on those items and materials that it imported. Here, despite India's economic interests, the costs involved in strategic policy were considered too great for India to concede. The Indo-U.S. nuclear deal rescued India from this quandary by offering India the option of returning to the status quo ante by dividing India's nuclear program into civilian and military sectors, with parts of the former open to safeguards. The intense debate in India over the nuclear deal reflected the internal dispute over whether the strategic costs were worth the economic benefits.[36] While India's choice reflects the importance of economic issues—in particular, power generation—in India's arms control and nuclear policies, the intensity of the debate also indicates the difficulty in this choice.

As India grows, the economic driver is likely to become even more important. Nevertheless, economic requirements will always be balanced against potential strategic costs, and the ultimate choice will depend on how high such costs are.

Implications for Multilateral Arms Control Efforts

These drivers have implications for India's approach to arms control multilateralism. This section examines these implications in three areas: the NPT regime, the Fissile Material Cut-Off Treaty, and the revitalization of the Conference on Disarmament.

The NPT and the Nonproliferation Regime

As stated earlier, the NPT is an issue on which domestic political opinion is strongly felt and deeply rooted; it is highly unlikely that any Indian government will be able to change policy and join the treaty as a non-nuclear weapon state. The alternative—joining as a nuclear weapon state—is equally unlikely, given global political opinion and the practical difficulties of making yet another exception for India after the nuclear deal.

But if the treaty itself is an area in which defensive multilateralism is most evident, the nonproliferation regime is another story. One of the areas where India has demonstrated the greatest amount of pragmatic multilateralism is on the associated elements of the nonproliferation regime. India did make some efforts to support the NPT, working not only on key problem areas such as Iran and North Korea but also on associated technology-denial regimes such as the NSG and others. In other words, India shifted from opposing the NPT outright to supporting at least the aims of nonproliferation. Thus, as noted earlier, India has attempted to work out a new deal that would allow both sides to work together without India joining the NPT formally. This is likely to continue. Indian decisionmakers now appear to support such a relationship with the NPT regime.

India and the FMCT

India has consistently supported the FMCT because it, like the CTBT, appeared to distribute obligations equitably, at least some versions of the FMCT. The difference over whether the "C" in the FMCT stood for "cut-off" or "control" indicates that "equity" is not an objective criterion. However, though India has supported a cut-off treaty, how this will proceed in an actual negotiation remains to be seen. The deadlock in the Conference for Disarmament since the late 1990s has meant that the complications that are certain to arise in the negotiations have yet to be faced and India's position on multilateral negotiation of the FMCT has yet to be tested. India's position is that it supports a multilateral, nondiscriminatory, and verifiable FMCT. While these appear straightforward requirements, each has potential problems. How these qualifications are to be met remains to be seen: India's position in the negotiations will be determined, at least in part, by whether India adopts a pragmatic or defensive multilateralism. For example, whether India will accept an FMCT negotiated outside the CD, even if it is negotiated multilaterally, is unclear because it depends on how both "multilateral" and "universal" are defined. "Nondiscrimination" is another difficult criterion. This issue came up in the earlier negotiations over the CTBT, which at least on the surface was equitable because the obligation—not to conduct any more nuclear tests—was borne by all parties. The inequity was that some countries had already conducted tests, which meant that the CTBT would freeze extant inequity.

India justified its refusal to sign the CTBT by invoking, probably forthrightly for the first time, national security interest. Whether India would take recourse once again to national security if equity is resolved is not clear.

Revitalizing the CD

The deadlock in the CD has persisted for almost fifteen years and shows little sign of easing. It is possible that some compromise on either the FMCT or one of the other issues might get the CD back to work again, although this is uncertain at present. Indian diplomats have declared that the CD is the only multilateral nuclear arms control negotiating forum, effectively scuttling some of the proposals for moving some of the key negotiations out of the CD. The deadlock is the result of disagreement not only over whether the focus should be nuclear disarmament or other measures such as the FMCT or PAROS (a pact to prevent an arms race in outer space) but also about what the form of an FMCT should be. What is of interest here is the Indian position on the CD: although India might benefit from taking the FMCT out of the CD or from changing the CD's consensus rule, which is blamed for the current deadlock, India has refused to accept either solution. The CD's consensus rule gives every member, however small or weak, a veto. This veto permitted India to scuttle the CTBT and remains an important source of security for India. Today, Pakistan's refusal to compromise on the FMCT is preventing the CD from working, forcing other states to consider alternatives. India has not supported such efforts, preferring to keep the CD as it is, with the risk that Pakistan—or another state—will continue to block it rather than find an alternative.

Conclusion

India may have moved from defensive multilateralism to pragmatic multilateralism for a period after the 1998 nuclear tests. However, it seems to be slipping from the pragmatic multilateralism of the last decade. In any case, the prospects for multilateral arms control have worsened for reasons that have little to do with India. Further multipolarization of international politics would make multilateral arms control efforts even more difficult. India's retreat therefore is likely to affect these efforts only marginally.

Notes

1. Manu Bhagavan, *The Peacemakers: India and the Quest for One World* (New Delhi: HarperCollins India, 2012).

2. Gary Milhollin, "Dateline New Delhi: India's Nuclear Cover-Up," *Foreign Policy* 64 (Fall 1986): 161–75.

3. David Albright and Susan Basu, "India's Gas Centrifuge Program: Stopping Illicit Procurement and the Leakage of Technical Centrifuge Know-How" (Washington: Institute for Science and International Security, March 10, 2006) (http://isis-online.org/uploads/isis-reports/documents/indianprocurement.pdf).

4. David Albright and Susan Basu, "Neither a Determined Proliferator Nor a Responsible Nuclear State: India's Record Needs Scrutiny" (Washington: Institute for Science and International Security, April 5, 2006) (http://isis-online.org/uploads/isis-reports/documents/indiacritique.pdf).

5. On the A. Q. Khan network, see Gordon Corera, *Shopping for Bombs: Nuclear Proliferation, Global Insecurity, and the Rise and Fall of the A. Q. Khan Network* (Oxford University Press, 2006).

6. On India's pursuit of a nuclear guarantee, see A. G. Noorani, "India's Quest for a Nuclear Guarantee," *Asian Survey* 7, no. 7 (July 1967): 490–502. For a richly detailed, more recent account of India's nuclear decisionmaking during this period, see Andrew Kennedy, "India's Nuclear Odyssey: Implicit Umbrellas, Diplomatic Disappointments, and the Bomb," *International Security* 36, no. 2 (Fall 2011): 120–53.

7. George Perkovich, *India's Nuclear Bomb: The Impact on Global Proliferation* (University of California Press, 1999), p. 21.

8. Sunil Sondhi, *Science, Technology, and India's Foreign Policy* (New Delhi: Anamika Prakashan, 1994), pp. 129–30.

9. Strobe Talbott, *Master of the Game: Paul Nitze and the Nuclear Peace* (New York: Knopf, 1988).

10. *Report of the Informal Group on Prime Minister Rajiv Gandhi's Action Plan for a Nuclear-Weapon-Free and Nonviolent World Order 1988 (RGAP 88)* (www.pugwashindia.org/images/uploads/Report.pdf).

11. UNGA, First Committee, 61st Session, "Working Paper by India on Nuclear Disarmament," A/C.1/61/5, October 6, 2006.

12. Michael J. Sullivan III, "Re-Orientation of Indian Arms Control Policy, 1969–72," *Asian Survey* 13, no. 7 (July 1973): 691–706.

13. C. Raja Mohan, *Impossible Allies: Nuclear India, United States, and the Global Order* (New Delhi: India Research Press, 2006), pp. 18–19.

14. Deepa Ollapally and Rajesh Rajagopalan, "The Pragmatic Challenge to Indian Foreign Policy," *Washington Quarterly* 34, no. 2 (Spring 2011): 145–62.

15. Ashley J. Tellis, "The Evolution of U.S.-Indian Ties: Missile Defense in an Emerging Strategic Relationship," *International Security* 30, no. 4 (Spring 2006): 113–51.

16. Shri Ranjan Mathai, keynote address at the "National Export Control Seminar," Ministry of External Affairs, Institute for Defense Studies and Analyses, April 18, 2012 (www.idsa.in/keyspeeches/AddressbyForeignSecretaryShriRanjanMathai).

17. On India's position on the ATT, see Rajiv Nayan, "The Politics of Arms Trade Treaty Negotiations," *IDSA Policy Brief*, July 27, 2012 (http://idsa.in/system/files/PB_PoliticsofArmsTradeTreaty_RajivNayan.pdf).

18. "India's Explanation of Vote by Ambassador Sujata Mehta, Permanent Representative of India to the Conference of [sic] Disarmament in Geneva during the UNGA Session on the Arms Trade Treaty" (www.mea.gov.in/Speeches-Statements.htm?dtl/21502/Indias+Explanation+of+Vote+by+Ambassador+Sujata+Mehta+Permanent+Representative+of+India+to+the+Conference+of+Disarmament+in+Geneva+during+the+UNGA+Session+on+the+Arms+Trade+Treaty).

19. Perkovich, *India's Nuclear Bomb*, pp. 103–04.

20. Kennedy, "India's Nuclear Odyssey," pp. 127–28.

21. Dinshaw Mistry, "Domestic-International Linkages: India and the Comprehensive Test Ban Treaty," *Nonproliferation Review* (Fall 1998): 25–38.

22. Arundhati Ghose, "Negotiating the CTBT: India's Security Concerns and Nuclear Disarmament," *Journal of International Affairs* 51, no. 1 (Summer 1997): 239–61. Ghose was India's permanent representative to the United Nations in Geneva and led the Indian team at the CTBT negotiations.

23. Sujata Mehta, remarks in the debate on "Revitalization of the CD," CD Plenary, Government of India, Ministry of External Affairs, August 21, 2012 (http://meaindia.nic.in/pmicd.geneva/?50031178).

24. Deepa M. Ollapally, "Mixed Motives in India's Search for Nuclear Status," *Asian Survey* 41, no. 6 (November-December 2001): 926.

25. Stanley A. Kochanek, "India's Changing Role in the United Nations," *Pacific Affairs* 53, no. 1 (Spring 1980): 48–68.

26. Bhumitra Chakma, "Towards Pokhran II: Explaining India's Nuclearisation Process," *Modern Asian Studies* 39, no. 1 (February 2005): 208.

27. Sullivan, "Re-Orientation of Indian Arms Control Policy."

28. Giri Deshingkar, "Indian Politics and Arms Control: Recent Reversals and New Reasons for Optimism," in *Nuclear Weapons and Arms Control in South Asia after the Test Ban*, edited by Eric Arnett (Oxford University Press, 1998) p. 26.

29. The first paragraph of the draft Indian nuclear doctrine released in 1999 begins by noting these two points. See National Security Advisory Board, "Draft Report of the National Security Advisory Board on Indian Nuclear Doctrine," August 17, 1999 (www.fas.org/nuke/guide/india/doctrine/990817-indnucld.htm).

30. Kennedy, "India's Nuclear Odyssey," pp. 126–27, and Chakma, "Towards Pokhran II," pp. 208–09.

31. "Ban on Landmines," Lok Sabha, unstarred question no. 2599, March 20, 2002 (http://mea.gov.in/lok-sabha.htm?dtl/13427/Q+2599Ban+on+Landmines).

32. David Cortright and Amitabh Mattoo, "Elite Public Opinion and Nuclear Weapons Policy in India," *Asian Survey* 36, no. 6 (June 1996): 558.

33. Rajiv Nayan, "Is NPT Membership as a Nuclear Weapon State an Option for India?" *Strategic Analysis* 31, no. 6 (2007): 869–87.

34. Mohan, *Impossible Allies*, p. 19.

35. On party fragmentation in India, see Christophe Jaffrelot and Gilles Verniers, "Re-Nationalization of India's Political Party System or Continued Prevalence of Region-

alism and Ethnicity? Evidence from the 2009 General Election," *Asian Survey* 51, no. 6 (November-December 2011): 1090–112.

36. For some of these debates, see P. R. Chari, ed., *Indo-US Nuclear Deal: Seeking Synergy in Bilateralism* (New Delhi: Routledge, 2009), and P. K. Iyengar, A. N. Prasad, A. Gopalakrishnan, and Bharat Karnad, *Strategic Sellout: Indian-U.S. Nuclear Deal* (New Delhi: Pentagon Press, 2009).

SANDEEP BHARDWAJ

12 Security in Cyberspace: India's Multilateral Efforts

Introduction

Cyberspace, governed by mechanisms difficult to understand and capable of impossible-to-assess disruptions, has significantly raised the uncertainty in the international system. Coupled with the contemporary shifts in the international balance of power, this uncertainty has posed unexpected challenges for states. On the one hand, governments are forced to develop a cooperative mechanism to govern cyberspace and the Internet.[1] On the other, nations need to develop a whole new framework for conflicts in a domain that adds a new degree of unpredictability in the international system and further complicates the existing concepts of national power, rules of engagement, and norms for state behavior.

Given these parameters, how has India sought security in cyberspace through multilateral means? Traditional accounts of the government's Internet policies, constructed in the media mostly by cyber-libertarian groups, have portrayed them as driven by the debates on freedom of expression and law enforcement concerns.[2] While pertinent to the contemporary national political discourses, these narratives fail to take into account the larger security concerns of India. As we will see, while the political and security threats from nonstate actors have been relevant factors in defining this policy, they have remained largely a secondary consideration.

This chapter posits that India's thinking has been driven by two phenomena. First are the post–cold war realities of a unipolar world where nations are forced to orient themselves to the gravitational pull of the United States and at the same time seek to "soft balance" their power by using "non-military tools to delay, frustrate, and undermine" unilateral U.S. policies.[3] Second is the rise of China, its geographic proximity to India, and the threat of relative gains within any multilateral framework created to enhance mutual security. These security considerations, combined with the government's steep learning curve of understanding the dynamics of cyberspace, have been the primary drivers of its policy.

India's rationale for engaging the cyberspace has gone through many twists and turns, driven largely by developments in the international scene. Recognizing this historical context is critical to understanding the current Indian policies. This chapter presents a historical account of the evolution of Indian policy over the last twenty-five years and its engagement with various multilateral organizations on issues relating to the Internet. It examines the internal and external factors that contributed to India's multilateral engagement and concludes that the current Indian position has been motivated by the government's heightened perception of threat and its ambitions to play a greater role in the emerging global order. Set against the backdrop of growing polarization in the world on the issue of Internet governance, these factors have led India to adopt a highly nuanced approach that both enhances its security in cyberspace and allows it to gain more influence in shaping and managing the evolving global arrangement to govern the Internet.

Prologue

Under the technophile administration of Rajiv Gandhi in the 1980s, India began experimenting with computer networking and rudimentary Internet technologies, well ahead of most other countries. In 1989 India established its first connection with the global Internet, six years before China. Nevertheless, the Internet failed to become a priority in the first of wave of International Monetary Fund (IMF)–induced Indian economic reforms of 1991. From 1991 to 1995, the Indian government followed a stifling regulatory Internet policy that contained the web's growth within the country. The monopoly of government-owned Videsh Sanchar Nigam Limited's (VSNL) over the international gateway for the Internet, the imposition of exorbitant licensing and royalty fees on e-service providers, and VSNL's refusal to extend Internet connectivity beyond certain technology parks and government institutions ensured that the Internet remained stillborn.[4]

To a certain extent, this had been a failure to mobilize and deploy appropriate technical know-how in conjunction with effective policies. (VSNL, having locked itself into obsolete technologies, failed to offer Internet service until 1995. It was, in fact, an experimental academic network funded by the United Nations Development Program that made the first connection with the international network and began offering first e-services in the country.) Yet it also betrayed a fear of the unknown that the Indian government harbored against this new uncertain development, and hence the government sought to address this uncertainty by treating the national telecommunications network as a "strategic resource."[5] For most of the 1980s, use of dial-up modems remained illegal in India. The National Telecommunications Policy in 1994, while calling for a certain level of liberalization of the sector, still listed the vague objective of "protecting the defence and security interests of India" among its priorities.[6] Despite a flourishing software industry, India's technical and economic footprint on the web remained minimal for the better part of the 1990s. By the time the government sought to turn it around, India was already falling behind other countries with regard to network penetration and sophistication of use.

First Phase: Joining the Global Network

The turnaround in Indian policy began in 1996 and gathered a sense of urgency by 1997 after the election of the new National Democratic Alliance government.[7] Bringing the Internet to India required not only developing technical infrastructure in the country but also building a legal and regulatory framework that met the international standards of the World Wide Web.[8] Given the interconnected nature of the Internet, its global expansion needed a baseline of laws and norms applied uniformly across the world. In the mid-1990s, the United States and the European nations were in the process of creating global economic and legal regimes to ensure this, and India eagerly sought to join them.

The political economy of the Internet demanded deregulation, limited liability, and strong copyright protection. India embraced all three as mantras. The Indian leadership was aware that it had nearly missed the boat and that to catch up it needed speedy reforms and quick entry into the international regimes. In 1996 the Internet treaties of the World Intellectual Property Organization were enthusiastically supported by India, one of the few developing countries to do so.[9] In 1998 India signed the World Trade Organization's Agreement on Basic Telecommunications, and within two years it had exceeded its commitments to the agreement.[10] This was followed by the Information Technology Act of 2000, paving the way for e-commerce and limiting the liability of Internet service providers (ISPs) for content. For good measure, the act also provided unchecked power with regard to government surveillance and interception.[11] The National Task Force on Information Technology and Software Development, created in 1998, came up with 108 recommendations of extensive reforms in a mere ninety days. The VSNL monopoly had already been broken; the recommendations sought even further liberalization, culminating in the National Telecom Policy in 1999. These developments capture the eagerness with which India wanted to be a part of the international Internet economy. If this meant indiscriminately following the United States, India was glad to pay the price.

Against the backdrop of this liberalization, the first round of debates over Internet governance emerged in Geneva and Washington, especially over the administration of the Domain Name System (DNS).[12] These debates resulted in the creation of the semiautonomous International Corporation of Assigned Names and Numbers (ICANN), which became responsible for the day-to-day administration of the DNS, while the ultimate authority to make changes in the root-zone file was retained by the U.S. Department of Commerce.[13]

India stayed out of this dispute, adopting a low profile on the issue in the 1998 International Telecommunications Union (ITU) plenipotentiary conference in Minneapolis, which had become the international forum for these debates.[14] Like most developing countries, India was yet to become a significant player in these debates. By 1998 India had only 0.1 percent Internet penetration compared with 31 percent in the United States, 13 percent in Japan, and 7 percent in South Korea.[15] The Indian software industry was developing few independent products for the emerging Internet economy. Even in 2001, a majority of the industry was engaged in "body shopping," essentially exporting highly skilled labor to foreign companies.[16] For the most part, India was happy to follow the U.S. lead, calling for greater "self-regulation"[17] on the issue of Internet governance and supporting stronger copyright laws across the world.[18] Partly this attitude was the result of the euphoria of liberalization in the late 1990s, and partly it stemmed from India's general reorientation toward the United States in the post–cold war setting. In fact, there is little indication that the Indian government recognized the potential of the Internet, initially seeing it as just another communication medium. The momentum of the late 1990s to develop Indian connectivity stemmed from the government's desire to boost its information technology (IT)—software—industry rather than to promote a true Internet-based economy. Accordingly, while it was quick to adopt the international regime and translate it into domestic laws, the government made little effort to develop a legal and regulatory framework that could support an Internet economy *within* the country. It focused instead on increasing the penetration and bandwidth of the Internet, not on increasing the sophistication of use or fostering innovation. An excerpt from the prime minister's national IT Task Force portrays how off the mark the government's thinking was regarding the Internet in 1998:

> If India has to take a lead in IT, then there is an immediate need to create a regional telecom hub in India. . . . Such an effort will not bring more revenues to Government, but [will] substantially bring more Internet/e-commerce traffic and also help connectivity, which is essential for future growth of software-driven IT industry.[19]

Second Phase: Switching Camps

This naïveté did not last. The government had already begun experimenting with Internet censorship in 1999.[20] By 2001 the challenges of an Internet society became evident through several incidents, most notably the government corruption scandals exposed by *Tehelka*, an online magazine. The need for the government to have a greater say in governance of the Internet, on both domestic and international fronts, was becoming evident.

Against strong U.S. opposition, the consensus among the developing nations of the need to seek greater multilateral control over the Internet emerged out of the 2002–03 regional preparatory meetings of the World Summit on the Information Society (WSIS).[21] India was slow to join the multilateralist bandwagon; most likely, its policy simply aped the general attitude among the developing countries. In preparatory meetings, Indian statements failed even to mention the issue of Internet governance.[22] It was only after the issue gained impetus among other countries that India followed suit. By the 2003 WSIS conference, India was squarely in the multilateralist camp. In his speech at the conference, the IT minister, Arun Shourie, said,

> A vast literature is already available—it is available on the Internet itself!—on how Information Technology can—and *should!*—be used to disrupt such progressively integrating systems. All of us together have to devise ways to prevent terrorists and other adversaries from doing so. [Italics and exclamations in original.][23]

Nevertheless, the 2003 WSIS failed to come to any agreement beyond establishing a Working Group on Internet Governance (WGIG) that would explore the issue and present its conclusion to the 2005 WSIS.[24] In the run-up to the next conference, India developed and refined its position, claiming, "India among developing countries is not at ease with limited influence of governments of various countries in ICANN." Additionally, like its fellow multilateralists, particularly China and Russia, India sought to expand the scope of the debate by including issues like spam.[25]

The WGIG final report was finished in July 2005, presenting four models of Internet governance that practically included all scenarios from maintaining the status quo to undertaking a complete overhaul.[26] At the 2005 WSIS, the debate continued without any resolution, as both sides stuck to their positions, including India, which claimed, "If the Internet is a shared resource, so must be its oversight and management."[27] The WSIS concluded with the status quo intact. In fact, given the absence of a resolution, it ended up lending legitimacy to ICANN, which vowed to include more multilateral involvement through its Governmental Advisory Committee (GAC). In addition, the conference also resulted in creating a new United Nations (UN) advisory body called the Internet Governance Forum (IGF), with little powers or mandate. India welcomed the IGF with limited enthusiasm. It offered to host the 2008 IGF meeting in Hyderabad, but took little part in the meeting itself.

Parallel to it, since 1998 Russia had been proposing talks on arms control in cyberspace in the UN and bilaterally, in the face of stiff U.S. opposition.[28] Nevertheless, years of Russian efforts in the UN led to the formation of the first Group of Governmental Experts (GGE) in 2004 to explore the possibility of arms control, which eventually collapsed because of American opposition. While part of the fifteen-member GGE, India remained noncommittal. Although India had had its own contentious resolution on regulating advanced technologies with military applications in the United Nations General Assembly since 1988, it was once again slow to catch onto the significance of Internet security.[29]

The fact is, even by 2005, India had not developed a real stake in the global management of the Internet. Internet penetration remained abysmally low at 2 percent, and Indian exports of information and communications technology (ICT) made up only 1 percent of the Indian economy.[30] Digitization of the critical national infrastructure was similarly moving at a slow pace.[31] Joseph Nye has observed that institutional learning in cyberspace is likely to be "lumpy and discontinuous."[32] India serves as a perfect example of this thesis. If crisis is a prerequisite for governmental learning, then the Indian experience with the Internet until 2005 offers little pedagogical insight. Almost all challenges that came to dominate the Indian government's thinking in a few years were either yet to crop up or ignored.[33] Additionally, given the extremely submissive private industry[34] and lack of a domestic cyber-libertarian movement, the government was able to implement its domestic priorities for national security and cultural policing without many political or technical impediments.

Therefore, in multilateral debates on Internet governance, India pushed for greater international recognition of the nation's right to exercise control within its borders; however, on multilateralization of Internet governance, it was yet to articulate its preferred outcome in detail. While it wanted multilateralization, it did not specify what shape or form such an approach would take. It was happy to follow the agenda set by other countries like China and Russia. The push for multilateralization was partly due to the fact that Bush-era unilateralism had accelerated the process of soft balancing against U.S. hegemony. Partly it was the intuitive recognition of the potentially disruptive capacity of the Internet. Internet-related issues remained a low priority for the government, with the full gravity of the situation yet to be internalized.

Interlude: Something Must Be Done

Three developments in the years following the WSIS changed these circumstances and forced India to develop a more nuanced multilateral policy. First was the sudden surge in the perceived threat of cyber security. Once India's cyber security agency CERT-In (established in 2004) began functioning, the number of reported cyber security incidents rose exponentially, from 254 in 2005 to 1,237 in 2007 and to 8,266 in 2009.[35] These official figures barely scratched the surface; a Microsoft survey in 2009 found that just the number of malwares on Indian computers was close to 200,000.[36] But the CERT-In figures were big enough to alter signficiantly India's perception of cyber threats. Meanwhile, with cyber attacks on Estonia and Georgia, military use of cyberspace was fast becoming a reality.[37] In 2009 a group of Canadian researchers announced their discovery of a Chinese cyber espionage network, GhostNet, that had infected at least seven Indian embassies as well as other offices in India, catching the government unaware.[38] In 2010 the allegedly American-Israeli worm Stuxnet (possibly inadvertently) infected close to 7,000 hosts in India, making India the third biggest victim of the malware after Iran and Indonesia.[39]

These developments prompted an overhaul of the Indian cyber security and cyber defense establishment, bringing forth a stream of policy documents, institutional changes, and amendments to the Indian IT Act. In 2010 the Indian military, which even in 2006 perceived ICT to be merely a tool to improve wartime communication,[40] was ordered to develop contingency plans for cyber attacks.[41] However, there were limits to what India could achieve unilaterally. After the discoveries of GhostNet and Stuxnet, the government hesitated to respond and tried to minimize the gravity of the attacks.[42] This tendency stemmed from the inherent problem of attribution in cyber warfare, making states unsure how to respond to an anonymous cyber attack. It was becoming evident that the world needed "rules of the road."

From 2010 onward, India began supporting multilateral efforts to create rules and norms for cyber warfare. In 2011 the Indian national security advisor, Shivshankar Menon, speaking at the Munich security conference, said,

> Common law, I am not sure, is the guide in this case [cyber warfare]. . . . Do, or when do, laws of governing the legality of war and laws of conduct of war apply to cyber attacks? A broader issue still is what the emergence of this domain and these new threats, capabilities, and forms of war mean for the balance of power.[43]

Twelve years after Russia introduced the UN resolution calling for cyber arms control, India began co-sponsoring the resolution. This turnaround coincided with a U.S. policy shift in the same direction. In the wake of the collapse of the first GGE, a second expert group was formed in 2009, with India again one of fifteen members. Unfortunately, while this GGE was able to reach a consensus, the resultant report was essentially a victory for the United States, with no mention of disarmament in cyberspace.[44]

The second development to shape the Indian position was the increasing complexity that the government was beginning to face in reining in transnational nonstate actors. The problem of regulating the behavior of actors not within a country's jurisdiction had been an oft-discussed issue among governments since the 1990s. However, in the late 2000s it became a real challenge. In the beginning of the decade, the government had been extremely successful in its surveillance and censorship efforts, largely through submissive ISPs.[45] The new technological advances, unbound by national boundaries, proved difficult to tame. Most notable of these was the showdown between the Indian government and Research In Motion (RIM), the service operators of BlackBerry. In 2010 India requested RIM to provide unencrypted access to the BlackBerry data services. RIM refused, forcing India to threaten an ultimatum. Part of the contention was RIM's claim that it had no access to the data themselves, which were heavily encrypted and routed through international servers beyond RIM's control. Although some kind of undeclared resolution was reached eventually, the event became a public relations disaster for both parties.[46]

Challenges like these highlighted the limits of state power in cyberspace. The 2010 U.S. diplomatic cables released by Wikileaks underscore this problem even further. Sachin Pilot, the minister of state for the Ministry of Communication and Information Technology, expressed this frustration in the Indian Parliament:

> Millions of users worldwide from all sections of society use Internet. The technology and the associated applications allow the users to post the content of their choice automatically after registration with such sites, without the role of service providers hosting such sites. Most of the large number of users logging on the sites and millions of pages on such sites make it practically very difficult to keep a vigil on all contents posted/hosted on these sites. Most of the sites are hosted outside the country.[47]

Another growing concern for the government was cyber terrorism, exacerbated after the 2008 Mumbai attacks carried out by terrorists adept in using technology to their advantage. Although there is little evidence of its existence, the fear of the untold damage made possible by such an attack was growing in New Delhi. Consequently, once again, the government sought to extend its powers by introducing the concept of cyber terrorism to its 2008 amendments to the Information Technology Act as well as introducing new cyber security rules and policies.[48] However, these initiatives had little control over nonstate actors beyond national borders. Although an alphabet soup of multilateral cyber security agencies had emerged since 9/11 (a selective list identifies at least seventeen such agencies), without any high-level international consensus on issues such as jurisdiction and sovereignty, they could be of little use.[49] Additionally, without any progress on the development of international rules and norms of cyber security, like defining legal grounds for hack back, the government was restricted in its capability to defend the country.[50]

India needed greater capacity to regulate the Internet on a global level, and this could only be achieved through creation of a multilateral regime for Internet governance. The WSIS left the world with the IGF, but the advisory body had failed to make an impact. It had remained aimless since its creation, failing to attract most of the important stakeholders or substantive debates to its arena.[51] In 2010 India complained in the UN, "Almost five years [since WSIS], we are yet to meaningfully discuss or operationalise the enhanced cooperation process. In the meantime, the reach and influence of the Internet on public policy issues has grown dramatically. Hence, in our view, these consultations are long-overdue and much-needed."[52] India suggested a review of the situation, hoping to restart the dialogue.

The third factor that forced India to refine its policy was the evolving balance of power in the world. By 2008 two important developments had changed the Indian perspective: the improving Indo-U.S. relations, solidified by the Indo-U.S. Nuclear Deal, and the 2008 global economic crisis predicating the relative decline of America. This meant that there was growing space for Indian ambitions in the international order. Moreover, the United States was no longer a hegemon favoring unilateralism, but a power amenable to forging partnerships, especially in the realm of international institutions. It was in this international context that India developed its policy after 2009.

Third Phase: Status Quo 2.0

The new decade began with a world divided on the issue of Internet governance, with the first bout scheduled at the ITU treaty renegotiations at the World Conference on International Telecommunications 2012 (WCIT-12). India was generally associated with the multilateralist camp of developing nations. However, there were two reasons for India not to follow the Sino-Russian lead. First, calling for a complete multilateralization was a losing position. As failure of the IGF had demonstrated, any arrangement without U.S. support would not work. Moreover, given the significance of the Internet in the American economy and security, the U.S. government was unlikely to give up its unique authority over the web.

The second reason was China. India's relationship with China had always demanded a tightrope act, improving bilateral relations while searching for new ways to balance the rise of Beijing's might; the same dynamics dominated the issue of Internet governance. As in every other economic domain, China's growth in the Internet field had been phenomenal. Its cyber espionage activities, national firewall, and superiority in emerging technologies like IPv6 had raised security concerns for other countries since the late 2000s.[53] China had always been a strong opponent of the U.S.-dominated Internet governance regime, and over the years it had become the silent leader of the multilateralist camp, which first included Russia and other Shanghai Cooperation Organization countries and later began coordinating with Middle Eastern countries as well.[54] In a scenario of complete multilateralization, with, say, the ITU as the Internet governing body, a one-nation-one-vote system would have practically ensured Sino-Russian leadership of the developing nations, leaving little space for India to gain influence. Moreover, it would result in an agenda far too focused on content censorship and surveillance for India's comfort.

However, siding with the U.S. and European nations would have been a public relations misstep, as it would have pitted India against the rest of the developing countries. Additionally, India needed to have some say on Internet governance. As the events in the previous years had shown, the status quo was not completely desirable.

Faced with these hard choices, India decided to adopt a compromise position, hoping to assume the role of a "bridging power" between the two camps.[55] The new Indian policy, which began to take shape by 2010, was three-pronged. India distanced itself from the Sino-Russian camp, deliberately stressing democratic values and freedom of expression as critical parts of the Internet; it sought new partners; and it proposed a new Internet governance regime that would allow other nations to have limited influence on Internet issues, while retaining America's unique position in administration of the Internet. According to India, what the world needed was not a new Internet regulator, but a forum where issues could be discussed among nations and "tangible movement towards effective policy development processes" achieved.[56]

The first step was to reform the IGF, which India had been pushing for in the UN. In December 2010 the UN's Commission on Science and Technology for Development (CSTD) established a working group that received proposals from various stakeholders. India tabled the most detailed position, in effect turning the agenda into a discussion of the Indian proposal.[57] The proposal suggested organizational reforms to make the IGF a more effective forum for discussing issues and reaching a consensus. It also recognized that as the IGF was not "a policymaking body, its contributions must come in the form of policy advice and recommendations." This proposal essentially legitimized the status quo and asked for much less than what multilateralists had been demanding.

As a second step, India sought to gain support from outside the binary camps of the United States and China-Russia. In September 2011 it developed a united position along with Brazil and South Africa at an India, Brazil, and South Africa (IBSA) meeting on Internet governance held in Rio de Janeiro. The meeting emerged with a set of recommendations that called for creating a new UN body on Internet governance. This new body would develop international public policies, arbitrate disputes, and oversee the agencies responsible for technical management of the Internet.[58] The meeting then resolved to move ahead with "follow-up action."

The Rio recommendations were a test balloon to gather international reaction and draw other countries into the debate. India followed up the recommendations by proposing the creation of a new body in the UN in

October 2011. The new body, the Committee for Internet-Related Policies (CIRP), was presented as a UN advisory body, in the vein of agencies like the Organization for Economic Cooperation and Development.[59] While, controversially, it still proposed to "coordinate and oversee" technical functioning of the Internet, the tone of the rest of the proposal suggested that this was a bargaining position rather than an actual demand.[60] The important features of this proposal were, first, it gave governments the ultimate say, thereby giving them greater authority over other stakeholders; second, it limited the number of member-nations on the committee (to be chosen or elected) to fifty. The second feature would contain Chinese and Russian influence by keeping the discussion between major countries instead of giving each country a vote.

The proposal generated a severe backlash from civil society, as it was misinterpreted as a naked grab for government control of the Internet.[61] The failure of the Indian government to communicate its intent clearly became a severe handicap in pushing the agenda further. India also failed to gain the necessary diplomatic momentum to initiate a global debate among nations. For the time being, the Indian proposal is yet to take off.

Epilogue

The Indian attempt to alter the debate preemptively failed. A scheduled round of the old debate was held in December 2012 at WCIT-12, with deepened polarization between the West and the developing nations.[62] Under these pressures, the negotiations at WCIT-12 collapsed. A new treaty was passed by a majority vote, which included a resolution calling for an "enabling environment for the greater growth of the Internet," essentially adding the issue of Internet governance to the ITU's agenda.[63] The resultant treaty was signed by 89 of the 152 countries, including most developing countries in Africa, Asia (including China), Latin America, the Middle East, and Russia, with an option for other nations to sign the treaty by 2015. However, the U.S.-led bloc refused to sign it and walked out of the conference. Without U.S. support, the treaty is unlikely to be of much significance. While the developing nations may have scored a symbolic victory, the status quo remains until negotiations reopen between the two sides.

For its part, India was noncommittal. In the preparatory meetings of WCIT-12, it remained silent, failing to submit any proposals.[64] At the conference, proposals submitted by India, while pressing for greater control of the "ICT network" at a national level, steered clear of the issue of including Internet governance on the ITU's agenda.[65] In the deliberations, it adopted a low-key presence, while privately distancing itself from the proposals of China, Russia, and the Arab states.[66] The treaty that resulted from the collapsed negotiations was signed by most developing nations. India became the only major developing country not to sign it on the spot. However, unlike its fellow nonsignatories (the European Union, Japan, and the United States), which forcefully criticized the treaty, India pleaded that it needed more time to consider the issue at home. Making its position even more ambiguous, India stated that it supported "the broad thrust of Resolution Plen/3 [the resolution that mentioned the term "Internet"]."[67]

By refusing to take sides, India is attempting to reach out to both camps in the hopes of brokering an agreement through its own compromise solution in the direction of CIRP. From the Indian standpoint, neither a U.S.-dominated, self-regulated system without any multilateral oversight nor a completely mulilateralized Internet is a desirable outcome. In the long term, neither position is sustainable. As the world grows more invested in the Internet, the American unilateral control over it will become increasingly unpalatable to other nations. At the same time, complete multilateralization would threaten Western security too much to be acceded by the European Union or the United States. Faced with the situation, India's attempt to reach a compromise presents a preferred alternative to the Balkanization of the Internet, which otherwise is bound to follow.

However, India's strategy has limitations of its own. Not only is the Indian proposal faced with a severe perception problem, it also has failed to generate much enthusiasm among other countries, most likely because of the inability of the Indian government to communicate it well. More significant, India has always lagged behind China and the West in technological advancements. As new innovations bring forth new governance challenges, such as deep-packet inspection and cloud computing, Indian leadership is unlikely to be able to keep up with the fast-paced emerging debates.

Finally, Indian interests do not align with those of any of the other major countries, which will prove to be an impediment in New Delhi gaining support from others. India's software industry has failed to become a major player in the Internet economy. In addition, a large English-speaking population has led India to adopt most international Web services instead of providing a market to a domestic industry of search engines, blogging services, social networking, and so forth in local languages, as has happened in Russia, China, and Japan. In short, India has little economic stake in the Web. Accordingly, the government's position has been motivated largely by its larger geopolitical agenda and its domestic security concerns. While this neutrality on contentious economic issues makes India a perfect arbitrator or a "bridging power," it also creates a mismatch of interests between India and other major countries.

Failing the CIRP route, the other alternative for the government is to seek more influence within the current U.S.-dominated regime. To a certain extent, this has been happening through the ICANN GAC, which has traditionally been driven by American and European concerns, but lately has given India a few victories. In October 2009 ICANN began issuing new internationalized domain names (IDNs) in non-Latin characters.[68] India has been given seven new country-code top-level domains in various Indian languages, more than any other country. This represents a huge surge in India's Internet real estate and revenues from registry fees. In the coming years, ICANN GAC may be able to snare India by offering innovations such as IDNs or allowing pre-screening of new domain names.[69] Such arrangements would undoubtedly be beneficial for India, at least in the short term.

Most likely, India will try to follow both alternatives, pushing for greater multilateralization through a nuanced body like the CIRP, while trying to maximize its advantage within the ICANN GAC framework. However, such a policy is constrained by time: it cannot be sustained forever without any concrete resolution. In the context of interstate warfare, India has fallen behind other nations in the buildup of capacity, and, barring development of any norms or institutions, it will be forced to enter the arms race eventually. Similarly, India remains exposed to the threat of non-state actors, which may attack from beyond its borders with impunity, in the absence of any international mechanism. Given these challenges and failing to secure an international consensus, India is likely to fall back on its last alternative. As we have seen, national level control over the Internet is one strategy that has consistently paid off for the government. Faced with an uncertain international environment, the government would seek to exercise greater unilateral control over the Internet within its borders and to regulate the connections between its national network and the global Internet. This would undeniably hurt the economy by raising Internet transaction costs, but it may be the only option left for the government.

Notes

1. The web requires not only a high degree of global uniformity on various levels, from international peering and domain name management to communication protocols and software standards; it also has high costs for even minor disruptions, leaving little negotiating room. Accordingly, achieving international cooperation on such issues is a task without parallel in the world's institutional history. For instance, the slightest difference in technical standards or even nomenclature can significantly diminish the Internet's universality. An equivalent of, say, international variations in measurements (metric vs. nonmetric systems) in cyberspace would raise transaction costs to a degree as to result in a system completely different from the present-day Internet.

2. Unfortunately, most literature on the subject has been prescriptive rather than analytical. For instance, see Institute for Defense Studies and Analyses Task Force, *India's Cyber Security Challenge* (New Delhi: Institute for Defense Studies and Analyses, 2012).

3. Robert A. Pape, "Soft Balancing against the United States," *International Security* 30 no. 1 (Summer 2005): 7–45.

4. Peter Wolcott and Seymour Goodman, "Global Diffusion of the Internet - I: India: Is the Elephant Learning to Dance?" *Communications of the Association for Information Systems* 11 (2003): 560–646; Larry Press, William Foster, Peter Wolcott, and William McHenry, "The Internet in India and China," *Massachusetts Institute of Technology Information Technologies and International Development* 1, no. 1 (Fall 2003): 41–60.

5. Historically, such a knee-jerk reaction is common among states when first confronted with the challenges of the Internet. Cuba, for example, simply outlawed the sale of personal computers to individuals until 2008; Myanmar banned personal ownership of modems until 2002.

6. National Telecommunications Policy 1994 (www.dot.gov.in).

7. Unfortunately, a comprehensive history of the advent of the Internet in India is still to be written. Wolcott and Goodman, "Global Diffusion of the Internet," is a good beginning.

8. The World Wide Web is just one of many cyber networks that were developed in the 1980s. It was only due to several economic and political factors that *this* Internet graduated to become a global commercial and cultural medium that is today known as *the* Internet. Accordingly, the legal and regulatory requirements of the World Wide Web were defined by its inventors and initial users.

9. "Bruce Lehman on New Intellectual Property Treaties" (Washington: United States Information Agency, April 4, 2004) (www.usia.gov).

10. Krishnan Venugopal, "Telecommunication Sector Negotiations at the WTO: Case Studies of India, Sri Lanka, and Malaysia," paper presented at the "Regional Seminar on Telecommunications and Trade Issues," ITU, ESCAP, and WTO, Bangkok, October 28–30, 2003.

11. Information Technology Act 2000 (www.deity.gov.in); C. M. Abhilash, "E-Commerce Law in Developing Countries: An Indian Perspective," *Information and Communication Technology Law* 11, no. 3 (2002): 269–81.

12. The DNS, often advertised as the "phonebook of the Internet," is the international network of thirteen servers that matches the domain names of every entity on the web to its physical location, thereby allowing the Internet to function. The servers, in turn, are managed through a master file known as the root-zone file.

13. For the history of these debates, see Milton Mueller, "ICANN and Internet Governance: Sorting through the Debris of 'Self-Regulation,'" *Info* 1, no. 6 (December 1999); Wolfgang Kleinwächter, "Beyond ICANN vs. ITU: How WSIS Tries to Enter the New Territory of Internet Governance," *Gazette: The International Journal for Communications Studies* 66, no. 3-4 (2004): 233–51; for detailed history, see Milton Mueller, *Ruling the Root: Internet Governance and the Taming of Cyberspace* (MIT Press, 2002).

14. International Telecommunications Union, "Documents of the Plenipotentiary Conference (Minneapolis, 1998)," Documents 1-356, DT 1-55, and DL 1-34 (www.itu.int).

15. Statistics from the International Telecommunication Union website (www.itu.int).

16. In 2001, 56 percent of the Indian IT industry's workers were working on-site at foreign locations. Nagesh Kumar, "Indian Software Industry Development: National and International Perspectives," in *ICTs and Indian Economic Development*, edited by Ashwani Saith and M. Vijaybhaskar (New Delhi: Sage Publications, 2005), pp. 93–130.

17. While the U.S. government claims that the current model of Internet governance by ICANN is "self-regulation," almost all scholars agree that the creation of ICANN was a result of the U.S. government's intent to retain its control over the Internet rather than give it up to a multistakeholder agency. For instance, see Mueller, "ICANN and Internet Governance." Similar U.S. influence can be seen across administration of the Internet. For example, the chair of the Internet Engineering Task Force, which authorizes the updating of the Internet protocol suite, is currently co-sponsored by the U.S. National Security Agency. See Carolyn D. Marsan, "Q&A: Security Top Concern for New IETF Chair," *Network World*, July 26, 2007 (www.networkworld.com).

18. For instance, see T. C. James, "The Internet as a Challenge for Intellectual Property Protection: An Indian Perspective," paper presented at the "Seminar for Asia and the Pacific Region on the Internet and the Protection of Intellectual Property Rights," World Intellectual Property Organization, Singapore, April 28–30, 1998 (www.wipo.int).

19. National Task Force on Information Technology and Software Development, "Basic Background Report—I: Internet/VSNL-Based Issues," June 9, 1998 (www.it-taskforce.nic.in).

20. The first recorded attempt to censor the Internet in India was the banning of the Pakistani newspaper *Dawn*'s website in the aftermath of the Kargil conflict. See "Grateful Dawn Group Writes to Express," *Indian Express*, July 15, 1999.

21. Kleinwächter, "Beyond ICANN vs. ITU"; on U.S. policy, see Kenneth N. Cukier, "Who Will Control the Internet? Washington Battles the World," *Foreign Affairs* 84, no. 6 (November-December 2005): 7–13.

22. Vinod Vaish, statement by the delegation of India at the Preparatory Committee I meeting of the WSIS, Geneva, July 1–5, 2002 (www.itu.int); Vinod Vaish, statement at the Asian Regional Conference, WSIS, Tokyo, January 13–15, 2003, Document WSIS/PC-2/CONTR/69-E (www.itu.int).

23. Arun Shourie, statement at the WSIS, Geneva, December 11, 2003 (www.itu.int).

24. See Markus Kummer, "The Results of the WSIS Negotiations on Internet Governance," in *Internet Governance: A Grand Collaboration*, edited by Don MacLean (New York: United Nations Information and Communication Technologies Task Force, 2004), pp. 53–57.

25. "Input from India for the Working Group on Internet Governance (WGIG) Meeting," Geneva, February 14–16, 2005 (www.wgig.org).

26. See William J. Drake, ed., *Reforming Internet Governance: Perspectives from the Working Group on Internet Governance* (New York: United Nations Information and Communication Technologies Task Force, 2005).

27. Dayanidhi Maran, statement at the WSIS, Tunis, November 16, 2005 (ww.itu.in).

28. The Clinton administration had rejected the Russian proposal in the late 1990s. From 2005 to 2008, the United States was the only country in the UN General Assembly's First Committee to vote against a resolution, sponsored by Russia every year, calling for multilateral talks on the issues of "information security." Tim Maurer, "Cyber Norm Emergence at the United Nations: An Analysis of the UN's Activities Regarding Cyber-Security?" Discussion Paper 2011-11 (Harvard Kennedy School, Belfer Center for Science and International Affairs, September 2011); see also Eneken Tikk-Ringas, "Developments in the Field of Information and Telecommunication in the Context of International Security: Work of the UN First Committee 1998–2012," Cyber Process Policy Brief (Geneva: ICT4 Peace Publishing, 2012); for a Russian perspective on the issue, see Sergei Komov, Sergei Kortokov, and Igor Dylevski, "Military Aspects of Ensuring International Information Security in the Context of Elaborating Universally Acknowledged Principles of International Law," *Disarmament Forum* 3 (2007): 35–44.

29. The latest version of the resolution was adopted in 2006: UN General Assembly, "Role of Science and Technology in the Context of International Security and Disarmament," Sixty First Session, A/RES/61/55 (New York: United Nations, December 6, 2006) (www.un.org); for an Indian perspective on the resolution, see S. S. Palanimanickam, "Introduction of the Resolution Role of Science and Technology in the Context of International Security and Disarmament," *Statements in the 55th Session of the General Assembly (Millennium Assembly)* (New York: United Nations, October 18, 2000) (www.un.int/india).

30. World Bank, World Development Indicators (worldbank.org).

31. For instance, by 2005 only 53 percent of the Indian bank branches had Internet banking. For the government-owned banks, the figure was an abysmal 20 percent. Dhiraj Sharma, "Does Technology Lead to Better Financial Performance? A Study of Indian Commercial Banks," *Managing Global Transitions* 10, no 1 (Spring 2012): 3–28.

32. Joseph S. Nye, "Nuclear Lessons for Cyber Security?" *Strategic Studies Quarterly* 5, no. 4 (Winter 2011): 18–38.

33. For instance, the government's cyber security agency, Indian Computer Emergency Response Team (CERT-In), was only created in 2004 and had very little impact in the first few years.

34. For instance, see Amit Agarwal, "The Case of Overzealous Indian ISPs," *Wall Street Journal: India Real Time*, August 23, 2012 (http://blogs.wsj.com/indiarealtime).

35. CERT-In, *Annual Report: 2009* (New Delhi: Government of India, Department of Information Technology, 2010), p. 4.

36. "Microsoft Security Intelligence Report," *Microsoft* 8 (July-December 2009): n.p.

37. Ian Traynor, "Russia Accused of Unleashing Cyberwar to Disable Estonia," *The Guardian*, May 17, 2007; Travis Wentworth, "You've Got Malice," *Newsweek*, August 23, 2008.

38. "Tracking GhostNet: Investigating a Cyber Espionage Network," *Information Warfare Monitor*, March 29, 2009.

39. Nicolas Falliere, Liam O. Murchu, and Eric Chien, "W32.Stuxtnet Dossier: Version 1.4," *Symantec Security Response,* February 2011 (www.symantec.com).

40. Narendra Kaushal, "Information Warriors," *Sainik Samachar* 53, no. 4 (February 15, 2006): n.p.

41. "Antony Asks Service Chiefs to Prepare a Coordinated Crisis Management Action Plan for Countering Cyber Attacks" (New Delhi: Government of India, Press Information Bureau, April 16, 2010).

42. For instance, see "Cyber Warfare Strategy" (New Delhi: Government of India, Press Information Bureau, December 13, 2010).

43. P. D. Samanta, "India Wants Rules of 'Cyber War' Defined," *Indian Express*, February 7, 2011.

44. For instance, the first GGE, which had failed to come to an agreement, was split over two issues: (a) the desire of the Russian bloc to control "content" along with infrastructure and (b) the position of the American bloc that talks of disarmament should not be included in the GGE. The second GGE (2009–10), which had a successful outcome, did not mention either issue in its recommendations, essentially following the U.S. policy on both points. See Office for Disarmament Affairs, "Fact Sheet: Developments in the Field of Information and Telecommunications in the Context of International Security" (New York: United Nations, November 2012) (www.un.org).

45. See Rebecca MacKinnon, "Corporate Accountability in Networked Asia," in *Access Contested: Security, Identity, and Resistance in Cyberspace*, edited by Ronald Deibert, John Palfrey, Rafal Rohozinski, and Jonathan Zittrain (MIT Press, 2012), pp. 202–05.

46. Vikas Bajaj, "India Warns It Will Block BlackBerry Traffic That It Can't Monitor," *New York Times*, August 12, 2010; Phred Dvorak, Amol Sharma, and Margaret Coker, "RIM Offered Security Fixes," *Wall Street Journal*, August 14, 2010; S. Ramadoral, "Don't Disconnect India," *Hindustan Times*, September 21, 2010; Euan Rocha, "RIM: BlackBerry Security Not Compromised in India," Reuters, August 2, 2012.

47. "Cyber Attacks" (New Delhi: Government of India, Press Information Bureau, November 30, 2011).

48. The Information Technology (Amendment) Act 2008 (www.deity.gov.in); Department of Information Technology, "Discussion Draft on National Cyber Security Policy" (New Delhi: Government of India, 2011); various notifications issued by the Government of India, Department of Information Technology, under IT (Amendment) Act 2008.

49. Jeremy Ferwerda, Nazli Choucri, and Stuart Madnick, "Institutional Foundations for Cyber Security: Current Responses and New Challenges," Working Paper CISL 2009-03 (Massachusetts Institute of Technology, Composite Information Systems Laboratory, September 2010).

50. Hack back is when the victim of a cyber attack tries to go on the offensive against the attacker. On ethical issues of cyber security by governments, see Dorothy E. Denning, "Ethics of Cyber Conflict," in *The Hand Book of Information and Computer Ethics,* edited by Kenneth Einar Himma and Herman T. Tavani (Hoboken, N.J.: Wiley, 2008), pp. 407–28.

51. For a report card of the IGF, see Jeremy Malcolm, *Multi-Stakeholder Governance and the Internet Governance Forum* (Wembley, Australia: Terminus Press, 2008); see also Milton L. Mueller, *Network and States: The Global Politics of Internet Governance* (MIT Press, 2010), pp. 107–26.

52. Manjeev Singh Puri, statement during the UN secretary general's consultations on enhanced cooperation on international public policy issues pertaining to the Internet, Permanent Mission of India to the UN, December 14, 2010.

53. See Christopher R. Hughes, "Google and the Great Firewall," *Survival* 52, no. 2 (2010): 19–26; Bryan Kekel, "Capability of the People's Republic of China to Conduct Cyber Warfare and Computer Network Exploitation" (U.S.-China Economic and Security Review Commission, 2009); Kevin Werbach, "The Centripetal Network: How the Internet Holds Itself, and the Forces Tearing It Apart," *University of California Davis Law Review* 42 (2008): 343–412; see also Tim Wu, "Network Neutrality, Broadband Discrimination," *Journal of Telecommunications and High Technology Law* 2 (2003): 141–78.

54. Unfortunately, the scholarship has yet to tackle the issue of China's current position on Internet governance. For the Chinese perspective in the early years, see Christopher R. Hughes and Monika Ermert, "What's in a Name? China and the Domain Name System," in *China and the Internet: Politics of the Digital Leap Forward*, edited by Christopher R. Hughes and Gudrun Wacker (London: Routledge, 2003), pp. 127–38.

55. For the rationale of "bridging power," see Sunil Khilnani, "India as a Bridging Power," in *India as a New Global Leader* (London: Foreign Policy Centre, 2005).

56. Commission on Science and Technology for Development, "India's Inputs to the Questionnaire Circulated by the Chair of the CSTD Working Group on Improvements to Internet Governance Containing Broad Elements of the Final Report" (Geneva: United Nations, n.d.) (http://www.unctad.info/upload/CSTD-IGF/Contributions/M1/India.pdf).

57. For the proposal, see ibid. For discussion on the issue, see "Transcripts of TS Workshop 10: Reflection on the Indian Proposal towards an IGF 2.0," Sixth Annual Meeting of the Internet Governance Forum, Nairobi, September 29, 2011; for a comparison of India's position with that of other nations, see Commission on Science and Technology for Development Working Group, "Compilation of Contributions Made by Members of the Commission on Science and Technology (CSTD) Working Group on Improvements to the Internet Governance Forum Circulated at Its Third Meeting" (Geneva: United Nations, October 3, 2011) (www.unctad.info).

58. IBSA, "Recommendations," Multistakeholder Meeting on Global Internet Governance, Rio de Janeiro, September 1–2, 2011.

59. Dushyant Singh, "India's Proposal for the United Nations Committee for Internet-Related Policies," Sixty-Sixth Session of the UN General Assembly, New York, October 26, 2011; for analysis of the proposal, see Milton Mueller, "A United Nations Committee for Internet-Related Policies? A Fair Assessment" (Syracuse University, Internet Governance Project, October 29, 2011) (www.internetgovernance.org).

60. Nevertheless, the proposal was toned down from the Rio recommendations that called for the body to "integrate and oversee."

61. For instance, see Sandeep Bamzi, "Internet Censorship: Goodbye Freedom," *India Today*, September 2, 2012.

62. See Larry Downes, "Why Is the UN Trying to Take over the Internet?" *Forbes*, September 8, 2012; Patrick S. Ryan, "The ITU and the Internet's *Titanic* Moment," *Stanford Technology Law Review* 8 (2012): n.p. For a more nuanced understanding, see the Internet Governance Project's coverage of the issue at www.internetgovernance.org.

63. ITU, "Final Acts" (Dubai: World Conference on International Telecommunications, 2012) (www.itu.int). On the collapse, see Wolfgang Kleinwächter, "WCIT and

Internet Governance: Harmless Resolution or Trojan Horse?" December 17, 2012 (www.circleid.com). Experts remain divided on whether the treaty actually holds any significance for Internet governance. While some maintain that the treaty can be interpreted to build ITU's case to take over Internet regulation, including DNS management and deep-packet inspection, others argue that it does little to alter the ITU's position.

64. Council Working Group to Prepare for WCIT-12, "Draft Compilation of Proposals with Options for Revisions of the ITRs," Document CWG-WCIT12/DT-62-E, May 8, 2012 (www.wcitleaks.org).

65. WCIT-12, "India (Republic of): Proposals for the Work of the Conference," Document 21-E, November 3, 2012 (www.wcitleaks.org); point-by-point comparison of India's final proposals with others can be seen at WCIT-12, "Proposals Received from ITU Member States for the Work of the Conference," Document DT/1-E, November 30, 2012 (www.itu.int/en/wcit-12).

66. ITU, "Finished Transcripts of WCIT-12," Plenary Sessions 1–17 (www.itu.int/en/wcit-12); Shalini Singh, "Now, Russia, UAE, and Others Want Direct Government Control of Internet," *Hindu*, December 10, 2012.

67. "India's Officially Submitted Stand on ITR at WCIT-2012" (New Delhi: Government of India, Press Information Bureau, December 14, 2012).

68. ICANN, "ICANN Bringing the Languages of the World to the Global Internet: Fast Track Process for Internationalized Domain Names Launches Nov. 16," October 30, 2009 (www.icann.org).

69. Milton Mueller, "Early Warnings of Corruption in ICANN's GAC" (Internet Governance Project, January 11, 2013) (www.internetgovernance.org).

DEVESH KAPUR

13 India and International Financial Institutions and Arrangements

Introduction

India's engagement with international financial institutions (IFIs) and other institutional arrangements governing global finance commenced even before independence, when the country participated in the Bretton Woods conference in 1944. Recently discovered transcripts of the Bretton Woods conference reveal that even though India was still a colony, the Indian delegation, led by Sir Chintaman Deshmukh, the first Indian governor of the Reserve Bank of India (RBI) and later finance minister, was particularly vociferous, questioning voting rights skewed toward Western countries and making it amply clear (to the consternation of the British) that the United Kingdom owed India money and India wanted to be repaid—soon!

Subsequently, over the next half century, India's principal engagement with these institutions—the International Monetary Fund (IMF), the World Bank, and later the Asian Development Bank (ADB)—was as a borrower. Its economic model of import substitution industrialization eschewed reliance on private foreign capital and international trade, ironically increasing its reliance on official sources of international finance. Although India did initiate international borrowing from private banks in the 1980s, it was only after the onset of economic reforms in 1991—when the country moved to integrate with the global economy—that India became open to foreign capital, whether as foreign direct investment, portfolio flows, or overseas debt borrowings by

Sections of this paper have benefited immensely from discussions with K. P. Krishnan and T. V. Somanathan. I am also grateful to W. P. S. Sidhu for his inputs and patience and to Saba Jafri for excellent research assistance.

Table 13-1. *India and the IFIs*

Institution	*India's shareholding (%)*	*India's current world ranking*	*China's shareholding (%)*
Global			
International Monetary Fund	2.75 (current quota share: 2.44)[a]	8 (current: 11)[b]	6.40[c]
World Bank	2.97[d]	8[d]	3.46[e]
Bank for International Settlements	Became a member in November 1996[f]	Not applicable	Became a member in November 1996[f]
Regional			
African Development Bank	0.386[g]	43[h]	1.931[i]
Inter-American Development Bank	Not a member	Not applicable	0.002[j]
European Bank for Reconstruction and Development	Not a member	Not applicable	Not a member
Asian Development Bank	6.35[k]	4[l]	6.46[l]
Subregional			
Caribbean Development Bank	Not a member	Not applicable	Not a member

a. Expected when the quota increases under the 14th General Review of Quotas becomes effective (www.imf.org/external/np/sec/pr/2010/pdfs/pr10418_table.pdf).

b. www.imf.org/external/np/sec/pr/2010/pdfs/pr10418_table.pdf.

c. www.imf.org/external/np/sec/pr/2010/pdfs/pr10418_table.pdf.

d. http://siteresources.worldbank.org/EXTANNREP2012/Resources/8784408-1346247445238/8817772-1346257698669/5.3_IBRDFinancial_Statements.pdf.

e. http://siteresources.worldbank.org/EXTANNREP2012/Resources/8784408-1346247445238/8817772-1346257698669/5.3_IBRDFinancial_Statements.pdf.

f. www.bis.org/about/chronology/1990-1999.htm.

g. www.afdb.org/fileadmin/uploads/afdb/Documents/Publications/AfDB%202012%20EN_WEB.pdf.

h. Out of seventy-seven member states, eighteen of twenty-four nonregional member-states.

i. www.afdb.org/fileadmin/uploads/afdb/Documents/Publications/AfDB%202012%20EN_WEB.pdf.

j. http://idbdocs.iadb.org/wsdocs/getdocument.aspx?docnum=36736798.

k. www.adb.org/sites/default/files/pub/2012/IND.pdf.

l. www.adb.org/sites/default/files/adb-ar2011-v2.pdf.

Indian firms. In turn, this led to a new engagement with global financial rules and standards and their institutional progenitors, first as a rule taker but increasingly as a participant with potential influence on rule shaping.

The chapter is divided into three sections. It first examines India's engagement with the IFIs as a borrower and the degree to which it has been able to adjust to taking a more strategic view of these institutions, beyond their ability to lend to India. The second section examines India's growing engagement with global governance "clubs," particularly the G-20 and intergovernmental rule- and standard-making bodies, focusing on the Financial Action Task Force (FATF). The third section focuses on private standard-setting bodies, which, while less visible, can have a considerable impact, focusing on International Financial Reporting Standards (IFRS). Finally, the chapter examines some overarching questions. Which institutions should India join? Under what conditions does power translate into influence, and when is it undermined because of seemingly mundane bureaucratic reasons such as institutional support from different ministries, degree of coordination among these ministries, bureaucratic capacity and competencies, and strategic mindset to bargain imaginatively with issue cross-linkages?

India's Engagement with the Multilateral Financial Institutions

For nearly six decades, India's primary engagement with multilateral financial institutions—the Bretton Woods institutions and the regional development banks—has been at the receiving end. These institutions were a source of external savings, much-needed foreign exchange, advice, and technical assistance—and, sometimes, arm twisting.[1]

India was one of the forty-four original signatories to the agreements reached at Bretton Woods that established the International Bank for Reconstruction and Development (IBRD) and the IMF. It was also one of the founding members of the International Finance Corporation (IFC) in 1956 and the International Development Association (IDA) in 1960. India later became a member of the Multilateral Investment Guarantee Agency in January 1994.[2]

IBRD lending to India commenced in 1949 with a loan to the Indian railways; the first investment by the IFC in India took place in 1959 and the first by the IDA in 1961 (a highway construction project). The World Bank has been India's largest source of external capital (from any one source); in turn, India has been the largest borrower from the World Bank, with loans accounting for 11.3 percent of total lending by June 2012. During this period, the World Bank lent India a total of $91.8 billion in 543 loans, with $48.3 billion in IBRD loans and $43.5 billion in IDA loans. This constituted nearly 8.5 percent of IBRD lending and 17.3 percent of IDA lending. Cumulatively, India's share of IFC loans was somewhat less ($8.5 billion for 340 enterprises; 6.7 percent of total lending and the second largest after Brazil).

India was also one of the founding members of the Asian Development Bank in 1966. At the time, it reached an informal agreement not to borrow, since, given the small size of the ADB and India's large borrowing requirements, it would have crowded out smaller Asian countries. While the informal agreement was that a Japanese national would head the ADB, India pushed for an Indian to run the institution, while the Philippines (supported by the United States) lobbied for the ADB to be located in Manila. India made a major mistake in not bargaining for the ADB to be located in New Delhi instead of insisting on a leadership role for its nationals in the organization. Physical location provides much greater benefits than leadership over the long run, with pecuniary and network externalities. It is also more permanent. The ability of the leadership of international organizations to advance national interests is limited, and its effects are more symbolic than substantive. Pressing for one's nationals in leadership positions is also more transient in that over time a single country will not be able to monopolize the leadership of an international organization.[3] But it does have payoffs for the elites of a country who fancy their own chances.

Following the third general capital increase in 1983, the ADB had enough capital to commence lending to India in 1986, and by end-2011 the ADB had financed 178 projects and lent nearly $27 billion in India. As with the World Bank, while there have been occasional hiccups in lending (usually because of pressures from the United States and some other G-7 members), these have waned in recent years. On the one hand, pressures from China have increased, which was apparent in 2009 when China strongly protested the ADB's lending program for India, arguing that it encroached on a territorial dispute between the two countries since it included projects in Arunachal Pradesh. China's foreign ministry spokesman Qin Gang put it bluntly: "China expresses its strong dissatisfaction over this. . . . The bank's move not only seriously tarnishes its own name, but also undermines the interests of its members." Following China's objections, India abandoned plans to obtain funding from the ADB and the World Bank for projects in Arunachal Pradesh.[4]

On the other hand, India has also engaged in similar behavior, blocking Pakistan from seeking financing from the ADB for construction of the Diamer-Bhasha Dam in Pakistan-occupied Kashmir, arguing that if the loan were granted, Pakistan could have a *locus standi* in waterworks and undercut Indian claims to the whole of Jammu and Kashmir under the Instrument of Accession.

After pressure from the government of India, the ADB asked Pakistan to obtain India's assent before approving the project, which Pakistan refused.

In the past, India saw these institutions through a North-South prism, where as a borrower it sought greater resources at minimal costs, both financial and nonfinancial (that is, conditionalities).[5] It sought to address these goals by trying to influence the governance of these institutions. However, despite being one of the five largest shareholders of the World Bank when it was established, the relative decline in India's economic fortunes meant that while it always had representation on the boards of these institutions, its shareholding per se did not provide it with much leverage. Since the 1970s India's shareholding in the World Bank declined, and this trend was reversed only in 2010, when India became the eighth largest shareholder of the Bank (it was the fourth largest shareholder in the ADB in 2012, with 5.4 percent of voting power).

While many in India (especially on the left) have been suspicious of the World Bank and its ideological baggage, the overall relationship between the World Bank and India has been characterized by symmetry and equality (with some notable exceptions). The relationship was particularly symbiotic in the first quarter century. As the first history of the World Bank put it in 1971, "No country has been studied more by the World Bank than India, and it is no exaggeration to say that India has influenced the Bank as much as the Bank has influenced India."[6]

The reality is that India has been treated more favorably than most other borrowers. The perceived sophistication of Indian policymakers, their ability to articulate programs (as distinct from their ability or willingness to implement them), and the caution that inevitably comes in dealing with a large country all played a role. India's democracy, the exigencies of the cold war, extreme poverty, and eloquent political and economic interlocutors made India the best argument for foreign aid for many years. On the flipside, criticisms of India would have weakened the general case for development aid. India's assigned role as an aid showcase added to the constraints the World Bank felt in pressing India for policy change. In addition, the Bank's limited leverage was also due to the reality that its resources were quite modest relative to the size of the Indian economy, whether that money was seen in per capita terms or as a percentage of both total government expenditures and gross domestic investment.[7]

Unlike with the World Bank, India's relationship with the International Monetary Fund has been more episodic—and in those relatively brief periods the IMF has been a political lightning rod within India. Indeed, the three main IMF programs that India undertook when beset by balance of payments problems—around the traumatic 1966 devaluation, in 1981–82 after the second oil shock, and the most recent program in 1991–93—were major turning points in India's economic policies. The 1981–82 program, when India borrowed SDR 3.9 billion under an Extended Fund Facility, was the largest arrangement in the IMF's history at the time and rolled back some of the more antibusiness policies of the Indian government.[8] The 1991–93 program (when India borrowed SDR 3.6 billion) marked the onset of a major turning point in India's economic policies.

A consistent theme in India's relationship with the IMF has been its insistence on expanding the IMF's resources and increasing the share of quotas for developing countries (and by implication itself). In recent decades, it has pressed its case more forcefully, arguing that the IMF quota formula, in which market exchange rates and "openness" (that is, the share of international trade in a country's economy) have a large weight, was biased against big countries like India that have large domestic markets and consequently a smaller role for international trade. But since China had faced exactly the same handicaps and had overcome them much more successfully that India, the argument did not cut as much ice. What mattered was (as with China) India's greater integration in the global economy and more rapid growth. When the fourteenth general review of quotas becomes effective, India's quota in the IMF will increase from the current 2.44 percent to 2.75 percent, making India the eighth largest quota-holding country at the IMF (from eleventh).[9] However, while India's quotas increased 0.31 percent, the financial cost to India was about 14,000 crores ($2.6 billion).[10] And following the 2008 global financial crisis, India joined the other BRICs (Brazil, Russia, and China, in addition to India) in contributing to the IMF's New Arrangements to Borrow to address the euro zone crisis, contributing SDR 8.74 billion (approximately $13.4 billion).[11]

At one level, this could be viewed as India's contribution to a global public good, while, of course, enhancing its private interests. It also reaffirmed that if financial contributions are a measure of participation in global governance, India's role in the IMF and World Bank via subscriptions is comparatively high and indeed ranks highest among the BRICs relative to its gross national income (GNI) and GNI per capita.[12] At the same it raises a question: if this is the marginal cost of power in the international financial system, are the marginal benefits commensurate with it?

In recent years, another issue has emerged in India's relations with the Bretton Woods institutions—the monopoly on leadership held by Americans in the World Bank and by Europeans in the IMF. The euro zone crisis and the need for greater resources for the IMF—this time to bail out the Europeans—resulted in a declaration by the G-20 leaders at the London summit in April 2009: "The heads and senior leadership of the international financial institutions should be appointed through an open, transparent, and merit-based selection process." In public India pressed for unity among developing countries in voting for a common candidate. However, when it came to choosing new leaders, India backed the French (in the IMF) and the American (in the World Bank) candidates. What mattered in the end was whether the candidates would be helpful to India's interests, not their nationality. Like Deng Xiaoping, India too appears to have come to the private conclusion that it does not matter whether the cat is white or black, as long as it catches the mice that India wants to catch.

In addition to leadership and shareholding, there are three additional channels of influence in the IFIs. These include the executive boards of these institutions; the Development Committee (in the case of the World Bank) and the International Monetary and Financial Committee (in the case of the IMF), which are ministerial-level forums for intergovernmental consensus-building on development and monetary and financial issues; and collective action through less formal "clubs," such as the G-24 in the 1970s through the 1990s and the G-20 more recently (which I discuss later).[13]

There is little doubt that an important reason that India punched above its shareholding weight in these institutions (especially in early decades) was the quality of Indian executive directors (and their advisers). While the degree to which the executive directors of these institutions shape their day-to-day governance is a matter of some debate, individual executive directors can at the margin shape the tenor of debate on institutional policies by force of the quality of logic, evidence, and persuasion, since decisions based solely on formal votes are rare. In this regard, in recent years the quality of Indian executive directors has been hit-or-miss, in part because decisions on who to send to represent India are personalized rather than institutionalized.

Until the new millennium, control of the key IFIs where India had primary interests was clear: the Japanese controlled the ADB, the United States controlled the World Bank, and the G-7 controlled the IMF. This mattered when India's relations with these powers were lukewarm. However, even as India, along with other emerging powers, especially China, has been acquiring greater weight in these institutions, India has been quietly strengthening its strategic relationship with Japan and the United States, in particular. Now their control of these institutions appears to be less detrimental to India's interests, especially since the only plausible replacement—China—seems even less likely to act in India's interests.

Although the primacy of the borrowing relationship with the IFIs is considerably lower today, India's strategic thinking about these institutions apparently has not shifted from a "borrower" mind-set to an "owner" mind-set. Ongoing discussions with regard to India's eligibility for IDA assistance illustrate the confusion. In 2012 the operational threshold for IDA eligibility was GNI per capita of $1,165 in real 2009 dollars (other considerations, such as capital market access, are not relevant for India today). India's GNI per capita was $1,170 in 2009. In practice, countries do not immediately graduate after breaching this income-based threshold—there is a five-year hiatus between exceeding the threshold and the cessation of new IDA lending (that is, formal graduation). This means that IDA-16 (2012–15) would be the last IDA replenishment in which India would be eligible for IDA lending and that the country would graduate in 2016 (the year in which IDA-17 would commence).[14]

In 2011 India informally agreed to "graduate" from IDA as per the policy. However, it subsequently reversed course and sought to remain an IDA-recipient country, arguing that although on average India is a lower-middle-income country with a per capita income above the IDA cutoff, it still has hundreds of millions of poor people. IDA undoubtedly faces a structural problem. With more than three-fourths of the world's poor now living in middle-income countries, there is a growing disconnect between poor countries and the countries where the majority of the world's poor live. Eventually an agreement was reached, with India continuing in IDA (through IDA-17) but with loans at less concessional rates to avoid a sharp reduction in the World Bank's overall financing to India.

But the decision, which was driven by just a few officials without any public discussion, also revealed a particular mind-set still prevalent in Indian officialdom. India wants to be recognized as a major global player, part of the G-20, a key player in global climate change and trade negotiations, a prospective member of the Nuclear Suppliers Group, and an emerging power. Yet in practice its behavior still has the hesitancy and defensiveness of a weak and poor country. India was recently asked to join the Asian Development Fund, with a nominal contribution of $10 million, barely a few million dollars a year. India reportedly declined on the grounds that doing so might have an adverse effect on its claims to the IDA. The larger point was lost: with China's inexorable rise, India needs to put itself squarely within Asian multilateral forums to provide a countervailing view.

Similarly, India was invited to join the Caribbean Development Bank. This entailed a payment of just a few million dollars to that Bank's capital. Again India declined. Despite the size of the Indian diaspora in that part of the world, the strategic imperatives of leveraging multilateral institutions to its own advantage apparently were not deemed important.

India was more forward looking when it was economically weaker. It was an early nonregional member of the African Development Bank, joining in December 1983, although in comparison to other nonregional members, India's financial commitments have been quite small. So far it has contributed $6.64 million toward the paid-up portion of capital stock and holds just 0.256 percent of total shares. However, it has been part of the Nordic constituency (Denmark, Finland, Norway, and Sweden), which commands 4.82 percent of voting power. India also has given $80 million to the African Development Fund since its inception (around 0.2 percent).

There is a growing contradiction between the idea that India is a poor country that cannot afford to support these modest multilateral initiatives and the relatively massive amounts it lays out for bilateral aid without hardly any public debate. Between 2003–04 and 2010–11, India provided $5.1 billion in lines of credit, of which $3.3 billion went to Africa, $1.8 billion to South Asia, and $131 million to Caribbean countries. In May 2011 India announced $5 billion in low-interest loans over the next three years for Africa and an additional $1 billion for education, railways, and peacekeeping efforts, a huge increase from the $25 million India provided as aid to Africa in prior years. It also provided $2.1 billion to its South Asian neighbors in grants and loans and $346 million to other developing countries. India has been among the top five donors to Afghanistan: it donated $1 billion from 2002 to 2010 and announced another $0.5 billion donation in 2011.

Yet when it comes to taking a strategic view on multilateral financial institutions, India has not yet adjusted to its more robust economic situation. While Indian foreign policy mandarins press for a "Look East" policy, they balk when it comes to taking a modest stake in the Asian Development Fund. India holds an annual jamboree for its diaspora with much fanfare, but despite a substantial Indian diaspora in the Caribbean, it does not deem joining the Caribbean Development Bank (again at modest cost) to be worthwhile.

At the time of writing, India was considering launching a BRICS (including South Africa) development bank focusing on infrastructure and perhaps green technologies. There could well be some advantages to launching such an initiative, but there are formidable conflicting interests even among these five countries, especially since only China has the deep pockets to finance an institution of any size—and why it would do so unless it has a commensurate say in the institution's governance is an open question.

Elite Clubs: To Join or Not to Join; The Case of the OECD

One way to understand India's changing relationships with international organizations is the inherent ambivalence and political and institutional challenges facing a country that is looming large in the international system but continues to be a poor country. India's relationship with the Organization for Economic Cooperation and Development (OECD) is a good example of this ambivalence.

The club of industrialized countries, the thirty-four-member OECD, represents more than 60 percent of global gross domestic product (GDP). In 2007 the OECD launched the Enhanced Engagement Initiative, aimed at advancing the OECD's relationship with five "key partners"—Brazil, China, India, Indonesia, and South Africa—by opening the full range of its work program to them. The OECD works through thirty-six committees on a wide variety of issues, and the five countries have taken a selective approach to picking their priorities. There is wide variance in the acceptance of invitations to participate in these committee deliberations, with Brazil the most enthusiastic, followed by South Africa, India in the middle, and then China, with Indonesia bringing up the rear.[15]

India became actively involved in the OECD Committee on Fiscal Affairs and its working parties in 2006. Since then, it has played a lead role in the Global Forum on Transparency and Exchange of Information for Tax Purposes and become an active member of the OECD's multistakeholder Task Force on Tax and Development and a full member of the OECD Network on Fiscal Relations across Levels of Government. In 2012 India ratified the Convention on Mutual Administrative Assistance in Tax Matters, a multilateral agreement developed jointly by the Council of Europe and the OECD.[16] With foreign direct investment becoming more important for India—both into and out of India—the variety of intercompany transactions has created multiple challenges for tax authorities. Hence understanding—and coordinating internationally—issues related to transfer pricing, global trends in tax reform, and the implications for international tax arrangements and international dispute resolution is of much greater importance.

Closer links with the OECD allow Indian officials to access forums for sharing experiences and expertise, for benchmarking national policies against best practices, and for identifying solutions to common problems, and the potential benefits are not confined to economic and financial issues. For instance, in 2011 India accepted the invitation of the OECD Council to be a full adherent to the OECD Council Act related to the Mutual Acceptance of Data (MAD) in the Assessment of Chemicals. An important consequence of India's full adherence to the MAD system is that nonclinical health and environmental safety data generated in India will be accepted by all OECD member-countries and other adhering countries, allowing India to develop contract research for evaluating chemicals and removing a potential trade barrier.[17]

But there are costs, whether financial costs (if India has to contribute to the budget) or subtle pressure to adhere to OECD conventions—for instance, on development assistance if India were to participate in the meetings of the Development Assistance Committee—or its self-identity as a leader of the Global South. In this case India's gradual, case-by-case approach makes sense: why join an organization when some of the same benefits can be derived without joining and when richer countries like Brazil and China have not done so?

New Interstate Economic Coordination Bodies: The G-20

The G-20 was originally promoted by Canada and the United States in the aftermath of steps to promote the G-22 and subsequently the G-33 in 1999.[18] Structural changes in the international economy and systemic vulnerabilities made it imperative that the G-7 model of collectivist cooperation be expanded to include the larger emerging-market economies. Even more, the growing weight of emerging markets (and commensurate reduction of some of the weaker members of the G-7) meant that if these countries were not included early as meaningful participants, global economic coordination would lack legitimacy and was unlikely to be effective. Gradually this led to a restructuring and the formation of the G-20, which first met in Canada in 2000.

In the wake of the Asian financial crisis, the G-20 focused on managing the global economy, addressing issues such as market volatility and exchange rates, emerging-market crises, domestic financial reform, and operations of the IFIs. Indeed, the creation of the G-20 was an explicit acknowledgment that such issues could not be tackled without including key emerging-market economies. Over time, however, the G-20's agenda has widened, and in recent years discussions have ranged more broadly across issues such as development and aid effectiveness, debt relief, energy security, and the like.

The G-20 does not promulgate rules or policies that are binding on its members. Given its relatively small size and the absence of a formal bureaucracy, the G-20 has institutional attributes that in principle provide an informal, consensual, and experience-sharing forum: "The G-20 highlights the importance of policy learning and transfer, the role of epistemic communities, and the discursive and policy activism of increasingly autonomous organizations."[19]

Five factors make the G-20 an important vehicle for India's current and future multilateral engagements. First, "Today, in almost every international forum, India has explicitly engaged with smaller groups of powerful nations to affect outcomes at the expense of the more broad-based universalist approach that it traditionally espoused (or claimed to)."[20] Second, the G-20 also dovetails well with India's traditional aversion to multilateral treaty-based systems. Amitav Acharya's characterization of Asia's "somewhat distinctive multilateralism" based on "organizational minimalism, preference for consensus over majority voting, and avoidance of legalistic approaches in favor of informal and process based socialization" rings true of India as well (India's perennial quest to be a permanent member of the UN Security Council is a notable exception).[21] Third, as an emerging power India is more comfortable with a "technical systems" approach than a pure "power politics" approach, as in the Security Council, in considerable part because the domestic politics are easier to navigate. Another reason is that India's policymaking in this area is led by officials with little political input, and they are more familiar with and feel on safer ground arguing about technical systems. Fourth, India's "finance diplomacy" (along perhaps with peacekeeping) has been one of India's strongest contributions to international relations, in part because it is less hamstrung by multiple domestic pressures and in part because the quality of talent in the Finance Ministry has been relatively strong. And finally, the G-20's emergence as a leader since 2008 has allowed India to put its best foot forward in that the format and subject matter were ideally suited to the skills and qualities of Prime Minister Manmohan Singh, whose deep knowledge of economic issues gave India considerable credibility in the small-group private discussions at these meetings. However, despite these advantages, the initiative to push for interactions at the leader level did not come from India, revealing just how cautious India has been.

While India's participation in the G-20 meetings opened opportunities for India to "help shape the new global economic architecture in line with its strategic interests" through both short-term crisis response actions and a medium-term agenda,[22] there is less agreement on the content of the actions and mechanisms for advancing these interests. While pressing for a political commitment to keep markets open or reforming the global financial architecture by strengthening the financial capacity of the Bretton Woods institutions and granting greater voting power to the emerging powers would advance India's interests, it is less clear how having China replace Japan (or the United States) would do so.

Having got a seat at the "high table," what have been India's achievements within the G-20? At one level, having a "seat at the table" has allowed India to quietly sink proposals not to its liking, such as discussing climate change commitments or a European proposal to adopt a tax on financial transactions as a way to generate aid for developing countries, joining forces with Canada and China. Whether opposing a "Tobin" tax was necessarily against India's interests is open to question, especially since India could instead have tried to steer the revenue stream to finance efforts to mitigate global climate change, of which it would be an obvious beneficiary.

On a more positive note, India (along with partners) worked within the G-20 for governance reforms in the IMF. The move gathered momentum at the G-20 ministerial meeting in China in 2005 and contributed to a two-stage governance reform package announced at the IMF's annual meetings in Singapore in 2006. It pitched for deeper tax information exchange agreements at the G-20 to facilitate the flow of crucial data on tax evasion. The resulting Convention on Mutual Administrative Assistance in Tax Matters allows governments to share information on bank accounts.

India's overt achievements at the G-20 appear to be modest; however, to be fair, the G-20's overall achievements have been rather limited. Indeed, global governance has been adrift, and by all accounts the prime minister's guidelines to the Indian delegations have been that it should act, keeping in mind that its power is still relatively modest. Nonetheless, there is little doubt that India feels that it is in its interest that the G-20 becomes the premier institutional mechanism for multilateral cooperation on global financial and economic issues. But can India do more as a rule shaper to make the G-20 more effective? The conclusion examines some options.

Interstate Rule-Setting Bodies: The FATF

As India's external economic linkages have grown, so has the need to align the Indian economy with global financial rules. India's interaction with the IFIs has been shifting, from an overwhelming concern with borrowing to global norms pushed by the Bretton Woods institutions such as capital account liberalization and to more recent concerns with global financial standards. These standards are increasingly being crafted in non-secretariat international bodies, both interstate and private, where monitoring and compliance are increasingly based on mutual peer review mechanisms. Their multiplicity and complexity pose considerable challenges for institutional capacity, goal setting, and internal coordination. At the same time, they offer an opportunity to use external standard setting to anchor and accelerate domestic reforms.

A good example where India has managed to meet these challenges is the Financial Action Task Force, an intergovernmental body set up by the G-7 in 1989 to create rules and standards to combat money laundering and terrorist financing. The FATF's global importance grew markedly in the aftermath of the 9/11 attacks. Since India was becoming increasingly open to international financial flows as well as a major target of international terrorism, the "need to combine an open approach to global capital alongside tough enforcement against terrorism and money laundering" made a compelling case for joining the FATF.[23] In addition, if India did not adapt and raise its standards to those espoused by the FATF, it would compromise the ability of Indian firms to compete in international trade in financial services.

In 1998 India became a member of the Asia Pacific Group on Money Laundering (APG), which conducted the first Mutual Evaluation Report (MER) of India in 2005. The weaknesses identified in Indian laws resulted in legislative actions to bring the Anti-Money Laundering Act and the Anti-Terrorism Act in compliance with FATF recommendations, which required amending the Unlawful Activities (Prevention) Act and the Prevention of Money Laundering Act (PMLA) in December 2008 and in June 2009, respectively.

India became an observer in the FATF in 2006 and initiated efforts to become a full-fledged member in 2008. The MER resulting from a joint APG-FATF effort in 2009 pointed out more than 100 deficiencies in financial laws and practices that India needed to address. To become an FATF member, India established a coordination mechanism, known as the Inter-Ministerial Coordination Committee, to coordinate more than forty ministries, departments, and regulators with a core ten-member working team from various stakeholder organizations.

The core of the actions required of India involved enlarging the scope of terrorist organizing and financing, extending the concept of proceeds of terrorism to nondesignated terrorist organizations, automatically including all designated individuals and entities as per United Nations (UN) Security Council Resolution 1267 (and successor resolutions), and promulgating rules clarifying the financial sector obligations of exchange houses, money remitters, payment gateways, and payment system operators.

India responded by providing an action plan to the FATF, divided into three timelines: immediate steps to be completed by June 2010, short-term steps to be completed by March 2011, and medium-term steps to be completed by March 2012. After completing the agreed immediate steps, India became a member of the FATF in June 2010 and a member of the Eurasian Group on Anti-Money Laundering and Terrorist Financing in December 2010. India was co-chair of the APG from July 2010 to July 2012 and, at the time of writing, co-chair of the Eurasian Group on Anti-Money Laundering and Terrorist Financing.

The medium-term action plan required amendment of two important pieces of legislation, the Prevention of Money Laundering Act and the Unlawful Activities Prevention Act. These were passed by Parliament in December 2012. The Banking Regulation Act was also amended. The amended PMLA in 2012 aligned India's definition of money laundering offenses with that of the Vienna and Palermo conventions. The issues covered included commodities futures brokers and other designated businesses and professions, and a broad range of sanctions were introduced, including sanctions against the designated directors and employees of such firms. The Unlawful Activities Prevention Act was similarly amended to include technical details such as having a more precise definition of "person," expanding the definition of "proceeds of terrorism" and "property," specifically including offenses committed by a company, society, or trust, extending the scope of the "offense of terrorism" to acts against an international or intergovernmental organization, and including offenses under the nine treaties annexed to the International Convention for Suppression of the Financing of Terrorism.

The FATF recommendations also led to the amendment of the Banking Regulation Act 1947: the Banking Laws (Amendment) Act 2012. The amended act addressed the deficiencies pointed out in the MER by sharply raising the penalties imposed by the RBI. In addition a host of amendments were made to the PMLA rules.

India also filed an application for entering into a multilateral memorandum of understanding in accordance with the procedures prescribed by the International Association of Insurance Supervisors to provide a legal gateway for appropriate information exchange and international cooperation. The FATF recommendations also required actions by the principal financial sector regulators, including the central bank, the securities markets, and the insurance regulator. The RBI amended the "know your customer" (KYC) and "anti-money laundering" (AML) manual and drew up new guidelines for internal policies for inspecting officers and new procedures for establishing correspondent banking relationships by banks.

New KYC rules had to be formulated for a host of other financial intermediaries such as the National Bank for Agricultural and Rural Development, the Securities Exchange Board of India, and the banking operations of India Post, while the Insurance Regulatory and Development Authority had to review and modify its inspection manuals to ensure compliance with the anti-money laundering and combating the financing of terror guidelines.

Stakeholders (including representatives from select banks, the RBI, the Indian Banks Association, and the Finance Intelligence Unit of the Ministry of Finance) were engaged to help banks to evolve common platforms and practices in dealing with KYC/AML–related issues under the PMLA and to suggest standard parameters for all banks to identify suspicious transactions. The KYC documentary requirements were made uniform for all financial intermediaries. Training and workshops were organized for thousands of banking and financial sector professionals.

India addressed all of the necessary issues in less than three years, a remarkable achievement given the complexity of the exercise and the endemic delays that often characterize the Indian system. Why did India become an enthusiastic member of a multilateral regime that it did not help to create and that was domestically intrusive (in that it required India to pass multiple pieces of domestic legislation)? And how did it manage to complete the complex exercises of coordination and legislation so rapidly without the usual protracted delays and domestic political fuss? First, the FATF reflected global regulatory practices that came within the ambit of UN Security Council resolutions on the financing of terrorism. Second, as a prime victim of terrorism, India's self-interest in improving its standards and practices to curb the financing of terrorism were obvious. Third, technical issues such as banking regulations bring together epistemic communities in which politicians and civil society activists have little interest precisely because of the technical nature of the rule changes. Fourth, the issue came squarely within the purview of the strongest ministry, namely, the Ministry of Finance. Finally, there was an element of happenstance in that the coordinating committee comprised an exceptional team.

Private Agents in Global Financial Governance: The IASB and International Accounting Standards

The last few decades have seen an enormous increase in the size, complexity, and degree of integration of global financial markets and a commensurate increase in the role of private regulators in global financial governance. From setting global benchmark interest rates (through the London Interbank Offer Rate process), to capital adequacy standards for international banking supervision (the Basel rules on capital adequacy), and to standards in cross-border securities market regulation by the International Organization of Securities Commissions, private sector self-regulation and public-private partnerships have emerged as an important pillar of global financial governance and transnational regulatory processes.

Several factors have driven this increase in global private regulators in international rules and standards, not just in finance but in a host of other areas as well, such as the role of the International Standards Organization (ISO) in setting international product standards. The domain expertise of such regulators gives them quasi-monopoly status that is largely uncontested—once such private bodies develop a standard, it becomes the global rule. This delegation of regulatory authority by governments to private international organizations is driven by recognition of the economic benefits of common global rules as well as by the reality that government regulators often lack the requisite expertise and resources, especially in specialized areas like complex financial products in internationally integrated markets. But it also reflects an ideological shift ("markets know best") and the sectoral business interests of powerful countries.

Private regulatory governance processes can leave public authorities vulnerable to dependence on the information and expertise provided by private agents, especially in rapidly changing market environments. This dependence can, in turn, result in financial regulation to align with private sector preferences and a tacit (if not more explicit) bureaucratic capture and loss of consumer welfare.[24] The outcomes for systemic stability can be potentially devastating, as the events of 2008 attest. Nonetheless, careful scrutiny of possible "regulatory capture," even of the institutions of global financial governance that have been subjected to intense private sector lobbying at the transnational level, such as the Basel Committee on Banking Supervision, finds that this access does not necessarily translate into capture; indeed, sometimes it has perversely led to "increasing regulatory stringency" rather than weakening regulation.[25]

The simultaneous internationalization and privatization of regulation have potentially far-reaching consequences, and therefore it is important to understand the actors who influence rulemaking in these private bodies and why some countries do better than others in transnational private rulemaking. Büthe and Mattli argue that influence in transnational regulatory institutions is less a function of the economic power of states and more a function of how well stakeholders are organized at the domestic level, that is, the ability of domestic organizations to "complement" international institutions.[26] They give the example of the International Accounting Standards Board (IASB), whose rules govern financial reporting by corporations in more than 100 countries. Although rulemaking has shifted to the international level, they argue that domestic institutions remain crucial for exerting influence over international standards, because they differ in how well they complement the private international regulatory bodies. Given the institutional structure and decision-making rules of bodies such as the IASB, it is essential for a country to grasp the international standardization agenda early and have a clear understanding of the implications of different accounting rules for the broad economy. This, they argue, fundamentally depends on the capacity of domestic institutions.

The International Financial Reporting Standards—originally known as the International Accounting Standards—were issued between 1973 and 2001 by the Board of the International Accounting Standards Committee (IASC). In 2001 the new IASB took over from the IASC the responsibility for setting international accounting standards that have come to be known as IFRS.

Accounting standards affect how costly it is for a company to raise capital, the incentives it has to invest in research and development, and how it calculates risks (and thereby what risks it takes). For an emerging market like India, the adoption of global accounting standards affects the ability of Indian firms to raise capital in global markets (one reason why some large Indian firms adopted Generally Accepted Accounting Principles) or the possibility of Mumbai emerging as a global financial center.

But accounting standards are not neutral. Take, for instance, the prioritization of "neutrality" (or the "absence of bias") over "prudence" (emphasizing judgment to avoid overstating capital or income), each of which has different legal and corporate governance moorings (the former in the United States and the latter in Europe). Accounting principles in Europe were rooted in a governance system that emphasized stewardship and ownership and depended on prudence and realizable values to ensure the protection of capital.[27] In the United States, in contrast, accounts evolved to facilitate trading in securities markets, which meant that more weight was given to neutrality and market valuations. There are serious questions concerning whether it is possible to have accounts that are both consistently prudent and neutral and whether the imposition of U.S.-style "neutrality" in Europe "risks removing the glue that binds together accounting and corporate governance."[28] And questions have been raised about whether the adoption of IFRS in banking prevented banks from provisioning for expected loan losses in the run-up to the 2008 financial crisis.[29]

India's representation in the IASC has been via the Institute of Chartered Accountants of India. While India has announced that a new set of standards convergent with (but not identical to) IFRS will be mandatory in India for financial statements (with a phase-in period depending on the size of the firm), the implementation date has been postponed twice, with April 1, 2013, as the new start date. There are a range of questions on whether India should adopt IFRS at once or gradually.

On the broader question of whether to move in the direction of IFRS, the fact that two of the largest market economies (Japan and the United States) have not adopted them or even committed to a time frame for adoption has influenced Indian thinking. Another crucial reason for the reluctance within important sectors of industry and the accountancy profession has been the potential effects on taxation. The two ministries involved have not had a common view, with the Ministry of Corporate Affairs pushing convergence and the Ministry of Finance preoccupied with the possible tax consequences and the methodology for preventing any tax reductions. The lack of clarity on tax implications has led to intense lobbying by companies that may suffer adverse tax consequences, which is believed to be the major reason for the postponement. At the time of writing, there were about forty differences between the converged accounting standards and the IFRS, reflecting, at least in part, technical disagreements.

The key question for India, given the size of its domestic economy and the predominance of domestic investment, is whether it should accept standards because they are international even when there are strong and defensible technical disagreements or they do not reflect India's underlying views on market and corporate governance. This is an important question in the area of accountancy because there is far less consensus among accountants on what the best approach should be. The reference earlier to "bias vs. prudence" is just one illustration of the debates and legitimate differences of opinion. A greater degree of professional judgment (which IFRS often requires) may have greater risks in a country like India where professional ethics and self-discipline are weak.

While the merits of IFRS can be debated, India has nothing to lose by exerting greater influence over the standard-setting process and moving it in the direction that Indian standard setters would prefer. Because of the process by which standards are drafted, this may require intense full-time participation at the IASB's headquarters through the secondment of Indian experts during formulation of draft standards rather than through high-level meetings. This is something India has not done.

Two broader issues emerge in respect of bodies like the IASB. First, if their pronouncements have impacts on the economy as a whole, it may not be in the country's best interest for representation to be led solely by a body representing one sectional or professional interest. In the Indian context, this may require the government (in the case of accountancy, the Ministry of Corporate Affairs) to engage actively with these nongovernmental bodies. A new protocol for these interactions is needed and should combine specialist technical input (from specialized bodies) with the representativeness and broader multidimensional view of the government. Second, given India's size relative to that of most other countries, India needs to make choices on standards that are widely followed internationally but not legally binding by treaty: are India's interests best served by completely following the international lead, by converging with it with some variations, or by going it alone? Smaller countries may have no choice, but India's size gives it greater room to maneuver, which it needs to exercise intelligently.

Conclusion

India's engagement with international financial institutions has been primarily with multilateral lending institutions. However, as its economy has grown and become more integrated globally, India has had to face up to the reality that an ever-increasing share of economic activity is governed by international rather than domestic rules or standards. This is exemplified by the new challenges of global finance, which are underpinned by a complex set of rules and standards that encompass a wide terrain from accounting to banking, from derivatives to debt instruments, and from insurance to securities. However, given the range of options among bilateral, plurilateral, regional, or global multilateral institutions through which India (and indeed other countries as well) will need to address its increasing global engagement, choosing among these options will require considerably greater analytical thinking and coordination among a wide range of domestic institutions, both public and private.[30]

India's changing relationships with the multitude of IFIs—those that lend money and those that set rules and standards, ranging from interstate to private—reflect the inherent tensions for a country that is looming large in the international system but continues to be low income. Getting out of old habits is rarely easy. Thus in engaging the IFIs, there is little strategic thinking about their budgets, uses of net income, or research priorities and how shaping them may better serve long-term interests. Leveraging these institutions to shape their lending (or nonlending) to other countries is an even farther cry.

While much of the more breathless discussions on the role of the big emerging markets like China and India focus on how they might "behave" at the global summit table—as rule takers, deal breakers, bridge builders, or even rule shapers—there is much less understanding of the domestic constraints that might affect which of these roles is happenstance rather than strategic. The limitations and caution also reflect the limited capacity in the Indian system, from the bureaucracy to academia to civil society, to coordinate and analyze the burgeoning number of issues that a serious engagement with the international system demands.

Notes

1. An institution that might be regarded as an IFI—the International Fund for Agricultural Development (IFAD)—was set up in 1977, as the thirteenth specialized agency of the United Nations, and India was one of the founding members. IFAD funds are primarily derived from member contributions. Since its inception, India has contributed $96 million toward the resources of IFAD, and IFAD has funded twenty-five projects in India, committing nearly $750 million.

2. IBRD loans are nonconcessional, while IDA is the concessional lending arm of the World Bank Group. In both cases, the loans require sovereign guarantees. The IFC makes nonguaranteed loans to the private sector, much like an investment bank. The World Bank here refers to the IBRD and IDA.

3. See Devesh Kapur, "Who Gets to Run the World?" *Foreign Policy* (November-December 2000): 44–50. The U.S. hold on the presidency of the World Bank, the European on the IMF, and the Japanese on the ADB are the only exceptions.

4. Kalyan Barooah, "Chinese Shadow over Arunachal Projects," *Assam Tribune*, January 15, 2013 (www.assamtribune.com/scripts/detailsnew.asp?id=jan1613/at05).

5. As financial institutions, the Bretton Woods institutions have to be satisfied that a potential borrower can meet its repayment obligations. However, as intergovernmental organizations, they are limited in their ability to emulate private creditors whose loan covenants use mechanisms such as higher risk premia, greater collateral, and shorter-duration agreements to reduce repayment risks. Hence they try to structure the agreement itself through stipulations that restrict the borrowing country's freedom of action, which are termed "conditionalities." However, not infrequently, these conditionalities reflect the interests of major shareholders rather than repayment risks per se.

6. Edward Mason and Robert Asher, *The World Bank since Bretton Woods* (Brookings, 1973), p. 675.

7. Devesh Kapur, John Lewis, and Richard Webb, *The World Bank: Its First Half Century* (Brookings, 1997).

8. The SDR (or special drawing rights) serves as the IMF's unit of account in which its loans are denominated and is a weighted basket of currencies (comprising the U.S. dollar, the euro, the British pound, and the Japanese yen).

9. As of June 2013, the reforms agreed to in 2010 were still pending because only members having 75.35 percent of total voting power had consented to the amendment on reform of the Executive Board, as against 85 percent required.

10. In absolute terms, India's quota will increase from SDR 5.8 billion to SDR 13.1 billion. While the cash component is 25 percent of this quota increase (about 14,000 crores paid in a reserve currency), the remaining 75 percent is in the form of securities (non-interest-bearing note purchase agreements issued by the RBI) that can be encashed when required by the IMF. It is only when the IMF encashes some fraction of these notes that there are any cash outflows.

11. The New Arrangements to Borrow is a contingent facility activated only in times of a major economic crisis when the IMF needs to supplement its quota resources for lending purposes.

12. Hongying Wang and Erik French, "China's Participation in Global Governance from a Comparative Perspective," *Asia Policy* 15 (January 2013): 89–114.

13. The G-24, more formally the Intergovernmental Group of Twenty-Four on International Monetary Affairs and Development, was established in 1971 to coordinate a common stance of developing countries on international monetary and development finance issues in international negotiations. India was one of the founding members and took an active leadership role. However, having obtained a seat at a more exclusive table (the G-20), India is less active in the G-24.

14. This discussion is taken from Devesh Kapur, "Graduation Day at Bretton Woods," *Business Standard*, March 12, 2012.

15. See OECD, "The OECD's Relations with Its Key Partners" (Paris, 2012) (www.oecd.org/general/50452501.pdf).

16. The Convention on Mutual Administrative Assistance in Tax Matters provides a multilateral basis for a wide variety of administrative assistance, including information exchange on request, automatic exchange of information, simultaneous tax examinations, and assistance in tax collection. The convention provides governments with a tool to fight offshore tax evasion and avoidance. India became the first country outside the membership of the OECD and the Council of Europe to become a party to the convention.

17. The REACH Regulation of the European Union requires that all chemicals exported beyond 1 ton need to be tested in a good laboratory practice (GLP) environment. In 2001 India achieved GLP-compliant certification by the OECD. This means that OECD countries will accept test data generated by Indian GLP-certified facilities, putting an end to evaluation of Indian labs by foreign inspectors. The National GLP Compliance Monitoring Authority was set up in 2002 under the Department of Science and Technology. There are currently eighteen GLP-certified facilities for pharmaceutical, agrochemical, and contract research.

18. The formation of the G-22 (also known as the Willard Group) was announced at the Asia-Pacific Economic Cooperation summit in Vancouver in November 1997 amid the firestorm of the Asian financial crisis. The goal was to organize a gathering of finance ministers and central bank governors from the G-7 industrial countries and fifteen other (mainly larger developing) countries to advance the reform of the architecture of the global financial system. It first met on April 16, 1998, and was superseded first by the G-33 in early 1999 and by the G-20 later that year.

19. Mark Beeson and Stephen Bell, "The G-20 and International Economic Governance: Hegemony, Collectivism, or Both?" *Global Governance* 15 (2009): 78.

20. David Malone and Rohan Mukherjee, "From High Ground to High Table: The Evolution of Indian Multilateralism," *Global Governance* 17 (2011): 311–29.

21. Amitav Acharya, "Regional Institutions and Asian Security Order," in *Asian Security Order*, edited by Muthaah Alagappa (Stanford University Press, 2002), pp. 210–40.

22. Arvind Subramanian and Aditya Mattoo, "India and Bretton Woods II," *Economic and Political Weekly*, November 8, 2008, pp. 62–70.

23. K. P. Krishnan, "India on the FATF High Table," *Economic Times*, August 10, 2010. Dr. Krishnan headed the Inter-Ministerial Coordination Committee on behalf of the Ministry of Finance.

24. Geoffrey Underhill and Xiaoke Zhang, "Setting the Rules: Private Power, Political Underpinnings, and Legitimacy in Global Monetary and Financial Governance," *International Affairs* 84, no. 3 (May 2008): 535–54.

25. Kevin Young, "Transnational Regulatory Capture? An Empirical Examination of the Transnational Lobbying of the Basel Committee on Banking Supervision," *Review of International Political Economy* 19, no. 4 (October 2012): 663–88.

26. Tim Büthe and Walter Mattli, *New Global Rulers: The Privatization of Regulation in the World Economy* (Princeton University Press, 2011).

27. Ben Levenstein and Robert Talbut, "The Pernicious Influence of U.S. Audit Rules," *Financial Times*, November 22, 2012.

28. Ibid.

29. Under IFRS, banks were required to implement an "incurred loan loss provisioning" model, which only permitted funds to be set aside for loans that were already going bad. Since riskier loans are associated with higher interest payments, banks were able to "cash in" higher margins up-front without allowing for the costs of expected defaults. In effect, banks failed to present a "true and fair view" of their economic health.

30. For a good summary of the challenges India faces in addressing global governance issues, see Working Group on India and Global Governance, *Understanding Complexity, Anticipating Change: From Interests to Strategy on Global Governance* (New Delhi: Council on Energy, Environment, and Water, December 2011).

NAVROZ K. DUBASH

14 Of Maps and Compasses: India in Multilateral Climate Negotiations

Introduction

India has taken a remarkably consistent approach to global climate negotiations: a principled position on climate change founded on attention to equity dimensions of the problem. This stance, which is the setting on a metaphorical compass that has guided the last two decades of Indian climate policy, has strong implications for India's arguments for the relative mitigation burdens of the industrialized and developing world and therefore for India's approach to multilateralism applied to climate change. Rooted in ethical claims, this view has served Indian interests well in staving off pressures for premature mitigation commitments and placing the emphasis for mitigation action on industrialized countries. However, the geopolitical terrain has shifted considerably over the last two decades. A more definitive science of climate change, growing alarm among vulnerable nations, an ascendant Asia, and a struggling West all have implications for how India should strategize to achieve its goals in climate negotiations and climate policy more generally. This new context, this chapter suggests, calls for updated cartography, even as the compass setting remains valid. With an updated map, India's climate journey may no longer traverse a straight line, even though the overall direction remains the same. In this chapter, I seek to explain the reasons for the persistence and continued validity of India's climate compass setting but also argue for rethinking our map of climate diplomacy.

The chapter begins with a discussion of exactly why climate multilateralism is such a challenging task. There is good reason why India, like many other countries, has struggled to deal with the complexities of global climate politics.

I then review in brief the trajectory of Indian climate policy, focusing on international positions but also tracing the growing significance of domestic climate policy. The third section seeks to interpret recent positions and strategies adopted by India, drawing on a growing literature. I conclude by expanding on the theme of an Indian climate position in a changed global context.

The Challenges of Climate Multilateralism

After two decades of effort at multilateral coordination on climate change, greenhouse gas emissions are relentlessly rising; it is hard to claim even moderate success on international cooperation to limit climate change.[1] The roots of this failure lie in at least five underlying characteristics of the climate challenge: the scale and scope of adjustment, the challenges of complexity and communication, the need to trespass across policy silos, the porosity of international and national categories of action, and uncertainty about who will bear the costs of climate change. First, the scale and scope of the climate challenge are unprecedented. Addressing climate change requires nothing less than reversing the entrenched pattern of industrialization built around accessing and using fossil fuels. The United Nations Environment Program estimates that in order to keep global average temperature increase to below 2° Celsius (the minimum threshold considered safe by science), global greenhouse gas emissions would have to peak well before 2020, and carbon dioxide emissions from industry and energy would have to decline at the rate of about 3 percent a year until 2050.[2] To put the latter figure in perspective, a 3 percent rate of decline in emissions translates to about a 6 percent rate of decarbonization—gross domestic product (GDP) per unit of carbon—with a GDP growth rate of 3 percent.[3] All of this would have to be accomplished in a world where developing countries legitimately assert the right to develop and grow in the most cost-effective way, which currently is a pathway dependent on the use of fossil fuels. In short, addressing climate change requires completely reengineering industrial development and reconceptualizing industrial society.

Second, the complexity of climate science and the challenge of communicating about climate change exacerbate the problems of building domestic political consensus for action and impede the construction of a common narrative around which to negotiate global action. The challenge begins with the complexity of climate science, which operates on carefully calibrated statements of probability—the Intergovernmental Panel on Climate Change (IPCC) uses statements such as "high agreement, much evidence" to indicate the extent of evidence and agreement among experts on the causes of and mechanisms to address climate change.[4] But, in addition, as Hulme notes, different attitudes to risk and technology, different perspectives on what is "fair," different interpretations of what constitutes development, and different visions of the future all place obstacles in the way of communicating about climate change.[5]

Third, to achieve this scale of change requires revising policy across an enormous range of sectors and breaching traditional policy silos. Domestically, mitigating and adapting to climate change involve departments that deal with agriculture, forests, urbanization, health, rural development, energy, water, and coastal protection, to name just a subset. Moreover, linkages across departments will have to be made to address climate change; concerns of water are tied to those of forests and agriculture, for example.

Fourth, climate change requires policymakers to move back and forth across domestic and international policy arenas. Internationally, climate change intersects with the work of ministries of trade, as questions of sanctions related to the greenhouse gas content of trade increasingly come into play.[6] Ministries of finance are also salient; India's Finance Ministry has recently set up a climate cell.[7] Constructing global climate negotiating positions requires diplomats to develop a close understanding of national policies across a broad range of sectors. Conversely, domestic policymakers need to be aware of the nuances of global climate debate, particularly as the international negotiation veers toward a regime based on "measurement, reporting, and verification" of domestic actions.[8]

Finally, central to the challenge of garnering global agreement is a lack of agreement on the costs of addressing climate change and how those costs will be divided. A contentious principle at the heart of the United Nations Framework Convention on Climate Change (UNFCCC) applies the idea of "common but differentiated responsibility and respective capabilities" (CBDRRC) as the basis for sharing burdens, but there is considerable contention on how to apply this principle and its continued salience.[9] As discussed later, CBDRRC is a central plank in India's negotiating approach. Coming out of this principle is a substantial literature on "burden sharing" in the climate context.[10] Two decades of debate and thinking, however, has not led to agreement. Climate change continues to defy both domestic policymaking and global agreement.

India in Climate Negotiations: A Brief Historical Tour

From the early days of climate negotiations in 1990, India was instrumental in shaping the underlying principles to guide the emergent global regime. Indian research organizations played an important role in framing the climate problem as one of allocating rights to the global commons.[11] From this idea came the corollary that any allocation should be on the basis of equity. At the very outset of substantive negotiations in 1991, India's delegation leader stated, "The problem . . . is caused not by emissions of greenhouse gases as such but by *excessive levels* of per capita emissions of those gases. . . . It follows, therefore, that developed countries with high per capita emission levels are responsible for incremental global warming . . . the principle of equity should be the touchstone for judging any proposal."[12]

By the conclusion of the framework convention, India had helped to formulate the position of the Global South along these lines; India's compass setting was largely the compass setting for the Global South. Building on the ideas articulated above, India had modified the IPCC's formulation of "common responsibilities" across countries to "common but differentiated responsibilities," reflecting the importance India placed on appropriately allocating responsibility across countries for causing the problem.[13] This formulation paved the way for introduction of this bedrock principle in the UNFCCC and reinforced its use as the compass setting for India's climate position. In addition, India worked with other developing countries to ensure that the negotiation process was held under the authority of the UN General Assembly through a specially constituted negotiating committee, judging that the UN framework would provide the best opportunity to articulate and defend these views. India also played a leading role in calling for new and additional funding and for a separate institutional mechanism for climate funding.[14]

These negotiations took place in the context of the early 1990s, when the global political map was dominated by an ascendant West. By contrast, developing countries had emerged from a decade of structural adjustment leading to perceptions and realities of political and economic disempowerment. Prior efforts in the 1970s and 1980s to build new forms of global cooperation to provide gains to the developing world had gone nowhere. In this context of limited faith in the ability of the international system to safeguard the interests of the South, the emergence of environmental concerns as a new agenda was viewed with deep suspicion. The potential for cooperation on global environmental problems demonstrated by the Montreal Protocol was built on differentiated commitments for North and South. This model of a "firewall" built around differentiation with corresponding financial obligations was seen as the most useful approach to defend Southern interests. Consequently, the climate regime that emerged from the UNFCCC was very much a product of its time, and India played a considerable role in crystalizing Southern concerns into legal architecture and form.

During the next significant moment in the buildup to the Kyoto Protocol, India played a significant role in defending the notion of differentiated responsibility. The context for these negotiations was growing pressure by vulnerable states for negotiation of a legally binding protocol and by industrialized countries for "advanced" developing countries to take on commitments. Faced with this situation, India convened a "Green Group" of seventy-two countries to support the idea of a legally binding protocol, but without any additional commitments for advanced developing countries.[15] The combined negotiating strength of the group was adequate to persuade the European Union (EU) and other champions of a legally binding instrument that in order to win the support of the Green Group, they would have to proceed on the basis of differentiated commitments.

While India's position in global climate negotiations has been defined largely within a foreign policy frame, the one significant exception is India's position on the Clean Development Mechanism (CDM) under the Kyoto Protocol. The CDM allows developing countries (non–Annex 1 countries, in the UNFCCC argot) to generate and then sell emission credits by undertaking projects to reduce greenhouse gases. India initially opposed this proposal, with the intent to keep exerting pressure for action on the industrialized world.[16] However, Indian business interests, led by the Confederation of Indian Industry, saw opportunity in the CDM and advocated a shift in India's position to embrace the mechanism, a position buttressed by research from Indian think tanks.[17] This revised position was reconciled with India's historical stance by locating it within the larger position that India would only take on mitigation actions when financially supported to do so.[18] This episode is noteworthy because it is one of the few cases where domestic interests have had an effect on shaping foreign policy on climate change.

The period starting in 2007 marked a new phase of the global climate negotiations process, when negotiations addressed the future of the global climate regime after the conclusion of the first "commitment period" of the Kyoto Protocol (from 2009 to 2012, when progress against commitments was to be assessed). This period of negotiations had three important moments: Bali in 2007, when a framework for negotiations was put in place—the Bali Action Plan; Copenhagen in 2009, when an effort to pull together an encompassing way forward narrowly foundered; and Durban in 2011, when a negotiating approach, the Durban Platform, was agreed upon. Throughout this period, a central and ongoing theme was whether negotiations would proceed on the basis of a unitary framework or whether differentiated responsibility would drive the form and architecture of the legal agreement.[19]

During this phase, large developing countries including India were placed under considerable pressure to articulate the conditions under which and the forms in which they would undertake climate mitigation commitments.[20] For their part, India and other large developing countries pressed the industrialized countries to commit to renew and enhance their commitments under the Kyoto Protocol for a second commitment period and pressured the United States (which has not ratified the Kyoto Protocol) to take on comparable commitments under a suitably stringent legal construct. Moreover, diplomatic pressures outside the UNFCCC process were also ratcheted up. Climate change became a regular feature of G-8+5 and G-20 discussions and pronouncements, particularly in the buildup to the 2009 Copenhagen negotiations.[21]

This period, with its heightened pressures, marked a turbulent phase of Indian climate politics and policy as, indeed, of climate policy in many countries. These are discussed under three categories: new statements and articulations of India's international stance, new and shifting alliances, and new frameworks for domestic policymaking linked to climate change.

First, the Indian government began experimenting with new formulations of India's climate policy, often in reaction to external stimuli, but occasionally in a proactive fashion. In response to pressure at the G-8+5, the prime minister announced that India's per capita emissions would never exceed those of the developed world.[22] This stance was consistent with India's long-standing position that long-term agreements should be based on per capita emissions, but represented a shift in that it introduced the notion of limits, albeit framed in per capita terms. The practical implications of this offer, in particular whether it binds India substantively, depend considerably on the rate of reduction in emissions in the industrialized world.

Equally if not more significant were tonal changes in the articulation of India's position. Many of these statements were associated with a new minister of environment and forests, Jairam Ramesh, whose broad approach involved positioning India as a forward-looking and positive player in climate negotiations. This stance is perhaps best summarized by a statement he made with regard to domestic environmental regulation, but that aptly summed up his approach to climate negotiations: he called for a shift to a "yes, but" approach instead of a "no" approach, indicating that the emphasis should be on the conditions for agreement.[23] Substantively, Minister Ramesh argued for shifting from a per capita approach to a "per capita plus" approach.[24] While this was never fully spelled out, the approach seemed to indicate sector-based plans and performance targets for action.

There was considerable domestic debate in the buildup to Copenhagen on whether this constituted a substantive shift in India's position, notably in the form of parliamentary debates, but also in the reporting and opinion pages of newspapers.[25] During those debates, Ramesh stated that India had three "red lines" going into the negotiations: no binding commitment to reduce emissions, no "peaking year" setting an upper bound on Indian emissions, and no scrutiny of domestic actions undertaken with domestic funds.[26] All of these flow directly from India's historical position emphasizing differentiated responsibilities consistent with the long-standing setting of India's climate compass. However, following a slew of voluntary pledges by other developing countries, notably China, on the eve of Copenhagen, India did announce a voluntary reduction in "emissions intensity" from 2005 levels by 20–25 percent by 2020.[27]

The intense pressure in the buildup to Copenhagen failed, however, to result in a formal agreement, achieving instead an "agreed outcome," for reasons discussed elsewhere, but this had to do with last-minute resistance by a small group of countries.[28] In the aftermath of Copenhagen, and notably at the Durban negotiating session in 2011, India continued to play a highly visible role, notably under a different minister of environment and forests, Jayanti Natarajan. The tonal quality changed, however, with India's emphasis shifting to arguing against initiating a process to reach a legally binding outcome. While the concerns were legitimate—the failure of industrialized countries to meet their commitments, the uncertain future of the Kyoto Protocol, the failure to mobilize adequate funds, and perhaps most important the failure to precondition legal stringency on substantive equity in the outcome—the shift in tone was palpable and left India open to criticism from small island and other vulnerable countries of being insufficiently supportive of global climate mitigation efforts.[29]

As these various statements and formulations suggest, the terrain for climate contestation has shifted considerably in recent years. Despite the lamentable failure of industrialized countries to meet their obligations, they have managed to ramp up pressure on large developing countries for action. While seeking to hold the line on differentiation, developing countries have been forced to articulate various ways in which they might contribute to mitigation efforts within their own countries. In the course of negotiating this terrain, India has continued to hew to the compass setting of common but differentiated responsibility, although some seasoned observers charged that Minister Ramesh was flirting with changing that course setting.[30] Whoever the minister, however, Indian climate policy has appeared somewhat reactive; the contours of a long-term strategic approach have not been particularly apparent.

A second implication of the changed context for climate politics was India's active engagement with new allies to manage the shifting geopolitical map of climate change. Most apparent was the emergence of Brazil, India, China, and South Africa (BASIC) as a new negotiating bloc.[31] The importance of BASIC came to the fore in Copenhagen, where the leaders of these four countries negotiated directly with the president of the United States, essentially sidelining the European Union and other regional blocs.[32] Notably, this new grouping also called into question the salience of the G-77 and China, which historically has sought to provide a unitary developing-country voice in climate negotiations. At Copenhagen and since, the BASIC countries have sought to defend a framework of differentiated responsibility, keep the process tightly tied to the UNFCCC, and make the case for equity a central element in forging a global climate agreement.[33]

Representing four of the most populous and fastest growing countries, BASIC is a powerful new presence in climate negotiations. While providing a bulwark against pressure from the industrialized world, the emergence of BASIC has also led to some expressions of alarm from vulnerable nations. At Durban, there was a direct statement challenging whether a morality of development, as articulated by BASIC countries, trumped the existential threat faced by small and island nations vulnerable to the impacts of climate change.[34] Moreover, as some observers comment, there are considerable differences between the four as well, and it is unclear whether their interests will converge over the long term.[35]

However, the battle lines drawn in climate negotiations do not necessarily extend to the world of diplomacy outside the UNFCCC. Concurrent with these negotiation-focused coalition-building efforts, India has also been engaged in pragmatic efforts at bilateral dialogue. India and the EU have a bilateral program of cooperation on energy, clean development, and climate change, and India and the United States have initiated creation of a joint clean energy research and development center.[36] These measures indicate not only a strain of pragmatism but also recognition that the arena for climate negotiation is not the only space in which climate issues will play out—many of the new developments will be in the broader arena of technology cooperation and energy policy.

Third, in response to pressure to demonstrate commitment to an effective global response, India, like other large emerging countries, has instituted a set of domestic policy processes on climate change. Even prior to the Copenhagen emissions pledge, India established a National Action Plan on Climate Change developed by an advisory group to the prime minister, which then spawned eight "missions" ranging from mitigation themes such as solar energy promotion to energy efficiency to adaptation efforts focused on water and agriculture.[37] Subsequently, India also set in place state-level processes to develop state action plans on climate change.[38] Finally, the government established an Expert Group on "Low Carbon Strategies for Inclusive Growth" to recommend approaches and policies for India's Twelfth Five-Year Plan.

All of these domestic measures signal a marked departure from the early days of Indian climate politics. They indicate a willingness to explore ways of internalizing climate change as one among multiple objectives, although very emphatically not the primary objective, of Indian development policy. Some of these efforts are open to criticism as dressing up existing policies in new garb, and some have undoubtedly received a stimulus due to their link with the climate agenda. This is particularly true of energy efficiency policies and renewable energy promotion measures, both of which are driven by energy security concerns as much as, if not more than, climate concerns, but which came to life as part of a climate action plan.[39] While the process of internalizing climate change into Indian development policy is somewhat ad hoc and lacks a conceptual structure, clear processes have been put in place, and some concrete initiatives are apparent.

Interpreting Indian Climate Policy

These changes in Indian statements, alliances, and domestic policies have led to a rash of efforts to interpret India's "new" climate policy and politics. While these reviews offer some insights into shifts in Indian climate politics and policies, they also tend to gloss over significant nuances in interpretation.

Several articles focus on a perceived shift in Indian foreign policy on climate change. Michaelowa and Michaelowa go so far as to pronounce India's approach as a shift from the "porcupine" to the "tiger," using a well-developed metaphor in the writing on Indian international relations, signaling a transition from a prickly and defensive stance in climate negotiations to a more dynamic and flexible one.[40] Atteridge and his co-authors interpret this shift in terms of growing political control displacing bureaucratic control.[41] Several scholars note that India's growing great-power aspirations and its desire to be seen as a responsible global actor explain much of the tonal shift in India's stance on climate negotiations.[42] However, there is a tendency to overstate the extent of this shift. While several authors acknowledge that tonal shifts have tended to be closely correlated with changes in the minister of environment and forest—with a flexible approach around Copenhagen associated with one minister giving way to a more traditionally Indian approach based on equity principles at Durban associated with another minister—the expectation of a long-lasting change in direction is more wistfully hoped for than rigorously argued.[43]

An important new direction in this emergent literature is an effort to link shifts in international climate policy to domestic changes and vice versa.[44] Atteridge and his co-authors, in particular, seek to paint a picture of Indian climate governance as an interplay between forces—material and ideational—at national (and subnational) and international levels. However, as I discuss further below, the links between national changes in climate politics and India's global positions are still tenuous, a point that Vihma also makes, drawing on earlier work by Dubash.[45] Among these reviewers, Getz stands out as particularly dismissive of domestic policy changes, arguing that these are essentially justified by domestic policy objectives such as energy security and therefore not to be taken seriously as climate policy. However, this criticism misses the point that in India political consensus is congealing around climate policy understood as an approach founded on "co-benefits" or the simultaneous achievement of climate and development policies. The important test of significance is whether this approach results in policies that would otherwise not have been formulated (or enhanced stringency or implementation of existing policies) and the impact of policy formulation on domestic and international climate policy. On both counts, the story is more complex (and affirmative) than Getz implies.

Interpretations Revisited

As this brief review suggests, the interpretive literature of the recent past has led to some significant insights, but the interpretations tend to be partial and swing from one extreme to another: India as obdurate climate player to climate tiger. Below, some further refinements in interpretation are suggested, building particularly on the link between domestic and foreign policy on climate change and on India's efforts to negotiate an ever more complex international policy and political debate.

First, while domestic policy on issues such as energy is now interwoven with processes and initiatives that are explicitly linked to climate action, these domestic policy initiatives insufficiently inform and shape international climate and energy policy in India. India's international climate stance remains focused rather single-mindedly on CBDRRC—the true north of India's climate compass. In the early days of negotiations, it was appropriate for this principle to form a single-point agenda. And even today, this principle should indeed be a starting point for India's international climate position, given long-standing and robust arguments about the historical responsibility of industrialized countries for the majority of greenhouse gas stocks in the atmosphere. In strategic terms, CBDRRC offers the best bulwark against any premature claims that India should offer absolute limits to greenhouse gas emissions.

However, in the current global context, it is increasingly incongruous as an exclusive guide for Indian climate policy. This context includes the emergence of a multipolar world within which India is claiming a louder voice, increasingly robust evidence of substantial impacts from climate change, and increasingly strident calls for action from small and vulnerable countries. In this context, calling *only* for differentiated responsibility leaves India open to criticism that it seeks a global climate agreement that puts off its own mitigation responsibilities indefinitely. Consequently, this stance fails to take diplomatic advantage of what is now the considerable cumulative weight of India's domestic climate policy. A position built around *both* CBDRRC as the bulwark against premature calls for absolute emission cuts from India—which would indeed seriously compromise future development prospects—and mitigation actions consistent with India's stated approach of co-benefits is likely to integrate domestic and foreign policy better and to serve India's short- and long-term interests.

Second, there is a growing tension between India's positions and its choice of allies, forcing constant adjustment. In forging a revised strategic vision, an updated map would need to take into account several new realities. As the least developed countries, small island nations, and other highly vulnerable countries have raised the pitch of their demands for an effective global climate deal, the coherence of the G-77 and China as a single voice of the developed world has come under pressure. As discussed earlier, the emergence of the BASIC grouping was, in part, an effort by rapidly developing large economies to articulate a shared position, one that was somewhat at odds with that of smaller developing countries. However, India is substantially different from its BASIC partners along several dimensions—considerably lower GDP per capita and social indicators, lower greenhouse gas emissions per capita by a factor of three to five, and greater vulnerability to climate change.

These differences in both capacity and responsibility suggest that the principle of CBDRRC is less defensible when applied to India's BASIC partners than to India itself, which shares considerably more characteristics with poorer and less developed economies. Consequently, there is a tension between partnering with BASIC and credibly defending and furthering the principle of CBDRRC. Indeed, there are indications that Brazil and South Africa, the two countries with the highest emissions per capita and GDP per capita in the alliance, are less wedded to the principle than are China and India. By late 2012, this tension had come out in the open, with China and India forging a new alliance of "like-minded developing countries," consisting of a curious collection of large Asian economies including China, India, Pakistan, the Philippines, and Thailand, oil producers such as Saudi Arabia and Venezuela, and several members of the Bolivarian Alliance for the Americas such as Bolivia and Ecuador.[46] While the glue binding this alliance can only be inferred, its press release suggests that a common commitment to preserving and defending CBDRRC is central to its purpose.

These shifting and overlapping alliances point to a larger challenge facing India in developing a foreign policy on climate change: India is simultaneously a country with large numbers of poor and vulnerable people and one that is rapidly growing and claiming an increasing share of globally available natural resources and carbon budget. From the former perspective, India's natural allies are the least developed countries; from the latter, they are the rapidly industrializing countries. This tension does not lend itself to easy solutions. In the absence of substantial progress on an effective global climate agreement, Indian decisionmakers appear to have swung toward placing higher priority on defending their access to the global carbon budget, calculating that a richer economy is also one that is better placed to adapt to climate change. Doing so, however, places India on a course of growing conflict with small and vulnerable nations.

Third, as a "premature power"—one where global reach has outstripped domestic indexes of development—India has limited means to exercise influence globally.[47] One option is, of course, for India to leverage its power by working with allies, as was successfully accomplished in Copenhagen through the BASIC alliance. However, this approach is limited by the schizophrenic nature of India's interests, as discussed above. Moreover, broader foreign policy considerations and broader strategic alliances inevitably limit India's options. Despite these limits, India has been remarkably assertive about its position, most notably at the Durban Conference of Parties (the annual meetings to take forward climate negotiations) in December 2011. On that occasion, India alone faced off against the European Union on the question of whether future negotiations would result in a legally binding document or not. Eventually India won the concession of somewhat weaker language on this point, but arguably lost ground on explicit articulation of the principle of CBDRRC in the final document.[48]

The Durban episode illustrated that India is failing to implement a strategy that brought considerable success in the early days of the negotiating process—framing issues in a manner that advances Indian interests and then building a coalition of support around that frame. Indeed, this approach enabled India to enshrine the CBDRRC principle at the heart of the UNFCCC process. More recently, India has provided little evidence of efforts to frame a forward-looking agenda that is strategically located within the current geopolitical context and then build support for it. Other nations similarly placed in the negotiations process have exercised great influence by developing concepts and building support for their ideas. The role of South Africa in floating the concept of "sustainable development policies and measures" that formed the basis for "nationally appropriate mitigation actions"—the accepted formulation for mitigation actions by developing countries—is a case in point. To link this point to the earlier discussion, the concept of co-benefits is ripe for such development, but India has invested very little by way of intellectual or political resources in promoting this concept as a legitimate basis for international action.

One potential reason for making relatively little effort to frame ideas and shape debate is the relatively low level of capacity devoted to climate change within government circles. During the first decade and more of negotiations, climate change was understood in India as a strictly foreign policy issue, which could be managed by a few skilled diplomats backed by a small number of specialists. In a context where climate change is closely interwoven with national energy strategy formulation, state-level development planning, and trade policy, the requirement is for climate policy that successfully draws on and integrates a range of additional policymaking arenas. Moreover, the climate regime is increasingly taking shape as a soft-law regime, where the role of international law is to nudge and induce rather than direct and enforce. Understanding and making use of this perspective requires skills and knowledge that go beyond traditional international law expertise.

All of these additional burdens require a broader range of skills and more coordination across different arms of the government. In addition, while nongovernmental think tanks played an important role in the early days of climate negotiations, as discussed earlier, and while the ecosystem of nongovernmental actors is far more dense, there is a degree of lock-in to existing positions. For a middle-level power like India to address the new landscape of climate politics will require refinements in substance (an integrative approach across policymaking arenas and scales of governance) and in policymaking process (alliance building with governments and engagement with influential nongovernmental actors in India and elsewhere to better represent Indian positions). Collectively, these observations suggest that while there is indeed a complex interplay between India's domestic and foreign policy on energy and climate, there is much scope for more intentional and strategic interaction, with considerable upsides for the effectiveness of India's foreign policy on climate change.

Recalibrating the Compass: Redrawing Maps

India's climate-negotiating approach has been marked by several high points, notably in the early years of negotiations, when India, along with other developing countries, managed to frame the climate debate around India's own compass setting to internalize considerations of equity. In Saran's phrasing, these early negotiators managed to structure the climate deal around the principle of nonreciprocity—the principle that obligations by the North need not attract reciprocal obligations by the South.[49] As Saran also notes, that world is long past; given the new geopolitical map, reciprocal commitments are now the order of the day, and concerns over economic competitiveness are foremost in the minds of Western democracies.

In this context, negotiating as if we lived in a nonreciprocal world is unlikely to be fruitful. This is not to say that the underlying principle of equity should be abandoned; it continues to have strong ethical resonance and enormous practical implications for India. But it may be productive to recalibrate India's negotiating compass and to reformulate both Indian objectives and consequent strategies.

The first step is to define Indian objectives clearly. A primary objective is surely to avoid a situation where India is forced to commit to absolute emission caps, which would likely cripple efforts at growth and poverty reduction, given that the cheapest energy sources continue to be based on fossil fuels. But equally, it is in India's interest, and that of India's vulnerable populations, to have an effective global climate agreement. Finally, climate policy has to operate in the context of India's larger concerns with energy security, given the country's limited energy resources and poor energy infrastructure. The principle of CBDRRC is a valuable instrument to ensure the first, but its updated articulation should be consistent with the latter two objectives. This more nuanced and multipart articulation could form the basis for a recalibrated climate compass.

Second, India's climate objectives have to be realistically located within the country's larger foreign policy objectives; climate policy does not operate in a vacuum. This redrawing and updating of the geopolitical map involves mapping not only global climate politics but also broader diplomatic objectives. It would serve India's interests to pay at least as much attention to the emergent coalition of nations most vulnerable to climate change—least developed countries (including many African nations) and small island states—as to its BASIC allies. While India straddles both categories, the insistence on donning the mantle of a rapidly industrializing economy alone risks subjecting India to demands for onerous climate obligations that it is least able to bear among large emerging economies and fails to reflect the strong interests of the poorest Indians in robust global climate mitigation. India must manage and perhaps even use productively its simultaneous status as a rising power and a vulnerable nation. Factoring in broader diplomatic objectives is a more complex issue. Climate considerations undoubtedly have to be leavened by ongoing strategic alliances. In the future, the thorniest issue is likely to be managing the balance between a recently warming relationship with the United States and the imperative of engaging a rising China. While unpacking the implications of a rapidly changing global context requires far more space than is available here, there is little doubt that Indian climate policy has to be informed by an updated geopolitical map.

Third, there is certainly room for India to develop and propagate alternative and more nuanced frames for climate negotiations. The need is for a frame that sidesteps the fraught North-South politics of global climate negotiations, while preserving substantive attention to concerns of equity and differentiated responsibility. The key to doing so might lie in India's "co-benefits"–based approach to domestic climate policy, which allows primacy of developmental objectives, even while making a substantive contribution to global mitigation.[50] This approach would need to be defined more carefully and formalized and could then be used as an important element of an updated version of differentiated responsibility across countries.

For the reasons outlined at the beginning of this chapter, solving climate change through multilateral negotiations has always been a tall task. Over the last two decades, the task has, if anything, become harder due to blurred boundaries: between international negotiations and domestic politics, entrenched North-South politics, and tectonic geopolitical shifts leading to a multipolar world. To achieve its goals, India cannot continue to deploy only old tools and techniques. These must be upgraded to reflect climate diplomacy in this far more complex environment.

Notes

1. International Energy Agency, "CO_2 Emissions from Fuel Combustion 2012: Highlights (Pre-Release)" (Paris, 2012) (www.iea.org/publications/freepublications/publication/name,4010,en,html).

2. United Nations Environment Program, *The Emissions Gap Report* (Nairobi: UNEP, November 2010), p. 28 (www.unep.org/publications/ebooks/emissionsgapreport/pdfs/GAP_REPORT_SUNDAY_SINGLES_LOWRES.pdf).

3. Ibid., p. 25.

4. Intergovernmental Panel on Climate Change, *Climate Change 2007: Synthesis Report* (Geneva, 2007) (www.ipcc.ch/pdf/assessment-report/ar4/syr/ar4_syr.pdf).

5. Mike Hulme, *Why We Disagree about Climate Change: Understanding Controversy, Inaction, and Opportunity* (Cambridge University Press, 2009).

6. Joanne Scott and Lavanya Rajamani, "EU Climate Change Unilateralism," *European Journal of International Law* 23, no. 2 (2012): 469–94 (www.indiaenvironmentportal.org.in/files/file/EU%20Climate%20Change%20Unilateralism.pdf).

7. See Ministry of Finance, Department of Economic Affairs, Climate Change Finance Unit (http://finmin.nic.in/the_ministry/dept_eco_affairs/economic_div/ccfu_index.asp).

8. Harald Winkler, "Measurable, Reportable, and Verifiable: The Keys to Mitigation in the Copenhagen Deal," *Climate Policy* 8, no. 6 (2008): 534–47; Angela Falconer, Pat Hogan, Valerio Micale, Alex Vasa, Yuqing Yu, Xuehua Zhang, Xiaolu Zhao, and Julia Zuckerman, "Tracking Emissions and Mitigation Actions: Evaluation of MRV Systems in China, Germany, Italy, and the United States," CPI Working Paper (San Francisco: Climate Policy Initiative, June 2012) (http://climatepolicyinitiative.org/wp-content/uploads/2012/05/Tracking-Emissions-and-Mitigation-Actions-Evaluation.pdf); Jane Ellis and Sara Moarif, *GHG Mitigation Actions: MRV Issues and Options* (Paris: OECD, March 2009) (www1.oecd.org/environment/climatechange/42474623.pdf).

9. Lavanya Rajamani, "The Reach and Limits of the Principle of Common but Differentiated Responsibilities and Respective Capabilities in the Climate Change Regime," in *Handbook of Climate Change and India: Development, Politics, and Governance*, edited by Navroz K. Dubash (London: Routledge, 2011), pp. 118–29.

10. Narasimha Rao, "Equity in Climate Change: The Range of Metrics and Views," in *Handbook of Climate Change and India*, edited by Dubash, pp. 147–56.

11. Anil Agarwal and Sunita Narain, *Global Warming in an Unequal World: A Case of Environmental Colonialism* (New Delhi: Centre for Science and Environment, 1991) (www.indiaenvironmentportal.org.in/files/GlobalWarming%20Book.pdf); Navroz K. Dubash, "The Politics of Climate Change in India: Narratives of Equity and Co-Benefits," *WIREs Climate Change*, March 15, 2013.

12. Chandrashekhar Dasgupta, "Present at the Creation: The Making of the UN Framework Convention on Climate Change," in *Handbook of Climate Change and India*, edited by Dubash, p. 89.

13. Sandeep Sengupta, "International Climate Negotiations and India's Role," in *Handbook of Climate Change and India*, edited by Dubash, p. 106.

14. Susanne Jakobsen, "India's Position on Climate Change from Rio to Kyoto: A Policy Analysis," CDR Working Paper (Copenhagen: Copenhagen Centre for Development Research, 1998) (www.kit.nl/library/documents/query.ashx?RecordID=231911).

15. Sengupta, "International Climate Negotiations and India's Role," p. 107.

16. Ibid., p. 106.

17. Dasgupta, "Present at the Creation," p. 89; Jakobsen, "India's Position on Climate Change," p. 39.

18. Sengupta, "International Climate Negotiations and India's Role."

19. Lavanya Rajamani, "The Changing Fortunes of Differential Treatment in the Evolution of International Environmental Law," *International Affairs* 88, no. 3 (2012): 615–20; Rajamani, "The Reach and Limits."

20. Navroz K. Dubash, "Copenhagen: Climate of Mistrust," *Economic and Political Weekly* 44, no. 52 (December 26, 2009): 8–11; Navroz K. Dubash, "Inconvenient Truths Produce Hard Realities: Notes from Bali," *Economic and Political Weekly* 42, no. 52 (December 29, 2007): 31–72 (www.epw.in/insight/inconvenient-truths-produce-hard-realities-notes-bali.html); Lavanya Rajamani, "The Cancún Climate Agreements: Reading the Text, Subtext, and Tea Leaves," *International and Comparative Law Quarterly* 60, no. 2 (April 2011): 499–519.

21. University of Toronto, "G20 Leaders Climate Change Conclusions: Analysis" (Toronto, February 15, 2011) (www.g20.utoronto.ca/analysis/conclusions/climatechange-l.html); Bryan Walsh, "G20 Leaders Agree, Broadly, on Climate Change," *Time*, September 26, 2009 (www.time.com/time/health/article/0,8599,1926384,00.html); Jonathan Weisman, "G-8 Climate-Change Agreement Falls Short," *Wall Street Journal*, July 9, 2009 (http://online.wsj.com/article/SB124704550659510745.html).

22. Manmohan Singh, "PM's Intervention on Climate Change at Heiligendamm Meeting of G8 Plus 5" (Heiligendamm, Germany: Consulate General of India, August 6, 2007) (www.indianconsulate.org.cn/site/?q=zh-hans/node/72).

23. Jairam Ramesh, "The Two Cultures Revisited: The Environment-Development Debate in India," *Economic and Political Weekly* 45, no. 42 (October 16, 2010): 13–16 (www.indiaenvironmentportal.org.in/files/Environment-Development%20debate.pdf).

24. Dipankar De Sarkar, "Slated at Home, Jairam Ramesh Is Praised by US, Britain," *Hindustan Times*, October 20, 2009.

25. Anu Jogesh, "A Change in Climate? Trends in Climate Change Reportage in the Indian Print Media," in *Handbook of Climate Change and India*, edited by Dubash, pp. 266–86; Suresh Prabhu, "Climate Change and Parliament," in *Handbook of Climate Change and India*, edited by Dubash, pp. 230–45; "Lok Sabha Debates: Impact of Climate Change" (Lok Sabha, December 3, 2009) (www.indiaenvironmentportal.org.in/files/debate-Climate%20change-Parliament-1.pdf); "It's a Sell Out; Cry BJP, Left on India's Stand at Cancún," *Economic Times*, December 10, 2010 (http://articles.economictimes.indiatimes.com/2010-12-10/news/27624379_1_binding-commitments-upa-government-india); "BJP Raps Govt for Its Negotiation Strategy on Climate Change," *Hindu*, December 4, 2009 (www.thehindu.com/news/national/bjp-raps-govt-for-its-negotiation-strategy-on-climate-change/article60151.ece).

26. Sengupta, "International Climate Negotiations and India's Role," p. 110; "Transcript of the Minister's Response in the Lok Sabha" (Lok Sabha, December 3, 2009) (http://moef.nic.in/downloads/public-information/LokSabha_trnscript.pdf); Press Information Bureau, "India Will Never Accept Legally Binding Emission Cuts at Copenhagen: Jairam Ramesh" (New Delhi: Government of India, December 4, 2009) (http://pib.nic.in/newsite/erelease.aspx?relid=55147).

27. Sengupta, "International Climate Negotiations and India's Role"; "Transcript of the Minister's Response in the Lok Sabha"; Saibal Dasgupta and Nitin Sethi, "India Offers to Cut Carbon Intensity by 20–25%," *Times of India*, November 28, 2009 (http://articles.timesofindia.indiatimes.com/2009-11-28/india/28084110_1_carbon-intensity-energy-intensity-emissions); Ananth Krishnan, "After China, India Considers Setting Emissions Intensity Target," *Hindu*, November 27, 2009 (www.thehindu.com/news/national/after-china-india-considers-setting-emissions-intensity-target/article55960.ece).

28. Dubash, "Copenhagen: Climate of Mistrust"; Lavanya Rajamani, "India and Climate Change: What India Wants, Needs, and Needs to Do," *India Review* 8, no. 3 (August 6, 2009): 340–74; Daniel Bodansky, "The Copenhagen Climate Change Conference: A Postmortem," *American Journal of International Law* 104, no. 2 (April 2010): 230–40.

29. D. Raghunandan, "Durban Platform: Kyoto Negotiations Redux," *Economic and Political Weekly* 46, no. 53 (2011) (www.epw.in/commentary/durban-platform-kyoto-negotiations-redux.html); Saleemul Huq, "Well Done in Durban," *Daily Star*, December 12, 2011 (www.thedailystar.net/newDesign/news-details.php?nid=213803).

30. Prodipto Ghosh and Chandrashekhar Dasgupta, "Smoke 'n Mirrors," *Financial Express*, December 14, 2011 (www.financialexpress.com/news/smoke-n-mirrors/887407/0); Chandrashekhar Dasgupta, "Sweet Surrender: Jairam Ramesh Has Turned India's Climate Change Policy on Its Head," *Telegraph*, January 17, 2011 (www.telegraphindia.com/1110117/jsp/opinion/story_13451487.jsp); "Oral History: Climate Change Negotiations; Guarding the 'Overriding Priorities,'" *Indian Foreign Affairs Journal* 6, no. 2 (2011): 9 (www.associationdiplomats.org/publications/ifaj/Vol6/6.2/ORAL%20HISTORY.pdf); "It's a Sell Out."

31. Xinran Qi, "The Rise of BASIC in UN Climate Change Negotiations," *South African Journal of International Affairs* 18, no. 3 (December 2011): 295–318 (www.tandfonline.com/doi/pdf/10.1080/10220461.2011.622945); Karl Hallding, Marie Olsson, Aaron Atteridge, Marcus Carson, Antto Vihma, and Mikael Roman, *Together Alone? Brazil, South Africa, India, China (BASIC), and the Climate Change Conundrum* (Stockholm: Stockholm Environment Institute, 2010) (www.sei-international.org/mediamanager/documents/Publications/SEI-PolicyBrief-Olsson-BASIC-ClimateChangeConundrum.pdf).

32. Sengupta, "International Climate Negotiations and India's Role"; Monica Alessi, Anton Georgiev, and Christian Egenhofer, *Messages from Copenhagen: Assessments of the Accord and Implications for the EU*, European Climate Platform (Copenhagen: Centre for European Policy Studies, Climate Policy Research Program, April 2010).

33. Harald Winkler, T. Jayaraman, Jiahua Pan, Adriano Santhiago de Oliveira, Yongsheng Zhang, Girish Sant, Jose Domingos Gonzalez Miguez, Thapelo Letete, Andrew Marquard, and Stefan Raubenheimer, *Equitable Access to Sustainable Development* (Beijing: BASIC Expert Group, 2011).

34. Richard Black, "Climate Talks End with Late Deal," BBC News, December 11, 2011 (www.bbc.co.uk/news/science-environment-16124670).

35. Hallding et al., *Together Alone?*

36. Christian Egenhofer and Noriko Fujiwara, *Understanding India's Climate Agenda* (Brussels: Centre for European Policy Studies, February 23, 2010) (www.ceps.eu/book/understanding-india%E2%80%99s-climate-agenda); Indian Embassy, "India-US Agreement for Setting Up Joint Clean Energy Research and Devel-

opment Centre" (Washington, November 8, 2010) (www.indianembassy.org/prdetail1650/india-us-agreement-for-setting-up-joint-clean-energy-research-and-development-centre-); Narayan Lakshman, "India-U.S. Clean Energy Research Centre Established," *Hindu*, August 20, 2010 (www.thehindu.com/business/Economy/article584315.ece).

37. Prime Minister's Council on Climate Change, *National Action Plan on Climate Change, NAPCC* (New Delhi: Government of India, 2008) (http://pmindia.nic.in/climate_change.htm.

38. Ministry of Environment and Forests, "Summary of Discussion: National Consultation Workshop on Preparation of State Level Strategy and Action Plan on Climate Change" (New Delhi: Government of India, 2010) (http://moef.nic.in/downloads/others/SAPCC-workshop-summary-2010.pdf).

39. Navroz K. Dubash, "From Norm Taker to Norm Maker? Indian Energy Governance in Global Context," *Global Policy* 2 (special issue, 2011): 66–79.

40. Katharina Michaelowa and Axel Michaelowa, "India as an Emerging Power in International Climate Negotiations," *Climate Policy* 12, no. 5 (June 22, 2012): 575–90.

41. Aaron Atteridge, M. K. Shrivastava, N. Pahuja, and H. Upadhyay, "Climate Policy in India: What Shapes International, National, and State Policy?" *AMBIO: A Journal of the Human Environment* 41, no. 1 (2012): 68–77.

42. Ibid.; Joachim Betz, "India's Turn in Climate Policy: Assessing the Interplay of Domestic and International Policy Change" (Hamburg: German Institute of Global and Area Studies, March 2012) (www.giga-hamburg.de/dl/download.php?d=/content/publikationen/pdf/wp190_betz.pdf).

43. Michaelowa and Michaelowa, "India as an Emerging Power."

44. Betz, "India's Turn in Climate Policy"; Atteridge et al., "Climate Policy in India"; Antto Vihma, "India and the Global Climate Governance: Between Principles and Pragmatism," *Journal of Environment and Development* 20, no. 1 (March 2011): 69–94.

45. Vihma, "India and the Global Climate Governance"; Navroz K. Dubash, "Toward a Progressive Indian and Global Climate Politics" (New Delhi: Centre for Policy Research, September 2009) (www.cprindia.org/workingpapers/2701-working-paper-20091-september-toward-progressive-indian-and-global-climate-politi).

46. "Meeting of the Like Minded Developing Countries on Climate Change," press release (Beijing, October 18–19, 2012).

47. Shyam Saran, "Premature Power," *Business Standard*, March 17, 2010 (www.business-standard.com/india/news/shyam-saran-premature-power/388829/).

48. Navroz K. Dubash, "Looking beyond Durban: Where to from Here?" *Economic and Political Weekly* 47, no. 3 (January 21, 2012): 13–17; Rajamani, "The Changing Fortunes of Differential Treatment."

49. Shyam Saran, "Irresistible Forces and Immovable Objects: A Debate on Contemporary Climate Politics," *Climate Politics* 10 (2010): 678–83. Also see chapter 3 by Shyam Saran in this volume.

50. See Dubash, "The Politics of Climate Change in India."

ARUNABHA GHOSH *and* DAVID STEVEN

15 India's Energy, Food, and Water Security: International Cooperation for Domestic Capacity

Why Does Resource Security Matter for India?

In recent years, higher and more volatile energy and food prices have pushed natural resources toward the top of the international agenda, while water scarcity is a growing threat to industry, agriculture, and energy generation. According to one estimate, by 2030 worldwide demand for food, water, and energy will grow approximately 35, 40, and 50 percent, respectively. At the same time, climate change will worsen the outlook for the availability of these critical resources.[1]

Food, water, energy, and climate change are policy domains that are enmeshed in a global economy that does not respect national or sectoral borders. Energy drives climate change, while climate limits energy options. Food and energy markets are tightly interlinked, while water is essential to food and energy production and is directly affected by a changing climate. All of these issues touch on other contentious international policy challenges such as trade, finance, and technology transfer. Thus the world must confront three interlocking challenges of sustainable development: securing energy, water, and other minerals to support economic growth; meeting basic needs for food, fuel, and water for a growing global population; and managing the environmental constraints and consequences of increased resource use.

India's development imperative places it at the forefront of these challenges. By 2050 there will be as many Indians—around 1.7 billion—as the population of the whole world at the beginning of the twentieth century.[2] By some projections, the Indian economy will have grown by a factor of ten by mid-century.[3]

However, growth depends on securing access to energy and other strategic resources. India is already struggling to meet domestic demand for energy, food, and water and has 14 percent of the global population living without electricity and nearly a third of the global population cooking with traditional biofuels.[4] It has little spare land or water and is one of the world's most vulnerable countries to the impacts of climate change.[5] Over the coming decades, these challenges will intensify.

Given the speed of both its population and economic growth, India faces some hard resource limits in the years ahead. However, its major problems are a product of the intersection of dysfunctional markets and governance systems for natural resources. Energy and food subsidies are increasingly fiscally unsustainable.[6] And political gridlock continues to reduce the prospects of an effective domestic response to resource pressures.[7]

India is, of course, only partially in control of its destiny in this area, especially during periods when commodity prices are high and volatile. It is already exposed to global energy markets and will have increasing exposure to international food systems.[8] It shares climate and water risks with Bangladesh, Pakistan, and other neighbors. International drivers will frame India's options at home, while effective domestic policy will make it easier for the Indian government to assert its interests on the international stage. Conversely, an increasingly competitive international dynamic—on resource nationalism, export bans, trade in commodities, or policy toward major energy exporters such as Iran—could create a growing, and dangerous, sense of isolation and constriction within India.

India, therefore, has an *especially* strong national interest in well-functioning commodity markets. As it becomes an increasingly assertive international actor, its willingness to work with other major powers on energy, food, water, and climate could significantly improve the prospects for effective management of these issues. Its growing presence as a "rule shaper" and its willingness to engage on a multilateral, rather than solely a bilateral, basis offer it potential to influence the design of robust international regimes for resource security and the provision of global environmental public goods. It will find, however, that existing regimes and their underlying rules often offer contradictory policy signals. Thus India could play an important role in developing governance frameworks that increase the coherence of rules across institutional regimes relating to resources, the environment, trade, and security.[9]

In this chapter, we review the resource and environmental challenges facing India over the next twenty years, focusing in particular on their political and geopolitical dimensions. We then discuss drivers of change and possible trajectories for India's domestic and international policy on these issues. Finally, we discuss options for future Indian engagement on strategic resources and climate change, offering concrete suggestions for the Indian government to deepen its engagement and build stronger partnerships and governance arrangements with other countries.

Understanding India's Resource and Environmental Challenge

This section evaluates the energy resources that India needs to sustain growth and the economic impact of energy scarcity. It also assesses India's fuel, food, and water requirements to meet basic needs. Finally, it examines the environmental constraints that these resource demands will put on India.

Energy Resources for Growth

Energy security is, and will continue to be, a defining challenge for India. The country is currently a second-tier energy consumer, sitting alongside Japan and Russia, but far behind China, the European Union, and the United States. Between now and 2030, however, demand is projected to increase more quickly in India than in any other country in the G-20. Even under an aggressive, and politically infeasible, scenario of global climate stabilization, India would consume around 60 percent more energy in twenty years than it does today.[10]

India may struggle to acquire this additional energy at a reasonable price or to minimize interruptions in supply caused by market volatility. It already has much higher levels of import dependence than China and the United States, with 37 percent of all energy and 76 percent of oil coming from overseas. The Indian government expects this dependence to increase over the next five years.[11] Moreover, the Indian energy sector is already showing signs of strain, with a consistent pattern of tight supply, lack of investment, and policy and market failures across all major energy sources.

Biofuels, biomass, and waste still constitute a large share of energy (33 percent) thanks to the lack of access to modern cooking fuels for 772 million people or electricity for 293 million people.[12] Coal, oil, and natural gas account for 54 percent of India's final energy consumption.[13] But as more households demand modern sources of energy, demand for fossil fuels will rise, possibly at a more rapid rate than expected if middle-class lifestyles continue to proliferate.

India is the world's third largest producer of coal and has the world's fourth largest reserves.[14] Demand for coal has, on average, been increasing by approximately 7 percent a year since 2005, up from 5 percent between 2000 and

2005, with power generation and manufacturing as the main drivers.[15] Development of the domestic coal sector, however, is beset by a lack of investment, disputes over land acquisition, and environmental concerns.[16] Coal India, a state-owned company, produces 80 percent of the country's coal,[17] and production is both inefficient and riddled with corruption.[18] There are also links between India's sometimes fragile internal security and its coal industry. Within the coal belt, large numbers of mafia groups are thought to be active, some of which are then "taxed" by Naxalite insurgents, producing revenue for rebel groups.[19]

In addition, the lack of port and transportation infrastructure, combined with dysfunctional markets, has hindered imports of coal.[20] Only four major ports handle coal imports, providing a capacity of just 63 million tons, leaving minor ports to pick up the slack. The major coal ports are along the eastern coast, but the largest power plants are now being built in the western states. New infrastructure for transporting coal is, therefore, badly needed inland and along the western coast.[21]

As a result of these deficits, coal scarcity is a growing problem for India, with an estimated 15 percent gap between supply and demand in 2012.[22] The problem is especially acute in the power sector, which currently expects to receive only half of the coal needed for new electricity generation envisaged in India's Twelfth Five-Year Plan, 2012–17.[23] Imports are growing rapidly, with 15 percent of coal now coming from overseas, but this is still not enough to keep up with domestic demand. Import dependence is projected to reach 40 percent by 2030, based on current trends[24] and assuming that infrastructure is developed to bring more coal into the country. More recent government estimates suggest that this level of import dependence would be reached by 2016 if the gap between supply and demand in the power sector were to be closed.[25]

With a relatively modest domestic endowment, India imports about three times more oil than it produces.[26] Production has remained almost flat over the past decade, with import dependence certain to increase, given that demand is projected almost to double by 2030.[27] Public sector enterprises control around 80 percent of oil and gas production, hampering foreign investment in the sector.[28] These national oil companies have sought equity oil and gas opportunities overseas, with international production now equivalent to around 10 percent of domestic production.[29] This has dragged India into some of the world's most risky places, including politically fragile states such as Iran, Iraq, Kazakhstan, Libya, Nigeria, South Sudan, and Venezuela.[30] Investments have proved problematic in many of these countries and also in the

South China Sea, where energy cooperation with Vietnam has created tensions with China.[31] Moreover, little "equity oil" makes its way back to India; instead, it is sold in global markets, making overseas investments a poor use of scarce capital.[32]

In any case, dependence on imported oil will grow. Even with a massive increase in the use of coal, India's oil imports will increase four to six fold by 2030.[33] As a result, India is exposed to "supply" risks (wars, strikes, or political upheavals in oil exporters, deliberate blockades of supplies to India) and "market" risks (higher and more volatile prices). For India, oil will increasingly become one of its most important sources of exposure to broader geopolitical volatility.

In the 1990s there was considerable enthusiasm for prospects in India's gas sector. New domestic discoveries, however, have reached only 40 percent of the level projected for 2012, again due to a lack of investment and infrastructure and to pricing decisions that saw gas being sold to the power sector at below-market rates.[34] As a result, demand for gas is estimated to outstrip supply by around a third and is projected to increase at more than 5 percent each year between now and 2030.[35] There is little immediate prospect that this demand will be met by domestic production, as the sector continues to underperform. India will therefore become more reliant on imports,[36] with substantial investment needed in liquefied natural gas terminals and, potentially, in transnational pipelines, although they would have to pass through states such as Afghanistan and Pakistan and would increase competition with China for pipeline gas.[37]

Nuclear power is likely to play only a niche role in India, at least in the medium term. While the International Atomic Energy Agency still expects to see "significant" growth in nuclear capacity in India and the government remains committed to increasing investment, nuclear expansion has been slower than expected. The Fukushima disaster, domestic civil society protests, opposition from state governments, and cost overruns are limiting the sector's potential.[38] Even under the government's optimistic projections, nuclear power will provide only 1.2 percent of India's energy in 2016–17.[39]

Economic Impact of Energy Scarcity

India's current development trajectory suggests that, unlike other major economies, all of its major sectors will have to grow simultaneously. Agriculture, which has been largely stagnant for the past decade, will demand more energy for irrigation and other value-added agro-processing industries. Manufacturing is slated to grow from 15 to 25 percent of gross domestic product

(GDP) under the new National Manufacturing Policy. And the services sector, already a major contributor to national income, will be boosted by rising demand from a rapidly urbanizing residential sector. The energy consumption of households outstripped that of agriculture for the first time during the last decade and now accounts for a third of all energy use.[40] Coal imports grew 80 percent in 2011–12 and oil imports grew 75 percent, but this is not enough to keep up with rising demand.[41]

Energy scarcity is *already* hampering India's economy, with the government estimating that the country runs a 7.9 percent energy deficit (which rises to 13.8 percent at peak times).[42] The blackout on July 30–31, 2012, which affected more than half of India's population and twenty-two of its twenty-eight states, seems certain to have made an important contribution to the economic downturn India experienced in 2012, when GDP growth fell to 4.5 percent, while also raising questions about the sustainability of the Indian economy.[43] Although energy efficiency is projected to continue to improve,[44] aggregate demand will still increase rapidly. Subsidies have been used to mask some of this vulnerability, but at the cost of an unsustainable fiscal burden, with one estimate suggesting that fiscal profligacy has four times the long-term impact on Indian GDP growth than an oil price shock.[45]

India is one of the few major economies that has limited resources of its own and is not geographically contiguous to major sources of supply. Its vulnerability to geopolitical and geoeconomic shocks through global commodity markets will therefore remain high.

Fuel, Food, and Water to Meet Basic Needs

While India has experienced robust growth in recent years, it remains a poor country. By 2015 it is projected to have 288 million people who are still living in absolute poverty, more than a quarter of the global total.[46] Resources, or the lack of them, play a critical role in the lives of India's poor.

Diets have failed to improve at the same rate as the economy, with average caloric intake both falling and, in some way, being the lowest in the G-20.[47] Overall, nutrition standards remain among the worst in the world, especially among children.[48] An estimated 217 million Indians are malnourished, a quarter of the world's total,[49] while half of Indian children are thought to be stunted, around a third of the global total.[50] Before the current food crisis, more than a quarter of the population stated that they did not have enough money to buy food, while a fifth said that they regularly suffered from hunger.[51]

By 2030 Indians are expected to consume only between a third and half of average global per capita energy use (only around 10 percent of the average

American). An estimated 144 million people will be without electricity,[52] almost all of whom will live in rural areas.[53] Without a rapid acceleration in progress, around 40 percent of the population will lack clean cooking facilities by 2030, again mostly in rural areas.[54]

Over half of India's population lives in areas that are water stressed, while only 72 percent of the population has access to safe drinking water.[55] Arable land per capita was halved over the past forty years,[56] and farm size is shrinking.[57] In twenty of India's twenty-eight states, irrigation infrastructure now exceeds the potential left to be developed.[58] The implication: a largely supply-side approach, relying on more investment in building irrigation infrastructure, is unlikely to suffice, as there is little irrigation potential left to be developed. Demand-side efficiency measures have become an imperative. Thanks to the inadequate water from surface canals, farmers are turning to groundwater to maintain productivity, with 61 percent of land now irrigated by groundwater.[59] In northern India, groundwater is "disappearing," raising the risk of a "collapse of agricultural output and severe shortages of potable water."[60] There is also feedback between energy and other resource domains. Subsidized electricity allows farmers to over-extract water, for example, while subsidies are also used to control the price of agricultural inputs (fertilizers and energy, with 42 percent of the latter derived from oil).[61]

India still has less than a third of its population living in towns and cities and will not be majority urban until 2050. Between 1993 and 2010, rural poverty fell 2.5 percent, as agricultural wages rose 2.9 percent.[62] However, increased yields have been relatively slow to feed through to poverty reduction, due to relatively unequal land distribution.[63]

The government hopes to pass the Food Security Bill in 2013, which aims to provide subsidized grain to around three-quarters of the rural and half of the urban population.[64] The government estimates that the bill will bring the cost of subsidies to around $16 billion a year from $14.5 billion in 2011/12, while the Food and Agriculture Organization (FAO) projects costs as high as $67 billion.[65] It will require up to 64 million tons of grain, with the public sector purchasing around a quarter of the total crop of food grains.[66]

Subsidies have also played an important role in limiting the transmission of global food prices to Indian consumers. During the 2008 price shock, the price of Indian wheat rose by only 11 percent of the global average and the price of Indian rice rose by just 4 percent.[67] As a result, and due to the impact of rapid economic growth, self-reported levels of food insecurity and hunger actually *fell* slightly during the food crisis.[68] Indian production has also grown strongly since the crisis, with cereals forecast to be 10 percent higher in 2012 than the average for 2008–10.[69] Total central government subsidies doubled in real terms over the past five years, and this has had a significant impact on a deficit that is four times the average for emerging economies.[70] Subsidies, however, for both food and energy create a heavy fiscal burden (16 percent of government expenditure in 2010–11) and are not well targeted on the poorest.[71]

Environmental Constraints of Resource Demand

India faces similarly urgent challenges in the face of extreme weather events and other environmental disasters, which further complicate its resource pressures. Between 2000 and 2009, an average of around 30 million people were affected by flooding each year, leading to the loss of 17,830 lives,[72] while large parts of the country are also vulnerable to earthquakes and tsunamis. In addition, the Drought Prone Area Program covers around three-quarters of a million square kilometers of the country,[73] with western and northern districts currently experiencing their worst drought in decades.[74] However, despite this vulnerability to drought, India has not experienced a famine since independence in 1947.

Given the shortage of land, India is vulnerable to any deterioration in the quality of that land. Land affected by soil erosion ranges from 0.1 percent in Goa to 21.6 percent in Rajasthan,[75] with erosion rates ranging from 5 to 20 tons of soil per hectare.[76] By 2050 India will need to support more than 18 percent of the global population on just 2.4 percent of the world's land, while the growing wealth of that population will continue to demand intensification of land use.[77] Demand for water is another growing problem, with India expected to be "water stressed" by 2025 and "water scarce" by 2050.[78] Water quality is also poor and will deteriorate without investment as cities grow. At present, only 31 percent of municipal wastewater receives treatment, while the rest is discharged into rivers, lakes, and groundwater.[79]

Beyond local environmental problems, India is one of the most vulnerable countries in the world to climate change, coming second on an index of vulnerability to Bangladesh.[80] A global temperature increase of 2–4° Celsius is expected to increase average annual precipitation by 7–20 percent a year. Central India and other semiarid regions in the country are expected to receive 5–25 percent less precipitation.[81] India's infrastructure, agriculture, and biodiversity are all susceptible to the impacts of climate change, as is its public health.[82]

Rising Demand and India's Role in Resource Markets

It seems inevitable that strategic resources and the environment will play an increasingly important role in shaping India's future. Over the next twenty years, energy security will be a defining challenge for India. Rapidly growing demand, energy poverty, high import dependence, and weak institutions guarantee that this issue will remain at, or close to, the top of India's political priorities. But, as a result of market failures in domestic energy sectors and volatile energy prices internationally, it seems unlikely that India's aspirations for rapid economic growth can be met given current energy policies. Poverty will remain a key driver of policy on resources. India's population is not expected to stabilize until the middle of this century, while it is projected to have significant levels of energy and food poverty for at least the next twenty years. Those who escape poverty and enter the middle class will be vulnerable to the erosion of their living standards by food and energy price inflation. No democratic government can afford to neglect these concerns, and India is likely to continue to favor an interventionist policy, at least in domestic resource markets. At the same time, it will be constrained in global markets for critical resources, where India's market-influencing power will often be limited.

To add to these challenges, the interactions between India's resource and environmental challenges will become more complex. Hydroelectricity links the energy sector with water, causing electricity shortages during times of drought. Agriculture in India is heavily dependent on oil, which accounts for 42 percent of all agricultural energy, with energy prices driving food inflation.[83] Subsidized energy allows farmers to over-extract water for irrigation, leading to both water and energy shortages and land degradation. Climate change multiplies the risks across all sectors, with energy infrastructure and agriculture vulnerable to extreme weather events, rising temperatures, and changes in the distribution and extent of rainfall.

National Pressures and Global Implications

Although energy, food, water, and climate all have obvious transboundary dimensions, more effective management of the country's dysfunctional resource markets is the most pressing priority. Reform, however, is blocked by a lack of consensus about future direction, by vested interests, and by the need to meet the basic needs of the poor.

Recent attempts to reduce subsidies have proved politically costly. While increased government intervention in food markets has the potential to reduce levels of hunger and malnutrition, it risks further distorting markets and creating an unsustainable fiscal burden. One attempt to reduce the distortions has been the introduction of direct cash transfers to beneficiaries, launched on a limited scale in twenty districts (in six states and three union territories) in January 2013.[84] The transfers will rely on another major program, the Unique Identification (UID) scheme, to ensure that the cash flows directly to beneficiaries identified by their UID numbers. The jury, however, is still out on whether cash transfers can be scaled up to cover the entire country effectively and with minimal leakage.

There is some evidence that the "social contract" on resources will continue to fray and widen existing fissures. These fissures are expected to manifest through demographic, regional, and intergenerational dimensions. In the worst case, natural resources and the environment could emerge as a significant threat to India's internal security. In rural areas, there is already a resource dimension to the Naxalite insurgency, while urban areas could experience unrest related to food and energy shortages. Across all resource industries, corruption and organized crime have a corrosive impact on legitimate political institutions.

It is quite possible that crisis will trigger badly needed reforms. High resource prices have placed the Indian government under increasing fiscal pressure and have already provided new impetus to reduce subsidies.[85] The power cuts of 2012 created fresh awareness of the need to invest in energy infrastructure, including off-grid systems that might improve energy access for the poor. In the future, dramatic evidence of the impact of land degradation, water scarcity, or climate change could make it possible for hard political decisions to be taken.

Global drivers will help to frame what is possible within India's domestic policy environment and how India might respond in global resource markets.

—*India's exposure to breakdown in global energy markets will continue to increase.* India is already heavily dependent on imported oil and is increasingly dependent on imported coal. Some of the measures it has taken to reduce its exposure to international markets, such as its investment in equity oil, have had limited impact, while its dependence on Iranian oil has already proved problematic. Moreover, India has, to date, been slow to engage in regime design to manage its resource dependencies, remaining outside all major multilateral and plurilateral energy regimes.

—*On food, India's size gives it considerable market power.* India is a dominant actor in the global rice market and plays an important role in other commodity markets. During the 2008 food crisis, Indian price stabilization and export controls played an important role in driving food prices higher for other countries, especially for rice.[86] India now plays a critical role in rice markets and soon is likely to be the world's third largest exporter. The country's reemergence as a rice exporter has helped to drive the rice price down, but continues to leave global markets vulnerable to any future resort to export bans.[87] While temporary export bans have shielded India's citizens from price rises, they have intensified the food crisis elsewhere. With an incentive to guarantee supply as import dependence grows, India is likely to play an active role in shaping food regimes and responding to supply interruptions and price volatility.

—*Transnational water stress will prove manageable in the short term.* It is plausible that water scarcity will heighten tensions with India's neighbors, especially if there are other causes of friction. However, it is more likely that water will provide a focus for cooperation rather than conflict, given the interest of all countries in managing shared water resources. (The India-Pakistan Indus Waters Treaty, signed in 1960, has survived three wars and many other dips in relations between the two countries.) However, in the longer term (2050 and onward), climate change could complicate matters, especially in the Indus and Brahmaputra river basins.[88]

—*The intersection between maritime and energy security is a potentially serious source of friction with India's neighbors.* By volume, 95 percent of India's trade depends on maritime routes (or 70 percent by value), making it highly sensitive to any risk of interruption.[89] These concerns feed into a potentially adversarial relationship with China, which is playing an increasingly assertive role in the Indian Ocean.[90] However, in the short term at least, China's ability to project naval power in the Indian Ocean is limited.[91] It is therefore possible that nontraditional security threats (from rising sea levels, pollution, and the decline of fisheries) could play a larger role. These—and the need for all countries in the region to secure energy imports—have the potential to spur cooperative action.

—*Climate change politics will be increasingly challenging for India.* As its emissions grow and "atmospheric space for emissions" shrinks, India will face international pressure to change the way it engages on climate. For twenty years, international climate politics has been strongly influenced by a steadfast alliance between India and China at the heart of the G-77 negotiating bloc. Indian per capita emissions are now far below China's, however, potentially leading to what could be a highly significant realignment. India will also have a growing incentive to shape international policy on climate adaptation, given its vulnerability to a changing climate and that of its neighbors.[92]

India will find that global governance regimes are both weak and contested for the issues that matter most to it. Energy governance is highly fragmented, with neither India nor China a member of the International Energy Agency.[93] The trade regime for food is better equipped to ensure market access than to prevent export bans when markets are threatened by collapse.[94] Thirty years of negotiations in climate change have failed to restrain the rapid growth in emissions of greenhouse gases.[95] The Indian government will therefore need to play a skilled hand if it is to meet its objectives in these sectors and, by doing so, reinforce its ability to implement reforms at home.

International Cooperation for Resource Security

India has long been an active participant in the processes and institutions of global governance.[96] Despite its growing economic and political power, India's engagement with the world will continue to remain contingent on how such engagement could produce outcomes that improve the human condition of citizens. This maxim will remain at the core of its diplomacy.

But India often lacks a clear strategy in its international engagement. This is compounded by the lack of capacity within the Indian system for contending with an increasingly crowded international portfolio. As the Indian economy grows, its interests become more complex. Often the government lacks the resources or the time to identify and further them effectively. With economic growth and greater resource demand, India's engagement with global institutions will change.

Despite the intertwined policy domains related to food, water, energy, and climate change, India seeks strategic autonomy in each of these areas. However, New Delhi is highly unlikely to find it, given the number and power of the other actors involved. At home, given its size and the nature of its political system, it is equally implausible that it will develop and implement a strategic, comprehensive, and integrated response to its resource and environmental challenges. It is much more likely that it will continue to muddle through, responding to the most pressing problems in a reactive fashion, gradually building increased institutional capacity, better-functioning markets, and more resilient communities. At best, international cooperation will support this process. At worse, it will make difficult domestic decisions even harder to take.

Domestically, we believe that a series of "mini-bargains" has the greatest potential to increase resource security, with each containing sufficient incentives for relevant interest groups to support—or avoid blocking—them. These mini-bargains could include, but not be limited to, reforming the most egregious of fossil fuel subsidies that have a negative impact on fiscal balances, public health, the environment, and social welfare (by being poorly targeted); reviewing critical food stocks to ensure that sudden supply shocks do not result in purely unilateral measures to secure them; and steadily strengthening the governance of energy and food markets, in order to increase supply while reducing the vulnerabilities in supply chains.

Multilateralism among Other Options

Recognizing that India is a major economy with large resource pressures, some resource-rich countries might find it attractive to apply strategic pressure on India to extract concessions in international forums. But such a strategy would only serve to alienate India. On the whole, the international community has a considerable interest in supporting reforms within India as a means to reduce its footprint on global resource demand. Both India and its allies have an incentive to look for opportunities for international cooperation on resource and environmental issues that will strengthen global regimes, while making India's search for domestic solutions more fruitful. Greater international engagement can accomplish the following:

—*Help to improve understanding of the risks that India faces.* Resource and environmental issues are highly complex, interacting with each other and with all aspects of India's society and economy. They also naturally cross borders, making a purely national perspective of little value. It is important for India to build a shared analysis of stresses, risks, and opportunities related to food, land, water, climate, and strategic commodities across countries in the region and internationally.

—*Provide India with a platform to share potential solutions with its partners.* Other countries in the region, as well as those in the G-20 such as Brazil and China, have important experience tackling resource challenges during a period of rapid growth and tackling resource poverty. Equally, India has its own successful models, which are relevant to emerging economies and poorer ones as well.

—*Provide a basis for Indian leadership in the G-20.* The G-20 turned its attention to energy in 2009 at the Pittsburgh summit, focusing on energy poverty, the need to phase out subsidies, and energy and climate security, while the 2009 L'Aquila summit laid the basis for international cooperation on food security. India has an especially strong incentive to keep the G-20 focused on both issues, ensuring that it does more to implement existing commitments, while exploring new areas for international cooperation. It is surely time for India to assume the G-20 presidency, possibly after Turkey in 2015. Energy and food would provide a natural theme for India to build its presidency around, while the intersection between maritime and energy security is another promising area for cooperation within the G-20.

—*Help India to influence the post-2015 development agenda.* Debate is currently under way about what should replace the Millennium Development Goals after 2015, with the new framework likely to focus both on poverty eradication and sustainable development.[97] Given that new goals will play an important role in shaping the international agenda for the next fifteen years or more, India has a powerful incentive to ensure that food, water, and energy poverty are at the heart of the new agenda and that progress is made on sustainable development and green growth, but not at the expense of countries such as India with consumption rates that are well below the global per capita average.

Preparing the Ground at Home

More decisive international engagement on resource issues will only be possible if the Indian government is prepared to enhance significantly its capacity to engage internationally. Indian diplomats increasingly recognize that, as an emerging power, India has to navigate four transitions in global governance: from taking rules to shaping them; from framing rules to designing regimes; from addressing issues in a single issue-specific institution to addressing them in complex regimes; and from undertaking diplomacy through formal forums to understanding the role of informal networks and groups of countries.[98] India will need increased capacity if it is to exploit the full potential that each of these transitions provides, while using them to construct an overarching strategic posture.

The first step is to invest in resource and environmental diplomacy and in the data and evidence needed to underpin this diplomacy. Indian diplomats often view foreign assessments of India's economy and resource consumption patterns with a degree of suspicion. They need to generate their own answers from sources they trust, while ensuring better information flows between resource-related departments, researchers outside government, and foreign policymakers.

India's diplomats then need to survey the full range of multilateral, plurilateral, and bilateral options, while assessing what markets can be expected to deliver without any government intervention. This will allow them to develop the basis for solutions and collaborations with foreign partners on specific problems and, thereby, lay the foundations for more robust international resource governance.

The National Security Council Secretariat is the natural focus for this iterative process of analysis and design of international engagement, but many others will need to be involved. Resource ministers and others are needed to monitor vulnerabilities in resource supply lines. Officials from all responsible ministries, including external affairs, need to be involved in the broader dialogue, creating a wider perspective on changing resource needs, markets, rules, and potential areas of tension. This will help to build a cadre of more strategically focused officers. Finally, the skills and knowledge of external actors must also be drawn on, including former diplomats, academics, think tanks, and industry representatives, providing a range of alternative perspectives on India's resource and environmental needs.

A strategic approach to India's resource challenges will not emerge overnight, but neither can the government afford to wait any longer. The pressure from energy, food, water, and climate is growing. It is time to engage on these issues with new vision, foresight, and determination, before signs of trouble turn into a crisis that threatens the country's prosperity, security, and international status.

Notes

1. National Intelligence Council, *Global Trends 2030: Alternative Worlds* (Washington, December 2012), p. iv.

2. United Nations, *World Population Prospects: The 2010 Revision* (New York: United Nations Department of Economic and Social Affairs, 2011).

3. Knight Frank and Citi Private Bank, *The Wealth Report 2012: A Global Perspective on Prime Property and Wealth* (London: Knight Frank Research, 2012).

4. International Energy Agency, *World Energy Outlook 2011* (Paris, 2011).

5. See Maplecroft, Climate Change Vulnerability Index 2012 (http://maplecroft.com/themes/cc/).

6. Grant Danise, Marc Lanteigne, and Indra Overland, "Reducing Energy Subsidies in China, India, and Russia: Dilemmas for Decision Makers," *Sustainability* 2, no. 2 (2010): 475–93.

7. "Indian Power Failure Shows Growing Political Gridlock," Bloomberg, August 3, 2012 (www.bloomberg.com/news/2012-08-02/indian-power-failure-highlights-growing-political-gridlock-view.html); "Now Finish the Job," *The Economist*, April 15, 2012 (www.economist.com/blogs/banyan/2012/04/indias-economic-reforms?zid=309&ah=80dcf288b8561b012f603b9fd9577f0e).

8. Planning Commission, *Faster, Sustainable, and More Inclusive Growth: An Approach to the Twelfth Five-Year Plan* (New Delhi: Government of India, 2011), p. 29.

9. Arunabha Ghosh et al., *Understanding Complexity, Anticipating Change: From Interests to Strategy on Global Governance*, report of the Working Group on India and Global

Governance (New Delhi: Council on Energy, Environment, and Water, 2011), pp. i–70 (http://ceew.in/pdf/CEEW_WGIGG_Report.pdf).

10. These calculations are based on energy demand projections of the International Energy Agency and Energy Information Administration to 2030. See International Energy Agency, *World Energy Outlook 2011*; Energy Information Administration, *International Energy Outlook 2011* (Washington, 2011).

11. Planning Commission, *Faster, Sustainable, and More Inclusive Growth*, p. 29.

12. International Energy Agency, *World Energy Outlook 2012* (Paris: 2012).

13. Central Statistics Office, *Energy Statistics 2012* (New Delhi: Government of India, 2012).

14. International Energy Agency, *Energy Technology Perspectives: Scenarios and Strategies to 2050* (Paris, 2010); World Coal Institute, *The Coal Resource: A Comprehensive Overview of Coal* (London, 2009).

15. International Energy Agency, *World Energy Outlook 2011*.

16. Saurabh Chaturvedi and Rakesh Sharma, "Coal India Trims Outlook on Environmental Issues," *Wall Street Journal*, December 21, 2010 (http://online.wsj.com/article/SB10001424052748703581204576033112469285354.html); "Coal India Mines Face Closure over Environmental Concerns in Jharkhand," *Economic Times*, August 24, 2011 (http://economictimes.indiatimes.com/news/news-by-industry/indl-goods/svs/metals-mining/coal-india-mines-face-closure-over-environmental-concerns-in-jharkhand/articleshow/9720497.cms); H. B. Sahu and S. Dash, "Land Degradation due to Mining in India and Its Mitigation Measures," in *Second International Conference on Environmental Science and Technology IPCBEE*, vol. 6 (Singapore: IACSIT Press, 2011); Shiv Pratap Raghuvanshi, Avinash Chandra, and Ashok Kumar Raghav, "Carbon Dioxide Emissions from Coal-Based Power Generation in India," *Energy Conversion and Management* 47, no. 4 (March 2006): 427–41.

17. International Energy Agency, *World Energy Outlook 2011*.

18. Comptroller and Auditor General of India, *Performance Audit: Allocation of Coal Blocks and Augmentation of Coal Production* (New Delhi, 2012) (http://saiindia.gov.in/english/home/Our_Products/Audit_Report/Government_Wise/union_audit/recent_reports/union_performance/2012_2013/Commercial/Report_No_7/Report_No_7.html); "PMs Response to Report," *Wall Street Journal*, August 8, 2012 (http://blogs.wsj.com/indiarealtime/2012/08/27/transcript-prime-minister-singh-counters-coalgate-allegations/); Vikas Bajaj and Jim Yeardley, "Scandal Poses a Riddle: Will India Ever Be Able to Tackle Corruption?" *New York Times*, September 15, 2012 (www.nytimes.com/2012/09/16/ world/asia/scandal-bares-corruption-hampering-indias-growth.html?pagewanted=all&_r=0); "India Story Alive and Kicking: Jyotiraditya Scindia," NDTV, January 28, 2013 (http://profit.ndtv.com/news/economy/article-india-story-alive-and-kicking-jyotiraditya-scindia-316819).

19. William Magioncalda, *A Modern Insurgency: India's Evolving Naxalite Problem* (Washington: Center for Strategic and International Studies, 2010) (http://csis.org/files/publication/SAM_140_0.pdf).

20. "New Pricing May See Cut in Higher-Grade Coal Imports," *Economic Times*, February 2, 2012 (http://bit.ly/xsRzpp).

21. Arunabha Ghosh, "Industrial Demand and Energy Supply Management: A Delicate Balance," in *Empowering Growth: Perspectives on India's Energy Future* (London:

Economist Intelligence Unit, October 2012), pp. 29–30 (www.managementthinking.eiu.com/empowering-growth.html).

22. Ajoy K. Das, "Coal Shortage Causes India's Electricity Generation to Slump," *Mining Weekly,* May 17, 2011 (www.miningweekly.com/article/coal-shortage-causes-indias-electricity-generation-to-slump-2011-05-17).

23. Sujay Mehdudia, "Coal Shortage to Hit Power Capacity Plans," *Hindu*, February 23, 2012 (www.thehindu.com/business/Economy/article2924660.ece); Sudheer Pal Singh, "Govt Expects Coal Shortage to Touch 15% by 2012," *Business Standard*, February 11, 2010 (www.business-standard.com/india/news/govt-expects-coal-shortage-to-touch-15-by-2012/385289/).

24. McKinsey and Company, *Environmental and Energy Sustainability: An Approach for India* (Mumbai, 2009).

25. Ministry of Power, *Report of the Working Group on Power for Twelfth Five-Year Plan (2012–17)* (New Delhi: Government of India, 2012), ch. 7, p. 5 (http://planningcommission.nic.in/aboutus/committee/wrkgrp12/wg_power1904.pdf).

26. Energy Information Administration, *International Energy Statistics* (Washington: Department of Energy, various years) (www.eia.gov/cfapps/ipdbproject/IEDIndex3.cfm).

27. International Energy Agency, *World Energy Outlook 2011*.

28. Planning Commission, *Faster, Sustainable, and More Inclusive Growth*, p. 33.

29. Ministry of Finance, *Economic Survey 2011–12* (New Delhi: Government of India, 2012) (www.indiabudget.nic.in/survey.asp).

30. Lydia Powell, "Do India's Equity Oil Investments Make Sense?" *Energy News Monitor* 8, no. 43 (April 10, 2012) (www.observerindia.com/cms/sites/orfonline/modules/enm-analysis/ENM-ANALYSISDetail.html?cmaid=35815&mmacmaid=35813).

31. Anilesh S. Mahajan, "World Wide Woe: ONGC Videsh's Overseas Woes: Could the Problems Have Been Avoided?" *Business Today*, August 19, 2012 (http://businesstoday.intoday.in/story/overseas-problems-of-ongc-videsh-other-oil-companies/1/186797.html); "ONGC to Continue Exploration in South China Sea," *Wall Street Journal*, July 19, 2012 (http://online.wsj.com/article/SB10000872396390444464304577536182763155666.html).

32. Powell, "Do India's Equity Oil Investments Make Sense?"

33. Planning Commission, *Integrated Energy Policy: Report of the Expert Committee* (New Delhi: Government of India, 2006).

34. Observer Research Foundation, *Dash for Gas: Opportunities and Challenges*, Policy Brief 13 (New Delhi, 2012), p. 3.

35. Ibid.; Anne-Sophie Corbeau, *Natural Gas in India* (Paris: International Energy Agency, 2010).

36. Energy Information Administration, *International Energy Outlook 2012* (Washington, 2012).

37. Anil Jain and Anupama Sen, *Natural Gas in India: An Analysis of Policy* (Oxford Institute for Energy Studies, April 2010).

38. Govindasamy Agoramoorthy, "Nuclear Power: India Should Exploit Renewable Energy [correspondence]," *Nature* 481 (2012): 145.

39. Planning Commission, *Faster, Sustainable, and More Inclusive Growth*, p. 29.

40. Ghosh, "Industrial Demand and Energy Supply Management," pp. 26, 29.

41. Amol Sharma and Megha Bahree, "Grinding Energy Shortage Takes Toll on India's Growth," *Wall Street Journal,* July 1, 2012 (http://online.wsj.com/article/SB1000 1424052702304331204577352232515290226.html).

42. Planning Commission, *Eleventh Five-Year Plan, 2007–2012,* vol. III: *Agriculture, Rural Development, Industry, Services, and Physical Infrastructure* (Oxford University Press, 2008).

43. International Monetary Fund (IMF), "World Economic Outlook Update: Gradual Upturn in Global Growth during 2013" (Washington, January 13, 2013) (www.imf.org/external/pubs/ft/weo/2013/update/01/).

44. International Energy Agency, *World Energy Outlook 2011.*

45. B.B. Bhattacharya and Sabyasachi Kar, *Shocks, Economic Growth, and the Indian Economy* (New Delhi: Institute of Economic Growth, 2005) (www.imf.org/external/np/res/seminars/2005/macro/pdf/bhatta.pdf).

46. United Nations, *The Millennium Development Goals Report 2011* (New York, 2011), p. 7.

47. Praduman Kumar, Anjani Kumar, Shinoj Parappurathu, and S. S. Raju, "Estimation of Demand Elasticity for Food Commodities in India," *Agricultural Economics Research Review* 24 (2011): 1–14.

48. Angus Deaton and Jean Drèze, "Food and Nutrition in India: Facts and Interpretations," *Economic and Political Weekly* 44, no. 7 (2009): 42–65.

49. Food and Agriculture Organization (FAO), *State of Food Insecurity* (Rome, 2012) (www.fao.org/docrep/016/i3027e/ i3027e.pdf).

50. Robert E. Black, Lindsay H. Allen, Zulfiqar A. Bhutta, Laura E. Caulfield, Mercedes de Onis, Majid Ezzati, Colin Mathers, and Juan Rivera, for the Maternal and Child Undernutrition Study Group, "Maternal and Child Undernutrition: Global and Regional Exposures and Health Consequences," *Lancet* 371, no. 9608 (January 19, 2008): 243–60 (www.thelancet.com/journals/lancet/article/PIIS0140-6736(07)61690-0/fulltext#article_upsell).

51. Julie Ray and Cynthia English, "Even before Crisis, Affording Food a Challenge for Many," *Gallup*, April 25, 2008 (www.gallup.com/poll/106807/Even-Before-Crisis-Affording-Food-Challenge-Many.aspx).

52. International Energy Agency, "World Energy Outlook: Energy Access Projections to 2030, Table 1" (Paris, 2012) (www.worldenergyoutlook.org/resources/energydevelopment/energyaccessprojectionsto2030/).

53. International Energy Agency, *World Energy Outlook 2011*, p. 469.

54. International Energy Agency, "World Energy Outlook: Energy Access Projections to 2030."

55. Günther Fischer, Harrij van Velthuizen, Mahendra Shah, and Freddy Nachtergaele, *Global Agro-Ecological Assessment for Agriculture in the 21st Century* (Laxenburg, Austria: International Institute for Applied Systems Analysis, 2001); Ministry of Finance, *Economic Survey 2011–12: Human Development* (New Delhi: Government of India, 2012) (www.indiabudget.nic.in/es2011-12/echap-13.pdf).

56. World Bank DataBank calculations based on FAO data, "Arable Land (Hectares per Person)" (Washington: World Bank, 2012).

57. Foreign Agricultural Service, *India Agricultural Economy and Policy Report* (Washington: Department of Agriculture, 2009).

58. Martin A. Burton, Rahul Sen, Simon Gordon-Walker, Anand Jalakam, and Arunabha Ghosh, *National Water Resources Framework Study*, research report submitted to the Planning Commission for the Twelfth Five-Year Plan (New Delhi: Council on Energy, Environment, and Water and 2030 Water Resources Group, September 2011), p. 152 (http://ceew.in/water).

59. Ibid., p. 219.

60. Matthew Rodell, Isabella Velicogna, and James S. Famiglietti, "Satellite-Based Estimates of Groundwater Depletion in India [letter]," *Nature* 460 (2009): 999–1002; Gretchen Cook-Anderson, "NASA Satellites Unlock Secret to Northern India's Vanishing Water" (NASA Earth Science News Team, August 12, 2009) (www.nasa.gov/topics/earth/features/india_water.html).

61. Derek Headey and Shenggen Fan, *Reflections on the Global Food Crisis: How Did It Happen? How Has It Hurt? And How Can We Prevent the Next One?* (Washington: International Food Policy Research Institute, 2010).

62. Anjani Kumar, Sant Kumar, Dhiraj K. Singh, and Issa G. Shivjee, "Rural Employment Diversification in India: Trends, Determinants, and Implications on Poverty," *Agricultural Economics Research Review* 24 (2011): 361–72 (http://mahider.ilri.org/bitstream/handle/10568/12418/AERR_rural.pdf?sequence=1).

63. FAO, *State of Food Insecurity*.

64. Sunil Prabhu, "Parliamentary Panel Clears Food Security Bill," NDTV, January 11, 2013 (www.ndtv.com/article/india/parliamentary-panel-clears-food-security-bill-316322).

65. Ministry of Finance, *Economic Survey 2011–12: Agriculture and Food* (New Delhi: Government of India, 2012) (www.indiabudget.nic.in/es2011-12/echap-08.pdf); FAO, *Food Outlook, May 2012* (Rome, 2012) (www.fao.org/fileadmin/user_upload/newsroom/docs/Final%20web%20version%202%20May%20(2).pdf).

66. FAO, *Food Outlook, May 2012*; Centre for Budget and Governance Accountability, *Unfulfilled Promises? Response to Union Budget 2012–13* (New Delhi, 2012), p. 54.

67. FAO, *Food Outlook, November 2011: Global Market Analysis* (Rome, 2011), p. 26.

68. Derek Headey, "Was the Global Food Crisis Really a Crisis? Simulation versus Self-Reporting," IFPRI Discussion Paper 01087 (Washington: Food Policy Research Institute, 2011) (www.ifpri.org/sites/default/files/publications/ifpridp01087.pdf).

69. FAO, *Food Outlook, May 2012*.

70. Ministry of Petroleum and Natural Gas, *Basic Statistics on Indian Petroleum and Natural Gas 2010–11* (New Delhi: Government of India, 2011), p. 36; IMF, "Nurturing Credibility While Managing Risks to Growth," *Fiscal Monitor*, July 16, 2012 (www.imf.org/external/pubs/ft/fm/2012/update/02/pdf/0712.pdf); IMF, "India: 2012 Article IV Consultation—Staff Report; Staff Statement and Supplements; Public Information Notice on the Executive Board Discussion; and Statement by the Executive Director for India" (Washington, April 2012) (www.imf.org/external/pubs/ft/scr/2012/cr1296.pdf).

71. James Lamont and Amy Kazmin, "Singh Aide Urges India to End Energy Subsidies," *Financial Times*, June 14, 2011 (www.ft.com/cms/s/0/7f48e1f8-96b7-11e0-baca-00144feab49a.html#axzz1pfwZAcMj).

72. Ministry of Statistics and Programme Implementation, *Compendium on Environment Statistics India* (New Delhi: Government of India, 2011) (http://mospi.nic.in/mospi_new/upload/compendium_2011_30dec11.htm).

73. Ibid.

74. R. S. Eshelman and ClimateWire, "India's Drought Highlights Challenges of Climate Change Adaptation," *Scientific American,* August 3, 2012 (www.scientificamerican.com/article.cfm?id=indias-drought-highlights-challenges-climate-change-adaptation).

75. Planning Commission, *Eleventh Five-Year Plan, 2007–2012,* vol. III.

76. Ministry of Environment and Forests, *State of Environment Report: India 2009* (New Delhi: Government of India, 2009), p. 13.

77. United Nations, *World Population Prospects*; Ministry of Environment and Forests, *Protected Area Network in India* (New Delhi: Government of India, n.d.) (http://envfor.nic.in/downloads/public-information/protected-area-network.pdf).

78. Institute for Defense Studies and Analyses, *Water Security for India: The External Dynamics; IDSA Task Force Report* (New Delhi, 2010).

79. See Aquastat (www.fao.org/nr/water/aquastat/data/query/results.html).

80. Maplecroft, "Big Economies of the Future: Bangladesh, India, Philippines, Vietnam, and Pakistan; Most at Risk from Climate Change," October 21, 2010 (http://maplecroft.com/about/news/ccvi.html).

81. Divya Sharma and Sanjay Tomar, "Mainstreaming Climate Change Adaptation in Indian Cities," *Environment and Urbanization* 22, no. 2 (2010): 451–65 (http://eau.sagepub.com/ content/22/2/451.full.pdf).

82. On infrastructure, see Prakriti Naswa and Amit Garg, "Managing Climate-Induced Risks on Indian Infrastructure Assets," *Current Science* 101, no. 3 (August 10, 2011): 395–404 (www.currentscience.ac.in/Volumes/101/03/0395.pdf). On public health, see Indian Network for Climate Change Assessment, *Climate Change and India: A 4x4 Assessment; A Sectoral and Regional Analysis for 2030s* (New Delhi: Government of India, Ministry of Environment and Forests, 2010).

83. Headey and Fan, *Reflections on the Global Food Crisis.*

84. "Govt Launches Direct Cash Transfer Scheme in 20 Districts," *Business Today,* January 2, 2013 (http://businesstoday.intoday.in/story/govt-launches-direct-cash-transfer-scheme-in-20-districts/1/191196.html).

85. IMF, *World Economic Outlook, April 2012: Growth Resuming, Dangers Remain* (Washington, 2012) (www.imf.org/external/pubs/ft/weo/2012/01/index.htm).

86. David Dawe and Tom Slayton, "The World Rice Market in 2007–08," in *Safeguarding Food Security in Volatile Global Markets,* edited by Adam Prakesh (Rome: FAO, 2011) (www.fao.org/docrep/013/i2107e/i2107e13.pdf).

87. FAO, *Food Outlook, May 2012.*

88. Walter W. Immerzeel, Ludovicus P. H. van Beek, and Marc F. P. Bierkens, "Climate Change Will Affect the Asian Water Towers," *Science* 328, no. 5984 (2010): 1382–85.

89. "National Level Infrastructure: Maritime Transport" (New Delhi: Government of India, n.d.) (http://business.gov.in/infrastructure/maritime_transport.php).

90. C. U. Bhaskar and G. Kemp, *Maritime Security Challenges in the Indian Ocean Region: A Workshop Report* (Washington: Center for the National Interest and National Maritime Foundation, 2011).

91. M. J. Green and S. Shearer, *Defining U.S. Indian Ocean Strategy* (Washington: Center for Strategic and International Studies, 2012) (csis.org/files/publication/twq12springgreenshearer.pdf).

92. See chapter 14 by Navroz Dubash in this volume.

93. Ann Florini, "The International Energy Agency in Global Energy Governance," *Global Policy* 2, no. 1 (September 2011): 40–50.

94. Alex Evans, *The Feeding of Nine Billion: Global Food Security for the 21st Century* (London: Chatham House, 2009).

95. Alex Evans and David Steven, *Hitting Reboot: Where Next for Climate after Copenhagen* (Brookings, 2010). See also chapter 14 by Dubash in this volume.

96. Parts of this section draw extensively on the first report on India and global governance. See Ghosh et al., *Understanding Complexity, Anticipating Change.*

97. Alex Evans and David Steven, *Beyond the MDGs: Agreeing a Post-2015 Development Framework* (Brookings; New York University, Center on International Cooperation, 2012). See also David Steven, *Goals in a Post-2015 Development Framework: Options and Strategic Choices* (New York University, Center on International Cooperation, 2013).

98. Ghosh et al., *Understanding Complexity, Anticipating Change.*

NITIN PAI

16 India and International Norms: R2P, Genocide Prevention, Human Rights, and Democracy

Introduction

The doctrine of responsibility to protect (R2P), India's permanent representative to the United Nations declared in a speech in October 2012, "is the most important challenge that the international community, anchored in the United Nations, is going to face."[1] Arguing that the initial suspicion of many developing countries toward the newest norm in international relations was misplaced, he supported the need for a "collective response by the international community to ensure that mass atrocities like genocide, ethnic cleansing, crimes against humanity do not take place." Explaining why India had abstained on a United Nations Security Council (UNSC) resolution authorizing military intervention in the Libyan civil war of 2011, he judged that implementation of the doctrine "gives R2P a bad name."

The Indian diplomat's arguments are a good example of India's attitude toward international norms infringing on state sovereignty in furtherance of human security, human rights, or liberal democratic goals. This chapter argues that India takes a middle path, supporting the evolution of human rights and democratic norms, but exercising caution in the manner of their implementation. It delves into the foundations of India's policy approach toward two sets of norms: those concerning human security and those pertaining to liberal democracy. It interrogates these norms as they have evolved and examines them from an Indian perspective. It concludes by exploring how Indian foreign policy in the context of these norms might change as India emerges to become a more powerful player in international politics.

The Middle Path

Constitutional values, a democratic political culture, and a diverse, plural society make India generally supportive of defending the world's people from oppression and promoting human rights and democracy. New Delhi's foreign policy orientation is at the very least consistent with a rules-based international order and is underpinned by liberal democratic values. The Indian republic's subscription to liberal international norms, however, has been tempered both by competing norms and by reservations about the nature of international interventions. The result is a foreign policy that treads a middle path.

An Idealistic Orientation

Part of the orientation toward liberal international norms is inherent in the Indian republic. Both its birth from a nonviolent struggle for freedom that focused on moral high ground and the values of its influential founding fathers have created a grand narrative that upholds freedom, human rights, and democracy. While this has not translated into a political impetus for promoting the Indian republic's political values abroad, it is nevertheless a reference point from which to measure departures from policy positions.

In fact, in the years preceding and immediately after independence, Gandhi's pacifism and Nehru's One Worldism put the pursuit of liberal internationalism on a higher pedestal than mere national interest.[2] India's first foreign policy debates marked the triumph of the high idealism of Mohandas K. Gandhi and Jawaharlal Nehru over the realism of Abul Kalam Azad[3] and Vallabhbhai Patel. While even during Nehru's early years this idealism came to be tempered by its unfavorable outcomes—for instance, over Pakistani aggression in Jammu and Kashmir (J&K)— it was the debacle of the India-China War of 1962 that jolted the New Delhi establishment into investing in pursuit of national interest.[4]

Independent India's early foreign policy agenda therefore was loaded with a broad range of normative issues: from support for the United Nations (UN) and the Universal Declaration of Human Rights to the contribution of troops for peacekeeping operations and championing of disarmament negotiations.

Nehruvian Dominance

Nehru's legacy lives on in the form of a strong internationalist constituency in India, among the policymaking elite, the media, and indeed the society at-large.[5] This constituency is concerned with defending human rights, protecting oppressed people, and opposing oppressive regimes. It upholds the UN as an important, though imperfect, institution of global governance, favors multilateralism, emphasizes international treaties and conventions, and supports international laws, rules, and norms to change the world for the better.[6] This is, arguably, the dominant tradition in Indian foreign policy, although its dominance has been increasingly contested over the last two decades.[7]

Safeguarding sovereignty from predations of great powers was a major priority in the decades after independence. Solidarity with fellow victims of colonial rule drove India to attempt to organize the "third world" politically around common interests. It also caused India to ignore massive violations of human rights or democratic norms by its co-travelers, as was the case with several postcolonial regimes of the 1950s–80s.

The not unfounded suspicion that freedom and democracy were and remain guises under which Western powers promote their interests is another major reason for India's reservations. To the extent that there is a divergence in interests between India and the West, these reservations become more acute. Furthermore, given the handicap of not being a permanent member of the UNSC, India is prudent not to empower further a body of which it is not a member.

New Delhi's reservations also arise from the risk that promoting international norms can backfire on India's own interests, especially if India needs the political support of other UN member-states or veto-wielding members of the UNSC. The experience of referring to the UN Pakistani aggression in J&K in 1947 and of pursuing nonproliferation negotiations in good faith, only to have lasting counterproductive outcomes, has made the Indian establishment suspicious of the motives of the great powers and generally defensive in its policy outlook.

This has not prevented India from acting purposefully in support of new norms. For instance, New Delhi championed the UN Human Rights Council despite being under constant attack by international nongovernmental organizations for its record in J&K and other areas. However, at the margin, Indian diplomacy tends to regard the promotion of norms with caution.

India's approach therefore is unique—normatively, it seeks both to promote human rights and to defend sovereignty. This tradition is in contrast to the West, which tends to prioritize human rights over sovereignty, and also of authoritarian powers like China, which do the opposite.

Interrogating Norms

There is a tendency in public discourse to pack human rights, humanitarian intervention, promotion of liberal democracy, and to a lesser extent market capitalism in the same basket of international "morality." It is, however, necessary to examine them separately.

This chapter limits itself to examining the responsibility to protect and the prevention of genocide as well as the promotion of a particular political order (democracy). The issue of human rights straddles these two broad categories, the former concerned with preventing the most egregious abuses and the latter with promoting political systems that respect human rights.

Crimes against Humanity

Of the two human security themes, prevention of genocide is the older and better understood. India was among the early signatories of the Genocide Convention, which it signed in 1949 and ratified in 1959, with a caveat stating that the consent of all parties to a dispute should be required before submitting it to the International Court of Justice.

India was the first—and arguably the only—country to have intervened militarily in time to prevent a genocide. There are several explanations for the decision of Indira Gandhi's government to send troops into a conflict in East Pakistan in 1971, which led to the birth of Bangladesh. Among the official ones offered was the need to stop the flow of refugees fleeing the Pakistan army's genocidal campaign in East Pakistan, creating political and socioeconomic burdens that India was incapable of bearing beyond a point.[8] Even if the official rationale is discounted, the fact is that the Indian army prevented further loss of life in conditions that would qualify as genocidal under international law.[9]

What is interesting here is that the Indian intervention was unilateral, lacked the normative legitimacy of a UNSC resolution, was carried out in the face of diplomatic opposition and military coercion by the Nixon administration, and was supported by the Soviet Union in the Security Council. India's action in East Pakistan, along with Vietnam's in Cambodia in 1979, Tanzania's in Idi Amin's Uganda, also in 1978–79, and to a lesser extent the North Atlantic Treaty Organization's in the Balkans in 1999, provides a powerful counterargument to the efficacy of the UN as an agency that can prevent mass atrocities and loss of life before they occur.

The failure to prosecute anyone for the Pakistan army's genocidal campaign in East Pakistan stands as an indictment of international mechanisms to prevent genocide. In March 1973 Pakistan applied to the International Court of Justice seeking jurisdiction over 195 of its military personnel charged with genocide and held as prisoners of war in India.[10] India had sought to hand them over to Bangladesh for trial. Pakistan contested this on the basis that the alleged crimes had occurred in Pakistani territory. India did not consent to the jurisdiction of the International Court of Justice in this case. In the event, the matter was settled out of court, as part of a broader set of settlements among Bangladesh, India, and Pakistan.[11] Consequently, the accused were repatriated to Pakistan and escaped charges of genocide or even lesser crimes.

How Many Deaths Will It Take?

The Indian experience in 1971 raises some difficult questions that continue to vex the international community: When is genocide a genocide? Can external intervention take place early enough and still be considered legitimate? Can multilateralism act swiftly enough to prevent genocide or resolutely enough to punish perpetrators? Should the legitimacy of an external intervention be subject to the balance of interests of the Security Council members, specifically its permanent members? Should it be exempt from a veto?

From the Indian perspective, these questions warrant deep skepticism of the UN's potential to prevent genocide and punish perpetrators without selectivity. The tragedies in the Balkans, Cambodia, Rwanda, and Sudan bolster this view.

The international community's response to these failings was to introduce and institutionalize a new norm: responsibility to protect. The UN's 2005 world summit outcome document recorded a "clear and unambiguous acceptance by all governments of the collective international responsibility to protect populations from genocide, war crimes, ethnic cleansing, and crimes against humanity [and a] willingness to take timely and decisive collective action for this purpose, through the Security Council, when peaceful means prove inadequate and national authorities are manifestly failing to do it."[12] R2P was enshrined in the resolution adopted by the General Assembly in September 2005.[13]

R2P's proponents have held that the norm was conceived as a formula to reconcile sovereignty with human rights.[14] Its skeptics warn against turning it into "a tool legitimizing big-power intervention on the pretext of protecting populations" and "codifying a system of coercion, providing a tool in the hands of powerful governments to judge weaker states and encourage regime change primarily on political considerations."[15]

The first of R2P's three pillars is relatively unobjectionable—every state has a responsibility to protect its own citizens against genocide, ethnic cleansing, crimes against humanity, and war crimes. The second pillar begins to tread contentious ground when it holds that the international community has a responsibility to build capacity to prevent mass atrocities in states where such capacity does not exist. The third, and most contentious, pillar binds the international community "to timely and decisive collective action, in ways that are consistent with the UN Charter."

To the extent that the second and third pillars involve external intervention, the questions raised in the preceding section come into sharp relief. Yes, the international community has a responsibility to build capacity in states to prevent mass atrocities, but implementing this mandate is extremely hard in practice. Which states qualify for external support and at what time? Who pays? What if the states that most need this capacity—from the international community's perspective—do not agree or refuse such assistance? Also, given the scarcity of funds, resources, and political capital, where does capacity building to prevent mass atrocities rank with respect to the international community's other priorities? Indeed, it may well be argued that the ambitions of the second pillar have created obligations and expectations that are way beyond the capability of the international system to meet. Unmet promises undermine the credibility of the agency making them.

Inevitably, the question of where and when the international community must intervene is answered through a process of geopolitical bargaining. For instance, an observer in India might wonder why violent suppression of protests against authoritarian regimes in Iran, Libya, and Syria attract the UN's attention, while those in Bahrain, Balochistan, and Tibet do not.

While the allegation of "double standards" does not perturb amoral subscribers of realism, it does rankle liberal internationalists in New Delhi's establishment, media, and civil society. The selectivity in the choice of theaters in which to intervene leads to skepticism about the motives of the world's major powers. It also provides another justification for New Delhi's own policy positions with respect to the conflicts in its immediate neighborhood. Whereas India had intervened forcefully in Bangladesh, the Maldives, and Sri Lanka in the 1970s and 1980s, it adopted a less activist military role in the conflicts in Myanmar, Nepal, and Sri Lanka thereafter and relied mainly on politics and diplomacy.

Therefore, the unrealistic ambition of the R2P norms, the inability of the international system to measure up, the necessary geopolitical bargaining within and outside the United Nations, the consequent selectivity of the interventions, and the perceived subversion of the letter and spirit of the authorizing norms by the great powers strengthen the reservations that inform India's approach to this norm.

Despite the obvious shortcomings of international norms on genocide prevention and R2P, India's foreign policy continues to take the cautious middle path. Dismissing the initial skepticism over R2P as "short sighted," India has moved toward being a scrupulous watchdog of the fairness of external interventions measured against the letter of UNSC resolutions.[16] India is, of course, unable to influence the agenda significantly with regard to which conflicts attract the Security Council's attention. How India's positions might evolve in the future is discussed in the next section.

It is important to ask whether R2P norms as they are today will actually prevent genocides or mass atrocities. Will a marginal state—one that is powerful enough, has enough at stake, and is prepared to use military force—unilaterally intervene to head off massive loss of life in a nearby country? This was India's approach in East Pakistan in 1971 and Jaffna in 1987.

It is likely that R2P norms will deter such unilateralism. A state like India might be persuaded to let the UN processes take their course, while attempting to influence the geopolitical bargaining in a manner that protects its own interests. Such an approach might result in a legitimate external intervention, but is unlikely to result in a timely external intervention that prevents suffering and loss of lives. Among the many causes of India's nonintervention in the conflicts in Nepal and Sri Lanka post-1991 is that unilateral interventions would not only have attracted international opprobrium but also have militated against the evolving narrative on the norms of international intervention. Unlike what its champions claim, however well-intentioned it might be, R2P might not be an improvement over the status quo ante.

Championing Liberal Democracy

Why has the Indian republic, which proved that populous, poor, diverse, and socially complex countries can sustain a robust, flourishing democracy, been so reluctant to promote the model abroad? The reluctance is as old as the republic itself—even as Nehru set about trying to shape an international system that was itself inspired by India's constitutional framework, early India's enterprises to shape political order in other countries were limited to opposing colonialism. Apart from providing technical assistance—in drafting constitutions and conducting elections—to countries that request it, India has eschewed bold projects and even strong rhetoric promoting liberal democracy in other countries.[17]

India's reluctance has been explained as arising from three broad considerations. Maya Chadda summarizes these succinctly:

> First, protection of its "strategic autonomy" has compelled India to reject attempts to set any general precedent of collective intervention on behalf of intervention in the domestic affairs of other states; it does not wish to set a precedent of intervention in the name of normative principles. Second, pro-democracy coalitions (for much of the cold war period) were military alliances in disguise led by the United States to promote U.S. interests. India was reluctant to participate in these. Third, challenges such as insurgencies and terrorist violence arising from ethnic demography in Punjab, Indian-administered Kashmir, and many parts of the Northeast have made India vulnerable to charges of human rights violations. India has therefore been reluctant to support any blanket endorsement of international human rights regimes.[18]

There is a more basic reason: India's fundamental orientation is directed inward. New Delhi's grand strategy—like that of the subcontinent's empires before it—is to keep the country united under one rule.[19] Liberal democracy, with all its shortcomings and compromises in the Indian edition, is well suited to this end.[20] So while the Indian state is deeply committed to democracy at home, it is not interested in promoting democracy abroad because the abroad does not concern it, except as a threat to its domestic integrity.

New Delhi's centuries-old grand strategy is unlikely to change in a hurry, unless promoting liberal democracy becomes necessary to maintain national unity. How this might transpire is discussed in the following sections.

In the absence of a policy imperative for proactively bringing about democratic change, New Delhi's perspective toward political transformations around the world is instrumental. While India supports struggles for political freedom and democracy in principle, the practical considerations involve evaluating interests on a case-by-case basis.

The first concerns the well-being of Indian nationals resident in the country. Large numbers of Indian nationals live in countries under nondemocratic regimes. Where such a diaspora exists, this is usually the first factor that weighs in the minds of the political leadership and policymakers when faced with political unrest abroad. The commercial interests of Indian enterprises and nationals figure in the calculations, but to a lesser extent.

Second, regimes that support India or those that India needs to engage to manage the balance of power receive sympathetic treatment from New Delhi. There is also a solidarity quotient for political leaders and regimes that have supported India in the past. This solidarity quotient increasingly works at the margin, in the shadow of realpolitik considerations.

Third, sections of the New Delhi establishment remain highly suspicious of "revolutions," which they see as masking ulterior motives of domestic and political actors. In contemporary times, the replacement of authoritarian rulers in the Middle East by Islamist regimes that acquired power through elections is seen, with some justification, as a threat to India's national security. Similarly, the transformation of Nepal from a monarchy to a republic has taken place amid concern that a revolutionary Maoist state on India's borders is inimical to India's domestic stability.

Finally, with regard to states in its immediate neighborhood, India confronts a paradox of proximity:

> Having a fragile state in the neighbourhood makes it important for you to intervene, but there are structural constraints to your ability to do so . . . For India, history and proximity turn what might have been largely matters of foreign policy into a number of inter-connected issues of domestic politics. Given that domestic policy outcomes (in its parliamentary democracy) are generally resultants of the complex interplay of political forces, there are limitations on the timeliness, coherence, and effectiveness of India's response.[21]

Prospects

To what extent will India continue to tread the middle path? How might India's foreign policy change in the future in the context of further normative development and its own accumulation of power?

Values, Interests, and Power

Foreign policy, especially in the context of these norms, is an outcome of an interplay of values, interests, and the state's own position in the international system. Governments of liberal democracies confront a fundamental tension between their values and their interests. At the same time, their power relative to other states circumscribes their policy options. Therefore, if India acquires greater power over the next decade, New Delhi will enjoy greater latitude in foreign policy. (The converse is true: if India's growth stalls, its policymakers will find themselves with little additional policy space. We shall, however, consider the optimistic prognosis, as it is more likely.)[22]

The Indian republic's middle path approach to international norms is at one level indicative of the tension between values and interests. Greater prosperity and power will widen the range of possibilities that policymakers have. India will, however, have to contend with an intensification of the tension between values and interests.

First, as India's geopolitical interests cover a larger geographic footprint, its governments, corporations, civil society, and individuals will need to grapple with the local and regional politics of the places and people with which they are engaged. India's "front office" interaction with the world is increasingly conducted along many more dimensions than the purely official and commercial lines of the past. Violent conflicts and human suffering in many parts of the world are no longer remote events that Indians read about in newspapers and watch on television. They are palpable because Indians are involved as bystanders, victims, or participants. This trend moves foreign policy firmly into popular public discourse, bringing the debate about values versus interests into sharp relief.

Second, the penetration of Internet connections and mobile telephones not only has made information flows rapid, inexpensive, and less susceptible to government control but also has created radically networked societies. Events in one part of the world can echo elsewhere and have surprising political effects. For instance, attacks on Rohingya Muslims in Myanmar led to violent riots in protest in Mumbai, catching political and law enforcement authorities unprepared.[23] This particular event did not significantly influence India's position with respect to the unrest in Myanmar. Nor will all cases of ill-treatment trigger reactions or even evoke public sympathy in India. Rather, as Indian society becomes even more radically networked, we can expect there to be greater potential for distant events to influence foreign policy.

Both of these trends will be tempered by domestic politics and the predisposition to the local. At the margin, though, increasing numbers of Indians will engage with the external world, strengthening the influence of the social vector in foreign policy. India's decision in March 2013 to vote in favor of a U.S.-sponsored resolution concerning accountability for human rights violations and loss of civilian lives in Sri Lanka is a case in point: with political parties in the Indian state of Tamil Nadu competing in their demonstration of solidarity with their ethnic Tamil counterparts and with a coalition ally withdrawing support to the federal government, New Delhi voted against Colombo, albeit after watering down the resolution.

Changing Attitude toward Norms

At the dawn of its creation, the Indian republic was a political newborn, economically weak, with its society scarred by the violence of partition. What it lacked in material power, however, it compensated with moral power, which it possessed in good measure due to the principles and practices of its nonviolent struggle to shake off colonial rule. Although the Gandhian and the Nehruvian worldviews were inherently idealistic, it is nevertheless possible to see India's moralpolitik as realpolitik, using the relative abundance of moral power at its disposal to pursue the national interest.

Over time, as India began to accumulate power, there was a declining reliance on the language of values. We can see this as the second phase in its power trajectory. On human security and human rights, foreign policy ranged from following the international consensus to pro forma or rhetorical support and indifference.

Throughout the 2000s, New Delhi steered away from taking any position on the human rights violations and political oppressions of populations in its neighborhood. It chose to engage a dictator who had seized power in Pakistan and ignored the Pakistan army's ruthless campaign in Balochistan. It remained silent over China's suppression of the Tibetan struggle, over King Gyanendra's seizing of absolute power in Nepal and the Maoists' campaign, over the Myanmar junta's violent repression of Buddhist monks, over the Bangladesh army's soft coup, over the Sri Lankan belligerents' depredations against civilian populations, and even over the suppression of pro-democracy protests in Myanmar.

In fact, the current phase does not exclude the undermining or rejection of norms, no matter how dear they are to its values.

As noted earlier, if India continues along the current trajectory in the coming decades, accumulating greater material power, engaging with the world deeper and along multiple dimensions, and becoming radically networked, the language of values is likely to be more pronounced in foreign policy.

All else being equal (particularly domestic political considerations), where values overlap with interests we can expect India to take the initiative in shaping and enforcing the former. India's motivation in being a key player in the formation of the UN Human Rights Council is a case in point. Such an institution not only was consistent with India's political values but also was an opportunity for New Delhi to reshape the prevailing international discourse on human rights that often put India on the defensive. That the venture did not turn out as India or other liberal democracies expected is another matter, attributable both to the nature of the UN system and the shortcomings of Indian diplomacy.

What happens where values and interests do not converge? Realism suggests that interests will determine the outcome. As noted, India's neighborhood policy over the past decade is a case in point. New Delhi's posture was often contrary to the palpable public opinion in favor of victims in Sri Lanka, Tibet, and to a lesser extent Myanmar. This is not new. Nehru's "mildly worded critique" of Soviet action in Hungary was a lot milder than public opinion at that time.[24]

Putting Norms in Action

In addition to the dynamics of values, interests, and position in the international system, India's future approach toward international norms will be affected by the extent of the restructuring of the UN and other international multilateral organizations, the fate of multilateralism, and the evolution of international norms.

The effectiveness and legitimacy of international multilateral organizations will depend on how accurately they reflect the standing of powers in the international system. India sees the current structure as unrepresentative and unfair. While some changes are occurring within the international financial institutions like the World Bank and the International Monetary Fund, the reform of the UNSC to admit India as a permanent member is the sine qua non in this respect. With its initial attempts to mobilize the international community to reform the Security Council having resulted in a failure to secure a permanent seat, India stands at a crossroads.

In all likelihood, New Delhi will persist on the course of patient but resolute persuasion within the UN framework. Therefore, as in the establishment of the Human Rights Council, of which India was a founding member, India's policymaking processes are likely to invest in the UN-focused approach to defining and enforcing norms. There is, however, another possibility: if India's Security Council aspirations are rebuffed, it can choose to invest instead in the high tables of which it is already a member.[25]

The example of the UN Human Rights Council is also a signal warning of what might occur if India lacks the diplomatic capacity and positional power to push through a normative agenda. Far from being a watchdog of human rights as they are understood in the post-Enlightenment world and in liberal democracies, the Human Rights Council has been undermined by the political and ideological agenda of its illiberal and undemocratic members.

Appointing some of the most authoritarian and oppressive states as members of the council has seriously damaged the credibility of the institution. While it may operate as another cog in the wheel of the complex UN system, its functioning is far from the letter and spirit of its creation.

A more prosperous India is likely to increase its financial commitments to the UN. While sections of the Indian establishment are likely to include these to bolster India's case for a permanent seat on the Security Council, it is unlikely that they will result in greater policy leverage within the UN system. This is both because India's financial commitments are unlikely to be anything in the nature of what bigger powers contribute and also because an unreformed Indian government bureaucracy will be unable to summon the unity of purpose to extract the leverage necessary to effect change within the complex UN system. The net effect of higher Indian contributions will ease the UN's budget constraints more than increase New Delhi's say in what the UN does.

Similarly, India's internal dynamics will continue to support contributions to UN peacekeeping in the near future, despite voices calling for review of this policy.[26] Over the longer term, however, rising standards of living, pay scales, and value of the Indian rupee could erode the attractiveness of UN peacekeeping for military personnel.

Regional groupings present a second route toward the evolution and enforcement of human security and liberal democratic norms. While at one level the relationship between regional groupings and the UN can be cooperative and even harmonious, the issues of human rights, foreign intervention, sovereignty, and democracy are controversial.

First, to the extent that the interests of the regional powers diverge from those of the great powers, regional blocs and the UN system will have different priorities. For instance, neither the South Asian Association for Regional Cooperation (SAARC) nor the East Asia Summit has taken a strong position on the crimes against civilians in Sri Lanka, even after the UN secretary general's panel submitted its report on the conflict.

Second, the mandate, internal dynamic, or balance of power within such groupings could militate against them being instruments of normative evolution or promotion. The Association of Southeast Asian Nations (ASEAN) had long been reluctant to engage the Myanmar junta over human rights, notwithstanding Western pressure and UN sanctions. Given that the principle of noninterference in the internal affairs of its member-states is one of the key organizing principles and often held out as a key to its effectiveness,

ASEAN is justified in being agnostic to gross violations of human rights and illiberal and undemocratic practices among its members.

The East Asia Summit, which has emerged as the Indo-Pacific's largest and most important high table, has an "ASEAN core." Its membership includes liberal democracies like India, Japan, and the United States, while the most powerful of its regional members is authoritarian China. It remains to be seen how effective it can be as an agent of normative change. The Shanghai Cooperation Organisation, set up under Chinese leadership, is unlikely to be a champion of human rights and democracy.

The effectiveness of SAARC and other "South Asian" ventures is likely to continue to be circumscribed by the bilateral equations of its smaller member-states with India. The paradox of proximity renders it an ineffective vehicle for India to champion norms, much less enforce them.

The social vector presents an intriguing third path for India—beyond the Indian government—to speak the language of values in international relations. So far, the focus and reach of Indian civil society have been limited to its boundaries. This could change as civil society groups become more interested in international developments and acquire domestic financial resources to pursue them. Transborder activism in ethnic, religious, or sectarian solidarity can now be efficiently mobilized over the Internet and social media. Indian human rights groups are beginning to engage in activism abroad. "Private foreign policy" of this kind, relying on the agency of nonstate actors, has the potential to cover the normative spaces left vacant by New Delhi's realpolitik-based foreign policy. We should not, however, overstate its prospects: the energies of Indian civil society will continue to be consumed largely by the myriad challenges at home.

Finally, there is the unilateral route. Like in 1971 in East Pakistan, India is likely to act unilaterally if conflicts in its neighborhood threaten to spill over into its own territory and threaten its integrity. Beyond the subcontinent, unilateral actions may be indicated in a future where India's relative power in the international system far exceeds its positional power in international multilateral institutions. This approach is also likely if great-power equations in the twenty-first century undermine multilateralism. The latter is unlikely, but not unimaginable.

Conclusion

Even as Indian foreign policy made the transition from Nehru's utopianism to the pragmatic realism of the post–cold war governments, it never abandoned its commitment to values. Normatively, New Delhi strikes a middle path. India is committed to genocide prevention, R2P, human rights, and liberal democracy in principle, but has serious reservations regarding their practical implementation. The commitment is born out of its own national values. The reservations are borne out by its experience too.

India has been supporting multilateral efforts—or has acted unilaterally on occasion—in response to international emergencies. It has been less enthusiastic in enterprises promoting liberal democratic norms, for it is a state primarily concerned with maintaining its own national unity, social transformation, and economic development.

To what extent will India deviate from the middle path if it becomes a bigger power in the international system? This chapter contends that the answer depends on whether the UN reforms itself to better reflect the contemporary global balance of power, the nature of India's geopolitical footprint, and the extent of internationalism in Indian civil society. Broad trends indicate that the Indian nation is likely to become increasingly global-minded and internationalist, even if at a pace that is sometimes frustrating and sometimes exhilarating. So the chances of the Indian republic becoming a rule taker in the international system will improve to the extent that it is more accommodating in the rule-making circles of a reformed UN. A richer, more powerful India may yet be a stronger defender of human security around the world, if not simultaneously a champion of liberal democracy.

Notes

1. Remarks by Ambassador Hardeep Singh Puri during a panel discussion on "NATO Intervention in Libya: Lessons Learnt," Syracuse University, October 19, 2012 (www.un.int/india/2012/ind2107.pdf).

2. Manu Bhagavan, *The Peacemakers: India and the Quest for One World* (New Delhi: HarperCollins India, 2012), p. 4.

3. Abul Kalam Azad, *India Wins Freedom* (New Delhi: Orient Blackswan, 1988), pp. 31–32. In the context of the Indian National Congress's debate over whether or not to support Britain's war effort against Nazi Germany, Azad declares that for him nonviolence was a matter of policy, not creed. For Gandhi, he writes, "the issue was one of pacifism and not of India's freedom."

4. Bhagavan, *The Peacemakers*, p. 162.

5. Quoted in Ramachandra Guha, "The Commanding Heights of Nehru," *Hindu*, November 13, 2012.

6. Shashi Tharoor, *Pax Indica: India and the World of the 21st Century* (New Delhi: Allen Lane, 2012), pp. 25–26.

7. David Malone, *Does the Elephant Dance? Contemporary Indian Foreign Policy* (Oxford University Press, 2011), pp. 257–58.

8. J. N. Dixit, *India-Pakistan in War and Peace* (London: Routledge, 2002), p. 181.

9. Nitin Pai, "The 1971 East Pakistan Genocide: A Realist Perspective" (Bangladesh Genocide Archive, 2008) (http://bit.ly/chaH3M).

10. International Court of Justice, Case Concerning Trial of Pakistani Prisoners of War, Case Record, 1976.

11. Pai, "The 1971 East Pakistan Genocide," pp. 9–10.

12. UN Department of Public Information, "2005 World Summit Outcome."

13. UN General Assembly, Resolution A/RES/60/1: 2005 World Summit Outcome.

14. Monica Serrano, "The Responsibility to Protect and Its Critics: Explaining the Consensus," *Global Responsibility to Protect 3*, no. 4 (December 2011): 2.

15. Remarks by Ambassador Hardeep Singh Puri at an informal interactive dialogue on the report of the UN secretary general on "Responsibility to Protect: Timely and Decisive Action," September 5, 2012 (www.un.int/india/2012/ind2058.pdf).

16. Puri, remarks at Syracuse University.

17. C. Raja Mohan, *Crossing the Rubicon: The Shaping of India's New Foreign Policy* (New Delhi: Penguin, 2003), pp. 61–65.

18. Maya Chadda, "Human Rights and Democracy in India's Emerging Role in Asia," in *Bridging Strategic Asia*, edited by Michael J. Green (Washington: Center for Strategic and International Studies, 2009), p. 350.

19. Nitin Pai, "Grand Strategy," Acorn, January 14, 2011 (http://acorn.nationalinterest.in/2011/01/14/grand-strategy/).

20. Sunil Khilnani, *The Idea of India* (New Delhi: Penguin, 2003), pp. 31–33.

21. Nitin Pai, "The Paradox of Proximity: India's Approach to Fragility in the Neighbourhood" (New York University Center on International Cooperation, April 2011) (www.cic.nyu.edu/mgo/docs/nitin_pai_paradox.pdf).

22. Charles Wolf Jr., Siddhartha Dalal, Julie DaVanzo, Eric V. Larson, Alisher Akhmedjonov, Harun Dogo, Meilinda Huang, and Silvia Montoya, *China and India, 2025: A Comparative Assessment* (Santa Monica, Calif.: RAND, 2011), pp. 37–54.

23. Yousuf Saeed, "How to Start a Riot out of Facebook," Kafila, August 13, 2012 (http://kafila.org/2012/08/13/how-to-start-a-riot-out-of-facebook-yousuf-saeed/).

24. Iqbal Singh, *Between Two Fires: Towards an Understanding of Jawaharlal Nehru's Foreign Policy*, vol. 2 (New Delhi: Orient Blackswan, 1998), p. 261.

25. See chapter 10 by Richard Gowan and Sushant Singh in this volume.

26. Brett D. Schaefer, "The U.N. Human Rights Council Does Not Deserve U.S. Support" (Washington: Heritage Foundation, September 5, 2012) (www.heritage.org/research/reports/2012/09/the-un-human-rights-council-does-not-deserve-us-support).

CHRISTOPHE JAFFRELOT *and* WAHEGURU PAL SINGH SIDHU

17

From Plurilateralism to Multilateralism? G-20, IBSA, BRICS, and BASIC

Introduction

What is India's preferred multilateral global order, and how does New Delhi seek to establish it? While this remains a work in progress, several strands of India's preference are discernible. Since the end of the cold war and the beginning of India's own economic reforms in the early 1990s, there has been a strategic shift from nonalignment to multialignment. This shift is premised on the recognition of two factors: the emergence of a multipolar world with several distinct poles of influence and the need for India to engage with each of these poles. Second, the importance of multialignment to sustain economic growth and the need to translate this growth into political power. However, this shift, like the economic liberalization program, has remained ad hoc, inarticulate, and piecemeal. Moreover, this transition is unlikely to be linear, evident in India's reluctant embrace of various plurilateral groupings.

This strategic shift and global vision were rationalized in some detail in 2009 by Prime Minister Manmohan Singh. In an essay ahead of the G-8 plus G-5 summit in L'Aquila, Italy, he stressed that India's preference was for a reformed United Nations (UN)–centered system of global governance and asserted that India "will continue to strive for the reform of the United Nations to make it more democratic." However, he candidly admitted, "efforts to reform the system have made little headway" and argued that the "unworkability of the existing structures has led to greater reliance on plurilateral groupings."[1]

Thus in the global political realm, India wants to emerge as one of the key decisionmaking poles and is keen to play a crucial role as a rule shaper, especially if it can work with other groups of countries. This strategy is apparent in India's membership in myriad plurilateral and minilateral groupings, including the G-20, IBSA (a group formed by India, Brazil, and South Africa), the BRICS (Brazil, Russia, India, China, and South Africa), and even the various export control cartels, such as the Nuclear Suppliers Group. At the same time, India continues to use these forums to pitch for its ultimate goal: a permanent seat on the United Nations Security Council (UNSC). This is evident, on the one hand, in persistent calls in almost all of these other plurilateral settings for UNSC reform and, on the other, in the aborted effort to hold a UN General Assembly (UNGA) vote for similar reforms during India's 2011–12 membership on the UNSC. However, New Delhi's quest to reform multilateral institutions through plurilateralism faces several challenges.

This chapter begins with an overview of how India is using the new plurilateral groupings, particularly the G-20, IBSA, BRICS, and other ad hoc groups, to further its interests and reform the structure for managing the global order. The following sections examine India's role in each of these groupings in some detail, seeking to address several key questions: Does the G-20 provide India with the ideal mechanism to move from plurilateralism to multilateralism? What does India get from IBSA in terms of South-South cooperation? Will BRICS emerge as a new, post–cold war anti-West structure? How does India continue its quest for strategic autonomy and sovereignty, while increasing its plurilateral and multilateral engagement? Can India befriend everyone and sustain strategic alliances with the United States but also with Russia and China? Or will the inherent contradictions between the various groupings and between strategic autonomy and plurilateralism limit India's role in shaping the global order?

G-20: Bridging the Gap between the West and the Rest?

Although the G-20 was formally established in 1999–2000 by G-7 members, its genesis lay in the 1996 Asian financial crisis.[2] However, the first summit was held only in 2008 against the backdrop of deteriorating global economic conditions. While India took little or no initiative in creating it, the G-20 was the first major minilateral group that was economically and politically relevant to India for at least three reasons.[3]

First, it demonstrated that the G-7 club could no longer protect the international economy from systemic vulnerabilities without including the bigger emerging-market economies, like India. Second, it provided India not only with a seat on a high table but also with the opportunity to try and restore the health of the global financial system, which would benefit India's economic growth. Finally, unlike IBSA and BRICS, which might be seen to be in opposition to the West, the G-20 provided a platform for working with key Western players within the existing system and for bridging the gap between them and emerging powers like India.

Given this mutual interest, could India and the G-20 work together to create a new world order? Clearly, despite its many limitations, the G-20 is the most effective instrument of the moment for addressing the immediate financial and economic crisis. However, three serious drawbacks are likely to prevent it from playing a significant role in establishing a new world order. First, the G-20 remains a disparate and inchoate group, which still does not share a common vision of a new global economic order, let alone a new global political order. While some countries, particularly from the West, see the G-20's role as preserving the existing order, other emerging economies, like India, want the G-20 to transform the present order to accommodate them. Second, even if there was a common objective among all of its members, the G-20 is much too unwieldy to manage all global governance and peace and security issues; these can only be addressed effectively by a much smaller and select group of no more than four or five countries (as is the case with the permanent members of the UNSC). Third, while the G-20 is designed to address the ongoing financial and economic crisis, it is not necessarily equipped to address other global challenges, such as climate change or cyber security.

However, a case can be made for the G-20 to move beyond the economic realm.[4] The first meeting of G-20 foreign ministers in Los Cabos, Mexico, in February 2012 indicated that the G-20 might be evolving toward an institution also concerned with international peace and security. This shift, which generated mixed reactions among G-20 members, could not have come at a more appropriate time.[5] With post-Gadhafi Libya in disarray, the bitter dust-up over Syria in the UNSC, and the looming war clouds over Iran, a forum like the G-20 is urgently needed to try and carve out a common, cooperative approach on all of these issues. But is it, perhaps, too optimistic to assume that the G-20 will succeed where other forums have failed? Yes and no.[6]

It is certainly optimistic to assume that a single meeting, even in the tranquil setting of Los Cabos, could overcome the deep divisions between the established powers and the BRICS in particular. Nonetheless, the G-20 meeting does offer a useful venue for the established and reemerging powers to try to bridge their differences and to engage at two levels: strategic and tactical.

At the strategic level, the G-20 members could explore normative areas of convergence, especially over the concepts of responsibility to protect, given that there was broad support for the principle (as apparent in UNSC Resolutions

1970 and 1973), but serious disagreement on how it should be implemented. In addition, the group could also consider the Brazilian idea of "responsibility while protecting," which needs to be elaborated further outside of the charged atmosphere of the UNSC setting. Moreover, there is also need to explore the responsibility for post-conflict reconstruction. As the Libyan case, including the killing of the U.S. ambassador, has amply demonstrated, a successful (albeit prolonged) military campaign and regime change alone do not guarantee greater security or better governance for a country.

Against the backdrop of these broader normative debates, which are likely to continue beyond Los Cabos, several tactical issues require urgent attention. Syria is prominent among them. Given that there appears to be overwhelming (if not unanimous) support for a political transition in Syria, could a common agenda be worked out within the G-20 framework, especially one that takes on board the IBSA and BRICS sensitivities as well as lessons from the Libyan experience? If it could be reached, such an understanding could contribute to a more cooperative approach among the key powers in the UNSC.

Here, it is worth remembering that a similar G-8 meeting in Berlin in June 1999 helped to resolve the tensions, particularly between Russia and the United States, over the bombing of Kosovo and paved the way for the consensus UNSC Resolution 1244 and post-conflict reconstruction. While it could be argued that a G-8 consensus was easier to achieve, given the smaller membership, if the G-20 were to achieve a similar breakthrough, it would carry greater conviction, given the more representative and diverse nature of the bigger group. Similarly, the representative characteristic of the G-20 might also be an important asset in dealing with the gathering storm over Iran.

Finally, given the present stalemate over the UNSC reform process and assuming that the G-20 foreign ministers meet regularly, this forum would be the only venue where the permanent members of the UNSC and the aspiring members, notably Brazil, India, and South Africa, would be able to interact on a regular basis on international peace and security issues.

While in recent years the G-20 agenda has broadened to include issues like development and aid effectiveness, debt relief, energy security, and even peace and security, there is pushback from countries, like India, that have sought to curtail the scope of the G-20 to financial and economic issues.[7] New Delhi was one of the key capitals that was uncomfortable with the Los Cabos initiative. India's approach to the enlargement of the G-20 agenda is in contrast to its support for the expanding agenda of IBSA and BRICS. Both of these groups now increasingly make pronouncements on international peace and security issues, ranging from Syria to Iran and the use of force. The Indian reluctance to support the expansion of the G-20 agenda to include peace and security issues is probably based on two reservations. First, given the deep divisions on some of the most contentious international issues, such as Syria, there is concern that the inability to reach consensus between the West and the rest might adversely affect the primary objective of the G-20, which is to ensure the stability of the global economy. Second, New Delhi might also be worried that decisions related to international peace and security—traditionally considered to be the remit of the UNSC—might weaken both the UNSC's role and India's efforts to reform the UNSC and attain permanent membership in this exclusive club.

While India has been reluctant to expand the scope of the G-20 beyond economic issues, it has been willing to diversify the agenda of more homogeneous clubs of emerging countries, such as IBSA and the BRICS, with the same objective in mind: to assert India's power in the UN system.

IBSA: A Concert of Southern Democracies

IBSA, the grouping with Brazil and South Africa, offers India a framework for South-South cooperation similar to the one that Prime Minister Jawaharlal Nehru promoted in the 1955 Bandung conference to reflect a sense of third worldist solidarity—minus the discordant presence of China.

IBSA dates back to 2003 and is thus the oldest representative of the emerging countries' "minilateralism."[8] It came together when the heads of state and government of these three countries got together in Brasilia in January 2003 for the inauguration of Luiz Inácio Lula da Silva as Brazil's president. South Africa's Thabo Mbeki reportedly first conceived the idea of this coalition.[9] But its official founding date was June 6, 2003, when the three countries' foreign affairs ministers met in Brasilia and produced the declaration named after that city. The document articulated the need for a cooperation mechanism among the three countries, which had decided to form an association in order to wield greater influence over the reform of the existing system of global governance.

The 2003 meeting took place in a context dominated by the efforts of emerging powers to resist the West at the World Trade Organization (WTO), even as they were reeling from the shock of George W. Bush's decision to wage "preventive war" in Iraq. Article 3 of the Brasilia Declaration stresses the importance of international law and the need to prioritize diplomacy as a means to maintain international security (a recurring theme in the IBSA narrative), while Article 14 regrets that "the major trading partners" of these three countries "are still moved by protectionist concerns."[10]

Another underlying strategic goal of the IBSA countries was to build an alliance to obtain permanent seats on the UN Security Council. Two of the members, Brazil and India, were already part of another group, the G-4, which was formed along with Germany and Japan and had the same objective. Article 4 of the Brasilia Declaration, moreover, calls for expanding the UNSC to include developing countries in the categories of both permanent and nonpermanent members, in deference to the African group's sensitivities on reforms.

But beyond this international involvement, IBSA has posed as a model of South-South cooperation from its very inception, recommending exchanges of experience "in combating poverty, hunger, and disease" (Article 6 of the Brasilia Declaration) and technology transfers. The ministers meeting in Brasilia in June 2003 not only set up a trilateral joint commission that they co-chaired but also opened it up to the members of their respective governments in charge of science and technology, defense, transportation, and civil aviation portfolios, consulting them to promote joint cooperation projects.

Although IBSA has no permanent structure or headquarters, contacts among officials of these three countries have become more frequent and institutionalized. Alden and Vieira have pointed out the effectiveness of a strategy that has consisted of embedding intra-IBSA relations within the various foreign affairs ministries. Beginning with Brazil, all three now have an "IBSA desk."[11] Such bureaucratic embedding within what is generally a highly professional and powerful diplomatic apparatus has helped to maintain the pace of a true rise in power, despite changes in titular ministers or parties in power.

In addition to the theoretically quarterly, but in reality annual, meetings of the trilateral joint commission, since 2006 annual summits as well as working groups have brought together the relevant ministers for deliberations on a growing assortment of areas: public administration, agriculture, development aid, trade and investment, culture, defense, social development, education, energy, the environment and climate change, taxation, health, science and technology, the information society, transportation, tourism, and town planning.[12] These working groups have been supplemented by several dialogue forums among these three countries, bringing together judges (particularly from their supreme courts), businessmen, legislators, women's groups, academics, and so on.

IBSA is undoubtedly one of the crucibles for cooperation and the shaping of a common foreign policy among three of the most important emerging powers. In terms of cooperation, the three countries' defense ministers, after meeting in Pretoria in 2004, discussed the development of a new generation of air-air missile and preparation of common naval exercises off the South

African Coast in May 2008.[13] While much of this remains on paper, it reflects the inherent desire of the three to cooperate more closely even on defense and security issues. As for diplomatic consultation, in addition to summits and trilateral commission meetings, the heads of state and government of IBSA have continued to meet at the margin of—and in preparation for—the multilateral meetings in which they take part, whether the UN General Assembly or Security Council, the G-20, or major summits on climate change or biodiversity.

Beyond these internal ties, IBSA has also sought to extend its aid to less developed countries. Thus in 2004 a "facility fund" of $250 million was created, for which each country provides $1 million a year. Its purpose is to fund various poverty reduction projects managed by the UN Development Program. This fund has been used, for instance, to introduce new rice strains in Guinea-Bissau, rehabilitate a derelict neighborhood in Port-au-Prince, and modernize two dispensaries in Cape Verde.

For India, IBSA is a potentially important grouping for at least three reasons. First, it offers a convincing way to reinvent Nehru's idea of South-South cooperation—all the more so as the IBSA countries are prepared to help other poor developing countries. While the present "facility fund" is limited in the support it can offer other developing countries, it provides IBSA members an opportunity to coordinate their development efforts. Second, it offers a concert of the largest democracies on their three continents, which have undergone dramatic economic, social, and political transformation; they offer an alternative narrative not only to the global North but also to China and even Russia. The decision to schedule the tenth anniversary IBSA summit in New Delhi in 2013—separately from the fourth BRICS summit at the same venue in 2012—underlines IBSA's democratic distinction and India's attempt to use the IBSA grouping to assert its international stature—the same way as China is using the BRICS.[14] Finally, given its democratic credentials, this coalition provides India with additional political leverage on the international scene.

BRICS: Neo Nonalignment?

The benefit that India expects from the IBSA plus China and Russia (BRICS) grouping is somewhat different and has more in common with another legacy of the Nehru years—the promotion of nonalignment. Although the BRICS present themselves as a "mechanism of current and long-term coordination on . . . the world economy and politics," there is greater emphasis on the former than the latter.

The original BRIC group (Brazil, Russia, India, and China) did not come together as quickly as IBSA. Their foreign affairs ministers began meeting at the margin of the UN General Assembly in 2006. Their finance and economic ministers started meeting at the margin of G-20 summits in 2008, and their heads of domestic security started meeting at least as frequently in 2009. From that time on, the group began to gain in substance.

At the first BRIC summit in Yekaterinburg (Russia) on June 16, 2009, apparently at the behest of the Russian foreign minister Sergei Lavrov, former ambassador to the UN in 1994–2004, there were indications of the intention to make the new coalition an anti-Western war machine.[15] As one scholar argued, the main role of the group appeared to be to counterbalance the existing power axis in the world with broader economic and political goals.[16] The Yekaterinburg meeting's final resolution, still very vague, called for at once "a more democratic and just multi-polar world" and commitment to "multilateral diplomacy, with the United Nations playing the central role in dealing with global challenges and threats."[17] This ambition plainly transpired in the demand for reform of the international financial institutions to "reflect changes in the global economy." In a line that implicitly referred to the BRIC refusal to see the United States and Europe dominate the leadership of the World Bank and the International Monetary Fund (IMF), the final Yekaterinburg Declaration stated, "The emerging and developing economies must have greater voice and representation in international financial institutions, whose heads and executives should be appointed through an open, transparent, and merit-based selection process." The first summit of the BRIC countries thus demonstrated a determination to convert their economic power into political clout in the wake of the 2008 financial crisis, which in this regard can be considered a real turning point. For many leaders of emerging countries, the subprime fiasco—along with the collapse of Lehman Brothers—revealed the negligence, even incompetence, of the Western powers in economic matters.

The communiqué of the second BRIC summit, held in Brasilia on April 16, 2010, while repeating what was to become a leitmotif regarding the essential role of the G-20, more directly emphasized the need to reform international financial institutions and opposed their domination by the West:

> Reforming these institutions' governance structures requires first and foremost a substantial shift in voting power in favor of emerging-market economies and developing countries to bring their participation in decision making in line with their relative weight in the world economy. . . . We do also agree on the need for an open and merit-based selection

> method, irrespective of nationality, for the heading positions of the IMF and the World Bank. Moreover, staff of these institutions needs to better reflect the diversity of their membership. There is a special need to increase participation of developing countries.[18]

A certain radicalization marked the third summit, held in Sanya, China, in April 2011. First, the political dimension of the coalition was affirmed with the admission of South Africa into the club and the enlargement of BRIC into BRICS. Co-opting South Africa, which could not be explained on the basis of economic criteria alone (even though it is the only G-20 member from Africa), indicated a desire for greater political representativeness: the group needed to include an African state.

Second, the four BRICS members of the WTO also endorsed Russia's accession to this organization to strengthen their economic and political clout. Regarding the IMF and the World Bank, not only did Brazil's president, Dilma Roussef, state during the summit that "governance at the IMF and the World Bank cannot be a systematic rotation between the US and Europe, with the other countries excluded," but the final communiqué did not settle for the adjustments agreed at the November 2010 G-20 summit in Seoul[19] and demanded that "the governing structure of the international financial institutions should reflect the changes in the world economy, increasing the voice and representation of emerging economies and developing countries."[20]

The fourth BRICS summit held in New Delhi on March 29, 2012, reiterated statements made regarding the G-20 and the UN but demonstrated that international financial institutions were the primary targets of the group's members. They expressed impatience at the slow pace with which the IMF quota and governance reforms approved in 2010 were implemented—the ratification process has been particularly long, especially on Capitol Hill[21]—and asked for a review of the weights of emerging countries in January 2013 and January 2014. Though the BRICS challenged the Western leadership of international financial institutions, they were either unable or unwilling to formulate and lead an alternative approach. Thus their call for "an open and merit-based process" of selection does not necessarily reflect their democratic instinct, but instead their inability to agree on a consensus candidate.[22] Similarly, although the Delhi Declaration also called for the reform of the UNSC, it fell well short of supporting the Indian case (along with that of Brazil and South Africa) for permanent membership in this exclusive club. It was certainly not as ringing an endorsement as that of President Barack Obama on his maiden visit to India.

The highlight of the fifth BRICS summit in March 2013 in Durban, South Africa, was the decision to set up a BRICS Development Bank—an idea first proposed by Prime Minister Manmohan Singh during the New Delhi summit—to mobilize resources for "infrastructure and sustainable development projects in BRICS and other emerging economies and developing countries."[23] In addition, the Durban summit also announced the setting up of a $100 billion contingency relief arrangement (CRA) to "forestall short-term liquidity pressures, provide mutual support, and further strengthen financial stability."[24] China will be the largest contributor to the CRA, with $41 billion, while Brazil, India, and Russia will each pledge $18 million, and South Africa will pledge a mere $5 billion.[25] These twin developments, coupled with the now pro forma call for reform of international financial institutions, particularly the IMF, reflects that the BRICS might be moving to establish new financial structures.

However, several influential Indian editorials expressed deep reservations about the BRICS Development Bank and the CRA. One described the bank as evidence that the group is "a clever investment-banker fantasy rather than a reality on the ground," while another explained India's backtracking on the idea on the grounds that New Delhi will be "subsidising Chinese soft power with Indian taxpayers' money."[26] In fact the bank may become a bone of contention between India and China if the latter does not show the kind of generosity that the former is expecting.[27]

Nonetheless, for India the BRICS contributes to its notion of the global order in two ways: first, it helps to counter the domination of the West in existing international institutions, particularly financial institutions, and, second, as examined in greater detail later, it defends the concept of state sovereignty. In the latter context, the veto-wielding power of China and Russia in the UNSC is distinctly appealing to the nonmembers of the council.

A Poor Man's G-20 and BASIC: Coalitions of Convenience?

Apart from the formal plurilateral groupings described above, India has also been instrumental in building and working with ad hoc coalitions of like-minded countries to strengthen its negotiating position on specific issues. Two such examples—the so-called G-20 group of countries in the WTO and the BASIC (Brazil, South Africa, India, and China) group formed during the Copenhagen climate change negotiations—are noteworthy.

After suffering from divisions in the WTO where each member (state or customs area) has one vote, Brazil, China, and India joined forces in reaction to the Declaration on Agriculture signed on August 2003 by the United States and the European Union in anticipation of the meeting at Cancún. As soon as the declaration was published, Brazil and India drafted a counterproposal demanding that "rich" countries lower their subsidies for agriculture and open up their markets more to agricultural products from developing countries. Twenty countries signed this text—including China, which was one of the first to support it—marking the birth of a new, poor man's G-20.[28] The group comprised countries at very different levels of development,[29] but it was formed not only against the West but also against the rich in the name of the poor. The emerging powers that dominated the debates shrewdly used their intermediary status, emphasizing that they were still "developing," to act as a credible mouthpiece for the many poor countries, particularly those of the G-77. The G-20's success at the WTO also lies in "the flexibility of allegiances that has allowed members to turn to other groups for particular issues that were incompatible with the collective agenda," according to Cornelia Woll.[30]

Similarly, India relied on an ad hoc coalition to defend its position against the Europeans in another multilateral context: the talks on climate change. The Copenhagen summit in 2009 represents a watershed in the assertion of emerging nations' influence on the international scene. Brazil, South Africa, India, and China formed the BASIC group so as not to commit to taking measures toward environmental protection advocated primarily by the Europeans. These measures were perceived by the emerging powers as an obstacle to their growth that should, at the very least, be financed by developed countries, which they hold responsible for the accumulation of greenhouse gases in the atmosphere, despite the fact that today the highest carbon emitter is none other than China. Some countries, such as India, also wanted to calculate emissions reductions on a per capita basis, which would give them a huge margin for progress. This does not mean that the BASIC countries are not aware of the ecological challenges confronting them, but they want to deal with them on their own terms.[31]

Copenhagen was a diplomatic turning point not only in substance, given the unprecedented isolation in which the Europeans found themselves (the United States having largely joined forces with BASIC). Copenhagen ended with a declaration of intention urging all countries to reduce their carbon dioxide (CO_2) emissions to stay within a warming limit of 2° Celsius since the beginning of the industrial age and admonishing rich countries to make the greatest effort.

After the Copenhagen summit, emerging powers deliberated within the framework of the BASIC contacts, which consisted of the four countries' environment ministers. During the three preparatory meetings in Bonn prior to the sixteenth United Nations Conference on Climate Change in Cancún, the members of the BASIC quartet reneged on certain commitments made in Copenhagen with regard to reducing greenhouse gas emissions.

In Cancún, from November 29 to December 10, 2010, emerging powers took the lead over a bruised and disunited Europe.[32] Jairam Ramesh, India's environment minister, played a key role—alongside Mexican foreign affairs minister Patricia Espinosa, representing the host country—in transforming an anticipated failure into a mitigated success. In fact, achievements were very slim, as each group remained unyielding. Global warming was acknowledged to be a reality, the goal of limiting temperature increase to less than 2° Celsius was announced, the Kyoto Protocol was renewed, and a Green Climate Fund of $100 billion per year until 2020 was discussed to help poor countries to reduce their CO_2 emission, but no plan of action was established.

In December 2011 the outcome of the Durban climate change conference was less inconclusive, but nevertheless deceptive. The BASIC group of countries and the United States indeed resigned themselves to reducing their carbon emissions as well as to setting up a legally binding mechanism to govern these reductions under UN supervision. But with the complicity of the United States, BASIC won its demand for the mechanism to be negotiated up until 2015 and not to take effect until 2020. Meanwhile, the parties to the "Durban platform" committed to reducing their emissions only on a voluntary basis, thereby increasing the likelihood that the temperature rise will be greater than 2° Celsius.[33]

At both the WTO and in climate talks, the emerging powers carried such weight in certain negotiations that they are now in a position to block any compromise that they do not co-author. In short, the only rules they are prepared to accept are those they have contributed to shaping. This analysis also holds true in the case of International Labor Organization norms, which India rejects for reasons that are almost as psycho-sociological as economic: they were codified by and for industrialized countries, whereas the emerging powers have to manage a large informal sector.[34] Such refusal of binding rules above all reflects the die-hard support for sovereignty, which is also characteristic of the positions taken by the emerging powers in the UNSC, especially on the enforcement of the "responsibility to protect" through military intervention.

Protecting Sovereignty

In addition to helping India to defend its interests vis-à-vis the West, the BRICS and IBSA are most useful to India for promoting a concept that has been dear to the country since its independence in 1947: state sovereignty.[35]

In 2010, in the wake of the so-called Arab Spring, President Obama in his address before the UNGA admonished emerging powers: "Do not stand idly by when dissidents everywhere are imprisoned and protesters are beaten. Because part of the price of our own freedom is standing up for the freedom of others."

The BRICS had virtually the opposite reaction, concerned as they are with defending sovereignty, which is hardly compatible with the concept of "responsibility to protect"[36]—a principle adopted unanimously during the sixtieth UN world summit in 2005—and which could be evoked to justify foreign military intervention. This was evident when all of them—apart from South Africa—abstained when voting on UNSC Resolution 1973, which invoked the responsibility to protect and made international military intervention possible.[37] During the Sanya summit, the BRICS, including South Africa, which had voted in favor of UNSC Resolution 1973, continued to oppose intervention in Libya.[38] The BRICS's final communiqué emphasized the need to maintain sovereignty:

> We share the principle that the use of force should be avoided. We maintain that the Independence, sovereignty, unity, and territorial integrity of each nation should be respected. We wish to continue our cooperation in the UN Security Council on Libya. We are of the view that all the parties should resolve their differences through peaceful means and dialogue in which the UN and regional organizations should as appropriate play their role. We also express support for the African Union High-Level Panel Initiative on Libya.

Similarly, in 2011, as Syrian demonstrators were enduring a fierce crackdown, all five BRICS, which were then members of the UNSC, refused for months to support any resolution against Bashar al-Assad. In August, while India held the council's rotating presidency, an IBSA delegation, comprising a representative from each country, was sent to Damascus. It came away siding with neither the Syrian regime nor its victims, but condemned violence from all sides and merely called for an end to the violence. The communiqué of the delegation mentioned that the foreign affairs minister of Syria "outlined in detail the political reforms that are in the process of being implemented and said that free and fair elections to the Parliament will be held in Syria before end 2011." The communiqué also reaffirmed the commitment of IBSA to the sovereignty, independence, and territorial integrity of Syria.[39] Subsequently, a senior IBSA diplomat admitted that the mission was a failure, as the violence continued and no dialogue had been initiated between the various sides in the conflict.[40] One indication of this is that the IBSA mission never briefed the UNSC, which it could very well have done.

In March 2012, during the New Delhi summit, as the death toll was nearing 30,000 in Syria, BRICS reaffirmed the same principles regarding Syria as it had in Sanya with respect to Libya: "Global interests would best be served by dealing with the crisis through peaceful means that encourage broad national dialogues that reflect the legitimate aspirations of all sections of Syrian society and respect Syrian independence, territorial integrity, and sovereignty." While there is much to be appreciated in promoting dialogue and diplomacy over the use of force, neither BRICS nor IBSA has followed through with concrete action, apart from sending one joint delegation.

This support for sovereignty also explains that the BRICS prefer the intervention of regional organizations to multilateral ones. Prior to the intervention in Libya, they had rallied around the South African proposal to let the African Union handle the issue (Jacob Zuma later protested against Western military action on the grounds that it smacked of colonialism). In the case of Syria, the BRICS systematically backed the Arab League's plan. The implication of their declarations was that if sovereignty of the incriminated states was to be violated, it was less objectionable if it was carried out by its neighbors rather than by Western powers.

The support for sovereignty exhibited by the emerging powers has roots in the past trauma they suffered at the hands of Western imperialism. In the twenty-first century, emerging powers interpreted the Bush doctrine of "preventive war" and "regime change" as a return to neocolonialism. The BRICS are all the more distrustful of the UN principles because, in the post–cold war world, countless interventions have taken place under one pretext or another that have finally shattered the sovereignty of the countries singled out, such as in the case of Iraq.

But support for sovereignty today can also be explained by the desire of emerging powers to settle well away from the public eye delicate issues in which human rights (and even a people's right to self-determination) are often at stake, such as for the Kashmiris, the Tibetans, Uighurs, and Chechens. For instance, Raja Mohan attributes India's refusal to support any intervention in Libya to three factors: the "postcolonial tradition of opposing Western interventions in the Middle East," India's reluctance "to concede political space in the developing world to China, by appearing to align uncritically with the West," and "India's strategy to prevent the internationalisation of its own domestic problems and regional disputes."[41]

Lastly, the refusal of outside interventions in such a specific case as Syria may simply reflect the limits of emerging powers' commitment to human rights, even when they are practicing democracies, as India's national security adviser Shivshankar Menon eloquently justified in a public lecture:

> Do we not have a responsibility to spread democracy and fight for our values abroad? Yes and no. Yes, if we have the means to actually ensure that we are able to spread them. And yes if having democrats as our neighbours contributes to the peaceful periphery that we need. But please remember that a people cannot be forced to be free or to practice democracy. They have to come to these values themselves if they are to be lasting. Such a crusade for one's values is often mistaken by others as the pursuit of self-interest couched in high-tone words. We have seen how high sounding phrases like the "right to protect" are selectively invoked and brutally applied in the pursuit of self interest, giving humanitarian and international intervention a bad name.[42]

The fact that sovereignty is the common denominator among emerging powers should not lead us to lump them all together. In fact, the situation in Syria gradually introduced an element of differentiation between China and Russia, on the one hand, which twice vetoed Western resolutions backed by the Arab League in February and July 2012, and India and South Africa, on the other, which, after consulting with Brazil, backed the resolutions or abstained.[43] While the IBSA countries may stand alongside their BRICS partners, they can also sing to their own tune.

Conclusion

The principal rationale for India's participation in various plurilateral or minilateral groupings is to push for reform of the existing UN-centered global governance structure, ranging from the UNSC to the international financial institutions, and also to establish new governance structures where none exists at the moment. In this context, the principal plurilateral groupings serve different objectives. The G-20, given the nature of its membership, has the potential to encourage a cooperative approach between the West and the emerging powers. However, the nature of its membership—on the one hand, it is more inclusive than either IBSA or BRICS, but, on the other hand, it is too unwieldy and disparate to address contentious issues effectively—means that cooperation will be constrained. Besides, India, which sees the G-20 solely as an instrument to address economic issues, is wary about expanding its agenda to embrace peace and security issues.

In contrast, the BRICS grouping serves India's purpose of challenging the West's domination of the existing international political and financial institutions of global governance. This has led to a perception that BRICS are likely to become anti-Western blocs. This may well be the outcome if these groups follow the established Western tradition of creating noninclusive structures. However, the BRICS countries are unlikely to follow the Western model of exclusivity. This is not because its membership is necessarily more enlightened or intuitively more inclusive, but because such an approach serves its objectives for at least three reasons.

First, major differences between BRICS countries prevent the possibility of creating a united front. This is particularly true of the India-China relationship. Apart from the divergent political ideologies, the presence of the longest disputed border (which has witnessed regular confrontations) and the shadow of Tibet (which manifested itself in the tragic immolation of a Tibetan protester on the eve of the March 2012 New Delhi summit) loom large and sustain mutual mistrust. This distrust is evident in the various BRICS declarations, which called for reform of the UNSC but fell well short of supporting the Indian case (along with that of Brazil and South Africa) for permanent membership in this exclusive club.

Second, although the BRICS group has started to challenge the dominant Western discourse on issues as diverse as the leadership of the World Bank and the IMF, as well as the crisis over Iran and Syria, it is either unable or unwilling to formulate and lead an alternative approach. Thus, in the case of the World Bank leadership, its call for "an open and merit-based process" of selection reflected not its democratic instinct but its inability to agree on a consensus candidate.

Similarly, while calling for an "inclusive political process" in Syria and "resolution . . . through political and diplomatic means and dialogue between the parties concerned" on Iran, the BRICS have been reluctant to lead this approach in either case. The latter is particularly ironic given that a peaceful resolution of the Iranian crisis would benefit China, India, and South Africa, which are significantly dependent on Iranian oil supplies.

Finally, given that all BRICS countries, including India, have strategic partnerships with the United States and value their relationship with Washington more than with each other's capitals, there is no incentive to confront the leader of the Western bloc. Moreover, any reform of the existing global governance structure or establishment of new ones will be well nigh impossible without the endorsement of the United States, which is still the biggest stakeholder in the present international system. Confronting the United States either unilaterally or collectively through BRICS is a nonstarter.

In contrast, the IBSA, as a coalition of Southern democracies, is expected to promote the same values in its neighborhood and globally. However, in the world of realpolitik, leading democracies of the world have often supported authoritarian regimes. The United States has been particularly guilty of this charge, backing odious undemocratic regimes from Chile to Pakistan and the Philippines. Washington justified this aberration with a quip that a dictator "may be a son of a bitch, but he's our son of a bitch."[44]

Similarly, even the multiethnic, multicultural IBSA democracies have been uneven in their promotion of democracy in their immediate neighborhoods. For instance, India's 1971 intervention in Bangladesh set the country on the long and winding road to democracy, while its 1988 role in the Maldives helped to prolong the life of an authoritarian regime. More recently, New Delhi cozied up to the military junta in Myanmar, while voting against Sri Lanka's human rights record in the UN's Human Rights Council. It also contributed to installing democracy in Afghanistan to hold its own against Pakistan.

This trend suggests three key characteristics that have determined democracy promotion and also apply to IBSA. First, no power, however principled, is likely to promote democracy to the detriment of its own national security. Second, as a corollary, democratic powers are likely to promote democracy only when it is expected to enhance or at the very least not undermine their national security or interests. Finally, most of the IBSA countries, which are able to determine their national interests in their immediate neighborhood, are finding it more difficult to make a similar determination outside their local areas of influence, leading them to follow their default position of practicing, but not promoting, democracy.

However, as IBSA economies, particularly India, become inexorably intertwined for resources and markets with countries out of their immediate area of regional influence, their comfortable policy of masterly inactivity is likely to become detrimental to the promotion of their own national interests. Thus there is a need to recognize the strategic importance of democracy promotion, particularly in areas undergoing profound political changes, such as the Middle East, for strengthening the economy and furthering the national interests.

While promoting democratic practices, such as rule of law, might be seen to be of limited relevance to the economy in the short term, such practices are likely to benefit the economic interest of rising democratic economic powers, such as India, in the long term, as opposed to the interest of undemocratic powers, such as China.

To promote democracy strategically, India will have to work closely with the other IBSA democracies as well as the democratic permanent members of the UN Security Council at the bilateral, regional, and multilateral levels. One option might be to work in countries in transition on joint low-profile, bottom-up approaches to promote local governance structures. A parallel option might be to enhance the role of the UN's Democracy Fund and the Community of Democracies. This would also require the rising democracies to insulate their efforts from the strategic instincts of the undemocratic members of the BRICS. Here India's decision to separate the IBSA summit from the BRICS summit is a good start and should be built upon in the coming months.

Subsequently co-opting the United States and the European Union into the IBSA groupings would also be essential to underline that this is not necessarily an anti-West alliance, but a new liberal democratic alliance. India, which perhaps has the best relations with Washington at the moment, is most suited to taking the lead on this approach. This would not only serve New Delhi's objective but also enhance the prospects for cooperative global governance.

Notes

1. Manmohan Singh, "PM's Vision of How the World Is Governed in the 21st Century," press release (New Delhi, July 7, 2009).

2. The G-20 members are Argentina, Australia, Brazil, Canada, China, the European Union, France, Germany, India, Indonesia, Italy, Japan, Mexico, Russia, Saudi Arabia, South Africa, South Korea, Turkey, the United Kingdom, and the United States. See also "G-20: Its Role and Legacy," G-20 Presidency (en.g20russia.ru/docs/about/part_G20.html).

3. See chapter 13 by Devesh Kapur in this volume for other factors that attract India to the G-20.

4. See Richard Gowan and Bruce Jones, "New Threats Demand a New Global Security Forum," Brookings Opinion, November 5, 2010 (www.brookings.edu/research/opinions/2012/02/17-g20-mgo).

5. See Celso Amorim, Rut Diamint, Shen Dingli, Michael Fullilove, Giovanni Grevi, Ambassador Wu Jianmin, Bruce Jones, Dong Hwi Lee, and W. P. S Sidhu, "Perspectives on the G-20 Foreign Ministers' Meeting," Brookings Opinion, February 17, 2012 (www.brookings.edu/research/opinions/2012/02/17-g20-mgo).

6. .This section is drawn from W. P. S. Sidhu, "Hope from a Meeting in Mexico," *Mint*, February 20, 2012 (www.livemint.com/Opinion/ritnZ3aUVh0Tdy5lOeKcZI/Hope-from-a-meeting-in-Mexico.html).

7. This was evident in the final declaration of the Los Cabos summit, which merely noted, "An informal meeting of G-20 Ministers of Foreign Affairs . . . explored the ways in which G-20 member countries could contribute more effectively to address key challenges in global governance," but did not mention any of the specific international security challenges that were discussed. See G-20 Leaders Declaration, Los Cabos, Mexico, June 2012.

8. On the notion of "minilateralism" applied to IBSA, see Christian Lechervy, "Coopération Sud-Sud et diplomatie tri-continentale: L'exemple du dialogue IBAS (Inde, Brésil, Afrique du Sud)," *Les Carnets du CAP 15* (Fall/Winter 2011): 185–94. See also Ruchita Beri, "IBSA Dialogue Forum: An Assessment," *Strategic Analysis* 32, no. 5 (September 2008): 809–31 (www.ipc-undp.org/ipc/doc/ibsa/papers/ibsa11.pdf).

9. Sarah-Lea John de Sousa, "IBSA: An Actor in a New Global Order?" in "IBSA: An International Actor and Partner for the EU?" edited by Susanne Gratius, Working Paper 63 (Madrid: Fundación para las Relaciones Internacionales y el Diálogo Exterior, July 2008), p. 3; Francisco Figueiredo de Souza, "IBSA: A Brazilian Perspective," in *Emerging Powers: India, Brazil, and South Africa (IBSA) and the Future of South-South Cooperation* (Washington: Woodrow Wilson International Center for Scholars, August 2009) (www.wilsoncenter.org/publication/emerging-powers-india-brazil-and-south-africa-ibsa-and-the-future-south-south). The trio formed at the margin of the G-8 summit in Evian, in June 2003, where French president Jacques Chirac had invited the heads of state and government of these three countries. See Paulo Sotero, "Introduction," in *Emerging Powers*, p. 1.

10. See Brasilia Declaration, June 6, 2003 (www.itamaraty.gov.br/temas-mais-informacoes/temas-mais-informacoes/saiba-mais-ibas/documentos-emitidos-pelos-chefes-de-estado-e-de/brasilia-declaration/view).

11. Chris Alden and Marco Antonio Vieira, "The New Diplomacy of the South: South Africa, Brazil, India, and Trilateralism," *Third World Quarterly* 26, no. 7 (2005): 1077–95 (www.ipc-undp.org/ipc/doc/ibsa/papers/ibsa9.pdf). In particular, see p. 1089.

12. The IBSA countries explain that they have much to learn from each other, due to the gap in revenues they face and the weight of the informal sector in their economies compared to developed countries such as France (which used to advise Brazil in these matters). See Carey Carpenter, "Global Governance, South-South Economic Relations, and Foreign Policy Strategies," in Emerging Powers, p. 4.

13. Lechervy, "Coopération Sud-Sud et diplomatie tri-continentale," p. 190.

14. C. Jaffrelot, "Under a Southern Sun," *Indian Express*, April 1, 2013 (www.indianexpress.com/news/under-a-southern-sun/1095677/).

15. This is in line with the impression that the BBC correspondent in Moscow had about him in 2007: "To hear Mr. Lavrov you would think the Cold War had never ended." See "Russia's Deep Suspicion of the West," *BBC News*, December 15, 2007 (news.bbc.co.uk/2/hi/programmes/from_our_own_correspondent/7144560.stm).

16. Alexandra A. Arkhangelskaya, "IBSA—Past? BRICS—Future?" (Moscow: Russian Academy of Sciences, n.d.) (www.brics5.co.za/assets/AAA2.pdf).

17. All BRICS declarations are made available by the BRICS Information Center on the University of Toronto website at www.brics.utoronto.ca/.

18. "Communique from BRIC Summit in Brasilia," Reuters, April 16, 2010 (www.reuters.com/article/2010/04/16/brics-statement-idUSN1513243520100416).

19. For instance, China's quota share was realigned, from less than 3 percent to more than 6 percent, and four of the BRICS are now among the ten largest shareholders in the fund (www.imf.org/external/np/exr/facts/quotas.htm).

20. The full text of the BRICS Declaration at Sanya is available at www.rediff.com/business/report/full-text-of-the-brics-declaration-in-sanya/20110414.htm.

21. The reform of the voting rights decided by the IMF and approved by the G-20 at Seoul are still to be implemented because of nonratification by several countries, including the United States.

22. W. P. S. Sidhu, "BRICS: Creating a New World Order?" *Mint*, April 1, 2012.

23. See eThekwini Declaration, "BRICS and Africa: Partnership for Development, Integration, and Industrialisation" (Durban, March 27, 2013), para. 9 (www.brics5.co.za/about-brics/summit-declaration/fifth-summit/).

24. See eThekwini Declaration, par. 10.

25. Pranab Dhal Samanta, "BRICS Bank, $100 Billion Contingency Fund Gets Nod," *Indian Express*, March 28, 2013.

26. "Beyond India's Grasp: The Many Problems with a BRICS Bank," *Business Standard*, March 31, 2013; "The Foundation Is a Bit Shaky," *Hindustan Times*, March 28, 2013.

27. See Samir Saran, "Generosity within BRICS Offers China Passport to Power" (http://samirsaran.com/2013/03/11/generosity-within-brics-offers-china-passport-to-power/), and Jaffrelot, "Under a Southern Sun."

28. Cornelia Woll, "Emerging Power Strategies in the World Trade Organization," in *Emerging States: The Wellspring of a New World Order*, edited by Christophe Jaffrelot and translated by Cynthia Schoch (Columbia University Press, 2009), p. 252.

29. The G-20 in fact varies in size. The founding members are Argentina, Bolivia, Brazil, Chile, China, Cuba, Ecuador, India, Mexico, Pakistan, Paraguay, Peru, the Philippines, and Thailand. Colombia, Costa Rica, Egypt, El Salvador, Kenya, Nigeria, Tanzania, and Zimbabwe are also members.

30. Woll, "Emerging Power Strategies," p. 252.

31. See chapter 14 by Navroz Dubash in this volume.

32. One of the participants, Laurence Tubiana, concluded, "The old world died in Copenhagen. In Cancún we saw the emerging countries become a real source of new ideas." Cited in Grégoire Allix, "Optimisme après l'accord sur le climat à Cancún. Les emerging countries ont joué un rôle moteur dans le succès de la conférence des Nations Unies," *Le Monde*, December 12–13, 2010, p. 4.

33. See the analysis of a disillusioned observer from Bangladesh—one of the least advanced countries that is the most threatened by rising sea levels: Ashfadur Rahman, "Durban Conference: Most Successful Failure!" *Daily Star*, December 11, 2011.

34. Organization for Economic Cooperation and Development anticorruption rules may also be rejected for the same reasons, and the BRICS already refuse any idea of a World Environmental Organization in keeping with an "every man for himself" attitude that the Rio+20 circus had considerable trouble concealing despite the virtuosity of the Brazilian diplomats.

35. See also chapter 9 by David Malone and Rohan Mukherjee in this volume.

36. The official title of this clause, also known by its abbreviation "R2P," is "responsibility to protect populations from genocide, war crimes, ethnic cleansing, and crimes against humanity." See chapter 16 by Nitin Pai in this volume.

37. The resolution justified the use of force to establish a no-fly zone to protect civilians.

38. Two of them, China and Russia, could have vetoed the resolution but did not. In 2011, in addition to these two permanent members, Brazil, India, and South Africa sat on the UNSC as nonpermanent members.

39. Embassy of India, "Syria: Press Statement; IBSA Delegation Visit to Syria" (www.indianembassysyria.com/english/whats-new/327.html).

40. Personal conversation with senior IBSA diplomat, Copenhagen, December 2012.

41. C. Raja Mohan, "India, Libya, and the Principle of Non-Intervention," *ISAS Insights* 122 (April 13, 2011): 7.

42. Shivshankar Menon, "India and the Global Scene," Sixteenth Prem Bhatia Memorial Lecture, New Delhi, August 11, 2011 (www.maritimeindia.org/article/india-and-global-scene).

43. Whereas in the October 2011 vote South Africa and India had abstained, in February 2012 they both voted in favor of the resolution, before parting ways again in July 2012, with India voting for and South Africa abstaining.

44. This insight is attributed to U.S. president Franklin D. Roosevelt and was in reference to Nicaraguan strongman Anastasio Somoza.

Contributors

SANJAYA BARU is Director for Geo-economics and Strategy at the International Institute for Strategic Studies, London, and Honorary Senior Fellow at the Centre for Policy Research, New Delhi.

KANTI BAJPAI is Professor and Vice Dean Research at the Lee Kuan Yew School of Public Policy at the National University of Singapore.

SANDEEP BHARDWAJ is Research Associate at the Centre for Policy Research, New Delhi.

NAVROZ K. DUBASH is Senior Fellow at the Centre for Policy Research, New Delhi.

ARUNABHA GHOSH is CEO of the Council on Energy, Environment and Water (CEEW), an independent policy research institution in India.

RICHARD GOWAN is Associate Director at the Center on International Cooperation, New York University, and Senior Fellow at the European Council on Foreign Relations.

CHRISTOPHE JAFFRELOT is Research Director at the Centre National de la Recherche Scientifique at Sciences Po (Paris), Visiting Professor at the King's India Institute (London), and Global Scholar at Princeton University.

BRUCE JONES is Senior Fellow in Foreign Policy and Director of the Managing Global Order project at Brookings Institution and Director and Senior Fellow at the Center on International Cooperation, New York University.

DEVESH KAPUR is Director of the Centre for the Advanced Study of India and Madan Lal Sobti Associate Professor for the Study of Contemporary India at the University of Pennsylvania.

TANVI MADAN is Director of The India Project and Fellow in the Foreign Policy program at Brookings Institution.

DAVID M. MALONE is Rector of the United Nations University, with the rank of Under Secretary General of the UN. He was Canada's High Commissioner to India and nonresident Ambassador to Bhutan and Nepal in 2006–08. He is the author of *Does the Elephant Dance? Contemporary Indian Foreign Policy* (OUP, 2011).

PRATAP BHANU MEHTA is President of the Centre for Policy Research, New Delhi.

C. RAJA MOHAN is Distinguished Fellow at the Observer Research Foundation, Delhi, Visiting Research Professor at the Institute of South Asian Studies, Singapore, and a Non-Resident Senior Associate at the Carnegie Endowment for International Peace, Washington.

ROHAN MUKHERJEE is a doctoral candidate in the Department of Politics at Princeton University and a Fellow of the Center for International Security Studies (CISS), also at Princeton.

NITIN PAI is Co-founder and Director of the Takshashila Institution, an independent think tank and public policy school in Bangalore.

SRINATH RAGHAVAN is Senior Fellow at the Centre for Policy Research, New Delhi.

RAJESH RAJAGOPALAN is Professor at the School of International Studies at Jawaharlal Nehru University, New Delhi.

ISKANDER LUKE REHMAN is a Research Fellow at the Center for Strategic and Budgetary Assessments, a PhD candidate at Sciences Po Paris, and a former Associate and Stanton Fellow at the Carnegie Endowment for International Peace.

SHYAM SARAN is former Foreign Secretary of India. He is currently Chairman, National Security Advisory Board; Chairman, Research in Information Systems for Developing Countries; and Senior Fellow at the Centre for Policy Research, New Delhi.

WAHEGURU PAL SINGH SIDHU is Senior Fellow at the Center on International Cooperation, New York University, a member of the editorial board of the *Global Governance* and *Peacebuilding* journals, and a regular columnist on international strategic issues for *Mint* newspaper in India.

SUSHANT K. SINGH is Fellow for National Security at the Takshashila Institution in Bangalore.

DAVID STEVEN is Nonresident Senior Fellow for the Managing Global Order project in the Foreign Policy program at the Brookings Institution and Nonresident Senior Fellow and Associate Director of the Center on International Cooperation at New York University.

Index

Accounting standards, 252–56
Acharya, Amitav, 248
Acharya, Shankar, 85
Achuthanandan, V. S., 106
ADB. *See* Asian Development Bank
Adeniji, Oluyemi, 46
Afghanistan: foreign aid from India, 61, 65–66; India's expanding role in, 70; India's interventions in, 335; security cooperation with, 66–67; Soviet invasion of, 81; UN role in, 185
Africa: democracy promotion in, 7; foreign aid from India, 245. *See also specific countries*
African Development Bank, 245
African Union, 332
An Agenda for Peace (Boutros-Ghali), 161
Agreement on Basic Telecommunications (WTO), 219
Agriculture: energy use by, 285–86, 289; subsidies for, 105
Ahluwalia, Montek Singh, 85
Albright, David, 199
Alden, Chris, 324
Allocation of Business Rules, 53
Amin, Idi, 306
Angola, Security Council interventions in, 161
Annan, Kofi, 168
Anti-access and area denial (A2/AD), 144
Anti-Ballistic Missile Treaty, 203
Anti-colonialism, 168. *See also* Decolonization
Anti-Money Laundering Act (India), 250
Antisubmarine warfare capabilities, 134
Anti-Terrorism Act (India), 250
APEC (Asia-Pacific Economic Cooperation), 18
APG (Asia Pacific Group on Money Laundering), 250
Arab Spring, 331
Arms control negotiations, 197–215; capacity for multilateralism in, 206–07; and defensive multilateralism, 201–02, 203–04; and domestic politics, 208–09; drivers of India's multilateralism in, 204–10; and economic issues, 209–10; evolution of India's multilateralism in, 200–04; historical experience with, 204–06; India as rule blocker on, 198–99; and national security concerns, 207–08; nuclear disarmament. *See also* Nuclear disarmament; and pragmatic multilateralism, 202–03. *See also* Comprehensive Test Ban Treaty (CTBT); Non-Proliferation of Nuclear Weapons Treaty (NPT)
Arms Trade Treaty (ATT), 203
ASEAN. *See* Association of Southeast Asian Nations
Asian Development Bank (ADB), 237, 240, 243, 244, 245

Asian financial crisis (1997–98), 82, 247, 320
Asian Relations Conference (1947), 26
Asia-Pacific Economic Cooperation (APEC), 18
Asia Pacific Group on Money Laundering (APG), 250
Assad, Bashar, al-, 331
Association of Southeast Asian Nations (ASEAN), 34, 36, 63, 88, 315
ATT (Arms Trade Treaty), 203
Atteridge, Aaron, 269
A2/AD (Anti-access and area denial), 144
Australia: Indian corporate sector's interests in, 104; and Trans-Pacific Partnership, 64
Australia Group, 8, 203
Azad, Abul Kalam, 304

Badal, Parkash Singh, 106
Baglihar Dam, 120, 126
Bajpai, Kanti, 115
Balance of payments, 77–78, 80, 84, 242
Bali Action Plan (2007), 48, 265
Banerjee, Dipankar, 180
Bangladesh: democracy promotion in, 6; foreign aid to, 61, 62; India's interventions in, 37, 160, 182, 308, 335; liberation of, 29; and maritime diplomacy, 143; regional initiatives by, 34; trade relations with, 61; UN role in 1971 crisis, 59; water security in, 282
Banking Laws Amendment Act (India), 251
Banking Regulation Act (India), 251
Baru, Sanjaya, 14, 75, 101–02
Basel Committee on Banking Supervision, 253
BASIC (Brazil, South Africa, India, and China), 49–50, 88, 268, 271, 328–30
Basu, Partha Pratim, 102
Basu, Susan, 199
Bay of Bengal Initiative for Multisectoral Technical and Economic Cooperation, 140
Bhagavan, Manu, 27, 197
Bhagwati, Jagdish, 89
Bharatiya Janata Party, 105, 202
Bhardwaj, Sandeep, 217
Bhaskar, Uday, 136
Bhutan: foreign aid from India, 61; free trade agreements with, 61; and riparian rights, 121; treaty with, 58
Bhutto, Zulfiqar Ali, 117
Bilateral trade agreements, 61, 63
Biofuels, 283
Black, Eugene, 120
Bolivarian Alliance for the Americas, 272
Border disputes, 116–19
Bosnia and Herzegovina, humanitarian assistance to, 162
Boutros-Ghali, Boutros, 161
Brasilia Declaration (2003), 323–24
Brasstacks crisis (1986–87), 123–24
Brazil: and BRICS Development Bank, 328; and Conference on Disarmament, 46; and Declaration on Agriculture, 329; energy security in, 293; in G-4, 11; and IBSAMAR naval exercises, 139; and Internet governance, 227; and Security Council reform proposals, 163, 171, 324; and UN peacekeeping operations, 177, 185; World Bank lending to, 82; and WTO, 86. *See also* BASIC; BRICS; IBSA
Bretton Woods institutions, 44, 79–83
BRICS (Brazil, Russia, India, China, and South Africa): India's participation in, 13, 88, 334; and international financial institutions, 9, 10, 83, 242; and nonalignment strategy, 325–28; and responsible multilateralism, 35; and Security Council, 10, 163; and sovereignty issues, 330–31, 332; and UN peacekeeping operations, 189
BRICS Development Bank, 328
Brzezinski, Zbigniew, 134, 143
Bush doctrine of preventive war, 323, 332

Cambodia: humanitarian interventions in, 38, 306, 307; Security Council interventions in, 161
Canada: and G-20, 247; and WTO, 86

Capacity for multilateralism, 95–114; in climate change negotiations, 106–07; and coalition politics, 100–01; and corporate sector, 103–04; and decentralization, 17; economic growth's impact on, 5; factors affecting, 98–100; and horizontal policymaking lines, 98–100; and human capital, 96–98; media's impact on, 101–02; and public opinion, 101–02; recommendations for, 108–10; and resource security, 294–95; in trade negotiations, 104–06; and vertical policymaking lines, 98–100
Cape Verde, IBSA projects in, 325
Capital adequacy standards, 252–53
Caribbean Development Bank, 244, 245
Carnegie Endowment for International Peace, 135
CBDRRC. *See* "Common but differentiated responsibility and respective capabilities"
CD. *See* Conference on Disarmament
CDM (Clean Development Mechanism), 265
Center on International Cooperation, 187
CERT-In (India), 223
Chadda, Maya, 310
Chahbahar port, 70
Chaudhuri, Rudra, 100, 101
Chemical weapons, 45
Chile: and Trans-Pacific Partnership, 64; U.S. support for authoritarian regime in, 335
China: and Asian Development Bank, 240; and BRICS Development Bank, 328; and climate change negotiations, 49, 267, 271, 272, 275; and Conference on Disarmament, 45; and cyber security, 218, 223, 226; and Declaration on Agriculture, 329; and East Asia Summit, 316; economic policy impact of, 89–90; energy security in, 283, 291, 293; Indian corporate sector's interests in, 104; and maritime security, 139, 142, 144–45; nuclear program in, 207–08; oil imports from Iran, 70; pluralism in, 18; and regional power, 61–62, 63; and responsible multilateralism, 35; and Security Council reform proposals, 171; "string of pearls" strategy of, 138; territorial disputes with, 9–10, 28, 58, 118–19, 159; and UN humanitarian interventions, 68; and UN peacekeeping operations, 177; U.S. relations with, 134; and WTO, 86. *See also* BASIC; BRICS; Sino-Indian War (1962)
Chouhan, Shivraj Singh, 52
CII (Confederation of Indian Industry), 103–04, 265
CIRP (Committee for Internet-Related Policies), 228
Civil society activism, 316
Clean Development Mechanism (CDM), 265
Climate change negotiations, 261–79; capacity for multilateralism in, 106–07; challenges for multilateralism in, 262–63; and energy security, 291; history of India's participation in, 263–69; horizontal and vertical policymaking lines for, 98; India's role in shaping policy on, 12–13; policy interpretations for, 269–74; practitioner's perspective on, 47–51; recommendations for, 274–75; regional cooperation on, 115
Clinton, Bill, 32, 124
Coalition politics, 100–01
Coal sector, 283–84, 286
Colombo Powers, 118
Combined Multinational Taskforce (CTF), 140
Commission on Peaceful Uses of Outer Space (UN), 31
Commission on Science and Technology for Development (CSTD), 227
Committee for Internet-Related Policies (CIRP), 228
Committee of the 34 (UN), 188
Commodity markets, 282, 290–91

"Common but differentiated responsibility and respective capabilities" (CBDRRC), 263, 264, 268, 271, 273
Communication technology. *See* Information and communication technologies
Community of Democracies, 336
Comprehensive Program on Disarmament, 45
Comprehensive Test Ban Treaty (CTBT), 162–64, 199, 202, 205, 208
Confederation of Indian Industry (CII), 103–04, 265
Conference of Parties, 48, 272
Conference on Disarmament (CD), 43, 44–47, 198, 205, 212
Congo. *See* Democratic Republic of Congo
Congress Party, 100, 105
Container Security Initiative, 203
Contingency relief arrangement (CRA), 328
Convention on Law of the Sea. *See* Law of the Sea, UN Convention on
Convention on Mutual Administrative Assistance in Tax Matters, 246, 249
Copenhagen Accord, 50
Corporate sector, 103–04, 105
Côte d'Ivoire, Security Council interventions in, 163, 191
Council on Climate Change (India), 99
Counterterrorism Committee (UN), 10
CRA (Contingency relief arrangement), 328
Crimes against humanity, 306–09
Crossing the Rubicon (Mohan), 163
CSTD (Commission on Science and Technology for Development), 227
CTBT. *See* Comprehensive Test Ban Treaty
CTF (Combined Multinational Taskforce), 140
Cyber security, 217–36; global network joining phase, 219–21; horizontal and vertical policymaking lines for, 98; and multilateral control of Internet, 221–23, 226–28; threat environment for, 223–26
Cyprus: Security Council interventions in, 161; UN mediation of conflict in, 159

Dalai Lama, 62
Decentralization, 16–17
Declaration on Agriculture (2003), 328–29
Decolonization, 44, 59, 159, 168, 181
Defensive internationalism, 31–35, 198
Deindustrialization, 78
Delhi Declaration (2006), 69, 327
Democracy Fund (UN), 168, 336
Democracy promotion, 6, 39, 309–11, 335, 336
Democratic Republic of Congo, UN peacekeeping operations in, 159, 178, 181, 183–87, 190
Deshingkar, Giri, 207
Deshmukh, Chintaman, 237
Devolution of powers, 17
Diamer-Bhasha Dam project, 240
Differentiated responsibility. *See* "Common but differentiated responsibility and respective capabilities" (CBDRRC)
Dikshit, Sheila, 52
Directorate of Foreign Cooperation (India), 139
Disarmament. *See* Arms control negotiations
Disaster relief operations, 139, 141, 148
Dixon, Owen, 117
Doha Development Round, 8, 51, 87, 88, 89, 104, 106
Domain Name System (DNS), 220
Domestic politics: and capacity for multilateralism, 100–01; and climate change negotiations, 107, 268–69, 270–71, 275; multilateralism impact of, 14–18; and political parties, 53; and resource security, 289–92; and trade negotiations, 105
Drinking water, 287. *See also* Water security

Drought Prone Area Program, 288
Dubash, Navroz K., 12, 13, 261, 270
Dubey, Muchkund, 84, 85, 86
Durban Platform (2011), 265, 272, 328, 330
Dysfunctional multilateralism, 28–31

East Asia Summit, 316
East Pakistan: humanitarian interventions in, 38, 123; India's intervention in, 160. *See also* Bangladesh
East Timor, Security Council interventions in, 165, 182
Economic policy, 75–93; and Bretton Woods institutions, 79–83; and China, 89–90; and energy security, 283–86; multilateralism impact of, 14–18; and rule-based multilateralism, 75–79. *See also* Trade
Egypt: and Conference on Disarmament, 46; and Nonaligned Movement, 28; official development assistance to, 77; UN mediation of conflict with Israel, 159
Eighteen-Nation Committee on Disarmament (ENCD), 202, 206
El Baradei, Mohamed, 46
Electricity subsidies, 287
Emission reductions, 48, 49, 329
Energy Coordination Committee (India), 99
Energy security: and climate change negotiations, 50, 274, 281, 291; as driver of multilateralism, 37, 53; economic value of, 283–86; and IBSA, 54; and maritime security, 137, 291
Energy subsidies, 287, 288, 289, 293
Enhanced Engagement Initiative, 246
Environmental constraints of resource demand, 288
Equity principle in climate change negotiations, 264, 274
Espinosa, Patricia, 330
Estonia, cyber attacks in, 223
Eurasian Group on Anti-Money Laundering and Terrorist Financing, 251
European Union: and Bretton Woods institutions, 326; and climate change negotiations, 49, 50, 265, 268, 272, 329; and Declaration on Agriculture, 328; energy security in, 283; and IMF, 81; and Indian corporate sector's interests, 103; multiculturalism in, 18; as rule maker, 12; and UN peacekeeping operations, 192; and WTO, 86. *See also specific countries*
Expansive internationalism, 26–28
Export pessimism, 84, 85
Extended Fund Facility, 242

FAO (Food and Agriculture Organization), 287
Federation of Indian Chambers of Commerce and Industry (FICCI), 104
Feigenbaum, Evan A., 100
Fernandes, George, 102
Financial Action Task Force (FATF), 239, 249–52
Fiscal Responsibility and Budget Management Act (India), 15
Fissile Material Cut-Off Treaty (FMCT), 198, 211–12
Food and Agriculture Organization (FAO), 287
Food crisis (2008), 80, 291
Food security, 29, 50, 80, 286–88
Foreign direct investment (FDI), 101, 237
France: Indian corporate sector's interests in, 104; nuclear agreement with, 9; and Suez crisis, 28; and UN peacekeeping operations, 189; and VARUNA naval exercises, 140
Free trade agreements, 61, 63, 88, 89
Friedman, Milton, 80

G-4, 11, 13, 171
G-7, 243, 250, 320
G-8, 14, 18, 266, 319
G-20: and capacity for multilateralism, 98; and climate change negotiations, 266; and energy security, 293–94; India's participation in, 13, 89,

320–23; and international financial institutions, 247–49; and trade negotiations, 328–30
G-77: and Bretton Woods institutions, 80; and climate change negotiations, 49, 106, 271; India's leadership of, 4, 35
GAAP (Generally Accepted Accounting Principles), 254
GAC (Governmental Advisory Committee), 222
Gandhi, Indira: and East Pakistan conflict, 123, 306; and economic liberalization, 101; foreign policy of, 30, 81; and IMF assistance, 80; and Indian National Congress, 29; and Soviet Union, 160
Gandhi, Mahatma (Mohandas K.), 165, 200, 304
Gandhi, Rajiv: assassination of, 182; and Internet infrastructure, 218; multilateralism efforts by, 31, 36; and naval forces, 135; and Sri Lanka civil war, 161
Gandhi, Sonia, 88–89
García Robles, Alfonso, 46
Gates, Robert, 124
General Agreement on Trade and Tariffs (GATT), 75, 78, 84–89, 169
Generally Accepted Accounting Principles (GAAP), 254
Genocide, 306–09
Genocide Convention, 306
Georgia, cyber attacks in, 223
Germany: in G-4, 11; Indian corporate sector's interests in, 104; and Security Council reform proposals, 163, 171, 324
GGE (Group of Governmental Experts), 222, 224
Ghosh, Arunabha, 281
GhostNet, 223, 224
Global Forum on Transparency and Exchange of Information for Tax Purposes, 246
Global public goods, 55, 167
Goa: India's military action in, 59, 159; soil erosion in, 288
Governmental Advisory Committee (GAC), 222
Gowan, Richard, 177, 188, 193
Graham, Frank, 117
Green Climate Fund, 330
Green Group, 265
Greenhouse gas emissions, 262. *See also* Climate change negotiations
Groundwater resources, 287
Group of 21, 45, 46
Group of Governmental Experts (GGE), 222, 224
Guinea-Bissau, IBSA projects in, 325
Gulf Cooperation Council, 68

Haass, Richard, 124
Haiti: IBSA projects in, 325; UN peacekeeping operations in, 177, 185
Hamas, 68
Hezbollah, 68
Hu Jintao, 137
Hulme, Mike, 263
Human capital, 96–98, 108
Human Development Index (HDI), 5
Humanist internationalism, 26
Humanitarian interventions, 32; in Bosnia and Herzegovina, 162; in East Pakistan, 38; naval forces used for, 139, 141, 148
Human rights, 27, 59, 68, 304–05, 313
Human Rights Council (UN), 6, 164, 305, 314
Hungary, Soviet invasion of, 28, 314
Hydroelecticity, 289
Hydrography, 142

IAEA. *See* International Atomic Energy Agency
IASB (International Accounting Standards Board), 252–56
IASC (International Accounting Standards Committee), 254
IBRD (International Bank for Reconstruction and Development), 82, 239

IBSA (India, Brazil, and South Africa), 323–25; and democracy promotion, 335, 336; and energy security, 54; India's participation in, 13; and Internet governance, 227; and responsible multilateralism, 35; and sovereignty issues, 330–31, 332
IBSAMAR naval exercises, 139
ICANN. *See* International Corporation of Assigned Names and Numbers
IDA. *See* International Development Association
Idealism, 76, 79, 304, 313
IDNs (internationalized domain names), 230
IFC (International Finance Corporation), 239
IFIs. *See* International financial institutions
IFRS (International Financial Reporting Standards), 239, 255
IGF (Internet Governance Forum), 222
IMF. *See* International Monetary Fund
Import-substitution development strategy, 77, 84, 85, 237
Indian Banks Association, 252
Indian National Congress, 29
Indian Ocean Naval Symposium (IONS), 140
Indian Ocean Rim Association for Regional Cooperation, 88, 140
India-Pakistan War (1965), 133
India Post, 252
Indonesia: economic growth in, 5; naval forces of, 133; UN mediation of conflict in, 159
Indo-U.S. nuclear agreement (2005), 9, 14, 36, 198–99, 203, 208–10, 226
Indus Waters Treaty, 119–22, 126, 291
Informal networks, 97
Information and communication technologies, 31, 222
Information Technology Act of 2000 (India), 219, 225
Infrastructure, 16, 284, 287
Institute for Defense Studies and Analyses, 135
Institute of Chartered Accountants of India, 255
Insurance Regulatory and Development Authority, 252
Intellectual property rights, 106
Interagency coordination, 99, 110
Inter-Dominion Accord (1948), 119
Intergovernmental Panel on Climate Change (IPCC), 262, 264
Inter-Ministerial Coordination Committee, 250
International Accounting Standards Board (IASB), 252–56
International Accounting Standards Committee (IASC), 254
International Association of Insurance Supervisors, 251
International Atomic Energy Agency (IAEA), 11, 69, 107, 160, 285
International Bank for Reconstruction and Development (IBRD), 82, 239
International Corporation of Assigned Names and Numbers (ICANN), 220, 222, 230
International Court of Justice, 120, 306, 307
International Criminal Court, 169, 173
International Development Association (IDA), 82, 239, 244
International Energy Agency, 292
International Finance Corporation (IFC), 239
International financial institutions (IFIs), 237–59; and Financial Action Task Force, 249–52; and G-20, 247–49; India's engagement with, 78, 239–45; and international accounting standards, 252–56; and OECD, 246–47
International Financial Reporting Standards (IFRS), 239, 255
Internationalized domain names (IDNs), 230
International Labor Organization, 330
International Maritime Organization, 137
International Monetary Fund (IMF): aid to India, 80, 81; and BRICS, 326, 327;

as financial and technological resource, 44; G-7 control of, 243; and G-20, 249; India's engagement with, 78, 239, 241–42; and international norms, 314; reform proposals for, 8, 79–83; in rule-based international order, 75
International norms, 303–18; changing attitudes toward, 313–14; crimes against humanity, 306–09; democracy promotion, 309–11; future of India's policy for, 311–16; and idealism, 304; and informal networks, 97; Nehru's influence on India's foreign policy, 304–05; UN implementation of, 314–16
International Organization of Securities Commissions, 253
International Seabed Authority, 137
International Standards Organization (ISO), 253
International Telecommunications Union (ITU), 220
International Tribunal for Law of the Sea (ITLOS), 137, 143
Internet: and civil society activism, 316; and cybersecurity, 221–23, 226–28; governance of, 218, 220, 221–22; infrastructure for, 219; international norms influenced by, 312; and social media, 101
Internet Governance Forum (IGF), 222
IONS (Indian Ocean Naval Symposium), 140
IPCC (Intergovernmental Panel on Climate Change), 262, 264
Iran: and BRICS countries, 10; Indian corporate sector's interests in, 103; nuclear program in, 69; oil exports to India, 69, 70, 284; sanctions against, 70, 71; Saudi Arabia's rivalry with, 69; Security Council interventions in, 161; and Syrian crisis, 68
Iraq: oil exports to India, 284; Security Council interventions in, 161, 165
Irrigation, 285, 287
ISO (International Standards Organization), 253
Israel: and cyber security, 223; and Middle East instability, 68; official development assistance to, 77; Security Council interventions in, 160, 161; and Suez crisis, 28; UN mediation of conflict with Egypt, 159; and UN peacekeeping operations in Lebanon, 186
ITLOS (International Tribunal for Law of the Sea), 137, 143
ITU (International Telecommunications Union), 220

Jaffrelot, Christophe, 319
Jaipal, Rikhi, 46
Jaitley, Arun, 87, 106
Jammu and Kashmir (J&K) conflict: and regional power, 58; and Security Council–India relations, 27, 158–59; and third-party engagement, 116–19, 122; and UN's humanitarian interventions, 32, 59
Japan: and Asian Development Bank, 243; and East Asia Summit, 316; economic growth in, 17–18; economic partnership agreement with, 63; energy security in, 283; in G-4, 11; Indian corporate sector's interests in, 104; and JIMEX naval exercises, 139; and responsible multilateralism, 36; and Security Council membership, 162, 171; and Security Council reform proposals, 163, 171, 324; and Trans-Pacific Partnership, 64; and WTO, 86
Jetley, V. K., 183, 188
JIMEX naval exercises, 139
Jones, Bruce D., 3

Kabila, Joseph, 186
Kalecki, Michal, 80
Kaplan, Robert D., 147
Kapur, Devesh, 98, 99, 237
Kargil War (1999), 124, 138, 166, 170
Karzai, Hamid, 66

Kashmir conflict. *See* Jammu and Kashmir (J&K) conflict
Kazakhstan, oil exports to India, 284
Kennedy, Andrew, 205
Keynes, John Maynard, 79
Khan, Abdul Qadeer, 199
Khan, Ayub, 123
Khilnani, Sunil, 98
Kishenganga Dam, 120, 126
Kissinger, Henry, 96
"Know your customer" (KYC) guidelines, 251–52
Korea. *See* North Korea; South Korea
Kosovo, NATO intervention in, 165, 182
Kosygin, Alexei, 123
Krishnasamy, Kabilan, 180, 184
Kumar, Nitish, 52
Kuwait, Security Council interventions in, 161
Kyoto Protocol, 47, 265, 266, 267, 330

Labor standards, 106, 330
Lagarde, Christine, 83
Lamy, Pascal, 9
Landmine Ban Treaty, 199
Lavrov, Sergei, 326
Law enforcement, 5, 67, 177
Law of the Sea, UN Convention on (UNCLOS), 117–18, 137
Lebanon: Security Council interventions in, 161; UN mediation of conflict in, 159, 186; UN peacekeeping operations in, 177
Liberation Tigers of the Tamil Eelam (LTTE), 126, 135
Liberia: Security Council interventions in, 161; UN peacekeeping operations in, 178
Libya: and G-20, 322; oil exports to India, 284; Security Council interventions in, 68, 161, 162, 163, 191, 303
Lilienthal, David, 120, 121
Liquefied natural gas, 285
"Look East" policy, 35, 62–63, 62–65, 169, 245
Los Cabos initiative (G-20), 322
Lula da Silva, Luiz Inácio, 323
Luttwak, Edward, 146

Madan, Tanvi, 95
MAD (Mutual Acceptance of Data) in the Assessment of Chemicals, 246–47
MALABAR naval exercises, 140, 147
Maldives: democracy promotion in, 6; foreign aid from India, 61; Indian corporate sector's interests in, 104; Indian interventions in, 135; India's interventions in, 37, 166, 182, 308, 335; naval assistance to, 142
Malone, David M., 14, 97, 157, 179, 191
Manufacturing sector, 286
Maran, Murasoli, 87, 105
Maritime Doctrine (2004), 139
Maritime Doctrine (2009), 141
Maritime peace dividend, 132
Maritime security, 131–53; and China, 144–45; as driver of multilateralism, 55; and energy security, 291; horizontal and vertical policymaking lines for, 98; and limits of integrative power, 140–44; and naval nuclearization, 145–47; and Non-Aligned Movement, 132–36; and Pakistan threat, 144–45; regional cooperation on, 115; shift in, 136–40; strategic flexibility in, 147–48. *See also* Law of the Sea, UN Convention on
Maritime Security Agency (Pakistan), 143
Maritime Strategy (2007), 141
Markey, Daniel, 108
Maternal mortality, 5
Mathai, Ranjan, 203
Mattoo, Aditya, 84
Mbeki, Thabo, 323
McNaughton, Bruce, 117
MEA (Ministry of External Affairs), 96, 99
Media: and capacity for multilateralism, 101–02, 109; on internationalism of Nehru, 304
Mehta, Pratap B., 3
Mehta, Sujata, 205
Menon, Shivshankar, 6; on cyber security, 224; on democracy promotion, 39; on

India's role as policy shaper, 13; on intervention vs. sovereignty, 333; on power projection, 11
MER (Mutual Evaluation Report), 250
Mexico: and Conference on Disarmament, 46; World Bank lending to, 82
Michaelowa, Axel, 269
Michaelowa, Katharina, 269
Middle class, 5, 16, 283
Middle East: and India's regional power, 65–71; regime change in, 311; Security Council interventions in, 159
MILAN naval exercises, 139
Millennium Development Goals, 294
Minilateralism, 323
Ministry of External Affairs (MEA, India), 96, 99
Ministry of Home Affairs (India), 99
Mishra, Saurabh, 179
Missile Technology Control Regime, 8, 203
Modi, Narendra, 107
Mohan, C. Raja, 25, 102, 108, 163, 180, 332
Mohan, Rakesh, 85
Montreal Protocol, 264
Mozambique, Security Council interventions in, 161
Mukherjee, Anit, 180
Mukherjee, Rohan, 157, 179, 191
Mukherji, Rahul, 101
Multilateral Investment Guarantee Agency, 239
Multilateralism in India: capacity for, 95–114; changing dynamics of, 25–41; and climate negotiations, 47–51; and Conference on Disarmament, 44–47; defensive internationalism phase, 31–35; domestic politics' impact on, 14–18; dysfunctional multilateralism phase, 28–31; economic policy's impact on, 14–18, 75–93; expansive internationalism phase, 26–28; future trajectory for, 36–40; perspectives on, 25–72; phases of, 25–36; policy in practice, 157–339; practitioner's perspective on, 43–56; recommendations for, 52–55; and regionalism, 31–35; responsible multilateralism phase, 35–36
Mutual Acceptance of Data (MAD) in the Assessment of Chemicals, 246–47
Mutual Administrative Assistance in Tax Matters Convention, 246, 249
Mutual Evaluation Report (MER), 250
Myanmar: and ASEAN, 315; diplomatic ties to, 6; India's interventions in, 308, 312, 335; and maritime diplomacy, 143

NAM. *See* Nonaligned Movement
Nambiar, Satish, 182, 190
Narasimham, M., 81
Nasser, Gamal Abdul, 28
Natarajan, Jayanti, 267
Nath, Kamal, 87, 104–06
National Action Plan on Climate Change (India), 51, 269
National Bank for Agricultural and Rural Development, 251–52
National Democratic Alliance coalition, 106, 219
National Intelligence Council (U.S.), 12
National Task Force on Information Technology and Software Development, 220
National Telecommunications Policy (India), 219, 220
NATO. *See* North Atlantic Treaty Organization
Natural gas, 283, 285
Naval forces, 134–36, 138, 139–40. *See also* Maritime security
Naval Strategic Forces Command (Pakistan), 145
Naxalite insurgency, 284, 290
Nayyar, Deepak, 86
Negative security guarantees, 45
Nehru, Jawaharlal: and arms control negotiations, 200; and collective security, 30; and expansive internationalism phase, 26, 28; external policy advice sought by, 80; foreign policy influence of, 4, 197; idealism of, 304; and international

norms, 304–05; and Jammu and Kashmir conflict, 158; and nonalignment strategy, 29, 134; and official development assistance, 77; and South-South cooperation, 323, 325; and sovereignty paradox, 165; on Suez crisis, 28; on UN-centered international order, 43, 58, 76; and Universal Declaration of Human Rights, 27; and UN peacekeeping operations, 180
Neo-Nixonian strategy, 142
Nepal: energy security in, 61; foreign aid to, 61, 62; India's interventions in, 37, 125, 126, 166, 308; and riparian rights, 121; trade agreements with, 61; treaty with, 58
Nigeria: and Conference on Disarmament, 46; oil exports to India, 284; and UN peacekeeping operations, 188
Nimitz, Chester, 117
Nixon, Richard, 134
Nonaligned Movement (NAM): and Conference on Disarmament, 46; India's leadership of, 4, 27; radicalization of, 29; and responsible multilateralism, 35; and UN peacekeeping operations, 179, 189
Nonalignment strategy, 4, 25, 134, 319
Non-Proliferation of Nuclear Weapons Treaty (NPT): India's challenges of, 8, 9, 30–31, 75, 159; and India's multilateralism, 198, 210–11; and Iran's nuclear program, 69; and Security Council–India relations, 159–60
Nonreciprocity principle, 274
North Atlantic Treaty Organization (NATO), 7–8, 165, 306
North Korea, UN peacekeeping operations in, 180, 185
Norway: official development assistance from, 77; Sri Lanka's civil war mediation efforts by, 125
Nottage, Hunter, 86
NPT. *See* Non-Proliferation of Nuclear Weapons Treaty
Nuclear disarmament, 36, 115, 200–01. *See also* Arms control negotiations; Comprehensive Test Ban Treaty (CTBT); Non-Proliferation of Nuclear Weapons Treaty (NPT)
Nuclear power, 285
Nuclear Suppliers Group (NSG), 8, 9, 160, 203, 211, 244
Nuclear testing, 200, 201–02
Nutrition standards, 286
Nye, Joseph, 222

Obama, Barack: endorsement of India's campaign for permanent Security Council membership, 11, 327; on intervention vs. sovereignty, 331; on nation building, 38
Official development assistance (ODA), 77
Oil, 284–85, 286
Ollapally, Deepa, 206
ONUC. *See* United Nations Operation in the Congo
Open-Ended Working Group (UN), 170
Order paradox, 157, 165–68, 169–72
Organization for Economic Cooperation and Development (OECD): and climate change negotiations, 49; India's disinterest in joining, 8; and international financial institutions, 246–47; UN budget allocations from, 47

Pai, Nitin, 303
Pakistan: and Afghanistan aid from India, 67; and Asian Development Bank, 240; and Bangladesh crisis, 38, 59, 123, 160, 308, 335; and Brasstacks crisis, 124; and climate change negotiations, 272; and Conference on Disarmament, 46; and Fissile Material Cut-Off Treaty, 212; foreign aid from China, 62; India's interventions in, 37; and Indus Waters Treaty, 119–22; and maritime security, 143, 144–45; naval forces, 138; nuclear program in, 199; territorial disputes with, 28, 58, 116–19; trade relations with, 61; U.S. relations with, 67, 335; water security in, 282. *See also* Jammu and Kashmir (J&K) conflict

Partial Test Ban Treaty, 27, 206, 208
Patel, Vallabhbhai, 304
Peacekeeping operations. *See* UN peacekeeping operations
Permanent Indus Commission, 120
Philippines: and climate change negotiations, 272; U.S. support for authoritarian regime in, 335
Pilot, Sachin, 225
Pipelines, 285
Planning Commission (India), 52, 53
Police, 5, 67, 177
Policy coordination, 98–100, 110
Political fragmentation, 100
Political parties, 53, 102, 107
Power sector, 284, 285
Prevention of Money Laundering Act (India), 250, 251
Preventive war doctrine, 323, 332
Private sector, 103–04, 105
Proliferation Security Initiative, 203
Proximity paradox, 311
Public opinion: and capacity for multilateralism, 101–02; on India's aid to Afghanistan, 66; on nuclear issues, 208; and trade negotiations, 105
Public-private partnerships, 104, 253
Puri, Hardeep Singh, 191

Qin Gang, 240

Radiological weapons, 45
Raghavan, Srinath, 57
Rajagopalan, Rajesh, 197
Rajiv Gandhi Action Plan for Nuclear Disarmament, 201
Ramesh, Jairam, 106, 107, 267; 330
Rann of Kutch dispute, 116–19, 122, 159
Rao, Narasimha, 117, 170
Rao, Nirupama, 103
Rao, P. Chandrasekhara, 137
RBI (Reserve Bank of India), 237, 251
Reagan, Ronald, 81
Realist approach, 75–79, 82, 83, 314
Regional disputes, 115–30; crisis, wars, and instability, 122–26; river disputes, 119–22; territorial, 116–19
Regionalism, 57–72; and defensive internationalism, 31–35; and domestic politics, 55; history of, 58–59; and "Look East" policy, 62–65; and Middle East, 65–71; and South Asia politics, 59–62. *See also* Regional disputes
Rehman, Iskander Luke, 131
Research in Motion (RIM), 224
Reserve Bank of India (RBI), 237, 251
Resource security, 281–301; and capacity for multilateralism, 294–95; challenges for, 283–88; and domestic politics, 289–92; and environmental constraints of resource demand, 288; and globalization, 289–92; horizontal and vertical policymaking lines for, 98; and India's role in resource markets, 289; international cooperation for, 292–95; need for, 281–83. *See also* Energy security; Food security; Water security
Responsibility to protect (R2P), 4, 32, 68, 169, 306–09, 331
Responsible multilateralism, 35–36
Rice, Susan, 164
Rikhye, Inderjit, 181
RIM (Research in Motion), 224
Riparian rights. *See* River disputes; Water security
River disputes, 119–22, 127. *See also* Indus Waters Treaty
Robbins, Lionel, 80
Roussef, Dilma, 327
R2P. *See* Responsibility to protect
Rule of law, 6, 335
Russia: and BRICS Development Bank, 328; and cyber security, 222, 226; energy security in, 283; naval forces in Indian Ocean, 135; nuclear agreement with, 9; and responsible multilateralism, 35; and UN humanitarian interventions, 68; and WTO, 86. *See also* BRICS; Soviet Union
Rwanda: humanitarian interventions in, 307; UN peacekeeping operations in, 182

SAARC. *See* South Asian Association of Regional Cooperation
Sakhuja, Vijay, 137, 141
Salal Dam, 120
Saran, Shyam, 43, 98, 274
Saudi Arabia: and climate change negotiations, 272; counterterrorism cooperation with, 70; Iran's rivalry with, 69; oil exports to India, 69; and Syrian crisis, 68, 164
Savings rate, 15
Schwab, Susan, 8
Schwebel, Stephen, 120
Seabed Treaty, 207
Securities Exchange Board of India, 252
Security Council (UN): and CTBT, 162–64; and Financial Action Task Force, 250; and Indian corporate sector's interests, 103; India's relations with, 157–76; and international order, 165–68, 169–72; and Jammu and Kashmir conflict, 158–59; and maritime security, 137; and NPT, 159–60; permanent membership quest of India, 4, 8, 10, 37, 75, 89, 315, 324, 327; and sovereignty, 164–65, 168–69; and UN peacekeeping operations, 190
Self-determination rights, 332
Services sector, 286
Shanghai Cooperation Organization, 226, 316
Sharif, Nawaz, 124
Shastri, Lal Bahadur, 123
Shourie, Arun, 221
Shroff, A. D., 79, 80, 83
Shukla, S. P., 86
Sidhu, Waheguru Pal Singh, 3, 187, 319
Sierra Leone: Security Council interventions in, 165; UN peacekeeping operations in, 182–83, 185, 187
SIMBEX naval exercises, 139
Singapore: free trade agreement with, 88; Indian corporate sector's interests in, 104; and SIMBEX naval exercises, 139; and Trans-Pacific Partnership, 64
Singh, Manmohan: on Bretton Woods institutions, 81–82, 82–83; career of, 97; on China, 89; and economic liberalization, 85–86; on export pessimism, 84; and G-20, 248; on justice in world order, 171; on maritime diplomacy, 141; and maritime security, 136; on multilateralism, 88; and Nonaligned Movement, 179; on regional cooperation, 64; and shift to multilateralism, 319; on trade relations, 61; on UN-centered governance system, 14, 78; and UN peacekeeping operations, 183, 187; and WTO negotiations, 87
Singh, Sushant K., 177, 193
Singh, Swaran, 117
Sino-Indian War (1962), 62, 304
Sir Creek dispute, 117–18, 119, 143
Skidelsky, Robert, 79–80
Social media platforms, 101, 109, 312, 316
Soft power, 139, 146, 273
Soil erosion, 288
Somalia: maritime security in, 143; Security Council interventions in, 161, 165; UN peacekeeping operations in, 182, 187
South Africa: and BRICS, 327, 328; and climate change negotiations, 273; and IBSAMAR naval exercises, 139; Indian corporate sector's interests in, 104; and Internet governance, 227; sanctions against, 27, 31, 44, 58, 160; Security Council interventions in, 161; World Bank lending to, 82; and WTO, 86. *See also* BASIC; BRICS; IBSA
South Asian Association of Regional Cooperation (SAARC), 34, 60, 88, 140, 315–16
South Asian Free Trade Agreement, 88
South China Sea, 64, 107–08, 285
South Korea: economic partnership agreement with, 63; free trade agreement with, 88; and responsible multilateralism, 36; strategic ties with, 64; UN peacekeeping operations in, 180, 185

South-South cooperation, 30, 323, 324, 325
South Sudan: oil exports to India, 284; UN peacekeeping operations in, 184
Sovereignty: and Bretton Woods institutions, 82; and human rights norms, 59, 305; and multilateral organizations, 18; promotion of, 330–33; and Security Council–India relations, 157, 164–65, 168–69; and UN humanitarian interventions, 68; and Universal Declaration of Human Rights, 27
Soviet Union: Afghanistan invasion by, 81; and arms control negotiations, 200; and Conference on Disarmament, 45; and defensive internationalism phase, 32; diplomatic ties to, 29, 134, 160; and East Pakistan conflict, 123; Hungary invaded by, 28, 314; naval forces in Indian Ocean, 134–35
Special and differential (S&D) treatment, 84
Special Committee on Peacekeeping Operations (UN), 188
Spykman, Nicholas J., 136
Sri Lanka: civil war in, 161, 166; and Conference on Disarmament, 46; democracy promotion in, 6; foreign aid from China, 62; foreign aid from India, 61; free trade agreements with, 61; and Indian Ocean zone of peace resolution, 132; India's interventions in, 37, 101, 125, 126, 135, 182, 308
State-owned enterprises, 103–04
Steven, David, 281
Stevenson, Adlai, 159
Stockholm International Peace Research Institute, 178
"String of pearls" strategy, 138
Stuxnet worm, 223, 224
Submarines, 134, 135, 145
Subramanian, Arvind, 84
Subsidies, 282, 286, 287, 288, 293
Sudan: humanitarian interventions in, 307; oil exports to India, 284; UN peacekeeping operations in, 184, 191
Sundarji, Krishnaswami, 124
Swaminathan, M. S., 8
Syria: and BRICS countries, 10, 331, 332; and G-20, 322; Security Council interventions in, 68, 163–64, 169, 191

Tagore, Rabindranath, 26
Taliban, 67
Tardy, Thierry, 178, 189
Tashkent Declaration (1966), 123
Ten-Nation Committee on Disarmament, 202, 206
Territorial disputes, 9–10, 116–19, 159
Terrorism: and cyber security, 225; and Financial Action Task Force, 250; financing of, 252; Indian Parliament attack (2001), 124, 166; and maritime security, 13; Mumbai attacks (2008), 166
Thailand: and climate change negotiations, 272; free trade agreement with, 88
Thakur, Ramesh, 161–62
Think tanks, 108–09, 295
Tibet: and Indo-China relations, 58; territorial dispute over, 62
Timor-Leste, Security Council interventions in, 165, 182
Tito, Josip, 133
TPP (Trans-Pacific Partnership), 64
Trade: capacity for multilateralism in, 104–06; and climate change negotiations, 51; development of, 77; and energy security, 281; and globalization, 17; horizontal and vertical policymaking lines for, 98; India's participation in multilateral trade regime, 84–89; and maritime security, 136–37; with Middle East, 65; regional cooperation on, 115; and responsible multilateralism, 36
Trade and Economic Relations Committee (India), 99
Trans-Pacific Partnership (TPP), 64
Turkey, World Bank lending to, 82
Turkmenistan-Afghanistan-Pakistan-India pipeline project, 66

Uganda, humanitarian interventions in, 306
UN Convention on Law of the Sea. *See* Law of the Sea, UN Convention on
UN Framework Convention on Climate Change (UNFCCC), 47–51, 263, 268, 273. *See also* Climate change negotiations
Unique Identification (UID) scheme, 290
United Kingdom: Indian corporate sector's interests in, 104; and Indus Waters Treaty, 120, 121; and Jammu and Kashmir conflict, 117, 122; and Kargil war, 124; and Suez crisis, 28; and UN peacekeeping operations, 189
United Nations: "agenda for peace," 32; budget of, 47; and Conference on Disarmament, 45; as conflict resolution mechanism, 159; and dysfunctional multilateralism phase, 29; on Indian Ocean as zone of peace, 132; and India's foreign policy, 58; India's participation in, 80, 181; international norms implementation by, 314–16; and Internet governance, 222; territorial dispute resolution via, 116–17. *See also* Law of the Sea, UN Convention on (UNCLOS); UN peacekeeping operations
United Nations Development Program (UNDP), 219, 325
United Nations Environment Program, 262
United Nations Operation in the Congo (ONUC), 181
United Progressive Alliance, 201
United States: authoritarian regimes supported by, 335; and Bretton Woods institutions, 79, 80, 81, 243, 326; and BRICS countries, 334; and climate change negotiations, 47–48, 49–50, 51, 268, 275, 329; and Conference on Disarmament, 45; and cyber security, 223; and Declaration on Agriculture, 328; and Durban Platform, 330; and East Asia Summit, 316; energy security in, 283; and G-20, 247; Indian corporate sector's interests in, 104; and Indus Waters Treaty, 120, 121; institutional framework in, 108; and Jammu and Kashmir conflict, 32–33, 117, 122; and Kargil war, 124; and Kyoto Protocol, 266; and MALABAR naval exercises, 140, 147; naval forces in Indian Ocean, 134–35, 142, 144; official development assistance from, 77; Pakistan relations with, 67; and regional disputes, 65; as rule maker, 11; and territorial disputes, 118; and Trans-Pacific Partnership, 64; and UN humanitarian interventions, 68; and UN peacekeeping operations, 189, 190, 192; and WTO, 86
Universal Declaration of Human Rights, 27, 44, 58, 304
Unlawful Activities Prevention Act (India), 250, 251
UN peacekeeping operations, 177–95; diplomatic dynamics for, 188–92; historical roots of India's involvement in, 180–83; and India's rule-taker status, 7, 38; reimbursement rate for contributions to, 192; responsibility burden for, 183–84; strategic logic for, 185–88
Uruguay Round of GATT negotiations, 85, 86, 87
Utopian multilateralism, 200–01

Vajpayee, Atal Behari, 124, 141
VARUNA naval exercises, 140
Venezuela: and climate change negotiations, 272; oil exports to India, 284
Verma, Nirmal, 142, 147
Videsh Sanchar Nigam Limited (VSNL), 218–19
Vieira, Marco Antonio, 324
Vietnam: energy cooperation with, 285; humanitarian interventions in Cambodia by, 38, 306; production-sharing contracts with, 64; and Trans-Pacific Partnership, 64; UN interventions in, 59
Vihma, Antto, 270
Vira, Varun, 178

Visibility/viability paradox, 146

Washington Consensus, 33, 80
Wassenaar Arrangement, 8, 203
Water security, 50, 286–88
WCIT-12 (World Conference on International Telecommunication 2012), 226, 228
WHO (World Health Organization), 5
Wikileaks, 224
Wilson, Harold, 117
WIPO (World Intellectual Property Organization), 219
Woll, Cornelia, 329
Working Group on Internet Governance (WGIG), 221–22
World Bank: aid to India, 80, 82; and BRICS, 326, 327; as financial and technological resource, 44, 239; India Country Strategy (2009–12), 82; India's engagement with, 78, 241; and Indus Waters Treaty, 121, 122, 126; and international norms, 314; on maritime security, 144; reform proposals for, 8, 79–83, 334; in rule-based international order, 75; U.S. control of, 243
World Conference on International Telecommunication 2012 (WCIT-12), 226, 228
World Health Organization (WHO), 5
World Intellectual Property Organization (WIPO), 219
World Summit on the Information Society (WSIS), 221–22
World Trade Organization (WTO): and IBSA, 323; and India's capacity for multilateralism, 8, 85–89, 104–06; Internet treaties of, 219; and order paradox, 169; in rule-based international order, 75; and trade liberalization, 33
WSIS (World Summit on the Information Society), 221–22
Wullar Barrage/Tulbul Navigation Project, 120, 122

Yadav, Subhash, 105
Yekaterinburg Declaration (2009), 326
Yemen, UN mediation of conflict in, 159
"Yen Diplomacy," 162
Yugoslavia, UN peacekeeping operations in, 182, 185

Zuma, Jacob, 332